Y0-BQD-675

HUMANISM AND THE CHURCH FATHERS

Traversari translating a Greek text. A detail of ms. Vat. lat. 394, s. XV, f. 1r, which contains Traversari's translations of Chrysostom's *Homilies on Titus, I and II Timothy*, and *Philemon*. The ms. originally belonged to Cardinal Marco Barbo (1420-91). *Biblioteca Apostolica Vaticana, Archivio Fotografico.*

HUMANISM AND THE CHURCH FATHERS

AMBROGIO TRAVERSARI (1386-1439)
AND CHRISTIAN ANTIQUITY
IN THE ITALIAN RENAISSANCE

CHARLES L. STINGER

Albany
State University of New York Press
1977

Published by State University of New York Press
99 Washington Avenue, Albany, New York 12246
© 1977 State University of New York
All Rights Reserved
Printed in the United States of America

Composed by
Typography Services
Loudonville, New York 12211

Library of Congress Cataloging in Publication Data

Stinger, Charles L., 1944-
Humanism and the church fathers.

Bibliography: p.
1. Traversarius, Ambrosius, Camaldulensis, 1386-1439.
2. Fathers of the church.
3. Renaissance — Italy.
I. Title.
BX4705.T737S85   282'.092'4 [B]   76-21699
ISBN 0-87395-304-5

For Pat

CONTENTS

LIST OF ILLUSTRATIONS

Frontispiece

Traversari translating a Greek text

Following page 172

Hermits' cells at the Eremo, Camaldoli

Mid-fifteenth-century depiction of S. Maria degli Angeli

Lorenzo Monaco, "L'Incoronazione della Vergine,"
Uffizi Gallery, Florence

Lorenzo Ghiberti, Reliquary for Sts. Protus, Hyacinth,
and Nemesius, Bargello, Florence

Miniature portrait of Traversari

Rough draft, in Traversari's hand, of his translation of
Athanasius' *De incarnatione Verbi*

The autograph ms. of Traversari's translation of
Chrysostom's *Homilies on I Timothy*

Example of the humanistic script produced at
S. Maria degli Angeli

Bessarion and Cesarini reading the
Decree of Union at the Council of Florence

Lorenzo Ghiberti, detail of the
"Gates of Paradise" to the Baptistry, Florence

PREFACE

No longer valid is the Burckhardtian view of the Renaissance as essentially neo-pagan in culture and spirit. The recent scholarship of Becker, Trexler, and Weinstein has demonstrated the centrality of Christian piety and ritual to the developing notions of the individual and the state, to affirming the value of the family and secular life, and to providing spiritual consolation and certainty to a world in which the medieval papacy and empire, and the corporate structures of guild and monastery, had diminished authority to define and sanction human experience. The burden of individual identity in the burgher world of the Florentine *polis* found support in new forms of lay piety; and in popular preaching and vernacular religious poetry charity and social justice joined in an exultant vision of the city as the destined New Jerusalem. Civic Christianity proclaimed *caritas* the expression of *humanitas*, and in so doing justified man's role as citizen and validated the temporal claims of the public world. [1]

Religion and the Church remained vital, then, to Renaissance urban life. But what place did Christianity have in the thought of the humanists? Nearly fifteen years ago Paul Oskar Kristeller pointed out the need for "further research on the religious element in Renaissance humanism." He added, "We need more work on the religious ideas of the humanists, and also on their Biblical, patristic, and historical scholarship as it affected the theology of the Reformation period, and finally on the humanist background of the sixteenth-century theologians." [2] Charles Trinkaus' magisterial *In Our Image and Likeness: Humanity and Divinity in Italian Renaissance Thought,* 2 vols. (Chicago, 1970) has done much to fill this gap. He has demonstrated the Italian humanists' concern for Biblical scholarship, spiritual counseling of the laity, and such theological matters as the sacraments and the status of the professional religious. Moreover he has shown the extent to which the Italian

xi

humanists utilized a Christian, specifically a patristic, view of man created in the image and likeness of God to affirm a new vision of *homo faber*. While stressing the fundamental importance of patristic theology to humanist religious thought, Trinkaus did not attempt to delineate the dimensions of humanist patristic scholarship as such, and he specifically excluded study "of the translations of the Greek fathers, in which Traversari played such an important role" (page 571).

The attention accorded patristic studies in northern humanism, especially in the scholarship of Erasmus, has long been recognized. Indeed interest in the Fathers was regarded as characteristic of the "Christian humanist" emphasis of the northern humanists. Again it was Kristeller who observed that the Italian Renaissance also had applied the new resources of critical philology and historical research to patristic as well as classical literature. He noted further that it was Traversari who was the first to bring the new scholarship to bear on the works of the Fathers.[3]

This book, enlarging on Trinkaus' and Kristeller's suggestive observations of Traversari's importance for the revival of patristic theology, is intended to describe fully the religious and intellectual context of Traversari's study of the Fathers, the aim and method of his patristic scholarship, and the efforts he made to apply his knowledge of patristic literature and of the early history of Christianity to the pressing spiritual and institutional problems of the fifteenth century Church.

The principal source for the study of Traversari is his voluminous correspondence, comprising nearly nine hundred Latin letters. It was Traversari himself, late in life, who began arrangements for the collecting and "publication" of his epistolary. In the autumn of 1434 he wrote to Cristoforo da S. Marcello, Bishop of Rimini, and a prominent official in the Roman Curia, that he was acceding to the prelate's repeated importunate requests to send him his letters. Much of his correspondence was personal in nature, Traversari remarked, and did not pertain to matters of Christian piety. Moreover, he had not preserved copies of his numerous letters to friends, and it seemed to smack of vanity to seek their return. Nevertheless, bowing to Cristoforo's insistence, he had done so, but he had not as yet had the leisure to emend the letters, nor to organize them. Before the prelate released the letters for public reading, they should be returned to him so that he could correct them and polish their style, lest they appear barbarous and unlearned.[4]

In the course of the next two years Traversari continued to recover his letters and to send them to Cristoforo.[5] By June 1436 he had completed the tentative organization of his correspondence into four books. Two books, consisting of letters to Pope Eugenius IV, to Cristoforo, and to his brother, Girolamo Traversari, pertained primarily to his work of monastic reform and to his activity as papal diplomat; the other two comprised the remainder of his epistolary. He remarked that he had still been unable to reacquire many of his letters.[6] By the summer of 1437 Traversari had collected ten additional books of letters. These he sent to Fra Michele, a fellow monk at S. Maria degli Angeli in Florence, and a practitioner of the new humanistic script, to transcribe into final form. To Michele Traversari gave explicit and detailed instructions regarding the appearance of the final copy, including margins, spacing, and titles. Michele was to use as a model the manuscript of St. Ambrose's epistolary which Traversari himself had transcribed.[7]

In 1438 Traversari arranged for one further disposition of his letters. Since Cristoforo had asked him to make a selection of his best letters to be compiled in a single volume, Traversari instructed Fra Michele to have Paolo Toscanelli and Filippo Pieruzzi, at the time Traversari's closest friends in the Florentine humanist community, assume the task of selecting the letters which seemed most worthy. He suggested that merely personal letters, in particular those to his brother, be omitted. It seems probable that the Traversari letters in ms. Vat. lat. 3911, a collection arranged in five books, are those selected by Toscanelli and Pieruzzi. This collection consists primarily of official letters sent to Cristoforo and Pope Eugenius, and to other lay and ecclesiastical dignitaries; reform letters sent to the abbots and monks of the Camaldulensian Order in the course of Traversari's activity as General of the Order; and his letters to his close humanist friends, the Florentine Niccolò Niccoli and the Venetian Leonardo Giustiniani. The contents of this manuscript, including Cristoforo's marginal notes, has been examined in detail by Giovanni Cardinal Mercati in his invaluable collection of studies on the Traversari epistolary.[9]

After Traversari's death Cosimo de' Medici asked Fra Michele to collect the complete Traversari correspondence. Michele remarks that Cosimo told him that just as the letters of the ancients had been preserved for their wealth of divine and human wisdom and for their genius and erudition, so the letters of learned men in their own time, including Traversari's ought to be preserved for posterity. Michele asserts that he made strenuous efforts, with Cosimo's help, to acquire additional Traversari letters for the collection, and that he rearranged the order.[10] Michele's collection consists of eighteen books. This begins with Traversari's letters to Cosimo de' Medici and his brother Lorenzo; continues with letters to Niccoli, Francesco Barbaro, Giustiniani, and Fra Michele – all related to Traversari's scholarship; proceeds to letters to Pope Eugenius and other Church officials and to the abbots and monks of the Camaldulensian Order; and concludes with the letters to Girolamo Traversari. Michele's collection is extant in a number of fifteenth century manuscripts, including Vat. lat. 1793, Laur. Strozz. CII, and Bibl. Capitolare Lucca 540.[11]

Another collection of Traversari letters, arranged in thirteen books, is also present in fifteenth century manuscripts, among them Bibl. Naz. Cent. Firenze, Conv. Soppr. G, 3, 35 (dated 1463), and Conv. Soppr. C, 2, 38 (dated 1468), which was originally at Camaldoli.[12] Individual Traversari letters were also included in numerous fifteenth century miscellanies of humanist writings.[13]

In the eighteenth century, two printed editions of Traversari's epistolary appeared. Both were based on the fifteenth century collections, supplemented with individual letters from other sources. The earlier edition was edited by Martène and Durand and printed under the direction of Mabillon in Paris in 1724.[14] The latter edition, edited by the Camaldulensian Abbot Petrus Cannetus, was published in 1759 in Florence by Laurentius Mehus, who prefaced the volume of letters with a separate volume which examines in detail the sources for Traversari's life and includes a lengthy literary history of

Florence from 1192 to 1440.[15] Mehus' Latin study remains an important work, especially for manuscripts of Traversari's translations which were present in Florentine monastic libraries in the mid-eighteenth century, but which were removed when the monasteries were suppressed under French rule in the early nineteenth century. I have used the Cannetus-Mehus edition of Traversari's letters for this study.

Modern scholarship has added nearly thirty letters to the Traversari epistolary.[16] In addition, F.P. Luiso has provided an invaluable chronological re-ordering of the letters.[17]

It is uncertain to what extent Traversari corrected and revised his letters prior to his death. Nor is it known if he decided deliberately to exclude letters from the collection. No extant letters date from 1400-15, the period of Traversari's spiritual and intellectual formation in S. Maria degli Angeli. From the internal evidence of his extant correspondence, numerous letters written to other humanists in the years 1415-31 are now lost. The overwhelming majority of the letters date from his election as General in 1431. Despite these problems, the Traversari epistolary remains an impressive source for the study of early Quattrocento Italian humanism, and deserves to be ranked in importance with such other notable humanist epistolaries as Leonardo Bruni's, Poggio Bracciolini's, and Guarino da Verona's.

Besides the epistolary, the other primary source for Traversari's life is his *Hodoeporicon,* the account of his journeys of monastic visitations undertaken from the autumn of 1431 to the summer of 1434. In 1912 Alessandro Dini-Traversari printed this work as an appendix to his biography, *Ambrogio Traversari e i suoi tempi* (Firenze, 1912), a book in many ways outdated, but useful still for the genealogical tables of the Traversari family and the good accounts of Traversari's work as monastic reformer and papal diplomat.

Just after Traversari's death, a friend and admirer, the Abbot Girolamo Aliotti urged first Carlo Marsuppini, then Leon Battista Alberti to write a life of Traversari. Each promised to do so, and Aliotti seems even to have gathered materials for Alberti, but neither in the end composed a life.[18] The first life of Traversari is that present in the *Vite di uomini illustri del secolo XV,* written by the Florentine book-dealer, Vespasiano da Bisticci (1421-98).[19] Vespasiano wrote his lives only after 1480, but in his account of Traversari he mentions incidents he learned from Cosimo de' Medici and Fra Michele. Therefore, despite its late date, it preserves a certain amount of first-hand material, and it provides a useful assessment of the significance Traversari's life and scholarship had for the later Quattrocento. The *Annales Camaldulenses* also contain information pertinent to Traversari's life within the context of a general history of the Camaldulensian Order.[20]

In this century two general assessments of Traversari's life and scholarship have appeared — Antonio Corsano, *Per la storia del Rinascimento religioso in Italia: Dal Traversari a G.F. Pico* (Napoli, 1935), and Pier Giorgio Ricci, "Ambrogio Traversari," *Rinascita,* II (1939), pp. 578-612. Traversari's activity at the Council of Ferrara-Florence has been examined by Jean Decarreau, "Un moine helléniste et diplomate: Ambroise Traversari," *Revue des études italiennes* (1957), pp. 101-43, and Costanzo Somigli, O. Camald., *Un Amico dei Greci: Ambrogio Traversari* (Arezzo, 1964). The most important studies of specific aspects of Traversari's patristic scholarship are E. Mioni, "Le *Vitae Patrum* nella traduzione di Ambrogio Traversari," *Aevum,* XXIV (1950), pp. 319-31; Sister Agnes Clare Way, "The Lost Translations Made by Ambrosius Traversarius of the Orations of Gregory Nazianzene," *Renaissance News,* XIV (1961), pp. 91-96; *id.,* "Gregorius Nazianzenus," in *Catalogus translationum et commentariorum: Medieval and Renaissance Latin Translations and Commentaries,* eds. Paul Oskar Kristeller and F. Edward Cranz, II (Washington, 1971), pp. 43-192; Agostino Sottili, "Autografi e traduzioni di Ambrogio Traversari," *Rinascimento,* 2nd S., V (1965), pp. 3-15; and *id.,* "Ambrogio Traversari, Francesco Pizolpasso, Giovanni Aurispa: Traduzioni e letture," *Romanische Forschungen,* LXXVIII (1966), pp. 42-63.

The initial research for this study was made possible by a Fulbright grant to Italy in 1969-70. Additional research was done as a Fellow at Villa I Tatti, the Harvard University Center for Italian Renaissance Studies, Florence, Italy, in 1972-73. I was aided also by a grant in 1971 from the Stanford University Committee on International Studies. I wish to express my appreciation to the directors and staffs of the Archivio di Stato in Florence, the Biblioteca Nazionale Centrale in Florence, the Biblioteca Laurenziana, and the Biblioteca Vaticana for their assistance. To the Biblioteca Nazionale Centrale of Florence and to the Biblioteca Laurenziana I am indebted as well for permission to reproduce photographs of manuscripts in their holdings. I am grateful for the helpful advice of Mr. Norman Mangouni, director of State University of New York Press, and especially for the skill of my editor, Mrs. Eleanor Sypher, whose suggestions were invariably sensible and constructive. Both greatly eased the work of publication. My debts to Renaissance scholars are many. Charles Trinkaus, Salvatore I. Camporeale, Heiko Oberman, William Bouwsma, Riccardo Fubini, Eugene F. Rice, Jr., Bernard Huppé, and Fred J. Nichols were generous in offering useful advice and suggestions. I am particularly indebted to Paul Oskar Kristeller who read the text, generously contributed additional bibliographic and manuscript references, and made improvements in the Latin translations. Finally, I wish to express special gratitude to Frank O'Laughlin of Hobart College, whose perceptive intellect and inspired teaching first stimulated me to further study of Italian Renaissance history; to Myron P. Gilmore, Director of Villa I Tatti, whose encouragement and kindness were instrumental to the accomplishment of this work; and above all to Lewis W. Spitz of Stanford University, whose scholarship has so fruitfully probed the links between humanism and the Reformation, and who first suggested to me Traversari's significance.

State University of New York at Buffalo
November 1975

HUMANISM AND THE CHURCH FATHERS

CHAPTER I
SPIRITUAL AND INTELLECTUAL FORMATION

In 1400, when he was fourteen, Ambrogio Traversari left his native village of Portico di Romagna, with its remote, cloud-shrouded peaks and plunging precipices, to enter the cloister of the Camaldulensian monastery of S. Maria degli Angeli in Florence. There, a year later, he made his profession as a monk.[1]

Little is known of Traversari's early years. He was descended from an ancient Romagnol noble family, related to the Traversari feudal magnates who had competed for rule of Ravenna in the thirteenth century. In *Purgatorio*, Canto XIV, lines 91-111, where Dante laments the passing of the ancient Romagnol nobility, he mentions the Traversari as among those families whose chivalrous *courtoisie* had been supplanted by the degenerate savagery of the corrupt new *signorie*.[2] The Traversari of Portico, along with other feudal magnates in the Romagna, suffered a decline in power and authority in the fourteenth century. In 1377 Portico fell to the hegemony of the expanding Florentine territorial state.

The young Ambrogio received his primary education at the Camaldulensian monastery at Galeata, near Portico. Perhaps this early experience induced him to follow the monastic life. Or perhaps the declining fortunes of his family impelled him in that direction. Regardless, the monastic vocation also proved attractive to Ambrogio's younger brother, Girolamo, who joined him as a monk at S. Maria degli Angeli in 1412.[3]

The Order that Ambrogio joined was founded by St. Romuald (952-1027), who established a hermitage at Camaldoli, high up in the Tuscan Apennines, from which the Order took its name. Characteristic of Camaldulensian monasticism was emphasis on the austerity of the eremitic life. Indeed Dante, in the sphere of Saturn in *Paradiso*, the domain of the contemplatives, has St. Benedict point out the presence of St. Romuald, the exemplar of western eremitic monasticism, as Macarius (c.300-c.390), the Egyptian desert father, was for eastern.[4] At the beginning of the fifteenth century the Camaldulensian Order comprised some fifty monasteries scattered through Tuscany, Umbria, the Romagna, and the Veneto.[5]

S. Maria degli Angeli was founded in 1293. Although it was an urban monastery − the third circle of the Florentine walls included it within the city − the foundation stipulated that the monks lead an eremitic life. The monks were to maintain a perpetual cloister, never leaving the grounds of the monastery except for grave circumstances, a stipulation which remained in effect until 1470.[6] In the early fourteenth century the monastery consisted of a Gothic cloister, composed of unadorned individual cells, and a Gothic oratory, a rectangular building with open-raftered roof illuminated through small slits in the upper walls. The simplicity of the buildings corresponded to Romuald's eremitic intentions. In the second half of the fourteenth century, with the revival of religious piety in the wake of the terrors of the Black Death, the monastery was enlarged with the addition of two new cloisters, a refectory, and an infirmary. The original cloister was plundered during the Ciompi rebellion of 1378, but in the last decades of the century this and the other buildings were embellished with altars, tabernacles, and fresco decoration donated by wealthy Florentine families.[7] During Traversari's stay in the monastery, some thirty monks lived there, including many from prominent Florentine patrician families.[8]

Traversari remained cloistered at S. Maria degli Angeli from 1401 until his election as General of the Order in 1431. Since his correspondence dates only from 1415, there is no direct knowledge of his early life in the monastery. Clearly, however, the life of solitude and prayer deeply affected his consciousness. In September 1433, he journeyed to Ferrara to urge the Holy Roman Emperor, Sigismund, to confirm the imperial privileges granted the Order. In his oration Traversari recalled his long years in the monastery:

> Most clement Emperor, I was nourished from boy-
> hood under the protecting grace of Christ in that
> celebrated monastery of S. Maria degli Angeli in
> Florence. There I spent thirty one years in observance
> of the Rule and in perpetual cloister. For my sins I no
> longer merit to enjoy that life of religious peace.
> From that protecting haven of quiet calm, from that
> most placid shore I am embarked by divine judge-
> ment upon the hostile open sea of worldly deliber-
> ations. By order of the Holy Roman Pontiff, Eugen-
> ius, I have been torn from that tranquillity and
> appointed General of our Order.[9]

As a young monk Traversari learned the liturgical chants and participated in singing the daily round of the canonical hours. In a letter to the Venetian humanist, Leonardo Giustiniani (1388-1446), Traversari wrote that while he had little voice for singing, he took great delight in music, not only the formal chants and liturgical music, but also vernacular songs in honor of God. Giustiniani, whose vernacular love songs were partic-ularly popular, had composed a number of vernacular lauds in honor of the Virgin and Christ for voice and instrumental accompaniment. Learning of these, Traversari asked that they be sent to Florence. As for Giustiniani's concern that attention to vernacular music might be beneath the dignity of humanist erudition, Traversari reminded him that

> those ancients, whom we admire, hardly despised this
> as uncultured. As is well-known, Socrates as an old
> man sang, accompanying himself with a lyre, a skill
> he had not cultivated before. Holy father Augustine
> wrote six books on music, and he intended to write
> six more on melody if leisure had permitted. I pass
> over those more ancient, namely holy King David,
> and others, who had a wonderful love for sacred
> music.[10]

From its origin S. Maria degli Angeli was celebrated as a center of the arts. Manuscript illumination was particularly important, especially during the latter fourteenth century when there flourished a "Camaldolese school" of miniatures, but the monastery also engaged in panel and mural painting and in making tapestries. From S. Maria degli Angeli emerged at least one artist of note, Lorenzo Monaco (c.1370-1425), the master of Fra Angelico.[11] Traversari took pride in the craft of manuscript illumination and regarded it as a worthy function of monastic life. When in 1429 he wrote to Giustiniani, requesting that he purchase in Venice and send to S. Maria degli Angeli a quantity of the rare and expensive ultramarine blue pigment used for miniatures, Traversari observed,

> there were always monks in our monastery (nor indeed are they lacking now) who used it in a most skillful and beautiful way for decorating manuscripts. This occupation is certainly not unworthy of religious repose.[12]

Traversari was himself a practitioner of this art, for on another occasion he informed Giustiniani that he was applying the finishing touches to the Venetian's manuscript with his own hand.[13] S. Maria degli Angeli as a center for copying and illuminating manuscripts was to contribute importantly to Traversari's scholarly work. Besides the choir books and other liturgical works to which the monks devoted most of their skill, they also produced copies of Traversari's translations, including beautifully decorated dedication copies. A number of the monks also learned the new humanist script and were able to transcribe both ancient codices and contemporary humanist works.

It was not music or art, however, which Traversari found most compelling about his cloistered life in the monastery, but rather the peace of its spiritual piety. During the trying years of monastic reform, Traversari wrote to Agostino da Portico, a monk at S. Maria degli Angeli:

> There comes back to my mind, son, that peace, and those former delights dazzle my senses. I cannot help but mourn being deprived of such joy, and the rich consolation which I experienced in the solitude of my heart when I celebrated with you the delightful Sabbath, when we sang to the Lord a new song and intoned psalms of joy. With Job I am forced to cry

out from the depths of my heart, "If only I could go
back to the old days, to the time when God was with
me." [14]

The piety of S. Maria degli Angeli is most strikingly revealed
in Lorenzo Monaco's triptych "The Coronation of the Virgin"
(now in the Uffizi), which originally stood on the high altar of
the monastery church. The central panel shows Christ crowning
the Virgin beneath an elaborate Gothic canopy surrounded by
singing angels, by Apostles holding open their books of
revelation, and by martyr saints with the instruments of their
torture. A large, tonsured figure kneeling on the right, garbed in
the white habit of the Camaldulensians, and holding the
rough-hewn staff of the hermit is St. Romuald. On the left
kneels St. Benedict, the Benedictine Rule displayed in his right
hand, and in his left the scourge for flagellation. The pastel
colors and gently flowing linear forms present in a symbolic
way the virtues of patience, humility, and obedience. No
internal life is suggested by any of the figures. Each simply
represents an aspect of the eternal, suprahistorical truths of
faith.

The hierocratic, timeless piety expressed in Lorenzo Monaco's painting was fundamental to Traversari's view of life.
His historical perspective and understanding of the concrete
reality of human activity, derived from his study of classical and
patristic literature, never completely overcame the earlier
assumptions of the monastic experience. Especially in times of
crisis he revealed the forms and ideas of traditional piety. His
rebuke to Niccoli for his angry quarrel with Leonardo Bruni is
characteristic.

Truly, dearest Niccolò, sacred revelation has taught
me patience and humility. Through the grace of
Christ I have devoted myself to each of these since I
was a boy, and I am prepared to the end to feel
humble, even when I perhaps may merit to be
numbered among the children of God. To merit this
exalted state, as you will recognize with me, no other
way lies open. Remember from the Gospels that the
Son of God descended from the bosom of the Father

> to earth to prepare by word, deed, and example for
> our ascent, and he demanded us to follow him with
> heart-felt humility. [15]

At a time when many Florentine humanists and artists were
exalting human achievement, Traversari reveals a deep pessi-
mism regarding earthly existence. He perceived a fragility in
human activity and designs, underscored by frequent recur-
rences of the plague, outbreaks of war, and civil strife. "You see
such vicissitudes, such inconstancy of fortune, which clearly
warn us that nothing in human affairs is to be gloried in, nor
any good fortune, for all that seems pleasurable and permanent
may suddenly fly away." [16] This *contemptus mundi* spirituality
of late medieval piety profoundly influenced Traversari's
humanist studies and patristic scholarship. He maintained a
clear distinction between "gentile" and sacred literature, and he
considered the latter as the proper object of his studies.
Indicative of the impact of monastic piety is that his first major
Latin translations of Greek patristic works, St. John Chrysostom's *Against the Vituperators of the Monastic Life* and St.
John Climacus' *Ladder of Paradise*, were intended to defend
and counsel the monastic vocation.

The ascetic piety of the monastic experience shaped Traversari's spirituality. But decisive for his intellectual conceptions
and for his cultivation of Christian antiquity was contact with
and commitment to the cultural-intellectual values of the *studia
humanitatis.*

In the last quarter of the fourteenth century it was Florence,
under the intellectual leadership of its Chancellor, Coluccio
Salutati (1331-1406), and the Augustianian monk, Luigi Marsili
(1342-94), which emerged as the center for the continuation of
Petrarch's conviction of the superiority of ancient widsom and
of his dedication to the revival of Ciceronian eloquence.

In the 1380's and early 1390's, the Florentine humanist
community, including Niccolò Niccoli, subsequently Traversari's closest friend, met daily in Marsili's cell in the Augustinian
monastery of S. Spirito. These gatherings may have served as a
model for the daily humanist meetings in Traversari's cell at S.
Maria degli Angeli in the 1420's. [17]

Did Marsili in any way inspire Traversari to focus his humanist scholarship on the Fathers? Marsili's intellectual interests are difficult to judge, for he wrote little. Salutati, however, asserts that Marsili lacked neither erudition, nor eloquence, nor virtue, and that he was learned both in human and divine knowledge. No one had a fuller grasp of "gentile" history or the classical poets and orators. Nor was anyone more fully versed in the "subtleties" and "obscurities" of modern scholastic philosophy and theology.[18] Marsili had studied philosophy and theology at the Universities of Padua and Paris for twenty years, an extensive experience in the late medieval scholastic curriculum. Yet contact with Petrarch, in Padua, in the 1370's exercised a deep influence as well. Indeed it was Marsili's Petrarchan commitment to the cultivation of Ciceronian oratory, classical poetry, and Roman history which seems to have most inspired Bruni, Poggio, Roberto Rossi and the other young Florentine humanists who gathered in Marsili's cell.[19] These studies were substantially aided by access to the extensive library of Latin classics which Boccaccio had bequeathed to Santo Spirito.[20]

Interest in the classics, however, did not mean that Marsili neglected religious studies. His concern for lay piety led him to promote the teaching of Aristotelian logic and philosophy and of Augustinian theology to the laity. The humanist Giannozzo Manetti began his studies, first in Aristotle's *Nicomachean Ethics*, then in Augustine's *De civitate Dei* under two Augustinian monks who preserved this tradition of lay teaching at Santo Spirito in the 1420's.[21] Marsili, who supported Florentine interests against the Papacy in the War of the Eight Saints, and who often served on diplomatic missions for the *signoria*, also wrote a short treatise, the *Regola per ben confessarsi,* intended to counsel the Florentine *popolo grasso* engrossed in the economic and political affairs of the urban republic. This work, written in the vernacular, and organized on the traditional medieval basis of the seven deadly sins, curiously reveals neither a concern for contemporary Augustinian theology nor offers a discussion of classical or Christian antiquity.[22] There is some indirect evidence, however, that Marsili was interested in patristic theology. In Giovanni da Prato's *Il Paradiso degli*

Alberti (1425-26), the imaginary reconstruction of Florentine literary society in 1389, Marsili is made to counter the Aristotelian theories concerning the true end and happiness of man put forth by the scholastic Biagio da Parma with arguments based on the authority of the Church Fathers.[23] Moreover, among the books Marsili acquired for Santo Spirito was a manuscript containing Basil's *Homilies on the Hexaemeron* in the late classical Latin translation of Eustathius and Gregory of Nyssa's *De opificio hominis* also in a late classical Latin translation, that of Dionysius Exiguus.[24] The library which Boccaccio bequeathed to Santo Spirito also included patristic manuscripts, notably Ambrose's *Hexaemeron*, Lactantius' *Divinae Institutiones*, Eusebius' *Chronicon* in Jerome's translation, and Augustine's *Enarrationes in Psalmos* as well as the *De civitate Dei*.[25]

If Marsili cultivated patristic theology, however, it does not seem to have been connected in a programmatic way to his interest in classical antiquity. Theology and the *studia humanitatis* remained separate enterprises, and of his wide-ranging intellectual interests the promotion of classical literature and history most impressed his young Florentine followers. Regardless, Marsili did provide for Traversari an influential Florentine precedent for the involvement of the regular clergy in the humanist movement.[26]

Especially vital for Traversari's engagement in humanist studies as a legitimate activity of the monastic vocation, and in particular for his cultivation of patristic studies within the intellectual context of the *studia humanitatis*, was Salutati's defense of classical studies against a series of anti-classical opponents who charged that the reading of pagan authors was impious. This controversy was particularly acute from 1397-1406. In 1397 it was rumored that the condottiere Carlo Malatesa, captain of the troops of the Florentine League, had, upon entering Mantua after his victory at Governolo on 31 August, ordered that an ancient statue of Virgil which had stood for centuries in the city be destroyed. Malatesta was alleged to have uttered imprecations against the classical poets and to have declared that only saints deserved statues. The circumstances surrounding the incident are unclear, and there is doubt it occurred at all, but it became a *cause célèbre* in humanist circles and was interpreted as an attack on the classical poets and on the study of literature in general.[27]

Earlier, in 1378, Salutati had defended Virgil against charges he was a false prophet by arguing, following medieval precedent, that Virgil should be read allegorically. For those who knew how to understand Virgil there were signs in his poetry of the highest mysteries of the Christian faith including the Trinity and the Incarnation.[28] More significantly he had stressed the Fathers' dependence on the pagan poets and classical orators for their art of eloquence. Unless Jerome had studied the classics he would never have been able to translate Sacred Scripture from Hebrew and Greek into elegant Latin. If Augustine had been ignorant of the poets, especially Virgil, he could not in the *City of God* have defended Christianity so eloquently against the false beliefs of the gentiles.[29]

In 1397 Salutati extended the scope of these arguments to the point of condemning the ignorance of scholastic theologians. Central to Salutati's case was once again an argument which had medieval precedent. He asserted that whoever condemns the nature of poetry condemns Scripture itself, which uses the figural and allegorical language of the poets:[30] Again it is significant that Salutati emphasizes the patristic dependence on the language of classical poetry.

> Is it possible that anyone can be considered so foolish and senile, so deceived by false opinion as to condemn the poets with whose words Jerome overflows, Augustine glistens, and Ambrose blossoms? Gregory and Bernard are not devoid of them, and on them the vessel of election himself [i.e. St. Paul] did not consider it foolish to rely.[31]

Further, unless one had studied the classics it was impossible to understand what the Fathers wrote. To their shame the scholastic theologians who had failed to study classical literature must run to schoolboys in order to learn what they could not comprehend in the teachings of the Fathers. In short, Salutati argued that knowledge of the classics, the curriculum of the *studia humanitatis*, was essential to the proper understanding of the nature of Scripture and of patristic theology.

The next stage of the controversy over classical studies was immediately proximate to Traversari, for it was Giovanni da Sanminiato (1360-1428), a monk at S. Maria degli Angeli from 1394 to his death, who attacked Salutati.[32] Shortly before 1400 Giovanni wrote to Salutati to attempt to dissuade him from further study of pagan poetry. In response Salutati urged Giovanni not to seek his withdrawal from those virtuous studies (*honestis studiis*), for he was not neglecting divine truth. He admired the eloquence of the poets indeed, but not for the vain pursuit of glory. His whole desire was to know and to communicate what God had taught. Giovanni's holy rusticity in the monastery might instruct other monks by his holy example, but Salutati's task was in the world, to instruct the laity to recognize their sins and to exhort them to shun the vanity of temporal pleasures.[33] Salutati did not oppose the monastic life. Indeed some twenty years earlier, in 1381, he had defended the superior sanctity and merit of the monastic vocation in the treatise *De seculo et religione*, written to deter a monk, recently entered into S. Maria degli Angeli, from regretting his decision and to strengthen his resolve to lead a severely ascetic existence.[34] Salutati admonished Giovanni, however, to remember that withdrawal to the monastery did not of itself bring one closer to God. Indeed, frequently — would it were not so often! — a monk is further from God than those who live amidst the dangers of worldly life. Regardless of one's state in life, whoever directs his mind to God and calls upon Him will not be lost, for God is everywhere.[35] Salutati did not denigrate the religious life. He simply stressed the validity of a Christian vocation within the world. In particular he pointed to the moral dignity of the humanist who counsels the spiritual life of the laity engaged in Renaissance civic life. It was this claim to mediate the needs of lay piety which was central to Quattrocento humanism.[36]

Five years later Giovanni returned to the fray. The center of the controversy now shifted from the question of the study of classical poetry to the legitimacy of the *studia humanitatis* as the curriculum for the education of youth. Giovanni warned Angelo Corbinelli, a young protégé of Salutati, to avoid as a trap of the devil the blasphemous and impious study of the pagan classics.[37] In response, Salutati defended the humanist curriculum at length and elaborated many of his earlier arguments regarding the figurative language of poetry and its usefulness in understanding the metaphoric and allegorical meaning of Scripture. Again he emphasized the patristic use of the classics and the importance of the Fathers' knowledge of pagan philosophy and literature, for it was this which made effective Christian apologetics against the gentiles. He pointed particularly to *eloquentissimus* Lactantius "singularly efficacious assailer of pagan religion. Deprive him of his education grounded in the poets, philosophers, and orators, and consider what, deprived of the testimony of the poets, his efficacious arguments would be worth."[38] As clinching evidence of the patristic support for classical studies, Salutati urged Giovanni to read St. Basil's *Homilia ad iuvenes de legendis libris gentilium*, a treatise which Leonardo Bruni had just translated (in 1400) from Greek into Latin, probably at Salutati's suggestion, and had dedicated to the Chancellor.[39] Basil argued that the study of pagan classical literature trained the intellect and inculcated virtue, essential preliminaries to prepare the mind and soul to comprehend the deeper mysteries of Holy Scripture. In the patristic age Basil's treatise had been decisive in influencing the receptivity of the Church to the cultural achievements of Hellenic antiquity.[40] Bruni recognized the importance of Basil's treatise as support for the humanists' cause. In the preface to his translation, he emphasized the authority Basil had among the Greeks who esteemed him both for the severity of his life and the sanctity of his ways, and for his devotion to knowledge and his learning in sacred letters. "I have willingly translated this work because through the authority of such a man I wished to put an end to the ignorant perversity of those who attack the *studia humanitatis* and regard it as wholly abhorrent."[41]

Basil's treatise, widely disseminated in Bruni's translation in the early fifteenth century, did prove a decisive support for the humanist position. But, before Salutati's death in 1406, the controversy had one more round. This time the opponent was Giovanni Dominici (1357-1419), an Observant Dominican, zealous monastic reformer, fervent ascetic, and fiery preacher who had lectured on Sacred Scripture at the Florentine Studio since 1399. Dominici was a more formidable opponent than Giovanni da Sanminiato, for he had a substantial following in Florence, and he had received university training in scholastic theology. His lengthy attack on classical studies, the *Lucula noctis* (Firefly), addressed to Salutati and probably written in 1405, used a systematic scholastic format and rigorous dialectical argumentation to assert as illicit any education based on the classics. Indeed he argued it was preferable to remain ignorant than to devote oneself to such studies, more useful for a Christian to plow the land than read the books of the gentiles.[42]

Salutati's planned systematic defense of the study of pagan letters was left incomplete on his death in May 1406. Enough was completed, however, to discern that the heart of his argument was that while sincerity of faith can be achieved without literacy, illiterate and uncultured holy rusticity cannot lead to a steadfast adherence to the truths of faith. Without study of the liberal arts, Scripture and its exposition by the Fathers and doctors of the Church cannot be known. "The *studia humanitatis* and the *studia divinitatis* are so interconnected that true and complete knowledge of the one cannot be had without the other."[43]

This extended controversy over the study of the classics marks a decisive phase in the growth of humanism. The attacks by the anti-classicists forced Salutati to articulate explicitly the nature and function of the *studia humanitatis* and to take a decisive attitude towards classical antiquity. While many of Salutati's arguments had medieval precedent — indeed it was really the obscuranticism of Dominici and other zealots which was novel — his emphasis on the decisive importance of classical studies for lay intellectual and moral formation was new. The *studia humanitatis* was espoused as the *paideia* for contemporary society. Stress fell not on dialectics, epistemology, and metaphysics — the systematic analysis of faith through the *scientia* of philosophic truth — which had marked the intellectual and spiritual efforts of scholastic theologians. Rather the emphasis was on grammar, rhetoric, educational curriculum, and moral philosophy — the arts of discourse and right living which made possible fulfillment in the social and political life of the Renaissance *polis*. With this emphasis Salutati recognized the Fathers as models intellectually and spiritually superior to the schoolmen. In their defense of Christianity the Fathers had imbibed the values of classical rhetoric, and the Fathers in general, and Basil in particular, had supported the *paideia* of a classical education. Moreover, for Salutati, the Fathers were not just Christian classics, but also the authoritative elucidation of an evangelical and Scriptural faith. [44] Finally, as Trinkaus has shown, Salutati utilized patristic theology, particularly Augustine's *De Genesi ad litteram* and *De Trinitate,* to resolve certain fundamental problems in fourteenth century nominalist thought, especially the paradox of human volition and divine providence. In Augustine, Salutati found an emphasis on the will, the volitional inner consciousness, as the source for both action and knowledge. Man's dignity consists in his freedom to will and to act, which in turn rest on his creation in God's image and likeness. Salutati's anthropology is thus an affirmation, based on patristic authority, of man's moral responsibility in individual and communal affairs. [45]

Nowhere does Traversari refer to this dispute on the study of the classics. Nor does he discuss Salutati's religious thought. Yet, in establishing the immediate context of Traversari's intellectual development, it is significant that precisely during his early years in S. Maria degli Angeli, Salutati, as spokesman for Florentine humanism, should focus attention on patristic literature, both as a defense of the humanist educational program, and as a source for responding to the spiritual needs of Renaissance civic culture. As shall be seen, Traversari embraced the intellectual and cultural values of the *studia humanitatis*. He was an enthusiastic student of the classics, and his patristic scholarship emphasized the rhetorical nature of the writings of the Fathers. He viewed the revival of Christian antiquity from the same historical perspective as the revival of classical antiquity — both were the regeneration of values superior to the "barbarity" of the middle ages. When Traversari as General established an academy to educate Florentine youths, he adopted the curriculum of the *studia humanitatis.* Finally, his first efforts in patristic scholarship — the emending of a Lactantius manuscript and the translation of a Basil letter —

concerned two Fathers given prominence in Salutati's second letter to Giovanni da Sanminiato, a letter widely circulated in the first years of the fifteenth century as a humanist manifesto. [46]

After Salutati's death, there is little knowledge of Giovanni da Sanminiato's life and activity in S. Maria degli Angeli, though it is clear he was a figure of some importance in the monastery. At his death he was Subprior. It is significant, moreover, that he made a number of vernacular translations for the "spiritual solace of those who can not read Latin." These included St. Bernard's *Sermons on the Canticles,* Petrarch's *Remedies for Both Kinds of Fortune,* and the latter half of the *Moralia* of Gregory the Great, done in 1415, and undertaken to complete the vernacular translation begun by the Florentine Zanobi da Strada in the 1350's. [47] The choice is intriguing. As Dufner points out, Salutati, in his reply to Giovanni Dominici had indicated the *Cantica Canticorum* and the Book of Job as two Scriptural works particularly poetical in nature. Moreover, he had praised above all "sanctissimus antistes Gregorius" for his elucidation, in the *Moralia,* of the multiple hidden meanings in Job. Did Giovanni in the end adopt Salutati's outlook? Or was the vernacular translation of celebrated patristic, medieval, and humanist spiritual works precisely the way to counter Salutati's objection to the "fruitless" monastic vocation? Further, and more importantly, did Giovanni's activity affect Traversari's pursuit of patristic studies? There is only one extant Traversari letter to Giovanni, dated 1420. This letter discusses the proposed reform of the Florentine monastery of San Marco, and makes no mention of humanist or patristic scholarship. [48] Nor does any other Traversari letter discuss Giovanni's scholarship. It is significant that Traversari's translations were all in Latin and intended to fulfill the literary expectations of humanists, not to satisfy the minds of those "che non sanno gramatica." As will be seen, Traversari did approve of Leonardo Giustiniani's efforts to provide vernacular works for the spiritual edification of the Venetian laity, and he admired and defended the preaching of San Bernardino. But these were not the ends of his own intellectual efforts. Rather his principal purpose was to begin to recover for the Latin West the patrimony of ancient Greek Christian literature, just as his humanist contemporaries were revealing the long-lost wisdom of the Greek philosophers. For inspiration and encouragement in this endeavor Traversari pointed not to Giovanni da Sanminiato, but rather to Matteo Guidone, Prior during his first twenty years at S. Maria degli Angeli, and above all to Niccolò Niccoli.

Matteo Guidone entered S. Maria degli Angeli at the age of seven in 1348, made his profession as a monk in 1354, was chosen Prior in November 1399, a year before Traversari's arrival, and died in May 1421.[49] We know little more about his life. Clearly, however, he provided incentive and support for Traversari's studies. This is evident from the prefatory letters to Traversari's two earliest major patristic translations, Chrysostom's *Adversus vituperatores vitae monasticae* (1417) and Climacus' *Scala Paradisi* (1419), both dedicated to Prior Matteo. In the preface to the Chrysostom translation, Traversari states that frequently he had become discouraged at ever being able to render Chrysostom's Greek into eloquent Latin, but that he had nevertheless persisted, recognizing that to abandon the undertaking would show extreme ingratitude to Matteo "when it is chiefly through your favor and help that I have pursued Greek and Latin letters."[50] More importantly Traversari attributes to Matteo the suggestion that it would be particularly appropriate to his monastic vocation to direct his attention to translating the literature of Christian, rather than classical, antiquity. In his concluding remarks Traversari underlines the importance of positive support from the Prior.

> It is my desire, if I recognize that this kind of exercise pleases you, if it is confirmed by your authority, and if you advise it as agreeable to our monastic repose, to translate by similar work and study many more works of this man (they are nearly innumerable) and to dedicate them to your name. In this minimal way may I return your incredible love for me . . . .[51]

The Climacus preface reveals how essential was Matteo's support for Traversari's patristic scholarship. The Prior, Traversari asserts, regarded the medieval translation of Climacus as difficult to understand. He therefore authorized Traversari to render a new one, anticipating that he would bring out more lucidly the meaning of the text. But this undertaking brought charges that it was rash and iniquitous to alter the translation which had been made by a man inspired by the Holy Spirit. Traversari's response was that the medieval translation was deficient in terms of scholarship, and that in offering a more intelligible translation he was satisfying the desires of the Prior and of the other monks in the monastery who avidly awaited its completion. The new translation was not therefore undertaken as a personal whim or for personal glory. In light of this he delegated to Matteo the responsibility for responding to his calumniators.[52]

Given this opposition to a humanistic translation of Climacus, and given the anti-classical attitude expressed by Giovanni da Sanminiato, Traversari's fellow monk, it was obviously of decisive importance that the Prior of S. Maria degli Angeli was a man who not only permitted, but encouraged, Traversari's humanist studies. Matteo seems to have recognized that Traversari's knowledge of classical Greek and Latin could, by being directed to patristic studies, contribute rather than detract from the foundations of piety in the monastery. Beyond this Traversari was an intimate of Matteo's. When he died in 1421, Traversari felt the loss deeply.

> It is hard to believe how seized with grief I am at his death, how covered with darkness my eyes. So strong was his love for me, so great his kindness, so welcome his presence, that I can hardly live without him. My life depended on his. I deny that any man was dearer, or more agreeable to him than I .... So much has grief seized me, dearest Francesco [Barbaro], that I admit that I have nearly abandoned all my former pleasures, that is the *studia humanitatis.* As yet I am scarcely able to recover and collect myself.[53]

That Traversari was to focus his intellectual energies on the study of the *Greek* Fathers stemmed from the arrival in Florence, in 1397, of the Byzantine scholar, Manuel Chrysoloras (c. 1350-1415). It was Salutati (with the financial help of

Niccoli and Palla Strozzi), who induced Chrysoloras to come to Florence to assume the chair of Greek studies at the Florentine Studio and to teach Greek to beginners. The Chancellor ardently sought, following the example of Cato, to acquire knowledge of Greek in his old age; and he hoped that through Chrysoloras' teaching, the rich sources of Greek wisdom that Cicero had admired — Homer, Plato, Plutarch — would be revealed to Florentine students. Chrysoloras' initial stay in Florence was brief, lasting from February 1397 to March 1400, but the extent of his impact on Florentine intellectual life can scarcely be exaggerated. Leonardo Bruni, who abandoned his study of civil law to experience the Greek classics, and later translated works of Plutarch, Demosthenes, Plato, and Aristotle; Pier Paolo Vergerio, author of an early treatise on humanist education; Roberto Rossi, humanist translator of Aristotle's *Posterior Analytics*; Palla Strozzi, leading patron of humanist studies and collector of Greek manuscripts; and Antonio Corbinelli, who amassed a large Greek library — all learned Greek from Chrysoloras. Besides teaching Greek, Chrysoloras provided the inspiration and method to translate Greek works into Latin, laid the basis for the purpose and content of the humanist educational curriculum, and sparked a whole generation of Italian humanists to pursue Greek studies. [54]

Traversari was undoubtedly affected indirectly by Chrysoloras' ideas through his friendship with Niccoli, who began Greek studies under Chrysoloras in 1397-99, but never became proficient in the language. There were, however, subsequent direct links between the young monk and the Byzantine apostle of Greek learning to the West. Chrysoloras was in Florence for several months in the summer of 1413 and again in January and February 1414 while attached to the court of the Pisan Pope, John XXIII. That Chrysoloras and Traversari met in 1413-14 is evidenced by a letter sent to Traversari in 1417 by Bartolomeo Arragazzi da Montepulciano from St. Gall, where he and Poggio were searching for manuscripts. Bartolomeo had learned Greek from Chrysoloras in Rome in 1411 and had conversed with him on a number of occasions at the Council of Constance prior to his death there in 1415. In the letter Bartolomeo states,

> That great man Manuel Chrysoloras, when he was
> with Pope John, used to speak very pleasantly with
> me about your renowned virtues. He did not hesitate
> to regard you as among the most eminent men of our
> age, not only for the holiness of your life, but also
> indeed for your genius and your learning in both
> Greek and Latin letters. He held that only men
> endowed with these virtues are wise, because they do
> not become insolent in prosperity and they suffer
> adversity with equanimity.[55]

By 1413-14 Traversari had not yet undertaken any translations of Greek texts, but Chrysoloras was impressed enough
with the young Traversari to address to him a long philosophical
letter, written in Greek, on the theme of friendship.[56]
Traversari in turn expressed the greatest admiration for Chrysoloras.

> . . . . it gives me the greatest pleasure to rejoice with
> you in his humanity, learning, and wisdom. Indeed to
> him belongs that facility and wealth of genius, so that
> after the ancients (whom we wonder at with the
> greatest admiration, and through whose books we are
> engaged in the *studia humanitatis*) he stands nearly
> alone. In my judgment he easily carries the palm of
> victory in learning . . . . I am indebted to him for,
> among many other things, his love and his singularly
> wonderful regard for me . . . .[57]

Chrysoloras is most famed for his inspirational teaching of
the Greek classics to members of the Salutati circle. But his
intellectual interests embraced theology and sacred literature as
well. He took part in the theological disputations at Constance,
translated from Latin into Greek the Collects of the Roman
Missal and the Mass attributed to Gregory the Great, and wrote
a work on the Procession of the Holy Spirit which upheld Latin
doctrine (perhaps an indication he had become a convert to
Rome). He was a strong advocate of the union of the Greek and
Latin Churches, an irenicism based largely on his conviction of
the importance of the cultural and intellectual bonds which
linked Greek East and Latin West in antiquity. Inspired by his

first visit to Rome in 1411, he wrote a treatise, addressed to the Byzantine Emperor, which compared the sacred memories of old and new Rome (i.e. Constantinople), and which stressed the glorious heritage shared by both civilizations.[58] In light of Chrysoloras' interest in sacred letters, it is particularly noteworthy that Traversari attributes to him the inspiration to translate Climacus' *Scala Paradisi*. In March 1416 Traversari wrote Francesco Barbaro seeking the Greek text of this work. He was eager to translate it, "for I have been informed by our Chrysoloras that in Greek it shines with the splendor of eloquence."[59]

How did Traversari learn Greek? He possessed a copy of Chrysoloras' widely diffused Greek grammar, the *Erotemata*, but it is clear he did not learn the language directly from him. Chrysoloras left Florence after his initial stay in March 1400, six months before Traversari's entry into S. Maria degli Angeli. He did not return to Florence until 1413-14, by which time Traversari already knew Greek.[60] Moreover, Traversari states that he taught himself Greek. He explains how he did so in response to a friend who sought advice and help in having his grandson learn Greek.

> . . . . I own nothing which contains both the Greek text and Latin exposition, neither of Plutarch and other gentiles nor of sacred letters. Since you state you have discovered that I pursued Greek letters without the help of a teacher, and since you seek my help and counsel in instructing the boy so that he can push forward on this uncharted journey by following my footsteps, I will reveal to you how I obtained my modest knowledge of this language. Through instruction in the religious rites of our Order, I was intimately familiar with the Greek Psalter. I began therefore to compare this with the Latin and to note individual verbs, nouns, and other parts of speech. As much as possible I committed to memory what these words signified. Then I pressed forward, turning first to the Gospels, then to the Epistles of Paul and to Acts, and studied these thoroughly. They contain a copious vocabulary and are translated faithfully,

diligently, and without awkwardness. Afterwards, to be sure, I wished to see books of the gentiles, but I did not understand them easily. Therefore it seems best to me . . . that he stick strictly to the ancient translations of sacred literature, which, since they are translated truthfully, are easier and more conducive to progress. He might indeed make use of a teacher; but unless he were exceptionally expert and knew the language thoroughly by experience, there would be no profit, but rather harm to the inexperienced mind. I judge it preferable to struggle along the certain, than to follow a doubtful and uncertain path. I speak from experience.[61]

Traversari's knowledge of Greek was acquired, evidently, on his own. But it is significant that Demetrio Scarano, a Greek from Constantinople, entered S. Maria degli Angeli in 1406, made his profession as a monk there in 1417, and died in the monastery in 1426.[62] To what extent did Scarano aid Traversari's Greek studies? In the period 1416-19 Traversari mentions that Scarano was transcribing for him Greek texts, both classical and patristic.[63] In 1424 Traversari sought to have Leonardo Giustiniani acquire for him in Venice a number of Scarano's Greek manuscripts, apparently left there. Among these were a Xenophon and Chrysostom's *Homilies on Matthew*.[64] Scarano's possession of Greek classical and patristic texts suggests that he was not a mere scribe, but rather a man of some learning. This seems corroborated by his desire to meet Johannes Chrysoloras, Manuel's nephew, when he arrived in Venice in 1415,[65] and more especially by Traversari's invitation to Niccolò Niccoli and Giovanni Aurispa to attend Demetrio's funeral rites.[66] While apparently Demetrio played no active role in Traversari's work of translation, his presence in the monastery was doubtless of considerable utility.

Salutati's stress on the patristic support for the *studia humanitatis*, and on patristic theology as an evangelical and Scriptural faith, the presence of the Greek-speaking Demetrio Scarano in S. Maria degli Angeli, Prior Matteo's deep affection and his sustained support for the humanist study of Latin and Greek — all were important for Traversari's intellectual formation. But it was undoubtedly Niccolō Niccoli (1364-1437) who was the most decisive intellectual influence.

In his zealous preoccupation with classical studies, and in his personal demeanor and daily life, Niccoli embodied the enthusiasm for the culture of antiquity which animated the Florentine humanists of the early *quattrocento*. From his youth, when he abandoned his family's flourishing wool textile business in order to devote himself wholly to the revival of antiquity, he was a passionate collector of ancient *objets d'art* and classical manuscripts. Vespasiano describes him dining from ancient porcelain and crystal amidst a vast collection of ancient bronzes and sculpture. He explored ancient ruins, copied Roman epigraphs, and ardently searched for ancient codices. For half a century, from the time he was a leading member of the Santo Spirito circle until his death, he was at the heart of the Florentine humanist movement. Moreover, he was in contact with all the leading humanists of Italy, who were eager to inform him of the latest archeological finds and the most recent recovery of ancient texts. For instance, it was Niccoli whom Poggio first informed of his spectacular discoveries of Quintillian, Lucretius, and Cicero manuscripts in Swiss monasteries during the period of the Council of Constance. Niccoli, first exhausting his own fortune, then drawing heavily on funds lent by Cosimo de' Medici, amassed the largest and finest classical and patristic library in Italy. His Greek collection, purchased from Giovanni Aurispa, Cristoforo Buondelmonti, and other travelers to the Greek East, was outstanding. And this library of Niccoli's provided the principal manuscript sources for Traversari's patristic studies. [67]

Niccoli wrote little, but his fastidious concern for the seeming minutiae of classical scholarship − for orthography, especially the correct use of diphthongs, and the use of ancient script − made him an arbiter of taste. Poggio, Marsuppini, and other humanists eagerly awaited Niccoli's judgement on their writings and scholarship. Traversari, too, looked to Niccoli as a critical judge of Latin style, and his usual practice was to send him first drafts of his translations. On one occasion when they met with Niccoli's approval, Traversari responded,

> I rejoice that you are pleased with the *Vitae Patrum*
> and [Chrysostom's] *Sermones contra Iudaeos* and
> *Quod Deus incomprehensibilis sit.* Because of your
> judgement, which I esteem, I will be more confident
> and bold to others. [68]

Another time, when the arbiter praised the eloquence of his
Latin style, Traversari replied,

> I might have used with regard to you (if my religious
> vocation permitted) that line of Naevius which Cicero
> used in writing to Cato, "Gaudeo laudari abs te,"
> brother, "laudato viro." [69]

Traversari regarded Niccoli as the man principally responsible
for the revival of Latin and Greek studies, and indeed for the
renaissance of antiquity in general. In a letter written shortly
after Niccoli's death, Traversari assessed the significance of his
life and activity.

> In particular all those who are dedicated to humanist
> studies lament that they have lost their progenitor
> and supporter. And indeed it is so, for in my
> judgment (which may be freely revealed) neither in
> our memory nor in the memory of our fathers has the
> Latin language owed more honor and praise to any
> man. Whatever erudition, whatever eloquence Italy
> has today (and I dare to say it has more than it has
> had for six hundred years), he was the founder and
> leader of it. He first brought about the revival of
> Greek studies which had been extinct here for many
> centuries. Almost alone it was his diligence and
> indefatigable devotion which brought to light the
> buried monuments of antiquity, when most men,
> especially those of leading stature, seemed indif-
> ferent. [70]

For Traversari, Niccoli was even more than the leading spirit
of the humanist movement. He was an intimate friend and the
man primarily responsible for his intellectual development and
scholarly achievements.

As for the fact that you rejoice so greatly in my studies, this is neither new to you, nor foreign to your character and custom. For my part I have long been convinced that you rejoice no less in my progress than in your own advantage and gain. I was sorry that you, disregarding dignity and long-established friendship, demean yourself so much as to assert that you regard yourself very fortunate to have deserved to become friends with me. Ought these be the words of my Niccolò? Did you not think I would blush at this? Have I deserved this from you? Do you think I could hear anything more disturbing? I believe from the depth of my being that you are no happier through my friendship with you than I am more illustrious, erudite, and blessed through your friendship with me. Indeed has anyone, after our venerable father [i.e. Prior Matteo], whose cordiality is worthy of memory, been more loving to me than you? You were, almost from the beginning, the patron, inspirer, and collaborator with my studies. However much progress I have made in Latin and Greek I owe primarily to you. I thus do not wish to be (may God prevent it) ungrateful for your benevolence and special kindness to me. Whatever progress I have made I owe to you from whom I received it. [71]

When and under what circumstances Niccoli first befriended Traversari is uncertain. But by 1416 Niccoli was a frequent visitor to Traversari's cell, and Traversari reported their friendship as especially close. [72] In the 1420's Niccoli was a daily visitor to S. Maria degli Angeli, and the two collaborated closely on humanist scholarship. For instance, Traversari emended the Greek in Niccoli's newly acquired manuscripts of Quintillian and Aulus Gellius, while Niccoli wrote down Traversari's dictated translations of Chrysostom's homilies on the Pauline Epistles. [73] Traversari worked hard to acquire manuscripts for Niccoli, while Niccoli in turn provided free access to his library. Indeed when Niccoli traveled to Rome in 1423-24, he left his library in Traversari's care at S. Maria degli Angeli. Niccoli originally intended to bequeath his library to S.

Maria degli Angeli, but when Traversari became General and was no longer permanently resident in Florence, he altered his plans, and in his last will named sixteen executors, headed by Traversari, and including the Medici and all the leading Florentine humanists, to provide for his library in a way which would be most beneficial to students. Traversari continued to have access to the library during the crucial years of the Council of Ferrara-Florence. After his death in 1439 Cosimo had Michelozzo build the famous library in the monastery of San Marco to house Niccoli's collection. [74]

Traversari's and Niccoli's friendship was more than intellectual. Indeed the younger monk acted as spiritual counselor for the strong-willed and often irascible elder humanist. In 1424 he rebuked Niccoli for his violent quarrel with Leonardo Bruni, advising him to examine closely the end of the ninth book of Augustine's *Confessions*, where the author treated the life of his mother. There he would discover much to the point regarding the virtues of patience and charity. [75] A certain coolness in their friendship is detectable in the mid-1430's, in part attributable to Traversari's long absences from Florence, first to make visitations to the monasteries of his Order, then as Papal Legate to Basel. But Niccoli also objected that Traversari's preoccupation with reform of the Camaldulensians and other ecclesiastical affairs would interfere with his patristic scholarship, which Niccoli regarded as more important. [76] In the last days of Niccoli's life their former intimacy was restored. Vespasiano relates that the two were together constantly. Each morning Traversari said mass in his friend's room, and then read from the Epistles of Paul. In the end Niccoli died in Traversari's arms. [77]

Niccoli, most famed for his cultivation of classical antiquity, developed a genuine concern for sacred letters, especially in his later years, and his devotion to Holy Scripture was praised by Alberto da Sarteano, the prominent Franciscan preacher. [78] Traversari also appealed to Niccoli's commitment to erudition in sacred letters in urging him to receive Easter communion, which he had neglected for many years. [79] More significantly, Niccoli encouraged Traversari's patristic studies, and in 1433 Traversari wrote that he "never ceases demanding that I, in the midst of perpetual occupations, translate Greek sacred texts." [80]

Niccoli's friendship was decisive for Traversari's commitment to the intellectual perspective and values of the *studia humanitatis*. Through him, Traversari shared the concern for the regeneration of antiquity and the cultivation of the ideal of eloquence. He also shared in the work of discovery, study, and translation of classical and patristic manuscripts along with the new ideas on education, speculation on ethical values, and interest in ancient art and architecture which occupied the minds of early Quattrocento humanists. Through Niccoli, Traversari made contacts with the humanist communities in Venice and Rome, and with such Florentine humanists as Bruni and Marsuppini whose classicizing intellectual interests did not involve patristic studies. As a consequence, Traversari was thoroughly familiar with the intellectual endeavors of the humanist movement as a whole, and his patristic studies were thoroughly rooted in the intellectual assumptions of the *studia humanitatis.*

In considering Traversari's intellectual formation, it is important to observe that he never attended a university. Unlike Marsili, who studied in the arts faculty at Padua, then pursued theology at Paris, before finally turning as a mature man to humanist studies, Traversari never was trained in the medieval *trivium* and *quadrivium*, nor did he attend lectures in philosophy, theology, or canon law. This is explicable in part because it was not the Benedictines, but rather the mendicant orders which dominated the university world. Once Traversari entered S. Maria degli Angeli, the option to pursue a university career was not open. But the absence of university training meant that Traversari was not shaped intellectually by the assumptions and concerns of late medieval scholasticism and was free to approach the Fathers and Christian antiquity from the new perspective of humanist thought.

For the impact of scholastic education in forming directions for humanist activity, it is instructive to take note of Traversari's contemporary, Andrea Biglia da Milano (c. 1395-1435). After entering the Augustinian Order in 1412, then studying literature and philosophy at Padua before coming to Florence in 1418, he lectured at the Florentine Studio on moral philosophy, poetry, and rhetoric for the following four academic years (1419-23); and he began theological studies, which he continued at the theological faculty of the university of Bologna from 1423-28, where he also lectured on natural philosophy and ethics. In 1428-29 he taught at Pavia, then went to Siena to teach at the Studio there. His early studies at Padua brought him into contact with Gasparino Barzizza, who lectured on the Latin classics, and who also taught Vittorino da Feltre. In Florence he became familiar with the leading humanists, including Traversari. [81] In Bologna he frequented the humanist household of Cardinal Niccolò Albergati, who also was patron of Tommaso Parentucelli, the future Pope Nicholas V. Biglia's letters and orations have been lost, but there is extant his humanist history of Milan from 1402 to 1431, the *Rerum mediolanensium historia*, modeled on Livy. Biglia also learned Greek, and he made a number of humanist Latin translations from the Greek, including Plutarch's *Vita Timoleontis*. His principal translations, however, were of Aristotle's *Physics* and *De anima*, works which reflect his education in scholastic philosophy and theology. A cycle of Biglia's sermons is extant, the *Sermones ab Adventu usque ad Resurrectionem Christi,* and he wrote a treatise attacking S. Bernardino's preaching. But neither his preaching, nor his involvement in the Bernardino controversy, nor his monastic profession directed him to Christian antiquity. Like Luigi Marsili his humanism was largely expressed in secular interests, and he kept distinct his humanist and his theological studies. [82] In contrast, Traversari integrated his commitment to monastic spirituality and his enthusiasm for the *studia humanitatis* by focusing on the renaissance of Christian antiquity.

CHAPTER II

THE STUDIA HUMANITATIS

In the summer of 1433 Traversari, then General of the Camaldulensians, was proceding from Padua to Mantua, continuing his journey of reform visitations to the monasteries of his Order. A short distance from Padua, he turned aside into the Euganean Hills "in order to see for myself in the village of Arquà the tomb of Francesco Petrarca. For he was a man renowned in our age whose dedication to letters began the awakening of the *studia humanitatis.* Thus I was easily induced to wish to see his mausoleum. Having paid my respects, and uttered prayers for his repose, I went on to the monastery." [1]

This incident is illustrative of Traversari's adherence to the cultural-intellectual values of the humanist movement, of which he felt himself a part. Just as he admired the genius and wisdom of the ancients, and believed it was his own age, initiated by Petrarch, which was creating their rebirth, so also he ignored as barbarous medieval culture, and had a scornful antipathy for scholastic thought. Like other humanists, Traversari gave primary emphasis to philology and textual criticism, regarded rhetoric as the central discipline of human discourse, strove for an elegant Latin style, and promoted the new educational curriculum. He shared also the implicit emphasis on the moral, as well as cultural, formation of the individual, and he made considerable, though hesitating, efforts to reconcile the ethical implications of the *studia humanitatis* with Christian piety and monastic spirituality. It is within this context of close association with other humanists, and a shared enthusiasm for the same cultural-intellectual goals, that Traversari's patristic scholarship must be understood.

Relation with Humanist Circles
in Florence, Venice, and Rome

Being cloistered in S. Maria degli Angeli did not mean that Traversari was isolated from contact with other humanists, since Florence in the first half of the Quattrocento was the center of the humanist movement. Many of its leaders lived there, and others from Venice, Rome, and elsewhere were frequent visitors. Niccoli's friendship was decisive for Traversari's initial introduction into the world of the humanists, but Traversari came to know personally nearly all those in Florence, many of whom frequented his cell, and several of whom became close friends. Moreover, through an extensive correspondence, he maintained close contact with those in Venice and Rome, until his travels as General made possible visits to these cities.

As early as the latter 1410's Traversari was actively cultivating humanist contacts. He was corresponding frequently with the young Venetian patrician, Francesco Barbaro (1398-1454), who had visited Florence in 1415, at which time they apparently met. Barbaro possessed an excellent Greek library, and encouraged Traversari to make free use of it, which he was delighted to do. Among the Greek classical texts he borrowed were Philostratus' *Life of Apollonius of Tyana* and a Nicander, both of which he had Demetrio Scarano transcribe. In return he sent a copy of Xenophon's *Agesilaus,* in Demetrio's transcription. More significantly Barbaro, who came to possess a number of Greek patristic texts, lent Traversari a Greek manuscript of St. Basil's *Letters.*[2] Besides exchanging manuscripts and information on current humanist scholarship — for instance, in 1418-19 Traversari informed Barbaro that Leonardo Bruni had begun a *Commentary* on the First Punic War based on Polybius, which he promised to send when Bruni finished it[3]— they exchanged copies of their translations. Traversari eagerly sought Barbaro's version of Plutarch's lives of Cato and Aristides, an undertaking he praised as particularly worthy for one who had chosen to model his life on the mores of the ancients.[4] Barbaro in turn sought Traversari's patristic translations; his admiration for the Climacus translation particularly gratified Traversari.[5]In 1416 Barbaro wrote *De re uxoria,* an elegant compilation of classical pronouncements on marriage, which he dedicated to

Cosimo de' Medici's brother, Lorenzo, as a wedding present. When Traversari read the work, he lavished praise on it. "You alone in our age are easily equal to that high, excelling genius of the ancients, and you may even be capable of surpassing them. Bravo! With this as your first effort, what light of genius will you reveal as an experienced orator? I do not know how to praise or admire your genius enough." [6]

In correspondence with Guarino da Verona (1374-1460) in this same period, Traversari displays a similar desire to bandy the elegant phrases of humanist discourse. Traversari probably became acquainted with Guarino in the period 1412-14 during which the latter, recently returned from an extended stay in the Chrysoloras household in Constantinople, taught Greek at the Florentine Studio. Traversari's relationship with Guarino was less intense than that with Barbaro, but they maintained contact by correspondence in the latter 1410's and early 1420's. In 1417 Guarino wrote, apologizing for the tardiness of his response to Traversari's previous letter. But he remarked, "We are linked by such long-established bonds of friendship that no matter where we happen to be our minds are present to each other. . . . Our love, founded on virtue, is so complete that words cannot augment nor silence diminish it." [7] To this Traversari responded:

> Yet your view . . . though wisely and splendidly expressed is too austere in my estimation, and is rather Catonian than Ciceronian. You know certainly how disagreeable the silence of absent friends was to Cicero, and rightly so. What indeed does friendship dread more than solitude? Is this not to be called solitude indeed when we are deprived of the sight and companionship of friends? But we are accustomed to alleviate and console this desire for friends through frequent exchange of letters. . . . I want you to know most charming Guarino — and also our Barbaro — that nothing brings greater pleasure or joy to me than frequent, delightful letters. [8]

By the early 1420's Traversari had gained a position of prominence among Florentine humanists. Guarino's student

Ermolao Barbaro (the Elder) had dedicated to Traversari his translation of Aesop's *Fables*, with effusive praise for Traversari's erudition in both Greek and Latin, and Bruni himself had brought to Traversari his just-completed Latin translation of Plato's *Phaedrus*.[9] Traversari now also added Poggio Bracciolini (1380-1459) in Rome and Leonardo Giustiniani (1388-1446) in Venice to his correspondents.[10] Moreover, a number of Florentine humanists began gathering daily in Traversari's cell for discussions, much as the previous humanist generation had met with Marsili at Santo Spirito. According to Vespasiano, this informal academy included — besides Niccoli — Cosimo de' Medici (1389-1464) and his brother Lorenzo (1395-1440); Carlo Marsuppini (1399-1453), the humanist from Arezzo, who came to Florence in the early 1420's as a tutor in the Medici household, and who eventually (in 1444) succeeded Bruni as Florentine Chancellor; Paolo Toscanelli (1397-1482), who returned to Florence in 1424 after seven years of medical study at the University of Padua, and who gained increasing fame for his knowledge of medicine, mathematics, and astrology; and Filippo Pieruzzi (1388-1462), Florentine notary, and student of Greek mathematics. Later, towards 1430, they were joined by Giannozzo Manetti (1396-1459), who had begun Greek studies under Traversari.[11]

Traversari enjoyed a close and sustained friendship with the Medici brothers. He had come into contact with Cosimo as early as 1416, for he wrote in that year to Francesco Barbaro praising Cosimo as "noster ornatissimus, atque sapientissimus adolescens."[12] As their friendship deepened in the 1420's, Traversari's esteem for Cosimo grew. When, in 1431, as division in Florence increased over the ill-fated war with Lucca, Cosimo resigned from the *Dieci di Balia* (war commission), Traversari wrote to Niccoli:

> We are in a worse way since Cosimo stepped down from the *Dieci*. He is esteemed and loved by the citizens, for he conducted himself in that office so that nothing, not even his own welfare, came before that of the country. The very stones seem to proclaim this! He has such generosity of mind that merely his appearance cheered the despondent, and bade those

wasting away with grief be of better hope. His vigilance had been such that whatever prospered was chiefly through his industry. Would that we had more such citizens! Never was any Republic happier and more prosperous. [13]

Cosimo's growing popularity and the debilitating war which eroded support for the Albizzi regime led Rinaldo degli Albizzi in the summer of 1433 to plan a pre-emptive coup against the Medici. When a Signoria favorable to the Albizzi regime was returned in the election of 1 September, Rinaldo decided to strike. On 7 September Cosimo was summoned to the Palazzo della Signoria, placed under arrest, and a *Parlamento* of Florentine citizens, dominated by Albizzi partisans, convened in the Piazza to decide his fate. Meanwhile Cosimo's brother, Lorenzo, was exiled to Venice. When rumors of the strike against the Medici reached Traversari on 12 September, he was in Ferrara, where he had just completed negotiations with the Holy Roman Emperor Sigismund regarding confirmation of the imperial privileges granted to the Camaldulensians. Traversari immediately hastened to Bologna, and there on the evening of the 15th met Lorenzo, who was on his way into exile. Lorenzo urged him to proceed straight on to Florence, and to exert whatever influence he could on Cosimo's behalf. Traversari left the next morning and arrived the evening of the 17th. The following morning he went to the Palazzo della Signoria and addressed the Priors. He was careful not to question the wisdom of their action. Instead he appealed to their humanity, urging them to feel pity for those who, once powerful and rich, had been struck down by fickle fortune and stripped of country, glory, and dignity. He asked them to have mercy on Cosimo, and urged his release from the grave discomforts and perils of imprisonment. Then he sought permission to see Cosimo, in order to console him. This request was granted. Traversari then relates:

> When I saw Cosimo imprisoned, I was filled with anguish, turning over in my mind the present state of affairs and past fortune. Nevertheless, I restrained my tears as much as possible. Indeed I discovered in him

such greatness of mind, such contempt for past fortune and worldly glory, that I could not desire more. He preserved his dignity of countenance and expression, so that he seemed rather to feel pity for the afflicted city than be concerned with his own injuries. Finally, after our lengthy conversation, I, who had come to console, came away much consoled, and I pitied the state which had lost such strong, magnanimous, and constant men. It was by men with this sense of devotion that the city had been wisely preserved. [14]

Despite Traversari's own deep concern for his brother, Girolamo, then gravely ill (and who indeed succumbed on 7 October despite all Toscanelli's efforts), he continued to work diligently on Cosimo's behalf. He met with the Venetian envoys, consoled the Medici wives, and even met with Rinaldo himself, but found him adamant. His influence exhausted, he returned to Cosimo, and discovered that liberal Medici bribes would lead to his prompt release. Traversari concludes his account:

After a few days, by God's mercy, he was released at about the fourth hour of the night. The day after he had departed a comet was seen in the sky which caused great anxiety. I gave thanks to God, who had adverted this threat from Cosimo, and who had relieved my perpetual worry and concern. [15]

Traversari's prestige may have proved of negligible help in Cosimo's hour of crisis, but his deep concern for Cosimo's safety is evident. Medici position and prestige by contrast, however, did prove valuable to Traversari's scholarship. In 1424, for instance, when Cosimo went to Bologna as Florentine envoy, Traversari turned to him to exert his influence with Niccolò Albergati, Bishop of Bologna, in order to procure a manuscript of Ignatius' *Epistolae* from the nearby Benedictine monastery of Nonantola. [16] More spectacular were the fruits of Lorenzo's embassy to Rome in 1431. While there he managed to procure on loan from Cardinal Giordano Orsini Latin volumes of Plautus and Tertullian. Both manuscripts had been discovered in Germany by Nicolaus Cusanus, who presented them to Orsini when he visited Rome in 1429. Traversari, at Niccoli's behest, had written Orsini in 1430, inquiring about the Plautus, but the Cardinal had not deigned to reply. When Traversari learned of Lorenzo's success, he rejoiced in his miraculous shrewdness in wresting the precious manuscripts from Orsini's "unworthy possession." [17] On a more mundane level, Traversari found the apparatus of the Medici Bank invaluable for the secure transport of manuscripts, or as places of deposit for manuscripts pledged for the return of borrowed volumes. [18] He also on one occasion turned to Cosimo to hire scribes proficient in writing humanistic script since he needed transcriptions of his translations. Cosimo may also have given financial support to the humanist academy Traversari founded at Fonte Buona. [19]

Cosimo, however, was more than simply a patron of humanist scholarship. As early as 1418 he had acquired a substantial library of Latin classical and patristic manuscripts. [20] When he was branch manager of the Medici Bank in Rome, he accompanied Poggio to Ostia and the Alban Hills to investigate the Roman ruins. [21] Moreover, it was Cosimo, along with Niccoli, who especially urged Traversari to undertake the translation of Diogenes Laertius. Traversari eventually did so, and dedicated his translation to Cosimo. He also dedicated to Cosimo his translation of the sermons of Ephraem the Syrian. [22] Both Medici brothers studied works of the Fathers. In 1424 Traversari wrote to Niccoli:

> I am extremely pleased with our Lorenzo's ardent study of sacred letters. That he has read avidly the *Moralia* of St. Gregory, and admired it highly, is in my judgement an indication of a good and sound taste. I shall send him not only willingly but with great pleasure Origen's *Commentary on the Epistle to the Romans* as you asked me; . . . and I will regard it as much benefit to myself if through your diligence, work, and support the youth gives himself to these studies, which alone are true and health-giving. Would that at last they would take heed, who until now have neglected these! [23]

Cosimo's interest in the Fathers was as strong as his brother's. Vespasiano states that when he was a youth he visited Cosimo at his villa at Careggi and found him engaged in two excellent tasks. First he spent some hours each morning pruning his vineyard, then he read Gregory's *Moralia,* completing the entire thirty-five books in six months.[24] Further, after Traversari became General, Cosimo repeatedly urged him to free himself from the onerous tasks of reforming his Order so that he could devote his energies to patristic scholarship.[25] While General, Traversari continued close contact with Cosimo, sending him the *Hodoeporicon,* an account of his journeys of monastic visitations 1431-34, and informing him of the situation at the Council at Basel, where Traversari was sent as Papal Legate in the fall of 1435. While at the Council of Ferrara in 1438, he promised to do all in his power to have the Council transferred to Florence as Cosimo desired. [26]

Traversari's association with the group of humanists which gathered in his cell involved him in the manifold intellectual and cultural interests of the humanist movement. For instance, Marsuppini — with whom, Traversari remarked, the Medici youths were no less happy, "than was Alexander with his first teacher Leonides or later with Aristotle"[27] — was particularly well versed in the Greek poets, and esteemed also for his own Latin poetry. When Traversari encountered difficulty in translating the enigmatic language of Diogenes Laertius, he turned to Marsuppini for help.[28] In 1429 Marsuppini made a Latin translation, first in prose and then in verse, of the *Batrachomyomachia* (The Battle of Frogs and Mice), the comic parody of the *Iliad,* attributed to Homer by the Romans, but undoubtedly written only in the fifth or fourth centuries B.C. It was then suggested that he turn to the *Iliad* itself. But Traversari opposed this, suggesting to Niccoli that Marsuppini instead translate the history of Diodorus Siculus. "I think it more useful to have him attend to this work than to have him translate the poem of Homer. True, he has a genius for composing elegant verse — and both a ready skill and a great command of the language — but in my judgement he would labor long before he could preserve in Latin the dignity of Homer, so that it would not be a dishonor."[29]

Similarly, friendship with Toscanelli and Pieruzzi involved Traversari in another humanist concern — Greek mathematics and engineering. In 1424 Traversari worked zealously, but fruitlessly as it turned out, to acquire an illustrated Greek work of Archimedes on military machines and hydraulics, reputedly in the possession of Rinuccio da Castiglione (c. 1395-after 1456), who had just returned to Italy from a lengthy stay in the Greek East. Eight months of careful inquiry among Traversari's humanist contacts in Bologna, where Rinuccio was staying, produced no results. Eventually Rinuccio came to Florence, and visited S. Maria degli Angeli. But rather than the anticipated genial discussion, Traversari was forced to endure in silence Rinuccio's assault on the Tuscan character (while he praised the Venetians to the skies), his vehement attack on Bruni as the plague and ruin of all studies, and his anger at Niccoli. Eventually Traversari extracted from Rinuccio a promise to send a complete index of all Greek volumes in his possession, and he borrowed and transcribed overnight a manuscript containing three Pythagorean letters. Moreover, Rinuccio did admit to having an illustrated Archimedes. Traversari's subsequent efforts to have the text produced, however, were unavailing, and the text, if it existed, was in all probability spurious.[30] Later, in the period 1425-27, Traversari did borrow from Giovanni Aurispa mathematical and engineering texts of Athenaeus and Pappus.[31]

The extent of Traversari's personal study of mathematics is uncertain. None of his letters discuss mathematical theory or engineering ideas. Mutual interest in mathematics and the engineering of antiquity, however, forged links between Florentine humanists and artists in the 1420's. It has been plausibly suggested, for example, that Toscanelli contributed to Brunelleschi's solution to the problem of linear perspective.[32] Traversari, himself, seems to have been involved to some extent with Florentine artists. In 1430 Lorenzo Ghiberti, the sculptor (who had completed a bronze reliquary for S. Maria degli Angeli in 1428), asked Traversari to reborrow for him from Aurispa Athenaeus' work on siege engines. The long exhortation to the study of all of natural philosophy with which Ghiberti opens his *Commentarii* (written during the 1450's) is, significantly, an unacknowledged translation of Athenaeus' preface.[33] More-over, Richard Krautheimer has built a plausible case that Traversari was responsible for the iconography, based on patristic scriptural exegesis, of Ghiberti's celebrated bronze "Gates of Paradise" to the Florentine Baptistry. [34]

Traversari's contact with the leading Italian humanist scholars of Greek thought was augmented in the latter 1420's with the arrival in Florence of Giovanni Aurispa (1376-1459) and Francesco Filelfo (1398-1481). Both men held the prestigious chair of Greek studies at the Florentine Studio, Aurispa from 1425 to 1427, Filelfo from 1429 to 1434.

Of all the Italian travelers to the Greek East in the early Quattrocento it was Aurispa who amassed the largest collection of Greek manuscripts. His first trip to Byzantium in 1413-14 produced a number of Greek texts, including a Thucydides, which Traversari mentioned that Niccoli bought in Pisa in 1417;[35] but it was his subsequent stay, 1421-23, which resulted in the largest and finest collection of Greek texts to reach Italy prior to Bessarion's arrival in 1438. Aurispa had gone to Constantinople as envoy of the Gonzaga of Mantua. While there he entered the imperial chancery and gained favor with the Emperor. When he returned to Italy in 1423 he wrote, in response to Traversari's solicitous inquiry, that he had brought to Venice 238 classical Greek manuscripts, including all of Plato, all of Plotinus, all of Proclus, and much of Iamblichus, many of the Greek poets, including Pindar, and much of Greek history, including the volumes of Procopius and Xenophon given him by the Emperor. Delighted with this fortuitous potential benefit to humanist Greek studies, Traversari readily arranged with the Medici the fifty florin loan Aurispa had requested to pay the freight charges for shipping his books from Constantinople to Venice. He also arranged for an exchange of Niccoli's transcriptions of the complete texts of Cicero's *Orator, Brutus,* and *De oratore,* discovered at Lodi in 1421, for Aurispa's transcriptions of the Greek texts of Aristotle's *Rhetoric* and *Eudemian Ethics.* Moreover, he joined Niccoli in exhorting Aurispa to abandon the teaching post he had assumed at Bologna and instead to take up the chair at the Florentine Studio. During Aurispa's year in Bologna, Traversari sought a number of Greek texts from him including a commentary on the *Iliad,* Herodian's *De linguarum varietate,* and a work of the grammarian Pollux. [36] During Aurispa's tenure in Florence, Traversari took advantage of his presence to borrow, besides the mathematical works of Pappus and Athenaeus, Proclus' *Platonic Theology.* [37] It is probable that Niccoli acquired a number of Greek volumes from Aurispa — Traversari mentions his acquisition of a beautiful manuscript of Aeschylus and Sophocles — [38] though the extent of these purchases is unknown. But at one point Aurispa professed his desire to have Niccoli's library surpass that of the Ptolemies'. [39] Aurispa's phenomenal collection, however, proved disappointing to Traversari in one significant respect. Except for a manuscript of Gregory Nazianzen, he had brought with him no patristic texts. He explained to Traversari:

> I have not brought any sacred volumes from Greece except the letters of Gregory [Nazianzen], which are, I believe, two hundred. This book is in faultless condition and all the pages can be read, but its beauty is hardly such as to invite the reluctant reader. Long ago I sent from Constantinople to Sicily a good number of very choice sacred volumes, for I admit frankly, they were less precious to me, and a number of malicious persons often brought charges to the Greek Emperor, accusing me of pillaging the city of sacred books. With regard to the heathen books it seemed to them not such a great crime. [40]

Traversari replied:

> I implore you to do what you can to have brought to us those sacred books which you sent from Byzantium to Sicily. You can imagine that I avidly await them. Moreover is it not possible that yet-to-be-revealed treasures of Babylon may lie hidden among them? [41]

By 1430 Aurispa had recovered from Sicily only one bundle of his manuscripts. This included a volume of saints' lives lent to Traversari, a Gregory Nazianzen lent to Niccoli, and volumes of the orations of Chrysostom, the Psalter, the Gospels, and the comedies of Aristophanes which Aurispa retained. He promised Traversari, who had repeatedly inquired about the sacred volumes in Sicily, that he would do all he could to recover the remainder, but his hopes were waning. There is no evidence Traversari ever managed to utilize that tantalizing hoard of sacred texts. [42]

Filelfo, who learned Greek in the Chrysoloras household in Constantinople from 1420 to 1427, also acquired a remarkable library of Greek classics, but the only patristic volume mentioned in the list he sent to Traversari on his arrival in Italy was a manuscript of Chrysostom homilies. [43] The Florentine humanists were eager to lure Filelfo to Florence to assume the chair of Greek studies at the Florentine Studio, again reopened after expenses of the war with Milan had forced its temporary closing. Again, as with Aurispa, Traversari wrote numerous letters encouraging Filelfo to come. Filelfo in response explained the conditions under which he would come to Florence, described his courses and the books used in his teaching, and sent copies of his Latin orations. He also sent Traversari the Latin translation he had made of the *Troica,* an oration of the Greek sophist and rhetorician Dio Chrysostom (A.D. 40-115) which attempted to prove Homer a liar and that Troy was never taken, as well as his Latin translation of Ps.-Aristotle's *Rhetorica ad Alexandrum*, on which he asked Traversari's critical opinion. [44] At length, in the spring of 1429, Filelfo agreed to terms and came to Florence. Four hundred auditors attended his public lectures, including Niccoli and Marsuppini. He was on excellent terms with Bruni, Palla Strozzi, and the Medici. It was only Traversari that he distrusted. [45] Traversari received Filelfo politely at first, though he regarded his salary as excessive. Two months later he described him to Giustiniani as a mixture of Greek levity and vanity, filled with self-praise. [46] Yet despite their mutual antipathy, Filelfo continued to come to S. Maria degli Angeli, seeking, according to Traversari, his help in polishing the Latin of his translations. Traversari explained:

> He has translated certain works from Greek, but with so much of my sweat that it can scarcely be told. His audacity has overcome my resolution to block completely his access to me, lest he disturb my leisure intended for other studies. [47]

In recompense for Filelfo's importunate demands Traversari overcame his customary reticence, as he wrote Niccoli, and shamelessly asked for his volume of Philo, to which Filelfo consented. [48] Traversari also asked Filelfo, who was a skilled Latin poet, to make verse translations of the epigrams in Diogenes Laertius; he twice agreed to do them, in 1430 and 1433, but they never appeared. [49] Already by 1430 he had openly quarrelled with Niccoli, and in 1431 the Medici had attempted to dismiss him from the chair of Greek studies, and replace him with Marsuppini. He became publicly identified with the anti-Medici forces, and by 1433 his relations with Traversari had degenerated to the point where Filelfo called him a hypocrite. [50] When the Medici returned from exile in 1434, Filelfo was dismissed and he left Florence.

There were other notable visitors to Traversari's cell in the 1420's. Indeed Vespasiano observed of Traversari:

> He acquired such a famous reputation, both for the holiness of his life and for his learning, that no person of quality would come to Florence without going to visit him at the Angeli. Not having met him it seemed that they had seen nothing. [51]

In 1424 Fra (later San) Bernardino da Siena and his fellow Franciscan preacher Alberto da Sarteano met with Traversari, who observed that Alberto was far from proficient as a Greek scholar, and criticized the lack of gravity in his sermon "De sacramento Corporis Christi" even though Guarino had praised it to the skies when it was preached in Verona. Nevertheless they embraced warmly, Alberto reported news of Guarino and other Venetian humanists and Traversari gladly fulfilled Alberto's request for a copy of Augustine's *De doctrina Christiana*. [52] In 1426 Tommaso Parentucelli (later Pope Nicholas V) came to Florence in the company of Cardinal Albergati, whom he served as humanist secretary. Parentucelli, with whom Traversari had previously corresponded, and whom he had referred to as "that brilliant, intellectually acute, and *humanissimus* man," brought Traversari two patristic manuscripts, an ancient Lactantius and a volume of Ambrose's *Epistolae*, both of them originally from the ancient Benedictine Abbey at Nonantola. [53] In 1428 Don Pedro, Duke of Coimbra, the second son of King John I of Portugal, was lodged in the recently completed Ospedale degli Innocenti, and since he was an enthusiast for classical studies, took advantage of his proximity to S. Maria degli Angeli to visit Traversari. In his dedication of his translation of Chrysostom's *De providentia Dei* to Don Pedro, Traversari expressed admiration for the Duke's character, and recalled their colloquy in his cell. [54]

By the early 1430's Traversari had entered the foremost rank of Italian humanists. When the young Lorenzo Valla (1407-57) revised his treatise *De voluptate* in Pavia and Milan in 1432-33, he sent the newly entitled *De vero falsoque bono* for criticism and comment to Pier Candido Decembrio in Milan, Guarino in Ferrara, and Bruni, Marsuppini, and Traversari in Florence. In the treatise Valla presented a radically new concept of human nature. He criticized Stoic moral idealism by defending Socratically and perhaps ironically, the ideas of the Epicureans, regarded by medieval thinkers as heretical. Valla asserted that man is a creature of will, immersed in a world of sensual and social experience, who finds only through faith in divine grace and the promise of immortality the impetus to struggle for virtue. Pressing affairs allowed Traversari only to scan Valla's work briefly. He thought the style pleasing and suited to the matter discussed, but he dared not from his quick reading bring forth a judgment on the ideas involved. He realized that Valla's opinions were controversial, but he noted that the ancients themselves regarded dissent as licit, and freely allowed men to defend their arguments whether against equals or superiors. "I do not condemn it, therefore, if we state somthing contrary to what the philosophers invented, if only we defend our opinions with true and plausible reasons." [55]

When Traversari was elected General of the Camaldulensian Order in October 1431, S. Maria degli Angeli was no longer his permanent residence. Instead he stayed principally at the monastery of Fonte Buona near the hermitage at Camaldoli. Fonte Buona was no more than a rugged two days' journey from Florence, and Traversari frequently visited the city. But except for two lengthy stays, June 1434 to February 1435, and January to September 1439 during the Council of Florence, his visits were limited to a few days or a few weeks. His activities as

General ended his daily meetings with Florentine humanists and curtailed his scholarship, but the journeys of reform visitations 1431-34 did enable him to renew personal contacts with humanists in Rome and Venice and to examine a large number of monastic libraries in search for ancient manuscripts . [56]

Traversari spent four months in Rome in the winter and spring of 1432 while awaiting Curial confirmation of his authority as General. He was cordially welcomed by the humanists of the papal secretariat — Antonio Loschi, Cencio de' Rustici, and especially Poggio, who frequently guided Traversari on explorations of the ancient Roman ruins. [57]

Even more congenial were the forty days Traversari spent in Venice in May-June 1433. There he stayed in the Camaldulensian monastery of S. Michele on Murano, the guest of a prior who shared his devotion to the study of sacred letters and his enthusiasm for restoring the ancient holiness of the Order. He was accorded an honorable procession of numerous Venetian lay and religious dignitaries for his formal reception by the Doge. Encouraged by Francesco Barbaro, Traversari explained in a Latin oration the purpose of his visit. The Doge cordially welcomed him and exhorted him to continue the work of reform for which he promised his support. In the midst of his visits to monasteries, there was ample opportunity to explore the sights of the city and to enjoy the company of the Venetian humanists, especially Francesco Barbaro and Leonardo Giustiniani. They conversed with him daily, were anxious to show him their libraries, requested copies of his recent translations, and made evident their esteem and affection. Barbaro presented him with a handsome gift of two Greek manuscripts, one containing the Old Testament books of prophets, the other orations of Gregory Nazianzen. While in Venice Traversari also met the Byzantine scholar George of Trebizond, whom he encouraged Niccoli to consider for a public appointment in Florence, since as a teacher of Greek and Latin he would be far superior to Filelfo. He also made the acquaintance of the romantic antiquarian Ciriaco d'Ancona (1391-c. 1455), who in a series of journeys throughout the Mediterranean and the Near East copied a vast number of Greek and Latin inscriptions, sketched ancient sites, and amassed a fabulous collection of ancient artifacts. Traversari examined his ancient gold and silver coins, and admired especially an elegant onyx stone engraved with the features of Scipio the Younger, the most beautiful stone he had ever seen. Traversari was introduced as well to the Venetian physician Pietro Tommasi, who possessed Greek texts of Galen and of Paul of Aegina (author of a first century B.C. medical text). When Traversari spoke to him of Toscanelli's knowledge and erudition, Tommasi became so eager to meet Toscanelli that he planned a trip to Florence, and moreover, agreed to give the Greek volumes to him. [58]

Of the new humanist contacts Traversari made in the 1430's, he was most impressed with Vittorino da Feltre (1399-1446). Traversari visited him in Mantua on several occasions, the first in July 1433 shortly after leaving Venice. This visit lasted only a few days, but this was enough for Traversari to develop a great affection for his humanity and learning. He examined Vittorino's noteworthy library of thirty Greek manuscripts, and arranged to have him transcribe and send to Niccoli a number of Greek texts, including the *Symposium* of Julian the Apostate. They also discussed Vittorino's educational methods, since Traversari was particularly impressed with the progress of his students in Greek studies, noting as praiseworthy one translation of Chrysostom. When he left Mantua, Vittorino accompanied him for several miles on the road to Verona, and Traversari reported that they conversed "de literis, de probitate, de modestia, de religione, de viris nostra aetate illustribus." [59]

Traversari made one further important intellectual contact in the 1430's, Nicolaus Cusanus. In 1433 Traversari wrote to Cardinal Cesarini, President of the Council of Basel, that Giovanni da Prato had recently returned to Florence from the Council, and that in the course of conversation with Niccoli and Marsuppini at S. Maria degli Angeli had mentioned seeing two volumes which Cusanus had with him at the Council. One was a volume, exceptional for its age and size, of the works of Aratus in the translation of Cicero or Germanicus. The other contained, according to Giovanni, all the works of Cicero except the letters. Traversari was skeptical about the latter, for Cicero's philosophical writings, rhetorical works, and orations would each fill a huge volume. Curious about this, he asked Cesarini to have an index made of these volumes and to send it to Florence. [60] Cusanus was not present at the Council in the fall of 1435 when Traversari was in Basel, but he did write Traversari asking for his support in gaining papal confirmation of his appointment as provost of Münster-Meinfeld. Traversari wrote in his behalf to the papal referendary:

Nicolaus of Trier [Cusanus], a zealous scholar, and distinguished for the large number of books in his possession, has written to me exhorting me to intercede with you. . . . Since as I hear he is a man of great erudition, and since his friendship which I am developing here by letter could contribute greatly to our cause, I ask you to approve his suit. [61]

Cusanus returned to the Council in 1436, but like Cesarini joined the minority party in the winter of 1436-37 in the dispute over the site of the council of union with the Greek Church. After the final rupture on 7 May 1437, Cusanus left Basel for Bologna to get papal confirmation of the minority decree, then joined papal emissaries to sail to Constantinople in order to accompany the Greek contingent on their journey to the Council. Traversari apparently again missed meeting Cusanus, for the papal ships left Venice at the end of July, and Traversari did not join the papal court in Bologna until mid-August. [62] Both men, however, were present together the following spring in Ferrara for the opening phase of the Council of Union, until Cusanus departed 6 June 1438 for Germany as papal emissary. What discussions may have transpired between them are unknown, but a little more than a year later, on 4 August 1439, Cusanus wrote to Tommaso Parentucelli while enroute to Frankfurt, rejoicing in the news of Greek union with the Latin Church, and adding, "I left in the possession of the General of the Camaldulensians Proclus' *De theologia Platonis* so that he might translate it. I beseech you, since he will now have more time for it, please urge him to do it." [63]

With the conclusion of the exhausting negotiations of the Council, Traversari did plan to return to scholarly work, and indeed made arrangements for remodeling his study at Fonte Buona, but whether translation of the Proclus was part of his plans is uncertain. Within a few months he was dead. [64] At some

point in 1438-39, however, Traversari in all probability translated several excerpts of the *De theologia Platonis*. These
excerpts appear in a manuscript which belonged to Cusanus, the
present Codex Strassburg 84. In 1462 Pietro Balbo translated
the whole of the *De theologia Platonis* for Cusanus, but the
Proclus excerpts in the Strassburg manuscript are distinctly
different from Balbo's version. Balbo translated nearly word for
word, whereas the excerpts are a freer and more humanistic
rendering of the Greek. Moreover they reveal not only a better
philological comprehension but also a superior spiritual understanding of Proclus' difficult text. Cusanus, who did not read
Greek, must have obtained a Latin version of at least part of
Proclus' *Platonic Theology* around 1440, for influence of the
work is clearly present in his *De coniecturis* (written c.
1443-44) as well as in a sermon he delivered for Christmas
1444. The most reasonable conclusion, as Haubst, who has
studied the excerpts, remarks, is that Traversari was the
translator, a supposition strengthened by the fact that Traversari had some familiarity with Proclus before contact with
Cusanus; in the mid-1420's he had borrowed a Greek manuscript of the *Platonic Theology* from Aurispa.[65] In the early
1440's Cusanus maintained contact with Traversari's scholarship. Indeed in 1443 he obtained from Paolo Toscanelli
Traversari's translation of Ps-Dionysius' *On Mystical Theology*.
Later he acquired the complete Ps.-Dionysius *Opera* in Traversari's translation, as well as Traversari's version of Diogenes
Laertius.[66] Since Ps.–Dionysius was a major inspiration for
Cusanus' central ideas, it is significant that he preferred to study
the works in Traversari's translation, even though he owned
several medieval translations of them.[67]

The sustained intellectual association which Traversari enjoyed with Florentine, Venetian, and Roman humanists was the
cultural ambience within which he thought and worked.
Humanist contacts were obviously vital for his scholarship, for
it was through humanist friendships that he had access to the
best Latin classical and patristic texts, many newly discovered
in Italian and trans-Alpine monasteries, and especially to Greek
manuscripts, most of which were brought directly from the
Greek East by Italian humanists. Even more important, Traver-

sari's enthusiastic involvement with the humanist movement meant adherence to a particular cultural-intellectual perspective – the conviction of the superiority of ancient wisdom, the rejection of the "barbarity" of late medieval culture, the emphasis on rhetoric, the dismissal of dialectic, and the stress placed on the discovery of Greek learning.

Other humanists clearly regarded Traversari as one of their leading scholars: they respected his classical erudition, especially his knowledge of Greek. Moreover, many humanists enthusiastically supported Traversari's concern for study of the Fathers. They sought his translations, collected Latin and Greek patristic manuscripts for their libraries, and some even engaged in patristic scholarship themselves. Guarino, for instance, included Jerome's letters and works of Lactantius and Cyprian in the curriculum of his famed humanist school at Ferrara (which Traversari witnessed himself in two brief visits in the summer of 1433).[68] Guarino also wrote a life of St. Ambrose (1434), which he dedicated to Alberto da Sarteano, and he translated several treatises of Basil and Cyril of Alexandria, including two of Basil's *Homilies on Fasting* (1438), dedicated to Pope Eugenius IV.[69] Vittorino also made study of the Fathers basic to the curriculum of his school.[70] Of Traversari's Florentine humanist friends, Giannozzo Manetti was most deeply involved with Latin and Greek patristic scholarship, though his studies found fruition only in the 1450's, more than a decade after Traversari's death. Trinkaus has demonstrated how patristic thought, especially that of Lactantius and Augustine, was the major inspiration for Manetti's philosophy of *homo faber,* expressed in his *De dignitate et excellentia hominis* (1452). Patristic studies, especially Eusebius, also were central to Manetti's textual history of Scripture and provided the context for his revised Latin translations of Psalms and the New Testament.[71]

Religious concerns, especially lay piety, were an important aspect of the thought of many of Traversari's humanist contemporaries. Giustiniani, for instance, worked to disseminate vernacular religious books for the spiritual edification of the "simpliciores." In so doing, he turned for help in procuring texts of the Old Testament, saints' lives, and confessional tracts to Traversari who encouraged his efforts, and had Florentine bookstalls searched, eventually locating a number of vernacular works, including an Old Testament. But he complained to Giustiniani that vernacular manuscripts cost more than those in Latin. [72] Even such a classicist as Marsuppini wrote a treatise of spiritual counsel on death and immortality, the *Consolatio* (c.1433), addressed to Cosimo and Lorenzo de' Medici, whose mother had just died. [73] A number of Traversari's patristic translations, especially the *Sermons* of St. Ephraem, were intended as spiritual counsel to the laity. [74]

Even more narrowly religious concerns, such as Church union, and monastic reform, drew humanist attention. Toscanelli, who conversed with an Ethiopian monk for whom Traversari had arranged lodging at S. Maria degli Angeli in the spring of 1438 while the monk was enroute from Rome to the Council of Ferrara, wrote Pope Eugenius urging him not to neglect the Coptic Christians in the irenical work of ecumenical union. [75] Pieruzzi, proscribed by the Medici regime in 1444, took up exile in the Cistercian monastery of S. Salvatore at Settimo near Florence, where he lived as a monk, studied Scripture, and taught Latin to the young monks. [76] Vittorino, widely respected for the sincerity of his Christian piety, encouraged Traversari's work of monastic reform. In 1432 Traversari wrote to Vittorino asking him to persuade one Jacobus Aldobrandus, who had fled to Mantua, the lone surviving lay brother from the sack of the Camaldulensian monastery of S. Michele in Bolognese territory, not to transfer ownership of the monastery to another Order as he had proposed.

> I have no doubt you will bring him over to your position for you are pre-eminent in oratorical excellence. You could persuade even a bitter enemy in a less good cause. Will you not, then, with little difficulty, and indeed meeting little resistance, win over a man we judge perhaps friendly and certainly not an enemy, and who moreover, as I hear, is not averse to *humanitas*? Add to this that God always lends strength to pious endeavors. [77]

Vittorino replied that he had willingly fulfilled Traversari's request, and that his efforts had met with success. He added,

> I grieve indeed, most exceptional man, for the cause of your learning, which you have never ceased to augment daily, and for which up to now you have had the leisure, so that now there are read a good many volumes of the Greek Doctors which you seized upon and published. I grieve, I say, that you are now so oppressed by affairs that you have no time left for this virtuous study. But I am consoled, and you with your prudence will similarly have consoled yourself, because in your exceptional conduct of affairs you will have earned a place of virtue beside other great and excellent men, since indeed it is the opinion of our Orator [i.e. Cicero] that all praise of virtue consists in action.[78]

Admiration for Traversari's religious concerns was by no means universal among Italian humanists. But Poggio Bracciolini's criticisms of Traversari's life and character were perhaps the most outspoken. Traversari may have known Poggio as early as 1413-14, for Poggio, as Papal Secretary, was with Pope John XXIII in Florence at that time. Subsequently, through Niccoli, Traversari kept abreast of Poggio's dramatic manuscript discoveries in trans-Alpine monasteries, and he passed the news on to Guarino and Barbaro in Venice.[79] Poggio then went on to England (1418-22), where he experienced a period of increasing intellectual discontent and personal difficulty. He reported to Niccoli that his enthusiasm for classical culture was waning and that he had immersed himself in patristic studies. Classical studies seemed vain, false, and insubstantial compared to sacred eloquence whose foundation was truth, the basis for all correct understanding and action. He mentions reading the works of St. Augustine, and especially the New Testament homilies of Chrysostom, which he admired for their gravity of doctrine despite the clumsiness of the medieval Latin translation.[80] Poggio longed to regain a post in the papal Curia, but he resisted the advice of Niccoli and others to take holy orders as a means to this end.

> ... that other office [of the priesthood] is not the
> beginning of liberty, but rather the workshop of
> servitude. Understand what I say. I do not seek that
> liberty which is free of all cares and worries; ... but
> rather that liberty in which I am subject to but a few,
> which is, as Cicero says, to live as you wish. The
> former is holier, but the Spirit blows as it lists, not
> according to our wish, but according to the mercy of
> God, whose power it is to act when He wills, not
> according to merits, but as He calls. In this life it is
> our Ambrosius [Traversari] whom I judge happiest,
> for he regards all things as dung, so that he may gain
> Christ. Lacking such strength of spirit, we desire to
> follow that middle way where following God we are
> not entirely a slave to the world.[81]

Once returned to the congenial world of the papal court in
1423, Poggio neglected sacred studies. At his death he owned
only a few patristic works, all of which (except for a
Lactantius) were ecclesiastical histories. He possessed none of
Traversari's patristic translations, though he did have his
rendering of Diogenes Laertius. Moreover, despite the admiration (ironic perhaps?) for Traversari expressed in the letter to
Niccoli, he quickly returned to anti-clerical and especially
anti-monastic polemics, of which the barbed, witty, and
salacious *Facetiae* (1450) is the most famous. While at the
Council of Constance Poggio had written a sharp attack on
clerical abuses in which he charged the clergy with avarice and
hypocrisy. In the *De avaritia* (1428), his first published dialogue, he returned to this theme, arguing, in refutation of San
Bernardino's preaching, that desire for wealth is natural to men,
and that the ideal of poverty as preached by the Franciscans
was meaningless and hypocritical. Merit lies not with these idle
drones, he asserted, but rather with those who build civilization
and preserve the human race. Traversari soon read Poggio's
work, but oddly seems to have responded only to the style,
which he criticized as less eloquent than Poggio's letters.[82]

Shortly after the publication of *De avaritia,* Poggio became
embroiled in a violent quarrel with the Observant Franciscans.

He charged that the devotion to the Name of Jesus which Bernardino inspired was idolatrous and heretical, and was preached by the "crude and uncultured two-legged asses" only to promote their own pride and ambition. Then he quarreled with Alberto da Sarteano, who had attacked him for personally intervening to block papal authorization to found a new Observant Franciscan monastery in S. Giovanni Valdarno, funds for which had been bequeathed by a wealthy Florentine. When Poggio again fulminated against medicant hypocrisy, Traversari attempted to moderate his vehemence, but Poggio replied:

> The charity of the many, who prefer public utility to private is a very great thing, for they corrupt and betray their souls so that they may save strangers. [83]

Sharp differences over Observant reform and Bernardino's preaching did not prevent congenial relations when Traversari was in Rome. Moreover, when Poggio was captured and imprisoned by the condottiere Niccolò Piccinino, who seized Rome in 1434, Traversari wrote an urgent appeal for his release citing his close friendship with him, and his deep respect for Poggio's erudition and *humanitas.* [84]

In 1447, when the more congenial atmosphere of the papacy of Nicholas V had succeeded that of Eugenius IV, who had strongly favored Observant reform, Poggio published another dialogue attacking clerical abuses, the *Contra hypocritas,* dedicated to Leonardo Bruni. In the dialogue, Carlo Marsuppini is the inveterate critic of the monastic life; and Girolamo Aliotti, the Benedictine, who had been in fact a friend and great admirer of Traversari, defends the monks. At the end of this work discussion turns to a judgment of Traversari's life and character.

> "What," Carolus said, "is your opinion of our Ambrosius. Did he pursue philosophy in a direct or devious way? Did he smell of hypocrisy to you?"
>
> "Not at all," said Hieronymus. "He was a man to be esteemed for his high character, who in his monastery was devoted to letters and wrote a great deal which was praiseworthy and learned. He was certainly endowed with the greatest humanity and virtue."

> "I praise his life," Carolus said, "and I consider
> him to have been beyond hypocrisy when he had
> leisure for the muses in the monastery in Florence.
> But when he was made Abbot [i.e. General], he
> diverged somewhat from his former way of life. He
> went about covertly, so that he seemed to seek
> something higher. I remember our Nicolaus [Niccoli],
> a man free in his speech and very close friends with
> him, used often to rebuke him for his useless cares, in
> which he involved himself of his own accord, and
> asserted that he was spreading out nets for a red
> hat."[85]

Intimately aware of moral duplicity in the papal Curia,
Poggio, unlike Manetti or Traversari, found no sustaining
spiritual ideal in patristic theology. Nor did he regard the
monastic vocation as peculiarly redemptive. His view of human
affairs was soberly pessimistic — men are driven by their own
uncontrollable inner drives and by the Heraclitean flux of
fortune. In the face of this, only Stoic self-control makes life
endurable.[86]

Leonardo Bruni, with Traversari the leading Greek scholar of
early Quattrocento Florentine humanism, was not an enthusiast
of Christian antiquity either. While in no sense anti-Christian —
in the preface to his translation of the *Phaedo,* Bruni argued for
the legitimacy of the study of Plato's philosophy on the
grounds that his belief in the immortality of the soul conformed
to Christian doctrine[87] — his central concern was with ethics in
the political life of the Renaissance *polis.* In his classical studies
he discovered the political and ethical *paideia* of the republican
city-state of antiquity, and in his translations of Aristotle's
Nicomachean Ethics and *Politics,* of Plato's *Gorgias* and *Apology,* of Demosthenes' orations, and of Plutarch's lives, as well as
in his own orations and *History of Florence,* he sought to
regenerate the ancients' civic virtue. His only work in patristic
scholarship was his translation of Basil's treatise on education, a
translation made, as we have seen, to support Salutati's defense
of the *studia humanitatis.* Lay piety and religious reform were
tangential to the cultivation of "civic humanism."[88] Moreover,
like Poggio, he believed the monastic vocation was rife with

hypocrisy.[89] Given their sharply different intellectual concerns, it is not surprising, then, that Traversari and Bruni were never close, despite Bruni's permanent residence in Florence from 1415 onwards.[90] Although Traversari and Bruni both emphasized rhetorical studies and believed in the superiority of antiquity, Traversari admired not the courage and political prudence of republican Athens and Rome, but rather the spiritual fervor of the Fathers and the more holy Christianity which animated the universal Church of the patristic age. This is not to deny Bruni's greatness, nor that he was undoubtedly the more original thinker, but merely to stress that early Quattrocento Florentine humanism cultivated Christian as well as civic humanism.

Philology, Textual Criticism, and Classical Scholarship

The humanists, in a conscious break with scholasticism, stressed grammar and rhetoric, rather than dialectics, as the basis for intellectual inquiry. Moreover, submission to the intellectual *auctoritas* of the ancients meant the necessity of returning to the original languages of the classics, of purifying Latin from the accretions of the "Dark Ages" of ignorance. Traversari shared this concern. In an early letter to Francesco Barbaro, he wrote, ". . . if that Grammarian, whom you have recorded in your index, seems to you not unworthy for my use (but certainly he will be most worthy if he smacks of antiquity and of that ancient, diligently pure Latin), send him to me."[91] Traversari was just as interested in Classical Greek. He acquired from Aurispa a manuscript of the Greek grammarian Julius Pollux, and Aurispa's transcription of Herodian of Alexandria's *De linguarum varietate;* and he asked as well for Aurispa's manuscript of the ancient scholia on the *Iliad.*[92]

Especially significant is Traversari's effort to learn the third ancient language, Hebrew. It is uncertain when he began to study Hebrew, though it was undoubtedly late in life, perhaps around 1430 when he was increasingly drawn to the study of Scripture. While he was in Rome in 1432, the young Roman noble Mariano Porcari gave him a Hebrew manuscript containing Psalms, Job, Daniel, the Lamentations of Jeremiah, Esther, and other Old Testament books. [93] Traversari was delighted with the gift, and the following fall, when he found time to return to patristic scholarship, he intended to use the manuscript in resuming his Hebrew studies as well. [94] In a letter, probably written in 1434-35, Traversari asked to have sent from S. Maria degli Angeli a manuscript of the conjugation of Hebrew verbs, so that in the enforced leisure occasioned by illness, he could undertake again his Hebrew studies, and begin to teach another monk who wished to learn the language. [95] It seems unlikely that Traversari acquired great facility in Hebrew — Vespasiano states, "he gave some effort to Hebrew letters, of which he had some knowledge" [96] — but Giannozzo Manetti, to whom Traversari taught Greek, was also probably influenced by him to take up the study of Hebrew. In the mid-Quattrocento Manetti was the leading Hebrew scholar of the Italian humanists, and he made a new Latin translation from the Hebrew text of Psalms. [97]

Traversari was not the first humanist interested in Hebrew studies. During the years of the Council of Constance, Poggio began to study the language, but he admitted of little progress. [98] Bruni, however, dismissed the study of Hebrew as useless and vain: neither Augustine nor Basil had known Hebrew; and, unlike Greek and Latin, Hebrew was a rude and uncultured language which had produced no philosophers, poets, or orators. [99] Traversari's concern for Hebrew, therefore, went beyond contemporary notions of the *studia humanitatis,* though the latter fifteenth and early sixteenth centuries emphasized the importance of Hebrew both for Biblical scholarship and for learning the arcane mysteries of the Hebrew Cabbala.

Closely connected to the study of the "pure" classical languages, and indeed largely an outgrowth of this effort, was the attention accorded textual criticism. The humanists wished to recover the vast patrimony of antiquity from the defiling hands of the medieval "barbarians." To accomplish this they pored through musty monastery libraries in search of ancient manuscripts, filled lacunae in the texts or expunged errors by carefully collating codices, transcribed classical works into what they thought was classical script, and by careful attention to style attempted to establish the authenticity of authorship. In all these areas of textual scholarship, we can see Traversari at work.

The search for classical manuscripts came at a particularly opportune time. In the revival of intellectual and scholarly activity in the West in the twelfth century, considerable attention had been given by the monasteries and cathedral schools to the copying of ancient texts. But as the focus of intellectual activity shifted from the monastery and cathedral schools to the universities, and as dialectics became the principal intellectual method, the ancient texts were no longer in such demand. Many Benedictine abbeys abandoned their scriptoria and their libraries were allowed to decay. When the humanists began searching through monastery libraries for ancient manuscripts, they found many torn, rotten, or crumbling with age. [100] While in Rome in 1432, Traversari made an excursion to the ancient Basilian monastery of Grottaferrata in the Alban Hills in order to examine the library. To his dismay he found much of the monastery in ruins, troops billeted there, the library holdings strewn about with many of the books in a deplorable state. [101]

In his monastic visitations and during his journey to the Council of Basel, Traversari searched diligently for ancient manuscripts. His discoveries were minor in comparison to Poggio's or Cusanus', but his careful scrutiny of monastic libraries indicates his participation in a central concern of humanist scholarship. So likewise does his diligence in seeking indices of humanists' libraries, in which he looked for a listing of the individual works in each codex and description of the script used. [102]

The humanists rejected Gothic script, asserting it had corrupted Latin texts, and promoted the return to *littera antiqua,* which was in fact the Carolingian script of the ninth through twelfth centuries, and not "classical" handwriting at all. [103] Concern for script was not merely the historicizing rejection of the immediate medieval past, for it also directed the humanists to a careful reconstruction of classical texts. Guarino da Verona, the greatest emender of texts in the first half of the Quattrocento, argued that the reasons for the fragmentary and corrupt state of codices transmitted through the Middle Ages were the neglect of Greek studies, the abandonment of diphthongs, the negligence in orthography which led to a conflation of different words, and the incorporation of marginal glosses into the body of the text. [104] Niccoli, who was particularly interested in classical writing, developed the "italic" script in which many classical texts were produced in the early period of printing. [105] In the letter in which he encouraged his brother Girolamo to undertake the *studia humanitatis,* Traversari stressed that he should not neglect the cultivation of classical script either. [106] A number of the monks at S. Maria degli Angeli learned the humanistic script, and it was in this script that Traversari's translations were disseminated. [107] Traversari also took a direct interest in the format and appearance of his published texts. When he arranged for the publication of his correspondence, he gave explicit instructions to his secretary, Fra Michele, with regard to margins, spacing, and titles, ordering him to follow the model of a volume of St. Ambrose's epistolary which he himself had written at S. Maria degli Angeli. [108]

Traversari's knowledge of Greek made possible the restoration of Greek words and passages in Latin manuscripts where medieval scribes, ignorant of the language, had either misrepresented the words or left them out entirely. In this work of reconstruction, he emended both classical and patristic texts. He collaborated with Niccoli, for instance, to restore the Greek to works of Quintillian and Aulus Gellius, and he emended the Greek in Barbaro's manuscript of Lactantius. [109]

Also essential to the task of reconstructing the ancient texts was the careful collation of extant manuscripts, a method which enabled the humanists to fill lacunae in the texts and to rectify garbled sentences or interpolated sections. In this, too, Traversari diligently adopted the standards of humanist critical scholarship. For example, he asked Guarino to send an emended text of Livy so that the could fill a lacuna in a Florentine manuscript. [110] More important, he gathered the oldest and best preserved codices on which to base his translations. For instance, though he already possessed two ancient manuscripts of Diogenes Laertius, he found it necessary to borrow yet a third from Giustiniani.

There are indeed two copies of this work, neither perfect, but both, as much as I can conjecture, full of faults and occasionally mutilated. . . . You know how necessary trustworthy sources are for translating. Since I have lacked this up to now in these two volumes, I seek from you, if you have the work, or any of your fellow citizens, to have it sent quickly to me, so that it will be possible for me to put the final touches to my labor. The comparison of three sources should be greatly conducive to emending and polishing the work. [111]

The careful observation of style, the consequence of the humanists' pursuit of eloquence, served also as a tool of critical scholarship. While in Rome in 1432, Traversari was able to identify, primarily from style, an ancient manuscript containing twelve homilies on Isaiah as a work of Origen. [112] Traversari's judgement was also correct that the *Synonyma* and *Differentiae,* which carried Cicero's name, were not his works. ". . . . I do not deny that the man is erudite, but he is far from Ciceronian dignity." [113]

It was not only the diligent study of classical languages, then, which distinguished the humanists of the early Quattrocento from medieval students of the classics, but also the greater sophistication of their scholarship. Thoroughly imbued with the intellectual and scholarly standards of his humanist contemporaries, especially the knowledge of classical rhetoric, Traversari was able to bring to his study of patristics greater powers of comprehension than had marked the efforts of the Carolingian or twelfth-century students of the Church Fathers, or than would mark the efforts of the Brethren of the Common Life.

Traversari held that study of languages and the new critical scholarship were not ends in themselves but simply the means to acquire the wisdom of the long buried Latin and Greek classics, which through the efforts of the humanists were coming to light again. [114] Although Traversari's energies were devoted principally to patristic studies, examination of his letters indicates his extensive reading in the classics. His references to works of the ancients are often parenthetical — borrowing or returning a volume, transcribing a work, the mention of a discovery — making difficult an assessment of the full range of his reading. In particular, it is often difficult to distinguish between his personal interest in a Greek or Latin text and an interest occasioned by Niccoli's avidity for an ancient volume. Moreover, there is no record of which classical volumes Traversari himself owned, nor is there an extant index of the library of S. Maria degli Angeli dating from Traversari's lifetime. [115] His principal source for classical manuscripts was, of course, Niccoli's splendid library.

From the evidence in his letters Traversari's reading in the classics centered on rhetoric and history, and especially Cicero. An extant manuscript of Cicero's *Letters to Atticus* contains marginal notes Traversari made while present at the Council of Basel in 1435; one reads: "Erat M. Tullius librorum avidus, sed in ea re cedebat tibi, Florentine!" – an obvious reference to Niccoli's insatiable desire for ancient manuscripts. [116] He was familiar with Niccoli's volume of this same work in which Manuel Chrysoloras had restored the Greek words, [117] and knew as well the eight orations of Cicero which Poggio discovered in 1417, and the complete texts of Cicero's *Orator, Brutus,* and *De oratore,* discovered at Lodi in 1421. [118] Besides restoring the Greek to Niccoli's manuscript of Quintillian, who with Cicero was the principal source for the humanists' understanding of classical rhetoric, he retained for some years Aurispa's copy of the complete text of *De oratoria institutione,* perhaps Poggio's most celebrated discovery. [119] Of the classical Latin historians, Traversari emended a text of Livy, knew Caesar's *Commentaries,* borrowed Curtius Rufus' *De gestis Alexandri,* [120] and had on loan from Aurispa a manuscript of Pliny the Elder's *Epistolae.* [121] Traversari's classical Greek studies also emphasized history, especially Plutarch, and he was familiar with the *Iliad* and the *Odyssey* as well as Ps.-Herodotus' *Life of Homer.* [122] He was eager as well to read the Latin translations made by his humanist contemporaries — Francesco Barbaro's and Leonardo Giustiniani's of Plutarch, Filelfo's of Ps.-Aristotle's *Rhetorica ad Alexandrum,* Bernardo Giustiniani's of Isocrates, and Bruni's of Plato. [123]

Clearly Traversari acquired considerable knowledge of classical antiquity, much of it from Greek or recently recovered

Latin sources, and he was able to enrich his discourses on contemporary affairs by citing the ancients. For instance, in 1434 Traversari remonstrated with the Bolognese Romeo Foscari regarding the continued refusal of Bologna to submit to papal rule; and in the course of his letter he quotes the opinions of Plato and Xenophon on the best form of government, and concludes, in characteristic fashion, that there was no king of loftier virtue than Pope Eugenius IV, nor did any rule provide greater liberty and felicity than *Ecclesiae Matris imperium.* [124] Traversari's revival of patristic theolory, then, was not isolated from the renaissance of classical antiquity, for this received his enthusiastic support.

'Elegantia' and 'Sapientia'

In scholasticism, Aristotelian logic and metaphyics were seen as the means to systematize truth as a coherent and objective entity. Just as scholastic theology, the *scientia de Deo,* stressed the objective power of grace (*gratia gratis data*) and the sacraments (*ex opere operato*), so faith was understood as composed of a series of propositions which could be analyzed intellectually and ordered into an objective science. Stress was placed on exploring the relation of Christian doctrine to problems of logic and conceptions of the cosmos, for theology and metaphysics were preceived as ultimately congruent approaches to wisdom, the *altissimarum causarum cognitio.*

With Petrarch there is a fundamental shift in the meaning of truth and the purpose of wisdom. Truth, for Petrarch, was not a logical or metaphysical entity, but rather a personal conviction, the psychological certainty of rightness. Correspondingly, the locus of truth shifted from the cosmos to man's recognition of his mortality and to his quest for virtue and salvation, and philosophy was to be evaluated not in the abstract coherence of its metaphysics or epistemology, but rather in its effectiveness in moving men towards piety and justice. What Petrarch saw in Cicero and other Roman authors was a love of virtue and their hortatory powers in urging its pursuit. Cicero had defined wisdom as the *ars vivendi,* and philosophy as the study of virtue, duty, moral worth, and honor. Moreover he had stressed the union of wisdom and eloquence, for without the orator's eloquence truth would lie mute and never relate to the reality of human affairs. Eloquence, then, was not mere harmony and beauty of expression, but rather persuasive power, the active force in shaping men's lives, even to evoking moral reform. Even more important was Petrarch's rediscovery of Augustine's emphasis on the moral, psychological, and spiritual dimensions of faith, The locus of faith shifted from the rational intellect to conscience, from the analysis of mind to the remedy of soul, for faith was the conviction that one could rise up from psychological despair because the redeeming miracles of the Incarnation and Atonement were true. This trust, for Petrarch, comes in the context of hearing the Word of Scripture and the testimony of the Fathers. Moreover, the impetus to an inward probing of conscience, to the consciousness of *accidia* and *superbia* and the commitment to effect their remedy, can only come through the exhortation of rhetoric, for only rhetoric commands the power to restructure human motivations. For Petrarch, *sapientia est pietas.* It is a learned piety (*docta pietas*), but the focus of learning is Scripture and the Fathers, not metaphysics and the celestial mysteries. Hence his denigration of scholasticism as arid *scientia.*

Petrarch's stress on rhetoric and his views of human nature were further developed by the humanists of the first half of the Quattrocento. In one of its dimensions, the stress of rhetoric met the psychic needs of civic life within the Renaissance *polis.* Salutati's perception that man is immersed existentially in a reality which is historical and contingent rather than logical and necessary correspond to the factual situation of secular activity in the Florentine city-state. Both he and Bruni stressed language as public discourse and education as the moral formation of the citizen. Since, for Bruni, the individual develops his potentiality and achieves his end only by participation in the *polis,* wisdom, the virtue of prudence, is ethical not metaphysical, active not contemplative, civic and lay rather than solitary and religious.

The humanists stress on a rhetorical culture was further stimulated by the recovery of the complete texts of Cicero's rhetorical works at Lodi in 1421, and perhaps even more importantly by the discovery of the complete text of Quintillian's *De oratoria institutione* in 1416. Quintillian not only argued a theoretical justification of the superiority of eloquence to philosophy, but he also established a curriculum for a rhetorical education based on the study of classical literature.

It is Lorenzo Valla, whose *Dialectical Disputations* depended heavily on Quintillian, who perceived most fully the opposing premises of the scholastic and humanist visions of man's nature. For Valla language and logic have to relate to the subjectivity of man as a creature of affections and passions, rooted in society and history. Man is distinguished from the animals by his immortality, not by reason, for man is also instinctual. Virtue is the classical *virtū* or *aretê,* the strength or energy of spirit which is identifiable also with Christian love. Hence scholasticism with its stress on forms and substances and its *a priori* ethics is remote and incomprehensible. It is rhetoric, drawing on the Scriptural revelation of faith, which makes tangible to man's imagination the invisible promises of salvation and which induces susceptibility to faith. [125]

The humanists discerned an adherence to rhetorical culture not only in the classics, but in patristic literature as well. Many of the Fathers had received classical educations, and a number of them, notably Augustine and Chrysostom, had been trained as orators. Valla, in the Proem to Book IV of his *Elegantiae* (written 1435-44), the leading Renaissance rhetorical textbook, argued in defense of the study of classical rhetoric that all the Latin and Greek Fathers — Jerome, Hilary, Ambrose, Augustine, Lactantius, Basil, Gregory [Nazianzen], and Chrysostom — ". . . praetiosas illas divini eloquii gemmas auro argentoque eloquentiae vestierunt." In so doing they followed the example of the Apostles, especially Paul, who was pre-eminent among the Apostles precisely because of his eloquence. Moreover, "in my judgement, whoever is ignorant of eloquence is entirely unworthy to speak of theology." [126] In the peroration to his *Encomium of St. Thomas Aquinas* — in fact a denigration of scholastic theology in comparison to patristic eloquence — which Valla delivered in 1457 to the Dominican Congregation in Rome to commemorate Aquinas' death, he depicted five pairs of Greek and Latin theologians playing a perpetual symphony before God. Basil and Ambrose sound the lyre, Gregory Nazianzen and Jerome the cithara, Chrysostom and

Augustine the lute, Dionysius and Gregory the Great the flute, and John of Damascus and St. Thomas clash symbols, an image of the inferiority of dialectics to rhetoric. [127]

It is clear that Traversari shared the humanist stress on rhetorical culture. As we have noted, he had studied the rhetorical works of Cicero and Quintillian. Moreover, he early emphasized the power of *elegantia.* In 1417 he wrote to Guarino:

> Would not even the most apathetic be aroused either
> by the dignity of the discourse or the subtle elegance
> of the arguments you have used? My breast is not
> iron, nor my heart hard as steel; nor were we raised in
> forests, the offspring of Hyrcanian tigresses. [128]

More importantly it was the eloquence of the Greek Fathers which inspired Traversari's translations. In 1424 he wrote to Niccoli of the powerful impression which his reading of the Greek text of Athanasius' *Contra gentiles, De incarnatione,* and *Disputatio contra Arium* had made on him.

> I turned to reading Athanasius, and I was so seized by
> admiration for this exceptional man that I could not
> tear myself away. I read his two books against the
> heathen. In the first he refutes heathen superstition;
> in the second he defends the ignominy of the Cross
> and the Incarnation with such forceful arguments and
> with such weighty thoughts, that though indeed this
> matter has been discussed by many, principally by
> our Lactantius, it does not seem, however, that it
> could have been done more worthily or divinely. I
> read next the first three books against Arius, for there
> are five books in all and large books at that. I was so
> refreshed by its fragrance of piety, nor can I
> remember having read anything that can be compared
> to this work. What is striking is a certain incomparable
> beauty in this man's writing, both in thought and
> words, which deserves everyone's admiration, vener-
> ation, and love. He pleads his case forcefully, as it
> deserved; and as he discloses, argues, and refutes all

the heretical objections, he elucidates so much of Holy Scripture that I could not be sated with reading him. What more? I have decided to devote myself entirely to this fervent and celestial man by translating what is before me (if I can find the time), for I would constantly affirm I could find nothing more salutary, nothing more fervent than his teaching. [129]

The fervent faith of the Fathers and the compelling power of their eloquence in exhorting men to the *studia pietatis* and the *studia virtutis* are persistent elements in Traversari's assessment of patristic literature. Moreover, he strove to preserve in his Latin translations the qualities which he discerned in the Greek (a concern we will examine in Chapter III). That he was not unsuccessful in writing eloquent classical Latin can be judged from Aeneas Silvius Piccolomini's remark in his *De liberorum educatione* (1450) that the humanists whose style was worth studying were Leonardo Bruni, Guarino da Verona, Poggio Bracciolini, and Ambrogio Traversari. [130]

It is significant that Traversari shared the humanist opposition to scholastic theology. We have seen that he never attended a university, nor did he study theology in any formal way. There is no evidence that he even read any works of the scholastics, though one volume of Aquinas at least was present in S. Maria degli Angeli. [131] Of the medieval theologians only St. Bernard, esteemed by the humanists as the "last of the Fathers," attracted his attention. Unlike Valla, he did not critically examine the intellectual premises of scholasticism. Nor did he attempt to make philology the new foundation for theological inquiry. Rather he condemned the sterility of scholastic theology in contrast to the efficacy of evangelical preaching. This can be seen in his support for San Bernardino da Siena, who in 1426 was summoned to Rome to face charges of heresy that his emphasis on devotion to the Holy Name of Jesus introduced a new cult. Devotion to the Holy Name was central to Bernardino's spirituality and preaching, and he popularized the devotion through an emblem which he himself designed — the gold letters YHS written on a blue ground, in the midst of a sunburst, surrounded by the circular inscription of Philippians 2: 10, "In nomine Jesu omne genu flectatur coelestium, terrestrium et infernorum." Inevitably the emblem, widely reproduced on churches, public buildings, and homes, acquired talismanic overtones in the popular consciousness, even though Bernardino stressed that what was efficacious was not the power of the sign but what the sign signified — Jesus as Saviour, Redeemer, and Son of God. He denied any intent to introduce a new cult, and he asserted that veneration for the Name of Jesus was to be found in the writings of St. Paul and St. Bernard, and in the teachings of St. Francis. "It is my intention," he said, "to renew and make clear the Name of Jesus as in the days of the Early Church." [132]

The early months of 1426 were difficult for Bernardino, for he was required to remain in Rome and refrain from preaching while the papal commission conducted its investigation. In this period Traversari wrote to Alberto da Sarteano, Bernardino's companion and fellow Franciscan preacher. He noted the great controversy which had arisen over the emblem and divergent opinions regarding its use. He believed there was no danger in having Bernardino summoned before the Pope and Cardinals, for there in the presence of Christ a just judgment would be rendered. If the cohorts of the devil whether from envy or malice should move unjustly against this good and God-fearing man, Christ as executor of divine justice would see to their punishment. He did caution that Alberto's intention to come to Florence to preach the following year presented difficulties, since there was considerable opposition in the city, "but I hope, however, Christ willing, and through the support of friends, you can perhaps take up again here the good work of repairing and restoring the spiritual edifice which was being built by our Father, Brother B." For his part he was certain that Bernardino had introduced the emblem for no other reason than the praise and glory of Christ. It had been rumored that Bernardino, in the face of the difficulties which had arisen, would relinquish the office of preaching, but he was certain Bernardino would retain his customary fortitude, and he reminded Alberto that by "the steadfast name of Christ the Apostles endured the savagery of the cruelest pagans and the insolent rage of other execrable men instigated by the devil." [133]

In April the case came to trial. In the presence of the Pope and the assembled pomp of Cardinals and Curia, Bernardino and two fellow friars found themselves confronted by fifty-two doctors of divinity. The case against him was presented in the syllogisms of scholastic disputation. In response Bernardino spoke simply, citing the words of the Gospels and the Fathers. He reiterated that what was essential in the emblem was not the shape or color of the sign, but rather the actual letters of Jesus' name and their significance. Martin V was convinced of his sincerity, pronounced him innocent of heresy, gave him his blessing, and permitted him to preach again. Seeking further details of Bernardino's triumph from an eyewitness, Traversari exulted in

> . . . . that immortal and magnificent flood of divine eloquence which always pours forth from the sweet and sonorous tongue of that divine man Fra Bernardino, who by the mighty eloquence of Sacred Scripture and by the omnipotence of the glorious and victorious Name of Jesus won over from emnity to friendship the Roman Curia and all the populace of the city. These he has led, from the depths of sin and perdition, the darkness of ignorance and the despair of salvation, into knowledge of divine things and the way of the Lord, and to devotion to the holy Name of Our Lord Jesus Christ.

He believed that the conversion of the minds and hearts of these men could only have occurred through the compassion of the Holy Spirit, who inflamed the tongue of Bernardino, and that through this preaching servant of Jesus, all Italy grew daily in devotion, in knowledge of heavenly things, and in desire for God. But he was eager for more details of Bernardino's victory. He wished to learn of the Pope's clemency and the admirable wisdom which was infused into him by Christ and the Holy Spirit. And he wished to hear of the benevolence and gentleness of many of the Cardinals.

> Finally, in your letter, reproduce before my eyes the conflict and confusion of those haughty minds consumed with prideful envy, the minds, I say, of those who attempt with simulated justice and puffed up knowledge to introduce a new foundation to the

Church of God, obliterating the name of Jesus; of
those who, devoid of all wisdom, prefer to have the
appearance rather than the reality of learning and the
Spirit. Describe to me their countenance and appearance, their shame and disgrace as repulsed they beat a
hasty retreat and sought shelter in snares and sub-
terfuges. If only I had been there to observe the
triumphal victory of Our Lord Jesus through Fra
Bernardino, that good, true, holy, and just man of
God; and to have seen those insolent, nefarious men
speaking against this holy man in outrage to Our Lord
Jesus, and in their usual rage carrying off to their
caves the little bundles of their puffed up learning
hidden under the cloak of the most magnificent
religion. Against these the Prophet chants, "Their
throat is an open sepulchre, they have flattered with
their tongues. God condemn them!" [Psalms
5:10-11]. [134]

Shortly after Bernardino's exoneration, the Bishopric of
Siena became vacant, and the government of the city urged
Martin V to name Bernardino bishop. The Pope agreed and
Bernardino was nominated. When Traversari heard this news he
wrote to Bernardino, "not without tears and with great grief in
my heart," that this was terrible news to those who had been
inflamed to Christ by his words. "I fear this is not from heaven
that you, preacher of poverty in Jesus Christ, edifier of
innumerable souls, seeker of the evangelical life, should be
nominated and pronounced Bishop." Bernardino could not wish
to uproot and destroy his holy work of reforming his Order. All
the people of Italy, who were devoted to Christ, would
stumble and perish, neglecting faith, hope, and charity, if
Bernardino, the trumpet of Christ, should accept this unhappy
dignity. This sacrifice of souls would only affirm the popular
rumors that he was seeking benefices. [135] Bernardino apparently gave no thought to abandoning preaching, for he refused
the nomination, as he later refused the bishoprics of Ferrara
(1431) and Urbino (1435). [136]

What Traversari perceived in Bernardino's preaching was the
renewal of early Christian spiritual fervor which joined the

praedicandi munus with ascetic piety and spontaneous charity. The Christianity that compelled men's hearts was the preached word of Scripture, not the subtle analysis of doctrine, or the legal power of episcopal office.

Just as scholastic theology drew the fire of humanists, so did the university study of civil and canon law. Bruni argued from the ancient parallel of Philip of Macedon, who sent Alexander to Aristotle not to study law, but rather literature and philosophy. Poggio attacked the Bartolists as avaricious, enmeshing truth in their cavilings and sophisms. Valla, in a philological critique of legal studies, demonstrated their a-historical use of legal terms. [137] Traversari shared this humanist opposition to contemporary legal studies, as is evident in a letter which makes clear also the strength of his admiration for antiquity, the importance he assigned to *elegantia,* and the emphasis he placed on education in classical culture.

> I have learned ... that you are giving attention to civil law. I approve of this, of course, but on these grounds: I advise you to seize upon and imitate the ancient lawyers rather than the idle commentators. The former possess great dignity and exhibit ancient elegance, which these modern expounders so lack — even if they could imitate it, for because of their ignorance of language often they do not even understand it. Otherwise you cannot be free for these studies without detriment to more cultured studies. For if those ancient and refined geniuses did not always praise this profession of law (though granted it was famous, and, witness Cicero, indispensable to an orator) and asserted that it lacked much of the grace of oratory (although the lawyers themselves were skilled in it), what can we say when merely scant remnants of ancient law survive and even these have been spoiled by the barbarism of the commentators. If one made a great effort, one could become a legal expert in three days, says Cicero in jest with regard to Servius Sulpitius, so it is clear how much they made of this exercise. You see what I feel about this. I am

pleased, certainly, that you are giving attention to
law, but I do not want you to allow harm to your
cultivation of the Latin language and the Muses. [138]

Traversari's attack on the *inflata scientia* of scholastic
theologians and on the ignorance of legal commentators
stemmed in part from the general humanist sense of cultural
and intellectual superiority to medieval learning. Like Poggio,
Bruni, and Niccoli, he contemptuously dismissed the schoolmen
as barbarous for the inelegance of their Latin. He reveals none
of the originality of Salutati's effort to reconcile an activist view
of man with nominalist conclusions about divine providence
and predestination. Nor like Valla, who was undoubtedly the
most fertile mind of the early Quattrocento humanists, did he
preceive in philology and rhetoric a new basis for theological
inquiry into a Scripturally-based faith which would supplant
scholastic dialectics. But Traversari's preference for the eloquence of the Fathers was not a vacuous admiration of classical
culture for its literary polish. He sincerely believed that
systematic analysis of doctrine was irrelevant to the religious
needs of his time. Men needed to be inspired and exhorted to
lead Christian lives, and to this end the eloquence of the Fathers
and the inspired preaching of San Bernardino were clearly more
efficacious. Much like Erasmus, he believed that Christian faith
was in essence simple and beyond dispute. What was often
difficult was to achieve from the depths of one's heart and
conscience a sincere and lively devotion to Christian piety. It
was this which the eloquence of patristic literature and the
fervent examples of the lives of the Fathers inspired.

The 'Studia humanitatis' and
the 'Studia pietatis'

Traversari actively promoted the *studia humanitatis* among
his fellow monks. Indeed in the 1420's he established an
informal school at S. Maria degli Angeli. There, according to
Vespasiano, he taught Latin to the monks, and Greek to Fra
Jacopo Tornaquinci, Fra Michele, and a number of laymen,
including most prominently Giannozzo Manetti. [139]   Prior to
1420 Traversari made an abridgement of Donatus' *De VIII*

partibus orationis for use by his students in learning Latin. [140]
In 1425 he wrote to Francesco Barbaro that Greek studies had
been begun by many in the monastery, and he asked him to give
the monastery a Greek psalter to enable these studies to be
continued. [141]

When Traversari became General of his Order, he turned to
education as a principal means of promoting reform. He
encouraged humanist studies for novices at a number of
different monasteries, but at Fonte Buona, near Camaldoli, he
established a new academy, on which he placed his highest
hopes for nurturing learned and holy monks. He named as
headmaster Fra Mariotto Allegri, whom he had encouraged to
pursue humanist studies as early as 1423 when Allegri was a
monk at Volterra. Traversari directed him to educate the youths
both "in timore Dei" and in "literis." [142]   While Traversari's
principal intent was to instruct future monks, the "novam
progeniem Christi," he encouraged Florentine patrician families
to send their sons to the academy even if they did not intend
them to pursue a monastic vocation. Regardless of whether the
students eventually chose a secular or a religious life, this
education in Christian virtue and piety and this early taste of
supernal grace, he argued, would bear good fruit, so that as
magistrates they would cultivate justice and as monks they
would remain virtuous, undeterred by the austerity of their
vocation. [143]   Traversari thus shared something of the humanist
notion of education for involvement in the active life of the
polis, but the life of the students at Fonte Buona had a
definitely monastic character. They were entrusted to the care
of a priest to whom they were to make frequent confession. On
Sundays and holidays the students assembled to recite psalms or
to sing hymns, a strikingly different custom from the frolicking
games and gaiety which schoolboys traditionally enjoyed on
such days, and which Traversari deplored. [144]   The stress on
inculcating piety and decorous behaviour was similar to the
aims of the youth confraternities established in Florence in the
early Quattrocento. Indeed these organizations earned Traversari's highest approval. [145]   But clearly as vital an inspiration for
the academy was the humanistic concern for moral formation.

It was precisely in the years 1433-35, when the school at
Fonte Buona was being established, that Traversari was able to

observe at first hand the schools Guarino had created at Ferrara (1429) and Vittorino at Mantua (1423). He was particularly impressed with Vittorino's school, where he observed that several of the students had made great progress in Greek studies. He noted also that Vittorino was educating even indigent youths if they showed intellectual promise. [146] In August 1435, while enroute to the Council of Basel, Traversari stopped briefly to visit Vittorino, and he described to Mariotto the great erudition of the Marquis' son Giovanni Lucido Gonzaga in Latin and geometry and the elegant Greek of his daughter Cecilia. In the course of conversation, the subject of the school at Fonte Buona came up, and the great humanist educator congratulated Traversari on the undertaking. [147]

Traversari had great expectations for his school, and he devoted considerable energy to it. Mariotto, who accepted the post of headmaster after much persuasion proved an excellent teacher, but financial problems occupied much of his attention, and the hostility of the Hermits to the project was disturbing. [148] When Pope Eugenius IV entered Florence in June 1434 after fleeing Rome, Traversari spoke to him about the academy. He found the Pope approved the project, but with straitened fiscal resources caused by the loss of much of the Papal States and the conflict with the Council, papal subsidies were another matter. At length Eugenius gave one hundred florins, enough apparently to remodel quarters in the monastery to serve as a school. [149] The Medici also may have contributed financial support. [150] What became of the academy is uncertain. Perhaps Traversari's work in humanist education at S. Maria degli Angeli was ultimately more important, for in the latter Quattrocento it continued to be a center of learning. Lorenzo de' Medici sent his sons there, and Pope Leo X spoke of the great attachment he felt towards this monastery in which he was educated as a youth. [151]

How seriously Traversari was committed to education in the *studia humanitatis* as an integral aspect of the monastic vocation is evident in a letter to his brother, Girolamo. "Not only with a willing spirit, but indeed with the greatest eagerness," he wrote, "have I read this letter of a loving brother, and this especially, that you are embracing so ardently and with

such avidity the *studia humanitatis.*" From his youth he had
counselled his brother to strive to be both a good and temperate
(*frugi*) man and also learned and devoted to wisdom (*sapientia
studiis*).

> I want you, my brother ... to apply yourself
> ardently and vigilantly to probity and virtue, nor to
> be content having begun, but to continue to pursue
> with all diligence and energy the noble name of
> erudition and holiness. Do not permit any time to go
> by without giving study to sacred letters; let time not
> be sufficient for your passion for pursuing the *studia
> humanitatis.* Let your principal concern be careful
> attention to the most knowledgeable and holiest men,
> those, that is, whom venerable antiquity commends,
> and commit to memory their precepts and principles.
> Enjoy their writings and become thoroughly familiar
> with them. I adhere to the teachings of the ancients
> which say that in reading over books you should not
> only consider the precepts of our own writers, but
> should also learn thoroughly foreign doctrine both
> for its copious knowledge and its elegant language.
> Many of these men were indeed eager for wisdom, so
> that they received the name, and indeed were so
> much lovers and honorable promoters of virtue, that
> they seem to have approached closely to our Relig-
> ion. [152]

When another fellow monk at S. Maria degli Angeli, Agostino
da Portico, began Greek studies, Traversari welcomed enthusiastically his eagerness and promised to give what aid he could.
Above all Agostino should strive more in daily spiritual
discipline, but he could pursue this and Greek learning at the
same time.

> For both can be properly accomodated, so that you
> progress both in spiritual devotion and in erudition,
> and daily become more advanced in holiness and
> more furnished with knowledge. Or, rather, I dare to
> say that increased grace of learning will be present
> where divine grace has abounded more, for among the

gifts of the Holy Spirit is knowledge, yoked to piety, and the Holy Spirit will illumine that mind, which it has filled, with all the splendor of knowledge. [153]

For Traversari, implicit in the renaissance of antiquity and in the *studia humanitatis* was an ethical imperative. Knowledge of ancient thought made men not only wiser, but more virtuous. In praising Niccoli for his fervent devotion to bringing forth from dust to light the buried writings of the ancients, Traversari wrote:

> ... you aroused nearly buried humanity. You first awakened the sleeping souls of men to this most virtuous study. Through the power of your ardent exhortation you caused youth, prone to sin, to bring themselves out of the foul whirlpool of pleasures to this most calm shore of learning. [154]

Moreover, the renaissance of antiquity, which had made Florence so illustrious and of such benefit to humanity, was clearly willed by God, for His gracious favor and loving devotion to the city defended it from the wicked and delivered it from grave dangers. [155]

Did Traversari, then, have no qualms about the pursuit of classical wisdom, no hesitation about the validity of studying pagan antiquity? Die he see no conflict between his Christian vocation as monk and priest and the cultivation of ancient thought? It was precisely these questions which he confronted in translating Diogenes Laertius, and he raised them himself in a letter to Cosimo written immediately after sending him the dedication copy of his translation. Cosimo should consider his condition, vow, and mode of life. Was such a task licit for a monk and priest, who wishes to respect truly his profession, who is often present at sacred altars and always engaged in divine duties, whose intercourse ought always to be with heaven, who does not leave the sanctuary, but by ancient decree is commanded to be continually in God's tabernacle and to live out his life there? [156] Before examining Traversari's conclusions, it is essential to understand the circumstances in which he argeed to make the translation, and the scholarly problems it presented.

By 1424 Traversari had established his reputation as a leading Greek scholar, and he began to receive appeals to devote his energies to the translation of Greek classics. The Archbishop of Genoa, for instance, had written asking for copies of his translations and encouraged him to take on the task of translating Diogenes Laertius and Plutarch. [157] Antonio da Massa, General of the Franciscans, who had journeyed to Constantinople in 1422-23 as Apostolic Nuncio to take part in preliminary discussions regarding the reunification of the Greek and Latin Churches, returned with a number of Greek manuscripts, including one of Diogenes Laertius. In the spring of 1424 he visited Traversari at S. Maria degli Angeli and urged him to undertake the translation of this work. [158] Meanwhile Niccoli seems to have suggested the translation of Diogenes Laertius or Philostratus. [159] After Antonio da Massa's visit Traversari wrote to Niccoli, then in Rome, that in this matter he would yield to no one more freely than to him or Cosimo, but he wished to wait until their return before agreeing definitely to the task. Moreover he was already fully burdened both with duties at the monastery and sacred translations previously undertaken. He hesitated to assume this fresh burden, not because he considered the study of Greek philosophers impious, but because he feared a prolonged distraction from sacred studies.

> You see how uncertain the human condition is, how fragile our life, liable each day to death. I ask you, especially now, to let me imbibe sacred letters, and be free for sacred concerns to which from youth I have devoted myself. I will obey your wishes if life attends me. [160]

Diogenes Laertius' *Vitae et sententiae philosophorum,* probably written in the first half of the third century A.D., provides not a systematic analysis, but rather a eulogistic narrative of the course of ancient philosophy from its origins among the pre-Socratics down to the epigoni of the four main classical schools, the Academy, Peripatetics, Stoics, and Epicureans. [161] Anecdotal and perhaps largely apocryphal in nature, still it gave to Renaissance humanists some conception of ancient philosophy, especially of Platonic and Epicurean thought; and in

Traversari's Latin translation, Diogenes Laertius seems to have been a key source for the emergence of Epicurean ideas in the Renaissance. [162] That Diogenes Laertius was not unknown to the medieval Latin west is attested by Henricus Aristippus, translator at the court of the Norman kings of Sicily, who promised in the preface to his mid-twelfth century translation of Plato's *Meno* a Latin translation of the *Vitae*. Attributable to him, in all likelihood, is the Latin version which formed the basis of Walter of Burley's early fourteenth century adaptation of Diogenes Laertius, the *Liber de vita et moribus philosophorum*. A medieval version was also known to the proto-humanist circle in early fourteenth century Verona, and to Petrarch's Augustinian friend and cultivator of classical studies Dionigi da Borgo S. Sepolcro (d. 1342). [163] In these medieval accounts Socrates and the other Greek philosophers appear strangely transmogrified into the guise of contemporary sages, much as the classical gods were depicted in medieval costume, a phenomenon Erwin Panofsky has termed the "principle of disjunction." [164] To the humanists of Traversari's generation, devoted to a restoration of classical ideas in a classical context, the medieval versions of Diogenes Laertius would certainly have been unacceptable, if indeed any was available. Traversari makes no mention of an extant translation.

Using two Greek manuscripts of the *Vitae*, one from Guarino's library, the other the text Antonio da Massa had brought from Constantinople, Traversari had made enough progress by May 1425 to seek yet a third manuscript from Giustiniani, hopefully intact where the other two were faulty, "so that final touches can be put to our labor." [165] But the work was proving far more demanding than he had imagined, and he asserted to Giustiniani that if he had read the work before agreeing to the translation, he would never, despite the entreaties of humanist friends, have assented to the task. He had thought it to be a simple historical narrative, but instead it discussed in detail the philosophical positions held by the various schools, and moreover did so often in an obscure or elliptical way. Especially difficult was the technical philosophical terminology of the Greek, much of which, he asserted, had no equivalent in Latin, and could only be rendered in an

inelegant way. [166] Nevertheless by August 1425, having diligently used Giustiniani's manuscript to correct a number of
errors, he had only the long final book on Epicurus to
complete. But he despaired at rendering the Greek into a Latin
acceptable to erudite readers, and he longed to return to sacred
studies. "Afterwards I will come back with a more ardent mind
and greater thirst to translating sacred letters, which I had
begun as a [spiritual] exercise, and with great joy I will sweetly
kiss these to which I have been accustomed nearly since
childhood." [167]

Despite his hopes that he would soon finish the translation, it
was not until 1433 that he actually presented the completed
version to Cosimo. Why the delay? He was forced repeatedly to
make corrections and revisions because he was a novice in
philosophy. He particularly regretted his ignorance of dialectics,
which he had never studied, and now realized would be of great
use — a great admission, indeed, for a humanist. He asked
Niccoli to send him Boethius' work on dialectics, if he had it in
his possession, for he anticipated this would be helpful. [168] The
final book on Epicurus, composed largely of selections of his
works, was proving particularly intractable, and in desperation
he turned to Marsuppini for help. [169] In 1428 Traversari sought
from Filelfo yet another manuscript of the Greek text of
Diogenes Laertius; and when Fifelfo came to Florence the
following year, he engaged him to translate the enigmatic
verse-epigrams. Filelfo promised the verses, but, as we have
seen, his relations with Traversari quickly soured, and he never
did them. When Traversari finally presented the translation to
Cosimo he left the verses untranslated. [170]

To return then to the "tribunal" — what justification does
Traversari give to Cosimo for this work of translation, which
proved so frustrating, absorbing his energies and distracting him
from sacred studies? He argues that in withdrawing from the
heavens to the depths he has committed no crime, for he had
grounds of charity. In service to friends it was proper to turn
aside briefly from his vocation and relax somewhat its rigors.
Nor would this be corrupting, for Christ had descended from
the bosom of the Father to our depths in order to bring back
the lost sheep to eternal pasture. St. Paul, his imitator, who was

taken up to the third heaven, descended readily from the summit of contemplation to set in order the commerce of the nuptial couch. So likewise have all the justified lived not for themselves, but for Christ, and they have soldiered to his gain. They have considered all things dung, so that they might win Him, and following his path they have done all for the cause of fraternal health.

> For who does not see that nothing should be preferred to holy charity? Yet, though charity is commended to us, and we are ordered by the law to love our neighbor as ourselves, we ought not, however, neglect our own salvation. It is necessary, therefore, to proceed along the middle way and to seek refuge in the protection of the Lord. May divine mercy, then, attend our pious endeavors, so that we may be regarded to have pleased the wishes of friends and done enough for our own salvation. [171]

In this letter, clearly, Traversari regarded the translation as disjunctive from his religious vocation and his patristic scholarship. This project was justifiable not by the nature of the book itself, for it concerned mere earthly matters, but only as a deed of charity for friends who desired it. Despite the examples of Christ and St. Paul, this letter reveals considerable uneasiness, especially in the closing prayer.

Quite different is the judgement Traversari expresses in the dedicatory letter to the translation, which he sent to Niccoli for approval before publication. [172] Again he states that this task was a temporary deflection from his religious vocation, but it was by no means reprehensible.

> On the contrary true reason suggested that by my labor the dignity of Christian grace and piety might become more evident and faith in God might sping up more readily and ardently. For when there is so much conflict of opinion about God and divine and human things among those who were foremost in pagan wisdom, so that they destroy one another in turn, nor can you discover where to make a stand, the mind embraces with greater liveliness indeed the grace of

divine dignity, and running to the font of truth pities the squalor of ancient errors. For even if scattered among them there are to be discovered certain things that are probable and consonant with truth, the intellect, fatigued by such variety of opinions gladly and gratefully finds refuge in the bedchamber of truth, and longs to hear continuously divine books and letters.

But does Diogenes Laertius provide merely this negative usefulness, demonstrating the error and confusion of the ancient philosophers in comparison to Christian revelation? No. Traversari continues:

In the writings of all the more notable philosophers, God, the heavens, the celestial bodies, and nature are truly and subtly discussed, and largely in agreement with Christian truth. Such singular effort of investigating truth, the work of such keen genius and celebrated study, did not deserve to be everywhere deprived of the fruit of its sweat. God permitting, from their testimony also the true faith might receive support and strength.

What Traversari really admired in the ancient philosophers was not their knowledge, however, but their pursuit of virtue.

You come across in them much said with gravity and done with constancy, so that not just from their books does the inviolable truth derive confirmation, but the examples of their lives also add on incitement for virtue to our religion. How destestable, how full of shame it is, if it chagrins Christian man, reliant directly on God, and having certain hope of eternal life, to strive for virtue and continence, when he has ascertained that the pagans, though alien from true worship of God and religion, were more zealous for probity, moderation, frugality, and the other ornaments of the human soul. There are many examples very close, I would say, to evangelical perfection, so that it should make a Christian blush and feel greatly ashamed if the philosopher of Christ exhibits this less than the philosopher of the world, and love of empty glory is more powerful in the breast of a pagan than desire of religious piety in the Christian soul. For these reasons I am easily persuaded that I not only might not despise this task of translation as useless, or flee it as noxious, but on the contrary might undertake it with calm conscience as proper and necessary. Of course, if admiration of these men seizes anyone more strongly than is right, and he wishes through examples to prefer or even to com- pare their deeds to our philosophy (which is nearly my only fear), he will be mildly admonished to admire rather that real virtue than the shadowy image of virtue. [173]

Study of Diogenes Laertius may, then, produce certain positive benefits, but Traversari cautions against excessive enthusiasm for the thought of the classical thinkers. Admiration for their wisdom and virtue must be tempered by the recognition that they were unaware of the true source of divine truth. There remained in Traversari's mind an unresolved tension between the revival of classical wisdom and Christian piety. This tension is all the more noteworthy since he was thoroughly familiar with Lactantius' *Divinae Institutiones* and Augustine's *De doctrina Christiana,* both of which had pointed to harbingers of Christian doctrine among the gentiles, so that ancient wisdom is regarded as *pia philosophia.* Salutati in his defense of Virgil had argued that his poetry contained signs of the Christian doctrine of the Trinity and the Incarnation; and Bruni, in the preface of his translation of Plato's *Phaedo,* had asserted that many believed Plato had known the Old Testa- ment prophetic tradition, either directly from Jeremiah in Egypt, or from the Greek Septuagint translation of the Old Testament. [174] Since it is difficult to imagine that Traversari was unfamiliar with the notion of *pia philosophia*, it must be that he was unwilling to press the syncretism of Christian doctrine and classical wisdom.

Paradoxically it was the Diogenes Laertius translation which was among the most widely diffused of Traversari's translations. Manuscript copies were present in most of the leading Italian humanist libraries and even in the library of Matthias Corvinus, the King of Hungary and a great humanist patron. Cusanus, as we noted, owned a copy which he annotated. Moreover six editions of the translation were printed in the fifteenth century, and six more appeared in the sixteenth century. [175]

Despite his reluctance to undertake the Diogenes Laertius translation, and despite the long and often frustrating task it entailed and his doubts about its utility, Traversari did not thereafter turn from classical scholarship to an exclusive preoccupation with patristic studies. He continued to read Greek philosophic texts and kept current with the philosophic interests of other humanists. [176] In 1437 he was considering translating Aristotle's *Eudemian Ethics;* [177] and he did complete one other translation of a Greek philosophic text, Aeneas Gazeus' *Theophrastus,* or *De animarum immortalitate.*

Aeneas Gazeus (450-534) was the principal figure in the efflorescence of Hellenic culture which occurred in the Palestinian town of Gaza in the fifth century A.D. The *Theophrastus,* written c. 484, like the work of Diogenes Laertius, belongs to the intellectual climate of the late Hellenistic world. In conscious emulation of Plato, the *Theophrastus* is written as a dialogue. Its setting is Alexandria where Eussiteus, a rhetorician and philosopher of Gaza — and spokesman for the author — has been forced to disembark when contrary winds blew his ship off course from its destined port, Athens, where he had intended to study philosophy. In Alexandria he finds Theophrastus, famed teacher of philosophy recently arrived from Athens. To him Eussiteus poses the question of the immortality of the soul. Theophrastus, standing for the whole tradition of Greek speculative thought, responds by citing the opinions of the Chaldeans, Egyptians, Eleatics, Pythagoreans, Plato, Plotinus, Porphyry, Iamblichus, and Proclus. By Socratic questioning Eussiteus gradually forces Theophrastus to recognize errors in his philosophy, particularly the Platonic idea of the pre-existence of the soul, which implies that birth is a fall from a superior state. For Aeneas the soul is not divine nor pre-existing, but it is immortal, and through the omnipotence of God the body also will be resurrected and join the soul in immortality. In the end Theophrastus bids adieu to the

Academy to follow God, and Eussiteus offers a prayer to the Christian Trinity. The dialogue is intended to show the inadequacies of Greek philosophy before the wisdom of the Christian God; but, in treating the problem of the immortality of the soul and of divine providence, Aeneas drew heavily on neo-Platonic metaphysics, especially Plotinus; and, like Gregory of Nyssa (whose *De opificio hominis* is an obvious source) and other of the more speculative Greek Fathers, he provides a synthesis of Christianity and neo-Platonism. [178]

When Traversari made his translation of Aeneas Gazeus is uncertain, though perhaps most likely is the prolonged stay in Florence from mid-1434 to early 1435. In July 1435 he dedicated the translation in gratitude to Andreolo Giustiniani (1392-1456), a wealthy Genoese patrician resident on the island of Chios, who had amassed an impressive library of Greek manuscripts and had just sent Traversari a generous number of Greek volumes. [179]

In the dedicatory letter Traversari states that when he had read the *Theophrastus* in Greek he decided to make a Latin translation because the beauty of the doctrine and dignity of the subject matter treated were such as to arouse even idle minds to admiration.

> The whole discourse is devoted to the Soul. His disputation treats this matter with great subtlety so that the learned, imbued with pagan philosophy, may gradually through reason attain the rudiments of Catholic faith and the sanctuary of piety. By true and rational arguments he refutes the empty, diverse and mutually conflicting opinions of the Philosophers and diligently and beautifully introduces the truth of Christian faith. [180]

Aeneas Gazeus, then, is not to be studied as a source for the philosophies of the soul of the esoteric *prisci theologi,* Plato, and the neo-Platonists, but rather as a work of Christian apologetics, and as a spur to turn from philosophy to Christian truth and piety. Again, as with Diogenes Laertius, Traversari was reluctant to press a syncretism of classical philosophy and Christian doctrine. This caution regarding the Platonic tradition is again somewhat surprising, for Florentine humanism had shown considerable interest in Platonic thought, especially the doctrine of the soul, In his consolatory letter on the death of Petrarch in 1374, Salutati criticized both Epicurean and Aristotelian doctrines of the soul, and drew on Platonic ideas, through Macrobius, Boethius, the Latin Fathers, and Chalcidius' commentary on the *Timaeus* to demonstrate the substantiality of the imperishable soul. In the preface to his translation of the *Phaedo*, Bruni argued, as we have seen, that Platonic doctrine of the soul conformed to Christian truth. In the early 1430's, Marsuppini, in his *Consolatio,* cited Plato's *Republic, Phaedrus,* and *Gorgias* in defense of the immortality of the soul. [181] The heyday of Florentine Platonism occurred, of course, in the latter Quattrocento with the establishment of the Platonic Academy, where ideas of the soul were a central concern. Since immortality of the soul is a principal subject of Ficino's *Theologia Platonica,* it is noteworthy that Ficino himself, in 1456, copied Traversari's translation of Aeneas Gazeus. [182]

As with the impetus to the study of Epicurus inspired by his translation of Diogenes Laertius, so in the utilization of Aeneas Gazeus by Ficino in his syncretism of Platonic philosophy and Christian doctrine, Traversari's scholarship in ancient philosophy did not serve the Christian apologetic function he anticipated. Rather than exploring the authoritative exposition of Christian doctrine as revealed in the Greek and Latin Fathers, the latter Quattrocento focused on finding identity between the gentile *prisca theologia* and sacred revelation.

In his admiration for the virtuous character of many of the ancient pagans, Traversari shared a sentiment common to the humanists of the early Quattrocento. His moral philosophy, like that of most of his humanist contemporaries (and a heritage from Petrarch and Salutati), was based largely on an eclectic stoicism such as was found in Cicero. The stress fell on fortitude in the face of adversity, moderation, a steadfast adherence to rectitude when tempted by worldly pleasures. Thus, as Traversari wrote to Mariotto Allegri, "that opinion of Hesiod also coincides with Catholic truth: 'the ascent to virtue is hard, arduous, and difficult, marked by the roughness of a rocky and tortuous route; in the beginning it demands the sweat of much effort and hard labor.'" So likewise had St. Benedict admonished his disciple Maurus. [183]

It was in the notion of *pietas* that ancient wisdom, for Traversari, approached the Christian idea of virtue. Writing to Giovanni Lucido Gonzaga, young son of the Marquis of Mantua, Traversari explained what he meant.

> And what indeed . . . is *pietas*? You will remember certainly that judgement of Cicero that it is a word of great gravity to which neither benevolence nor devotion can be compared. But indeed the meaning of this word seems to need our discussion. So that we may take our start from sacred letters, the Apostle Paul wrote to Timothy, the disciple in whom he was singularly pleased: "O Timothy, exercise yourself to *pietas*, for bodily exercise is of little worth, but *pietas* is conducive to all things" [I Timothy 4: 7-8]. This word which in Greek is $\theta\epsilon o\sigma\acute{\epsilon}\beta\epsilon\iota a$, can be translated into Latin as *"Dei cultus."* As Apollo attests, *pietas* is nothing other than *"Dei notio"* or *"Dei cultus."* You perceive surely that the name of *pietas* contains hidden within it the whole idea of virtue and probity. It is Cicero's opinion that it pertains to country and family and indeed to the gods themselves, even though it was the error of the gentiles to worship many and various gods. According to the true testimony of Paul this refers particularly to divine things, and this is what the oracle of Apollo proves. We, following this true teaching, and drawing on the admonition of the Apostle, understand *pietas* to be nearly a divine thing to which the Apostle exhorts his singularly meritorious disciple to exert himself. So that I may express in a few words what I mean, *"pietas"* is the same as cleanness or purity of heart, of which our Saviour said, "Blessed are the pure of heart, for they shall see God" [Matthew 5: 8]. Not by chance is it said that *pietas* is the way by which one reaches cleanness of heart, so that it is, as it were, the instrument of it. I, who have steadfastly asserted that both are the same, grant that they seem to differ in this. Cleanness of heart is as the destiny or $\sigma\kappa o\pi\grave{o}S$ we desire to reach so that whatever we do

is referred to this end; *pietas* is the action by which we seek this. [184]

Traversari continues his explication citing further passages from Romans and Corinthians, and observes that though many great men had treated the question of virtue, including Xenophon, none had done so with the diligence of St. Jerome. He exhorted Giovanni to read especially Jerome's *Epistles*. From his own experience he could attest to their exceptional nature, for when he was an adolescent of Giovanni's age he found nothing more inspiring or efficacious in arousing his devotion to virtue and execration of sin. He became so familiar with the *Epistles* that he came to know many of them by heart.

It was the stoic pursuit of virtue, then, which for Traversari most closely approached the Christian way of life. Hence his preference for the moral teachings of the Latins, especially Cicero, over and against the "seductions of Hellas," which he warned his brother were unable to enrich him as much as cultivation of Latin authors. [185] Moreover Traversari in large part identified Christian life, and especially the monastic vocation, with a stoic perseverence in the path of virtue in order to overcome the weakness and fragility of mortal life and to resist the defiling pleasures of the world. For the Christian devoted to the *studia probitatis,* however, in contrast to the pagan stoic, there is the hope of future beatitude and eternal felicity as the reward for persisting in virtue. [186] Further, and more importantly, Christ had supplanted the ancient moral virtues, or rather had fulfilled them and went beyond them in such a way that the imitation of Christ was the true Christian path to virtue.

> What indeed is true virtue except what the Apostle teaches, saying Christ is "*Dei virtutem*" and "*Dei sapientiam*" [I Corinthians 1: 18, 30]? He is the font of all virtues, the author of all perfection. I exhort and admonish you to draw on him with all your heart, so that according to his promise he "will be in you a well of water springing up into everlasting life" [John 4: 14]. You will lack no virtue if you receive and embrace its source. Not wisdom; how? when indeed he is the wisdom of God? Not fortitude since

he is "the Lord, strong and mightly in battle" [Psalms
23 (24): 8]; "who bound the strong man and took
away his spoils" [Matthew 12: 29]. Not justice, for
"he is made unto us by God the Father justice and
sanctification" [I Corinthians 1: 30]. Not prudence,
not temperance, for without him these are nothing.
Not glory, "when he is the King of glory" [Psalms 23
(24): 10]. Not wealth, for who can be richer than he
who merits to possess the King of eternity? It is clear
in short that one lacks nothing who possesses
him. [187]

Traversari, then, strongly promoted education in the *studia
humanitatis,* and even went so far as to yoke the *studia pietatis*
and the *studia humanitatis* together, for both learning and grace
are essential to the Christian. He admired the moral thought of
many of the ancients, and was greatly impressed with the
character of the ancient Romans to the point where he saw
correspondences between their pursuit of virtue and Christian
faith. He adopted an eclectic stoicism, of a quite unoriginal
kind, as the essence of Christian morality. But beyond this he
did not go. Though he seems to have read, at least hastily,
Valla's *De vero falsoque bono*, he was unaffected by the Roman
humanist's highly original preference for Epicurean moral
thought and by his critique of the profoundly anti-Christian
nature of the electic stoicism which humanists, including
Traversari, espoused. Traversari resisted any philosophical
syncretism of Christian doctrine and neo-Platonism, although
his translation of Aeneas Gazeus seemed to offer the opportunity to make such speculations. But Traversari was at depth
unfriendly to questions of metaphysics and epistemology. It
was the eloquence of the ancients, the forceful conviction of
their writings, which he admired. In the Fathers he discovered
this eloquence yoked to a profound, and for him "apostolic,"
piety, both in their lives and in their teachings. Hence the
revival of the spiritual and homiletical literature of Christian
antiquity was the real focus of his study and scholarship.

CHAPTER III

THE RENAISSANCE OF PATRISTIC STUDIES

In the winter of 1432, while Traversari awaited Curial confirmation of his authority as General, he occupied his enforced leisure by exploring the libraries of Roman monasteries. At S. Cecilia:

> . . . . I discovered Origen's thirty-nine *Homilies on Luke,* translated by Jerome. I was elated with such joy that I thought the wealth of Croesus to be surpassed, for these were known only by reputation, and I had found no one who had seen and read them. When this discovery was announced in Florence it aroused great excitement, especially with my devoted friend Niccoli. I immediately saw to having the work transcribed, together with the three *Homelies on Psalms* by this same author, although the volume was so rotting that hardly a few words could be read.[1]

A decade and a half earlier, in the preface to his first major patristic translation, St. John Chrysostom's *Adversus vituperatores vitae monasticae,* dedicated to Prior Matteo, Traversari wrote:

> You urged by your authority . . . that for the purpose of [spiritual] exercise I translate something of sacred letters from the Greek. For you said it would be highly auspicious if I would consecrate the first fruits of my studies to such monuments, and that it would be especially suitable to my vow and vocation if I were to exhibit no less devotion, labor, and diligence in translating the teachers of our philosophy than not a few brilliant and learned friends had done in our age and continued to do now in translating authors of foreign wisdom.[2]

These statements reveal the central thrusts of Traversari's patristic scholarship — the recovery of neglected writings of the Fathers, and making accessible to the Latin West what the Greek "philosophers of Christ" had elucidated regarding the nature of Christian faith and virtue. Before it is possible to assess the originality of Traversari's purpose, and the extent of his accomplishment, it is essential to grasp how widely Greek Fathers were known and studied in the Latin Middle Ages, and to ascertain the place of patristics in late medieval scholastic theology.

The Greek Fathers in the
Latin Middle Ages

An exhaustive account of the study of Greek patristic theology in the Latin Middle Ages is beyond the scope and purpose of this sketch. Rather the intention here is to indicate its general continuity in the Latin West until the mid- thirteenth century, and to consider interest in and access to works of the Greek Fathers in the late Middle Ages.[3]

Most of the early Christian writings, including the New Testament itself, were written in Greek. But in the patristic age Scripture, the Apostolic Fathers, and numerous works of the Alexandrian and Antiochian Fathers were translated into Latin. Greek theology and scriptural exegesis were studied closely by many Latin Fathers including Ambrose (339-97), whose *Hexaemeron* was largely an adaptation of St. Basil's similarly titled work. The principal achievements in translation, however, were made by St. Jerome (c. 347-420) and Rufinus of Aquileia (c. 345-410). Jerome, who studied under Gregory Nazianzen in Constantinople and who lived much of his mature life in the Greek East, not only provided the standard medieval Latin text of Holy Scripture, the Vulgate, but acquainted the Latin West as well with the state of Greek patristic Scriptural exegesis through numerous translations of Origen's homiletical works. Rufinus' patristic translations, which were even more extensive than Jerome's, also concentrated on Origen, though he provided as well Eusebius' *Ecclesiastical History,* works on Eastern monasticism, and some writings of Basil and Gregory Nazianzen.[4] As a consequence of Jerome's and Rufinus' activity, Origen was undoubtedly the most widely read Greek Father in the Latin Middle Ages; and despite the condemnation of his theology at the Fifth Ecumenical Council (553), his exegetical principles had a pervasive effect. His Old Testament commentary in particular influenced Latin theologians from Gregory the Great to Bernard of Clairvaux.[5] In the early fifth century Anianus translated the first twenty-five of Chrysostom's *Homilies on Matthew* as a defense of Pelagius' emphasis on the exercise of human will in the process of salvation. Whether this was a correct understanding of Chrysostom's thought led to further study and translation of his works with the result that next to Origen he was the Greek Father best known to the medieval Latin West.[6] St. Augustine used the Greek text of Scripture, and made great efforts to read the works of the Greek Fathers available in Latin translation, but not until the outbreak of the Pelagian controversy late in his career (415) was he forced to improve this knowledge of the language to the point where he could read and comment directly on the Greek Fathers. Consequently much of Augustine's theology was original and developed independently of the Greek tradition. Since Augustine was the preeminent doctrinal authority in Latin Christendom throughout the Middle Ages, the effect of his pervasive influence was to diminish the Latin desire to exploit the works of the Greek Fathers.[7]

The fifth century, which experienced such devastating barbarian invasions, saw the gradual disappearance of Greek culture in the West. Pope Leo the Great (440-61), for instance, was forced to rely on earlier translations for knowledge of Greek patristics. But then came a remarkable reflourishing of Greek studies in Italy under Theodoric in the first quarter of the sixth century. Boethius (c.480-524), whose translations of Aristotle's logical works and other writings on the *quadrivium* formed the core of early medieval philosophy, and Cassiodorus (c. 490-c.583) were the central figures in this "Hellenic Renaissance." After the Byzantine conquest of Rome in the mid-sixth century, Cassiodorus retired to the monastery of Vivarium in Calabria where he strove to place Greek literature and learning in the service of monastic culture. He instituted a program of liberal studies (described in his *Institutiones*) based on the curriculum at Alexandria; and under his direction translations were made of Chrysostom, Origen, Didymus, Clement of Alexandria, and Josephus which were disseminated over all of Europe in the seventh through ninth centuries.[8]

Late Latin antiquity thus made available to the West a considerable body of Greek patristic literature. Yet there were notable gaps. Few works of the Cappadocian Fathers — Basil, Gregory Nazianzen, and Gregory of Nyssa — were translated; and of Athanasius, only the *Vita S. Antonii* which in the translation of Jerome's friend Evagrius of Antioch became the model for Latin hagiography, was widely known.[9]

The mid-seventh to mid-eighth centuries saw a resurgence of Greek culture in Italy as Eastern clerics fled the onslaught of Islam, and Byzantine monks escaped the iconoclastic suppression of the Isaurian emperors. By c.800 more than a dozen Basilian monasteries had been established in or near Rome, including Grottaferrata. Moreover, the Papal See was occupied continuously in this period by Popes who were Greek in culture. This milieu saw the production of numerous Greek manuscripts, and a few new Latin translations of the Greek Fathers, but the overall impact on early medieval Latin culture was slight. By the eleventh century Rome's flourishing Greek colony had dwindled to insignificance, though the heyday of Basilian monasticism in south Italy and Sicily came during the Norman period. Indeed Greek culture remained prominent there until the fifteenth century in such places as the Basilian monastery of S. Niccolò di Casole, where Bessarion acquired important Greek manuscripts before its destruction by the Turks in 1480.[10] But south Italy had no impact on Greek studies in early Quattrocento Florence, where humanists were inspired directly by such Byzantine classicists as Chrysoloras, Plethon, and Argyropoulos. Except for Grottaferrata, Traversari made no effort to explore the library holdings of the Basilian monasteries in Italy.

The Carolingian Renaissance brought a renewal of Greek patristic studies. John Scotus Eriugena, the leading Greek scholar of the age, believed that in profundity of thought and power of expression the Greek Fathers were superior to the Latin, even Augustine. In the 860's he translated the works of Ps.-Dionysius the Aeropagite, the *Ambigua* of Maximus the

Confessor (c.580-662), which was a commentary on the orations of Gregory Nazianzen, and writings of Epiphanius and Gregory of Nyssa. In addition he wrote a commentary on the Gospel of John, strongly neo-Platonic in its emphasis, for which he used Greek texts of Scripture and drew extensively on Greek patristic exegesis. Eriugena's great work of philosophical and theological synthesis, the *De divisione naturae,* also drew heavily on the neo-Platonism of the Greek Fathers. Until its condemnation in 1225 this work continued to bring the influence of Greek speculative theology to bear in the West. His achievements were indeed impressive, but not without significant limitations: he seems to have conflated Gregory of Nyssa with Gregory Nazianzen; and his translations reveal an ignorance of the grammatical and syntactical niceties of the Greek. [11]

The twelfth century revival of learning also brought a renewal of Greek scholarship. Most decisive undoubtedly were translations of Aristotle, both from Greek and Arabic, which made available in Latin for the first time the full body of Aristotle's logic. This laid the basis for scholastic dialectic, the dominant mode of intellectual inquiry in the universities for the next four centuries. But influential translations of Ptolemy's *Almagest* and Galen's medical works were made as well. Much of this scholarship was patronized by the court of the Norman Kings of Sicily, where eclectic Byzantine and Islamic cultural influences remained strong. There Henricus Aristippus, celebrated translator of Plato's *Meno* and *Phaedo,* seems to have begun too a translation of Gregory Nazianzen. [12]

In the wake of the crusades and the establishment of Pisan, Genoese, and Venetian trading colonies in Byzantium and the Levant in the twelfth century, a number of theological disputations between Latin and Greek theologians were held in Constantinople. Among the Latins who came into contact with Greek theology there was Burgundio of Pisa (c.1100-93). At the request of Pope Eugenius III, Burgundio translated Chrysostom's *Homilies on Matthew* (c.1151) from a Greek manuscript which the Pope had sought and received from the Patriarch of Antioch. [13] He also translated Chrysostom's *Homilies on John* and *on Acts,* and the *De opificio hominis* of Nemesius of

Emesa (c.400), which he believed to be a work of Gregory of Nyssa. His most influential translation of Greek theology was John of Damascus' *De fide orthodoxa,* which was to form the basis of Peter Lombard's *Sentences.* [14] Yet the ultimate fruit of this renaissance of Greek patristics was slight. Burgundio's translations were not widely disseminated. More importantly the systematization of patristic theology in Lombard's *Sentences* was distinctly Latin, and indeed overwhelmingly Augustinian. Augustine is cited over a thousand times, and Hilary and Ambrose eighty each, while John of Damascus leads the Greeks with thirty, followed by Chrysostom with twenty, and such important Fathers as Athanasius and Cyril of Alexandria appear but once each. [15]

The thirteenth century, with the exception of Robert Grosseteste (1168-1253) and Roger Bacon (d. 1292), saw the neglect of the direct study of the Greek Fathers, and indeed a gradual abandonment of patristic theology, a consequence at least in part of the shift from Scriptural exegesis to systematic elucidation of doctrine as the primary focus of theological inquiry. Early in his career Grosseteste devoted his intellectual energies to a study of logic and natural science, in particular Aristotle's *Posterior Analytics* and *Physics.* But around 1230, and especially after he became Bishop of Lincoln in 1235, he turned his attention to Biblical and patristic studies, which he believed essential for sound preaching. He learned both Greek and Hebrew, and acquired substantial numbers of Greek patristic manuscripts, especially Origen and Chrysostom. He wrote a tropological exposition of the meaning of the Gospels, glosses on the Pauline Epistles, and a long commentary on Galatians, for which he drew on the Greek with an accompanying *catena* of Greek patristic commentary, and a commentary on Genesis, which made extensive use of Basil's *Hexaemeron.* In addition, he corrected Burgundio's translation of John of Damascus, and translated several other works of this eighth century systematic theologian, produced a revised translation of Ps.-Dionysius, along with Maximus' *Scholia* on it, and translated four apocryphal letters of St. Ignatius. [16] In the latter thirteenth century Roger Bacon also appealed for the study of the Greek New Testament and Greek patristic exegesis, but this went for nought. Even though Thomas Aquinas was said to have made so much of Chrysostom's *Homilies on Matthew* (in Burgundio's translation) that he would not have exchanged it for the whole city of Paris, no scholastic theologian knew Greek.[17] For Valla this was absurd, and he sharply criticized Aquinas' commentaries on the Pauline Epistles, where failure to know the Greek text, he argued, led to misinterpretation.[18] Late medieval theology in fact showed a livelier interest in Hebrew and in Jewish Old Testament exegesis than in Greek patristics. The Victorines, Hugh (d.1141) and especially Andrew (d.1175), had stressed Hebrew studies, and this effort was continued by such scholars as Nicholas de Lyra (d.1349).[19]

The last important achievement in medieval Greek studies was made by William of Moerbeke (d.1286), Aquinas' Dominican colleague. While a resident in Latin monasteries in Byzantium he learned Greek; he produced translations of all of Aristotle's works not previously made into Latin, and revised the earlier medieval versions, many of which had been made from Arabic rather than Greek sources.[20] The effect of Moerbeke's scholarship was to consolidate further the supremacy of Aristotalian philosophy and natural science in the universities.

Why were Greek studies neglected in the late Middle Ages? A partial explanation is Latin political hegemony in the Greek East in the thirteenth and fourteenth centuries. Western control of the Byzantine Empire in the wake of the Fourth Crusade lasted from 1204-64, while Latin possession of feudal principalities in Greece proper lasted into the fifteenth century. Latin bishops, predominantly Dominicans and Franciscans, occupied Greek sees and strove to submit the Greeks to Latin orthodoxy. Greek studies were promoted in a number of the Dominican and Franciscan monasteries established in the East, notably at the Dominican *studia* at Caffa, Pera, and Constantinople, but knowledge of the language was used as a weapon against Greek theological positions in the numerous disputations at Constantinople or in polemical tracts on the "errors" of the Greeks, particularly on the question of the Procession of the Holy Spirit.[21] Likewise the never-fulfilled provision of the Council of Vienne (1311) to establish chairs of Greek and of

Hebrew, Arabic, and "Chaldean" at the universities of Oxford, Paris, Bologna, and Salamanca, and at the Papal Court was intended less to insure the teaching of non-Latin thought than to encourage the language skills necessary to propagate Latin faith among "heretics" and "infidels".[22]

Even in Byzantium there is evidence of Latin cultural hegemony. The French courtly love romances of Alexander the Great were translated into Greek, an indication of Byzantine emulation of western feudal *courtoisie*; but, ironically, these romances derived from the mid-tenth century Latin translation of Ps.-Callisthenes' Greek account of the deeds of Alexander. [23] Byzantine intellectuals were attracted to Latin philosophy and theology. Maximus Planudes (1260-1310), prominent scholar of classical Greek lyric poetry, translated into Greek Cicero's *Somnium Scipionis* with Macrobius' late Latin neo-Platonic commentary, and Boethius' *De differentiis topicis*. Both works were enormously influential in the Latin Middle Ages, but they were thoroughly derivative of late Hellenistic thought. Hence it is odd that a Byzantine scholar should choose to translate these works when he had access to Porphyry and other neo-Platonists in their original Greek. Perhaps even more significant is that Planudes translated into Greek Boethius' *Consolation of Philosophy* and Augustine's *De Trinitate,* [24] a copy of which Traversari borrowed from Vittorino da Feltre in 1433. [25] Planudes was not alone. Demetrius Cydones (1315/20-1400), who lived to accompany Chrysoloras to Venice in the 1390's, translated Aquinas' *Summa contra gentiles* and part of the *Summa theologiae* from Latin into Greek (1353-58), while his younger brother Prochoros also translated parts of the *Summa theologiae,* several treatises of Augustine, and Jerome's Biblical prefaces. [26] George Scholarius, a participant in the Council of Florence, and later as Patriarch Gennadius a staunch opponent of union with the Latin Church, was nevertheless an ardent admirer of Aquinas. [27]

In the late Middle Ages the single exception to Latin neglect of Greek patristics was Angelo Clareno da Cingoli (d.1337). Clareno, a Spiritual Franciscan, travelled to the East as missionary to the Kingdom of Armenia in Cilicia (1290-94), where he visited the famous cave of St. Paul near Tarsus. In

1295-1305 he lived first in Latin-ruled Achaea, then in Thessaly where he learned Greek — according to legend, through the miraculous intervention of the Holy Spirit during the celebration of the office of Nativity. He subsequently translated the *Regula S. Basilii,* one of the spiritual homilies of Macarius whose work was important for Christian mysticism, and the *Scala Paradisi* of Johannes Climacus, a translation which Traversari sharply criticized. When Clareno returned to the West, he wrote several treatises of moral exhortation, a defense of the Spiritual Franciscans addressed to Pope John XXII, and an exposition of the Franciscan Rule. This last displays considerable erudition in Greek patristics and demonstrates that Clareno was familiar with Greek works of Eusebius, Athanasius, Gregory Nazianzen, Gregory of Nyssa, and Ephraem of Syria. [28]

Yet so absent was consciousness of patristic theology, especially the Greek Fathers, from Trecento religious thought that Dante in his enumeration of the Doctors of the Church in *Paradiso* depicts of the Greeks only "il metropolitano Crisostomo," besides Ps.-Dionysius; while Aquinas and Bonaventura, representatives respectively of Dominican and Franciscan scholasticism, are the principal luminaries. [29]

The pattern of Latin cultural hegemony over the Greek East ended in the latter Trecento with two simultaneous developments. In the West, Petrarch, followed by Salutati and the S. Spirito circle in Florence, broke with the intellectual assumptions of scholasticism. In their cultivation of the Latin classics, especially Cicero, they came to share the Roman admiration for Greek wisdom. Hence the extraordinary desire to study Greek and the remarkable reception accorded Chrysoloras' teaching in Florence. In the Greek East the Palaeologan renaissance cultivated a renewed emphasis on the Greek classics. By the mid-fourteenth century the consciousness of the formative influence of classical Greek culture led certain Byzantine writers to refer to themselves as "Hellenes," a term which hitherto had had pagan connotations and been regarded with opprobrium. [30] The most important figure in this "Hellenic" renaissance is George Gemistos Plethon (c.1360-1452), who at Mistra, near the site of ancient Sparta, established a school dedicated to the recovery of ancient Greek wisdom and to the revival of Hellenic

virtue. [31] Manuel Chrysolaras' relation to Plethon is unclear —
the years prior to Chrysolaras' arrival in the West are shrouded
in darkness — but like Plethon he promoted a return to the
Greek classics, and he developed a pedagogy which stressed that
a student completely absorb the text so that he might assimilate
a classical mentality. This approach dominated the intellectual
outlook of Italian humanists in the first half of the Quattrocento. [32] Quattrocento humanism thus brought a complete
reversal of late medieval attitudes to Greek studies. It was to the
steady stream of Greek scholars who came to the West —
Chrysoloras, George of Trebizond, Plethon, Bessarion, John
Argyropoulos — that the Italian humanists looked as authorities
in the analysis of Greek texts and as propounders of Hellenic
wisdom. [33] Kristeller suggests further that the Italian humanists
learned from Greek scholars not only classical Greek, but also
the method of interpretation of texts which had developed in
Byzantine philology. This influenced the choice of Greek works
read by the Italian humanists, the order in which they were
read, and perhaps also the study of philosophy and patristics in
a rhetorical rather than a dialectical context. [34] Certainly also
the Platonism of Plethon, Bessarion, and Chrysoloras had a
profound impact upon the humanists and encouraged their
break with the Aristotelian philosophy of the scholastics.

This new intellectual perspective on Greek thought brought a
reversal of attitudes towards the Greek Fathers. In a sermon
preached before King Charles VI of France in 1409, Jean
Gerson urged that the forthcoming Council of Pisa work for
union with the Greek Church, and he reminded the King that
the West owed the Christian faith itself to the Greeks and that
St. Denys, the Apostle to Paris, was a Greek. [35] A century later
Erasmus could write:

> . . . . Latin learning, rich as it is, is defective and
> incomplete without Greek; for we have but a few
> small streams and muddy puddles, while they have
> pure springs and rivers rolling gold. I see that it is
> utter madness even to touch the branch of theology
> which deals chiefly with the mysteries unless one is
> also provided with the equipment of Greek. [36]

It was in the context of this renewed enthusiasm for Greek literature and thought that Traversari turned to the study and translation of the Greek Fathers. Greek letters had not been extinct in Italy for many centuries, as Traversari asserted,[37] but more than two centuries had elapsed since the work of Burgundio of Pisa. Boccaccio, Marsili, and Salutati began to collect and read the late antique and medieval Latin translations of the Greek Fathers.[38] Poggio, too, while in England in the early 1420's wrote Niccoli that he was studying Chrysostom, in the translations of Anianus (early fifth century), Mutianus (associate of Cassiodorus), and Burgundio.[39] But, as will be seen, the humanists found the literal Latin translations unsatisfactory to their standards of elegance. It was precisely to reveal the profundity of Greek patristic wisdom in eloquent humanist Latin that Traversari saw as his intellectual and spiritual mission.

Patristic Theology in the Late Middle Ages

The Fathers, Augustine especially, remained for the late Middle Ages the authoritative sources of Christian doctrine. But the purpose and method of theological inquiry in scholastic thought departed sharply from patristic assumptions, and the scholastics ceased to immerse themselves in patristic writings. Systematic treatment of doctrine through Aristotelian logic and philosophy supplanted the patristic emphasis on Scriptural exegesis. The key steps in this transition occurred in the twelfth century.

The systematic treatment of doctrine began in the form of a more systematic approach to Scriptural exegesis. In the circle of Anselm of Laon c.1100-30 there emerged what came to be known as the *glossa ordinaria*, composed of interlinear and marginal glosses on the Biblical text. Patristic citation was prevalent, but the Fathers had been approached through Carolingian compilations of patristic *florilegia* and such eleventh century collections of glosses as Lanfranc of Bec. Moreover, Bede, and such Carolingians as Rabanus Maurus, Walafrid Strabo, and Scotus Eriugena were not distinguished in authority from the Fathers. Further, exegesis was not understood as the historico-critical means to discover the original meaning of the text, but rather the search for authoritative doctrinal statements, an approach analogous to the Bolognese glossators' treatment of Justinian's *Corpus iuris civilis* or Gratian's compilation of canon law, the *Decretum.* [40]

A second important development was that the identification of theology with the study of Scripture, the *divina pagina,* ended in the course of the twelfth century, as doctrine, *fides catholica* became separated from exegesis as a distinct subject. The key step in this process was Peter Lombard's *Quatuor libri sententiarum* composed 1150-51, and based in its conception on John of Damascus' *De fide orthodoxa* just translated by Burgundio of Pisa. The *Sentences* were intended to be a complete exposition of doctrine for theological students. Organized topically, it provided a synthesis of the "decisions" *(sententiae)* of the Fathers and Carolingians on such subjects as the Trinity, Creation, and the Sacraments. Extracts from Scripture, the Fathers, and medieval Doctors of the Church were arranged under each of these topics. By presenting a harmonious assembly of traditional and strictly orthodox doctrine, arranged in a systematic way, Lombard intended to combat the dialectical excesses he perceived in Abelard's logical speculation, but in fact the *Sentences* provided the raw material for a dialectical treatment of theology. The influence of Lombard's *Sentences* on medieval theology is difficult to overemphasize: it was the standard theological textbook in all university faculties of theology; indeed all Doctors of Theology were required to compose and defend a commentary on the *Sentences* as part of their theological training. The impact of the *Sentences* – and of the *Decretum* as well – was to "fix" what was of significance in the patristic tradition. The Fathers, then were not studied directly, but predominantly through these compilations of their doctrine. [41]

Reinforcing the systematic treatment of doctrine and the movement away from exegesis was the impact of Aristotelian logic. Theology came to be conceived as a speculative science proceeding to new conclusions from the premises of revelation on the model of the other sciences. Its method was argumentative, not exegetical. Thomas Aquinas, for instance, used the term "subalternated science" to indicate that theology was as much as science as music, for just as music derived its axioms from the prior science of arithmetic, so theology drew its principles from the higher, and prior, science, revelation.[42]

This whole approach to theology as *scientia*, which dominated the scholastic *via antiqua*, was sharply divergent from the theology of St. Bernard of Clairvaux (1090-1153), whom the humanists regarded as the "last of the Fathers." Bernard shared the patristic stress on theology as Scriptural exegesis, and his own great work of Scriptural theology, the *Sermones super Cantica* (1135-53), in its structure and principal themes was inspired by Origen's *Commentarium in Cantica Canticorum* (in Rufinus' translation). Bernard, like Origen, was passionately involved in the figural language of the sacred text. He feared that the reduction of revelation to certain "givens" analogous to the axioms of logical categories, and the substitution of dialectical terminology for the mystical symbols of Scripture deprived preaching of the means to nourish spiritual life and evoke a fervent faith. It was a betrayal of the pastoral function of theology in favor of abstract logical speculation.[43] To what extent Traversari knew Bernard's works is unclear, though he recommended the reading of the *Sermones super Cantica* and he had studied thoroughly the *De consideratione*,[44] but there is a striking similarity in their theological concerns. And Bernard was the only medieval theologian in whom Traversari showed any interest.

Aristotelian logic and philosophy dominated late medieval theology. In the fourteenth century Augustinian Order, however, there emerged a renewed study of patristic theology. Doctrinal clashes with other schools led the Augustinians to a more careful examination of the positive premises of their patristic sources and to increasing care in quoting patristic and scholastic references. Such figures as Thomas of Strassburg, Alfonsus of Toledo, and especially John Hiltalingen of Basel provide in the marginalia of their *Sentences* commentaries a rich historico-theological documentation of the Fathers and early medieval Doctors.[45] The most impressive single work to emerge from this renewed emphasis on the historico-critical examination of patristic sources is the *Milleloquium veritatis S.*

Augustini of Bartolomeo da Urbino (d. 1350). The *Millelo-quium* is a concordance to Augustine's works consisting of some fifteen thousand excerpts arranged under a thousand or so alphabetically arranged subject headings such as *fides, haeresis, iustitia*. The heading *ecclesia* for instance, includes some eighty excerpts from forty of Augustine's works. At the end Bartolomeo appended a list of Augustine's theological works, letters, and sermons, citing each by title, number of books, brief summary of contents and purpose, and *incipit* and *explicit*. In scope, completeness, and critical use of manuscript sources this work is clearly superior to Carolingian patristic *florilegia* or to the *Flores Beati Augustini* of Bartolomeo's predecessor Agostino (Trionfo) d'Ancona. The more than fifty extant manuscripts of the *Milleloquium* attest to its popularity and wide diffusion.[46] This work facilitated a much more thorough and systematic theological exploitation of the Augustinian corpus. On the other hand, as a topical compilation of Augustine's doctrine, it is similar in approach to other medieval encyclopedic works, and gives little sense either of Augustine as an individual or of the historical development of his theology.

The return to the *fontes Augustini* however, provided the context for the search for the *mens Augustini* and its application to the crucial theological issues of the fourteenth century. The principal figure in this recovery and reassimilation of Augustine's thought is Gregory of Rimini (c.1300-58). Through immersion in Augustine's works, Gregory restored the basic thrust of Augustine's conception of sin, grace, faith, justification, and predestination, though he transposed them into the form and idiom of nominalist disputation. His major work, a lengthy commentary on the *Sentences* (1342-44), opposes the fideism and scepticism in certain aspects of the *via moderna* and attacks especially the neglect of patristic tradition for excessive logico-critical subtlety. For Gregory, Augustine is the clearest defender of justification *sola gratia* and thus the restoration of his theology is the principal means to check the Pelagian excesses of certain nominalist thinkers. Moreover, Gregory broke with the thirteenth century view of theology as *scientia*. Theology must rest on divine authority as revealed in Scripture, not on logico-metaphysical demonstration, for it is impossible to infer eternal laws from the essentially contingent foundations of human perception. Since theology depends on divine authority, the task of the theologian is not to synthesize Aristotelian metaphysics with the truths of revelation, but rather to know the meaning of Holy Scripture. This led Gregory not only to an intensive study of Scripture (a no longer extant commentary on the Pauline Epistles is attributed to him), but also to a renewed emphasis on patristic and particularly Augustinian exegesis. [47]

In sum, the Augustinian theological school of the fourteenth century re-emphasized the authority of Scripture and the tradition of the Fathers and earlier medieval Doctors against philosophical speculation and the logical criticism of revelation and tradition. This movement, however, took place within and not against the scholastic approach to theology. Theology, the systematic elucidation of faith, remained attached to logic and ratiocination (though the limits of rational certainty were sharply reduced) rather than to grammar and rhetoric. *Sentences* commentary and scholastic disputation continued to be the mode of investigating theology. Moreover, authoritative tradition was perceived as on-going, and the contributions of the twelfth century Doctors were accorded attention equal to that of the Fathers. No effort was made to recover the Greek patristic heritage. Essentially this was a revival of Augustinian doctrine and its transposition into fourteenth century terms. [48]

It was Petrarch who broke with the intellectual assumptions of scholastic theology, and who embarked on a new vision of man's spiritual state. As we have seen, Petrarch marks the decisive shift to a humanist consciousness – to a stress on conscience, on faith as inward trust, and on rhetoric as the hortatory force which moves the human will to seek piety and justice. It was not on the scholastics, but rather in Scripture and the Latin Fathers, Augustine especially, that Petrarch focused his sacred studies. In part this was because the Fathers were "Christian classics," who partook of the Latin rhetorical tradition and wrote before the end of Roman civilization. Their combination of classical learning and Christian piety, in contrast to the "barbarity" of scholastic dialectics provided a model for Petrarch's own literary and spiritual aspirations. Equally important was that in Augustine Petrarch found solace for his spiritual dilemmas. The Augustine that Petrarch looked to for his fundamental religious outlook was not the medieval figure of pre-eminent doctrinal authority, nor the meta-historical theodicizing author of the *Civitas Dei*, which provided the basic historical vision of the Middle Ages, but rather the Augustine of the *Confessions*, with its intimate portrayal of searching self-analysis, moral ambivalence, despair, and ultimate conversion to trust in the grace of Christ. Petrarch was Augustinian in his stress on a theology of grace. He understood grace, however, not in objective or sacramentalist terms, but rather as the "mobilization of individual will through the miraculous or inexplicable intervention of something that causes the will to crystallize and take directions."[49] In the *Confessions* Petrarch discovered the acute psychological analysis of human motivations which went to the heart of his own spiritual state. Indeed, in the *Secretum*, the dialogue of confession to Augustine, Petrarch depicts much of his own spiritual turmoil in terms echoing those used by the historical Augustine. A more dramatic replication of a crucial experience of the saint occurs in Petrarch's "Ascent of Mont Ventoux". In *Confessions* VIII: 12, Augustine describes his conversion as the light of confidence which flooded his heart when in the moment of greatest anguish he opened Scripture and his eyes fell on *Romans* xiii: 13, a passage which spoke so clearly and directly to himself that instantly his darkness of uncertainty vanished. On the summit of Mont Ventoux, after admiring the tremendous vista, Petrarch opened his volume of the *Confessions* and hit upon X: 8, "And men go to admire the high mountains, the vast floods of the sea, the huge streams of the rivers, the circumference of the ocean, and the revolutions of the stars – and desert themselves."[50] Petrarch felt stunned, for the words were addressed to his own spiritual state; and he relates Augustine's crucial reading of Romans xiii: 13, and notes the parallel critical incident in St. Antony's life which Augustine had also recalled. It was the experience of grace in its full historical concreteness which had greatest meaning for Petrarch.

Does Petrarch's Augustinianism reflect in any way the contemporary return to Augustine's works within the theology of the Augustinian Order? This is an area incompletely explored, but there is clear evidence that Petrarch was acquainted with Augustinian theologians, such as Bartolomeo da Urbino, for whom he provided two sets of verses for his *Milleloquium*;[51] and, more importantly, Dionigi da Borgo San Sepolcro (d.1342), who studied theology at the University of Paris, and in the 1330's acted as spiritual adviser to Petrarch in Avignon. Besides his *Sentences* commentary of 1317-18, Dionigi wrote a *Postilla on Romans,* and commentaries on Valerius Maximus, Ovid's *Metamorphoses,* Virgil, the tragedies of Seneca, and the *Poetics* and *Rhetoric* of Aristotle (in their Latin translations). The Valerius Maximus commentary, particularly, demonstrates his wide reading in Latin classical and patristic literature available in the Papal Library at Avignon. Dionigi encouraged Petrarch's classical studies and supported his efforts to pursue the poet's laurel crown. Above all, it was Dionigi who gave Petrarch the pocket-sized volume of Augustine's *Confessions* which Petrarch kept as a constant companion, until shortly before his death he passed it on to Luigi Marsili. Significantly, it was to Dionigi that Petrarch addressed the "Ascent of Mont Ventoux.[52]

It seems unlikely that Petrarch ever read the theological works of the fourteenth century Augustinian school — scholastic discourse was abhorrent to his classicist taste — but there is a conjunction of spiritual outlook between Petrarch and Gregory of Rimini. Both stress the interior subjective experience of the individual human consciousness, and both stress the will over the intellect as the controlling element of the soul. What is present here, it seems, is not a question of influence, but rather a similarity of response to the spiritual problems of the fourteenth century. In Petrarch there is the probing *psychological* analysis of his situation caught between despair and grace, between the melancholy sense of human insignificance before the *potentia absoluta* of an abscondite God and the trusting faith in God's mercy which finds greatest assurance in the mystery of the Incarnation. Gregory of Rimini affirms a voluntarist view of human existence and an Augustinian stress on grace in confronting *epistemological* problems within the *via moderna.*[53] Fundamental to the thinking of both was a renewed stress on Scripture and on the tradition of the Latin Fathers. Indeed Petrarch asserts that it was through direct reading of patristic works, especially the *Confessions*, and Jerome's letters, but also of Ambrose, Gregory the Great, Lactantius, and Chrysostom that he was led from classical studies to Holy Scripture. [54] Salutati, much more deeply read in thirteenth and fourteenth century Augustinian theology than Petrarch, confronted in his *De fato et fortuna* the central problems of fourteenth century theology on human volition and divine providence. He found resolution to these problems through direct study of Augustine's works, and, as we have seen, he further underscored the crucial importance of patristic theology in stressing patristic support for the *studia humanitatis*. [55]

'Translate the Meaning'

Translation into Latin of Greek classical and patristic works was an intellectual enterprise of crucial importance to Quattrocento humanists. Since knowledge of Greek was exceptional until the sixteenth century, only by translation could the long neglected wisdom of the ancient Greeks become accessible to the Latin West. In the first half of the fifteenth century, Leonardo Bruni, Guarino da Verona, and Traversari were the most prolific translators, but almost every humanist knowledgeable in Greek turned his hand at some point to translation. The most zealous promoter of translations was undoubtedly Pope Nicholas V, who gave Lorenzo Valla five hundred gold *scudi* for his Thucydides, and a thousand to Guarino for his version of the first ten books of Strabo's *Geographica*. But Nicholas' patronage merely provided a brilliant climax to a half century of intense effort. A vast body of Greek literature and thought unknown to the Middle Ages became available. [56]

Translation was practised as a serious intellectual and literary art. It was Chrysoloras who first gave impetus to translation, urging that Plutarch, whom he regarded as the best exemplar of the cultural bonds which had linked Latin West and Greek East in antiquity, be rendered into Latin. Before leaving Florence in 1400 he had also begun work on Ptolemy's *Geography*, and later he collaborated with Uberto Decembrio on a translation of

Plato's *Republic*. [57] Chrysoloras also established the general principles of translation adhered to by all the humanists. He asserted that Cicero and his contemporaries had especially admired Greek culture, and since Cicero's style was considered exemplary, it was fitting that Greek authors be translated into Ciceronian Latin. Cicero himself had translated works of Plato, Xenophon, and Demosthenes into Latin — since largely lost — and Chrysoloras employed the Ciceronian term *transferre ad sententiam* to describe the correct method of translation. By this he meant that translation should preserve fidelity to the sense of the Greek text, yet should also meet the aesthetic demands of good Latin. Translators should preserve the thought and where possible the expressions and words of the Greek, but to translate according to the medieval principle of *de verbo ad verbum* was to distort the thought to absurdity. Nevertheless to stray too far from the quality of the Greek in the search for lucidity and elegance was not to translate, but rather to write an exposition of the Greek text. [58]

In classical antiquity, the rhetorical translation of Greek authors was preferred to the literal. Cicero and Horace both in theory and practice adhered to the method of translating for sense, not word for word, and wished to achieve an elegant effect. In their patristic translations, Rufinus and Jerome followed this standard. Indeed Jerome cited Cicero and Horace in support of the rhetorical method, but when it came to the translation of Scripture he stipulated a different principle. Since the very order of the words of Scripture is a mystery, he argued, and since this divine mystery transcends human knowledge, the translator must preserve the order so as not to endanger the profundity of the text. In practice Jerome did not rigorously follow this dictum, for his Latin Vulgate departed in places from the Greek and Hebrew in order to make a figure of speech intelligible. But he did renounce much of the rhetorical ornamentation which marked his other translations. [59]

The Middle Ages extended Jerome's advocacy of a word for word method for Scripture to all translations, even classical texts. Chalcidius' partial translation of Plato's *Timaeus,* the only Platonic dialogue known in the Latin West before the twelfth century, employed a virtual word for word method including numerous neologisms transliterated from the Greek which entered medieval philosophic terminology. A comparison of Chalcidius' literal rendition with the corresponding passages of the surviving fragments of Cicero's version of the *Timaeus* shows how far Chalcidius had departed from the classical conception of translation.[60] Boethius, whose intellectual influence was so decisive in the early Middle Ages, deliberately renounced a rhetorical method of translation. In the preface to his Latin version of Porphyry's *Isogoge* he justified instead a word for word translation—the method of the *fidus interpres*--as necessary in order to avoid introducing any alteration in the original thought. Cassiodorus and the translators of Vivarium also strove for a literal rendering, though they had a better comprehension of Greek syntax than any later medieval translators. John Scotus Eriugena, who cites Boethius' statement of method, applied a rigorous word for word literalism even to the point of violating Latin syntax. Doubtless his hesitant Greek contributed to his literalism, but he also tried consistently to translate each Greek word by the same Latin word in order to achieve a precise philosophic vocabulary. In the twelfth century Burgundio of Pisa explicitly avoided translation *ad sententiam* while striving for *de verbo ad verbum*, because he feared by a free translation to lapse into heresy. He cites Chalcidius, Boethius, Jerome, and John Scotus Eriugena in support of the *fidus interpres*.[61]

Chrysoloras' and the Quattrocento humanists' return to the classical *transferre ad sententiam* was therefore a distinct break with medieval practice. But Salutati, before Chrysoloras' arrival in Florence, had already rejected the medieval literal translations of Greek classical and patristic works, even though he knew but the merest smattering of Greek. He encouraged Antonio Loschi's effort to add rhetorical adornment to Leonzio Pilato's fourteenth-century translation of Homer's *Iliad*, though Loschi likewise knew no Greek. Moreover, Salutati himself revised the fourteenth-century translation of Plutarch's treatise *De ira*, made by Simon Atumano, a Greek-speaking Catholic from Calabria, who had become Archbishop of Catalan-ruled Thebes, and who taught Greek and Hebrew on his return to Rome in 1381. Writing to the Florentine Cardinal Corsini, who had sent him Atumano's translation, Salutati censured the translation as rough and obscure. He would have thought that the style of the *De ira* was uncultivated except that some of Plutarch had been beautifully translated in John of Salisbury's *Policraticus*. That it was Atumano's fault, moreover, was clear from his dedicatory letter in which it was evident he did not possess the slightest literary skill in Latin.

> A true Latin style is not, of course, to be expected after he has declared himself to be a Greek, especially in this age when even we Latins hardly get above the simple grammar. We have nowadays no Ciceros, Jeromes, Rufinuses, Ambroses, or Chalcidiuses, no Cassiodoruses, no Evagriuses, and Boethiuses, whose translations are of such grace and delicacy that no refinement or clarity can be lacking in the things that they have done. . . .Taking it amiss, therefore, that we should have even this bit of Plutarch in such shape that he can neither be read with pleasure nor his thought understood with ease, I decided to restore this little work from the darkness of its translation to the light of understanding by a clearer method of presentation, so that although we may not be able thus to read Plutarch verbatim [*ad litteram*], nevertheless nothing should escape us as to his meaning [*quo ad sententiam*].[62]

Even before Salutati and his circle had acquired knowledge of Greek, then, their stress on rhetorical culture had led them to consider medieval translations inadequate. Moreover, it is noteworthy that Salutati held up as exemplary the late antique patristic translations made by Jerome, Rufinus, and Evagrius, and that he regarded even Chalcidius, Boethius, and Cassiodorus as superior to medieval translators.

Poggio Bracciolini's remarks on medieval patristic translations are particularly relevant to Traversari's patristic scholarship, since it was in a letter to Niccoli in 1420 that he objected to Burgundio of Pisa's literalism.

> I had been reading Augustine previously. Now John Chrysostom is in my hands. I have read several of

his treatises and sermons translated with great beauty. Now I am scanning briefly others greatly inferior in eloquence, corresponding to their various translators. These are the thirty-five *Homilies on Hebrews*, and the seven *Homilies in Praise of Paul the Apostle* translated by Anianus, a quite learned man. The eighty-eight *Homilies on John* are exceptional. If the translator had been eloquent, you could read nothing more learned, more full of dignity, or more magnificent. But the translator was that Pisan, who admits in the preface that he translated *de verbo ad verbum*. The inelegance of the translator is not so great, however, but that the eloquence of the author shines through marvelously. [63]

Bruni, the leading Florentine translator of Greek classical texts in the first quarter of the Quattrocento, made a series of important statements defending the rhetorical method of translation. Shortly after 1400, when Salutati urged him to undertake a fresh translation of Plato's *Phaedo,* Bruni agreed; and in a letter to Niccoli he set forth his principles. He sharply criticized the medieval translation, made so ineptly, he asserts, that the translator (actually Henricus Aristippus) rightly suppressed his name. Whereas the medieval versions of Plato clung strictly to the syllables of the Greek, he tried above all to render the whole meaning (*omnes sententias*) of Plato's thought. Where it was possible to follow Plato word for word without awkwardness or absurdity, he freely did so, but where it was not possible he did not consider he had committed the crime of *lèse-majesté* if he departed from the literal to avoid absurdity and to preserve the meaning. Since Plato's language was extremely eloquent (*elegantissimi*) in Greek, it should certainly not seem inept and awkward in Latin. [64] Elaborating further in the preface to his rendering of Plutarch's *Vita M. Antonii* (1404/05), Bruni asserted that translation was a creative art. Above all the translator must recognize the divergent characterustics of Greek and Latin: Greek was copious and therefore capable of expressing ideas in a multitude of ways; Latin was pithy and precise. In seeking to recast Greek into Latin of equal merit the translator would therefore attain perfection by eschewing the richness of Greek expression and respecting the pithiness of Latin. [65] In a treatise of his mature years, the *De interpretatione recta* (1424/26), Bruni summed up the philological expertise and rhetorical sensitivity which marked proper translation. Only by a thorough familiarity with the literature of both languages could the translator achieve the mastery of figurative phrases and have profound knowledge of the intricacies of rhetorical tropes and the whole train of associations and meanings conjured up by the use of particular words and phrases. [66]

Bruni's theories of translation placed tremendous demands on the linguistic knowledge and literary sensitivity of the translator, but there is doubt whether in practice he consistently lived up to these standards – that is whether his translations were always a genuinely new and original response to the meaning of the Greek text, rather than merely a systematic revision of a medieval translation according to humanist rhetorical standards. In recasting Plato's *Phaedo* Bruni had before him Aristippus' version [67] and for Aristotle's *Nicomachean Ethics,* which he translated 1416-17, he had the scholastic text. [68] Of course, the bulk of the humanists' translations were of Greek works never previously made into Latin, and there can therefore be no question of their originality. But clearly the humanists approached the ancient Greek texts with certain preconceptions; and, indeed, Bruni's translation of the *Nicomachean Ethics* led to an important controversy with scholastic theologians which raised the whole issue of the aim and function of language, and the purpose of intellectual inquiry.

In the preface to his *Nicomachean Ethics* Bruni excoriates the medieval translator for failing to know either Latin or Greek and for producing a barbarous translation, half Latin, half Greek, devicient in both, complete in neither. His argument for the eloquence of the *Nicomachean Ethics* in Greek, however, derived not from the Greek text itself, but rather from Cicero's praises of Aristotle's eloquence and from Aristotle's own expressed enthusiasm for eloquence. [69] Bruni assumed that the extant Aristotelian corpus consisted of the works Cicero had praised for their elegant style; whereas, in fact, Aristotle's finished treatises had been lost since antiquity, and what survived as his major philosophical writings were technical discussions of philosophic problems in the form of lecture notes. But for Bruni it was the scholastics who were to blame for failure to recognize Aristotle as a man of eloquence and who thus presented him in an unintelligible way. [70]

Aristotle's *Nicomachean Ethics* in medieval Latin translation, often accompanied by Thomas Aquinas' commentary, had formed a basic text in scholastic philosophy and theology. To argue that the Middle Ages had misunderstood Aristotle was to strike at the underpinnings of a system of thought which had been elaborated over more than two centuries. The scholastic perception of Aristotle found its defender in Alonzo Garcia de Cartagena (1384-1456), made Bishop of Burgos by Eugenius IV in 1435. Although Alonzo had admired the eloquence of Bruni's translations of Greek oratory, he reacted differently when he first studied Bruni's translation of the *Nicomachean Ethics* c.1430. Alonzo knew no Greek, and therefore did not question Bruni's accuracy, but he did challenge the suitability of this version as a work of philosophy. The substitution of a Ciceronian Latin vocabulary for scholastic terminology made impossible, he argued, the precision and rigor essential to philosophic inquiry. Since ethics was a science, and since Aristotle had based his arguments on reason, the *Nicomachean Ethics* must be rational and systematic in its use of terms. Alonzo's arguments may seem strange to philologists, but, as Seigel points out, it is hardly less presumptive than Bruni's *a priori* belief in Aristotle's eloquence. Bruni's response to Alonzo was that one who was ignorant of Greek could hardly question the actual meaning of the Greek words or the appropriateness of their Latin renderings. The meanings of words could only be discerned through etymological analysis or the usage of trust-worthy authors, who, for Bruni, were Cicero and the classical Latin writers. [71] Essentially Bruni refused to think of language in metaphysico-logical terms. The Aristotle he attempted to restore to Latin consciousness was not the Aristotle of the *Physics* and *Metaphysics* but rather the author of the *Politics* (which he translated 1435), not the philosopher of the structure of being and of epistemology, but the great thinker on questions of human society and moral philosophy. In his translations of Plato – the *Gorgias, Crito, Phaedrus, Apology,* and *Letters*, as well as the *Phaedo* – Bruni likewise recovered not the constructor of a rational cosmology (the Plato of the *Timaeus*), but rather the "Socratic" teacher of the meaning of life and death, who sought answers to questions of justice and wisdom and of education within the context of the *polis.* Aristotle and Plato must therefore be rendered in a language accessible and meaningful as an educative force to men engaged in the *vita activa civilis*, and not in the abstract *vita contemplativa* of scholastic philosophy. For Bruni the *Nicomachean Ethics* did not form the authoritative basis for the "scientific" structuring of ethics as part of the cosmic order of God's will, but rather, linked with the *Politics*, provided the sum of Greek wisdom on man in society, of a philosophy conceived in anthropocentric not cosmic terms. [72]

For Bruni and the other humanists, rhetoric replaced logic as the essential linguistic characteristic. Language was seen as affective and empirical, relevant to man's position in historical terms, not as a logical symbol of metaphysical reality. The discovery of the ancients was, for the humanists, an encounter with ideas as active force, as the power to persuade, convince, and exhort. In contrast, for the scholastics, Aristotelian philosophy was the timeless system of cosmic order and the method of rational certainty in philosophic inquiry. [73] Hence the Hellenizing Latin medieval translations with their literal Greek syntax and numerous transliterated Greek words were not simply the result of a limited knowledge of classical Greek and Latin, but the consequence of a different concept of the uses of translation, particularly the need to establish a clear and systematic Latin philosophic vocabulary. This is the apparent principle behind James of Venice's new translation of Aristotle's *Posterior Analytics* (1130/40), which was the authoritative medieval translation of the work and was used by ten generations of Latin scholars. [74] This also was the concern of Robert Grosseteste, whose translations held fast to the exact order of the Greek words, even to the point of disregarding Latin idiom and syntax. He revised and corrected Burgundio of Pisa's twelfth-century translation of John of Damascus' *De fide orthodoxa* in order to provide a yet more literal rendering of the systematic theology of this Byzantine whose use of Aristotle and dialectical treatment of doctrine was so congenial to the Latin scholastic outlook. [75] William of Moerbeke also was strikingly consistent in his use of Latin scholastic philosophic terminology to render Greek. [76]

Traversari clearly shared the humanist rhetorical approach to language. Almost invariably the Greek patristic writings he chose to translate were selected for their persuasiveness, especially those of his favorite Greek Father, John Chrysostom, who, he pointed out, was given this cognomen for his golden power of speech. [77] Characteristic of his repeated expressions of admiration for Chrysostom's eloquence is the preface to his translation of *Adversus vituperatores vitae monasticae.*

> In this work this great man defends our philosophy against all vituperators and derogators so magnificently and with such dignity of expression, such power of argument, such wealth of opinions that it seems henceforth to have forced perpetual silence on all slanderers. I therefore gladly resolved to translate this work, and I judged this would be of great inspiration to our novices and would bring great comfort and be of utility to all monks everywhere when they realized that this extraordinary man supported their cause with such concern and defended it with such elegance and copiousness a thousand years ago. Meanwhile, I thought, those who are addicted to the pleasures of this life, and unceasingly carp against the monastic life would by this my study and labor be instructed in their ignorance or reprimanded for their audacity. . . . If these books might fall into their hands, they will abate somewhat their irrational fury and unconsidered indignation. And unless they are thoroughly senseless, they will yield when they see themselves enclosed and surrounded by so many and such variety of reasons of this most learned man.

Traversari's only concern is for the quality of his Latin translation.

> If in this you [Prior Matteo] discover anything said awkwardly (and you will indeed discover much), I want you to impute this to the ignorance of the translator. For I do not claim so much as to think myself able to translate this extremely eloquent man with equal lucidity of language. In my heart I do not doubt that I have made him seem greatly inferior in our language, whereas in his own, in Greek, there is an incredible fluency of expression, and it overflows with richness. If in this I have been unable to imitate what was the function of the best translator, you must first of all take the responsibility, for unmindful of my powers and estimating them by love rather than by reason, you sought this thing which belongs to the most learned men from one inexperienced. When I decided under no circumstances to refuse or reject your order, I chose rather to leave eloquence to be desired in me than faithfulness. [78]

These doubts as to the rhetorical quality of the translation were not shared by Traversari's humanist contemporaries. It received wide dissemination in humanist circles in Florence, Venice, and Rome. [79] When Paolo da Sarzana, young student of Guarino, and later Apostolic Secretary to Pope Calixtus III, read the work, he remarked to Traversari that it possessed such ancient eloquence that if he had not examined carefully the front of the manuscript he would have thought it a work of Cicero or one of the other ancients. Moreover, when he went to Mantua, he showed the work to Vittorino, who was seized with love for it and asked for a copy. [80]

As a matter of principle, Traversari rejected the medieval practice of literal translation, and he was able to cite patristic authority for doing so. Inspired by his reading of the actions of the early Church Councils, he decided to try his hand at translating from Latin into Greek a letter Gregory the Great had sent to the eastern patriarchates. "To accomplish this I considered what Gregory had diligently insisted upon from one who might translate his letters into Greek, that is he should translate not word for word, but the sense [*sensus*]".[81]

In the defense of his new version of Johannes Climacus' *Scala Paradisi* (c.1419), Traversari elaborated most fully his principles of translation. The initial inspiration to undertake the translation stemmed, as we have seen, from Chrysoloras, who told him that in Greek the work shone with the splendor of eloquence.[82] Seeking avidly the Greek text of the work, Traversari wrote in 1416 to Francesco Barbaro: "This work has indeed been translated into Latin, but so unskillfully that except for syllables no one can understand it. If I receive it, perhaps I can restore it to its original appearance, of which it was deprived in a certain measure by the ignorance and perversity of the translator."[83] In the dedicatory letter to Matteo Guidone, Traversari writes that the Prior regarded the medieval translation as unsatisfactory and difficult to understand. The reason, as Traversari states the Prior had prudently inferred, was that

> the one who translated it previously (whoever he was in the end, for I do not venture to designate him rashly) adhered to the letter and, contrary to the precepts of the ancients, translated word for word. You asked me to bring out more lucidly and suitably the meaning [*sensus*] of this man. . . . I have translated the work anew, wholly abandoning the footsteps of that earlier translator, and I have tried as much as my slight ability permits to express lucidly his meaning [*sensus*].

The medieval translator, whom Traversari criticizes in terms reminiscent of Bruni's indictment of the medieval translator of Plato's *Phaedo,* was Angelo Clareno de Cingoli, the Spiritual Franciscan who had translated Climacus 1300-05. In rejecting Clareno's rendition as inadequate, Traversari was criticizing not just a traditional medieval translation, but one venerated as the work of a man whose knowledge of Greek resulted from the miraculous intervention of the Holy Spirit. Traversari recognized this. "For there are not lacking those who may accuse me of arrogance and rashness for daring to translate anew this work after that former translator did so, who, they will assert with more pertinacity than consideration, was inspired by the Holy Spirit." In response to his anticipated critics, Traversari declared:

Meanwhile they will not in the least deny that his translation is extremely obscure. What therefore is my crime if what was translated obscurely I have tried to render more clear or rather more Latin? Moreover, is it necessary to say how erudite that translator was? They may contend that he revealed himself to be very learned in both languages. I, dissenting completely from them, will affirm truthfully that in neither was he fully adequate. For it will be easily established by anyone who has even a mediocre knowledge of the language that he did not understand correctly most of the Greek. And whoever affirms that he could have been erudite in Latin signifies with little doubt his own ignorance. If they will assert he was a holy man, easily and willingly I will agree. Because he was a saint, however, it does not follow that he was erudite and capable of translating. For holiness is one thing, erudition another. Indeed if he was a saint, he ought not to have attempted what he could not execute properly, nor to have approached this task which exceeded his powers. For one causes injury to a learned man by rendering his utterance in an ignorant and rustic way.[84]

Traversari was right in anticipating objections to his rejection of the medieval translation. Bernardino d'Aquila, a Franciscan, after recounting how Clareno was miraculously given the knowledge of Greek, took Traversari to task for criticizing the translation. He argued that although it did not sparkle with humanist eloquence, the medieval translation had made Climacus known to the Latin West, and had revealed the light of God and been a great consolation to many.[85]

Yet Traversari himself, when he sent his translation to Francesco Barbaro, observed that the *Scala Paradisi* was indeed an exceptional work for the salubrity of its thought, but that it was hardly splendid in style and indeed rather uncultivated. He asked Barbaro to excuse the "rusticity" of his translation, but this was unavoidable, for it was impossible to give beauty to the translation when it was missing in the original.[86] When Barbaro replied commending the translation, Traversari responded that he was pleased, for he respected the soundness of the Venetian's judgment. Again he noted that the work should be praised for its doctrine, not its style, "for this work is dense, compact, and little receptive to eloquence, and it is proper that it should be considered more useful than pleasant."[87] Similarly, when Traversari translated the *Vitae Patrum*, the lives and sayings of the Egyptian desert Fathers, he remarked, "my first concern was to preserve in Latin the simplicity of the Greek diction."[88] What Traversari seems to be expressing here is the principle of decorum, itself a notion basic to rhetoric. To render Climacus, a seventh century Byzantine ascetic, in Ciceronian language was inappropriate.

Once, however, Traversari did show concern for the medieval stress on the philosophical precision of language. At the request of Pope Martin V, Traversari translated in 1424 the treatise *Adversus errores Graecorum de Processione Spiritus Sancti* of the Byzantine theologian and Catholic convert Manuel Kalekas (d.1410). In his preface Traversari felt it necessary to apologize for the "obscurity" and "awkwardness" which the prudent reader would discover in the Latin text. This was due, he explained, in part to his immoderate haste (he completed it in a month), in part to the nature of the work. Since it discoursed on difficult theological matters of the loftiest sort, notably the Trinity, and employed technical terms in doing so, the translator must for safety not depart far from the author's footsteps. Such holy matters must be treated cautiously and the theological discussion rendered exactly *(accurate)*, rather than rhetorically embellished *(ornate)*.[89] Even though Traversari states he translated the work "faithfully" *(fideliter)*, he does not, however, define "faithfully" as "literally." Doubtless this was a work in which he had little interest. When he did confront the problem of rendering philosophic discussion in language suitable for a humanist audience, as in his translation of Diogenes Laertius, the difficulties in finding an appropriate

Latin philosophic vocabulary drove him nearly to despair.[90]

Traversari, then, while rejecting medieval literalism and adopting in general rhetorical principles of translation, was conservative in the amount of rhetorical embellishment he judged licit, particularly in rendering technical philosophical and theological discourse. Indeed he caustically criticized Bruni's translation of Plato's *Phaedrus* (1424), asserting to Niccoli that the "disfigured" (*deforme*) translation was crude, harsh, and uncultivated; he wished he had never seen it, for it was marked by excessive trumpetings, especially those Bruni made of himself.[91] Perhaps Traversari was implicitly distinguishing between two modes of non-literal translation, one for philosophy and theology which followed the text closely, the other for history and oratory where rhetorical embellishment was desired. His praise of the ancient translations of sacred texts, Jerome's Vulgate especially, which he used in learning Greek, as translated "truthfully" (*ad verum*) in contrast to the freer translations of classical texts, is an indication also of this distinction. It was Manetti in his *Apologeticus* (c.1458) who made explicit the distinction between translation *ad sensum*, which was proper for philosophy and theology, and a more ornate rendering appropriate to history, rhetoric, and poetry. Literal translation (*ad verbum*), however, was to be rejected as unclear and misleading. Moreover he cites Traversari's translations of Ps -Dionysius and Diogenes Laertius, along with Bessarion's translation of Aristotle's *Metaphysics*, as examples of humanist translations which had improved on the medieval literal versions in which the sense of metaphors and figures of speech had been lost.[92]

Latin Patristics

Traversari's Greek patristic scholarship was his most significant contribution to Quattrocento humanism, but in his effort to recover Christian antiquity, he did not neglect the Latin Fathers. Indeed he made great efforts to acquire manuscripts of their works, and became familiar with a considerable body of their writings. A full assessment of Traversari's Latin patristic scholarship is made difficult since there is no record of the manuscripts he owned or that were present in S. Maria degli Angeli during his lifetime. Doubtless passing references in his correspondence present an incomplete account of what he studied, but they do suggest the range and foci of his interests. Moreover, Niccoli's library contained at least eight manuscripts of Jerome, six of Gregory the Great, four of Hilary of Poitiers, three of Tertullian, three of Ambrose, and thirty-four of Augustine.[93] A number of these were acquired through Traversari's efforts, and all were accessible for his study. Perhaps the best indication of his wide-ranging scholarship, however, is the lengthy list of the Latin Fathers' statements on the Procession of the Holy Spirit, which he compiled for presentation during the debates at the Council of Florence.[94]

Traversari was familiar with at least a part of the vast corpus of Augustine's works. He knew, for instance, the *Super Genesim ad literam,* where the exegesis of Genesis 1:26 had led Salutati to an understanding of man's freedom as dependent on man's creation in divine image and likeness.[95] He lent a copy of Augustine's *De doctrina Christiana*, the work of synthesis between Christianity and classical culture so thoroughly exploited by Renaissance humanists, to Alberto da Sarteano, and had the text transcribed for Guarino.[96] S. Maria degli Angeli possessed an Augustine manuscript given by Pope John XXIII, containing: *Contra Academicos*, Augustine's response to philosophical scepticism; *De ordine* which treats the question of theodicy; and *De magistro* a discourse on education; and in 1437 Traversari wrote asking that this volume be sent to him for use in scholarly preparations for the forthcoming Council with the Greeks at Ferrara.[97] In 1424 he received from Giovanni Corvini, a humanist in Milanese service, Augustine's *De utilitate credendi.*[98] The Augustinian work he mentions most often, however, is the *Confessions.*[99] Yet there is the distinct impression that Augustine did not have the inspiring impact for Traversari that he had had for Petrarch and Salutati. Indeed when he began reading Gregory of Nyssa's *Homilies on the Canticles*, he remarked to Niccoli, "I dare to say this is a greater work than Augustine's *Super Genesim ad literam*. The style belongs to a man of great erudition and acute intelligence."[100]

What seems to characterize Traversari's study of the Latin Fathers is a concern for the whole of the Latin patristic heritage, not just Augustine. During the mid-1420's he and Niccoli were making intensive efforts to procure Latin patristic texts: in 1423, for instance, Traversari reported to Niccoli that he had received from a certain Antonio da Pistoia an index of manuscripts present in a monastery, probably Sant' Antonio in Padua, where Antonio had gone to fulfill a vow to St. Antony, but that the index listed only common and familiar works. [101] Niccoli, himself, while in Rome in 1424, obtained an index of the holdings in Montecassino, which he sent to Traversari. [102] At the same time, both men were anxious to learn what might be discovered at the ancient Benedictine monastery at Nonantola near Bologna, which was founded c.750 and did indeed possess an excellent library of the Latin Fathers. Even in the eleventh century it had forty manuscripts, and by the fifteenth century it probably contained over two hundred. [103] In March 1424 Traversari reported to Niccoli that Antonio had visited Nonantola and had examined the library, but that the few hours he had spent there permitted only time enough to count the volumes, not to make an accurate index. He saw forty-nine volumes of Augustine, seventeen of Jerome, sixteen of Gregory the Great, and nine of Ambrose, Hilary's celebrated *De Trinitate* — an important defense of Athanasian doctrine against Arianism and his most significant work, Hilary's *Commentary on Matthew,* his *Super aliquot Psalmos,* as well as Cyprian letters and treatises. Traversari was impressed with the wealth of manuscripts there, promised Niccoli that diligent efforts would be made to acquire its texts, and had high hopes that all the volumes unfamiliar to them would eventually come into their possession. [104]   Parentucelli did eventually procure a number of patristic manuscripts from Nonantola for Traversari's use, including one of Ambrose's *Epistolae*, which is the probably source for the transcription of Ambrose's *Letters* which Traversari made with his own hand. [105] Parentucelli also discovered in 1427-28 a manuscript of Hilary's *Super aliquot Psalmos* in the ancient monastery at Pomposa, located between Ferrara and Ravenna. He sent this to Traversari, who retained it until at least 1431, when Parentucelli asked to have it returned so that he could restore it to the monastery. [106]

Traversari's travels as General of his Order – to Rome in the winter and spring of 1432, to the Veneto in late spring and summer 1433, and to the Romagna in the winter of 1433-34 – enabled him to search personally for patristic manuscripts, as did his journeys as Papal Nuncio first to Basel, then to Austria in the last half of 1435. In Rome he searched primarily for Greek texts, though he planned, but actually never made, a trip to Montecassino. More productive was the journey to the Veneto: in Treviso he found an ancient volume of Augustine's letters; in Padua, where he was cordially received by the Bishop and humanist patron, Pietro Donato, he visited both the Dominican and Franciscan libraries and discovered a beautiful volume of Jerome's *Epistolae*. Also in Padua he came upon the letters of St. Antony in an ancient Lombard manuscript which he ordered transcribed. He looked one by one through the sacred volumes in both the church of S. Zeno and the cathedral in Verona, but turned up nothing new in either; nor did he find anything in the Dominican library in Vicenza. On his return trip to Florence he visited numerous monastic libraries in Bologna, where he discovered a volume of the *Acta* of some of the early Ecumenical Councils, and hoped, but was not permitted, to visit the monastery of Nonantola. According to Traversari, the Abbot, either from spite or ignorance, opposed the visit, claiming no manuscripts existed in the monastery. Traversari knew the contrary to be true, but he had heard that the books had been allowed to molder under dust and dirt. [107] His high hopes of making important discoveries in Ravenna were disappointed when he only came across an ancient volume of Cyprian which nonetheless had more letters than he had ever previously seen, and which he ordered transcribed. He also found an ancient Nicene Creed written on crimson parchment with gold letters, and was told that numerous ancient charters, including one of Charlemagne's, were present in the Cathedral Archives, but the absence of the custodian made examination impossible. This was unfortunate for the Archives also contained an extremely ancient (from the fifth to the sixth centuries) manuscript of Ambrose's dogmatic works. [108] While in Basel he saw in Pietro Donato's possession an ancient and beautiful volume of Eusebius' *Chronicon* in

Jerome's translation which he hoped to acquire for Niccoli. [109]
On the lengthy trip from Basel to Vienna, he mentions
particularly a splendid monastery at Ratisbon, where he
searched thoroughly the numerous volumes in the library but
discovered nothing new. [110] In sum, Traversari's discoveries
were slight in comparison to the spectacular finds of Poggio,
Cusanus, and Parentucelli, but his efforts to take advantage of
every opportunity open to him to investigate both monastic
libraries and humanists' collections indicate his concern for
Latin patristics.

Works of Augustine, Ambrose, Gregory the Great, and to a
lesser extent of Cyprian and Hilary, were known throughout the
Middle Ages. Manuscripts of their writings had been widely
diffused and were readily accessible, if not everywhere in such
numbers or of such quality as those at Nonantola. The great
Florentine mendicant monasteries, S. Croce, S. Maria Novella,
and S. Spirito, all possessed large collections of these Fathers,
though, as has been indicated, direct study of the Fathers
outside the Augustinian school tended to be neglected in the
late Middle Ages. Trecento humanism, however, had refocussed
attention on these Latin Fathers, and both Boccaccio and
Salutati possessed manuscripts of their works. [111] Hence
Traversari's interest in them broke no new territory, for
intellectual and spiritual concern for their writings was already
well-established. Yet if Krautheimer's thesis is correct that
Traversari used Ambrose's Old testament exegesis for the
iconography of the Ghiberti "Gates of Paradise," Traversari
was clearly approaching Latin patristic Scriptural exegesis in an
original way, one which stressed the historical concreteness of
the sacred history of the chosen people. [112]

Traversari's enthusiasm for the third century Latin Father,
Lactantius, also had antecedents in Trecento humanism.
Boccaccio cited him frequently in his works, especially the *De
genealogia deorum* and he owned a copy of Lactantius' most
important work, the *Divinae institutiones*. Salutati also
probably owned a copy of this and, while feeling free to
criticize Lactantius' doctrine of *fortuna*, singled him out as
"eloquentissimus." [113] The *Divinae institutiones* is both a
defense of Christianity against pagan religion and the first

attempt in Latin at a systematic exposition of Christian doctrine. It was precisely Lactantius' lack of metaphysical profundity coupled with his imitation of Ciceronian thought and oratory that made him a favorite of humanists. His stress on Christ as not just Savior, but as author of all wisdom, and his emphasis on prophecies of Christ's divine sonship not only in the Old Testament, but in the Sibylline oracles and in the *Corpus Hermeticum* as well, provided patristic support for the high valuation the humanists placed on classical culture. [114]

The admiration Bruni expresses for Lactantius in his treatise on education, the *De studiis et litteris* (1423/26) is typical of an early Quattrocento humanist for he names him along with Augustine and Jerome as theologians who joined their familiarity with letters to divine knowledge, and hence were vastly superior to the scholastics with their threadbare jargon. [115] Returning to praise Lactantius at a later point in this same work, Bruni concluded:

> Among all those who have ever written of the Christian religion, Lactantius Firmianus is preeminent for the wealth and brilliance of his language. He is without doubt the most eloquent of all Christians. His fluency and his figures of speech can provide superb instruction and nourishment to that talent of which we speak. I commend particularly those books which he wrote *Adversus falsam religionem* [i.e. *Divinae institutiones*], and also *De ira Dei* and *De opificio hominis*. If you love literature, read these, and in their delightful sweetness you will taste what seems like ambrosia and nectar. [116]

In the *De ira Dei* Lactantius opposes the Epicurean view of an impassive god, aloof from the world, saying that God by his very nature must be active in His creation. Against the Stoic notion of a solely beneficent god administering the forces of the universe, he stresses that God's providence for mankind necessitated His anger at human evil and that salutary fear of God's judgment moves men to seek good and avoid evil. The *De opificio hominis* celebrates God's creation of man, endowed with bodily beauty and perfection, with reason which elevates him above all the beasts, and with an immortal soul.

The transcription Traversari made of the *Divinae institutiones,* completed January 1415, is his earliest work in patristic scholarship. [117] A year later Francesco Barbaro asked Traversari to emend his manuscript, which contained the *Divinae institutiones,* the *De ira Dei,* and the *De opificio hominis*, and to give particular attention to the Greek words. Gladly accepting the task, Traversari replied:

> You really could have demanded nothing more worthy from yourself or more pleasant for me. I will exert myself to emend all of it, and the more willingly as I take great delight in the genius of the man who, in my judgment (which I have steadfastly declared), in the boundless golden flow of his eloquence cedes to none of the ancients, not even Cicero. [118]

Discovering Barbaro's manuscript carelessly written and full of errors, Traversari exclaimed:

> I pity the fate of this learned man, and I was silently indignant that his golden genius has been violated by ignorant hands. I praise your decision to liberate this man from this injury, and that you have sent him to me. Though my erudition may be slight, I am, however, diligent and studious. I repeat my vow to work zealously so that he whom you have sent to me full of faults will return to you fully emended. From ignorance, barbarity, and rusticity he will become, as much as my labor permits, erudite, Latin, and cultured. [119]

In January 1417, Traversari returned the emended manuscript to Barbaro; however, he had been able to edit only the *Divinae institutiones* since he could procure a trustworthy text of it alone. He was thus forced to leave the other two works "half-mutilated." [120]

During the 1420's Traversari maintained his interest in Lactantius. When Niccoli sent him two Lactantius manuscripts in 1424, Traversari (though giving no indication of what works were included in the manuscripts) agreed, significantly, to await Niccoli's return from Rome before inserting the Greek words.

Apparently the Greek had simply been left out, as was a common practice of medieval scribes. [121] In 1426 Parentucelli brought to Florence a remarkably ancient (from the sixth to the seventh centuries) manuscript of Lactantius' *De ira Dei, De opificio hominis* and part of the *Epitome,* Lactantius' own abridged re-edition of the *Divinae institutiones,* which he had acquired from Nonantola. [122]   In 1431, when Parentucelli demanded the return of the Hilary he had brought from Pomposa, Traversari anxiously wrote Niccoli urging him to amend his Lactantius as quickly as possible according to the reading of the ancient Nonantola manuscript. He feared Parentucelli would become angry at his and Niccoli's negligence in retaining the Lactantius so long, and he was concerned that they might be required to return it before their own text was corrected. [123] In 1433 Traversari discovered in Bologna, and had transcribed for himself there, the text of Lactantius *De ave phoenice,* the Latin Father's poem on the legendary phoenix, in which he saw the prophetic symbolism of Christ's resurrection, [124] and with the acquisition of this text, Traversari had procured manuscripts of all the important Lactantius writings.

Lactantius had a great impact on early Quattrocento humanist moral philosophy. Not only was he clearly part of the Ciceronian rhetorical culture, but his celebration of man's perfection and God-like reason, and his stress on free will and the necessity to seek moral virtue were also congenial to humanist views. Manetti's celebrated *De dignitate et excellentia hominis* drew heavily on Lactantius' works. The Florentine neo-Platonists also admired his notion of *pia philosophia,* that is the belief in a Gentile prophetic tradition whereby divine wisdom was transmitted from Hermes Trismegistos to Pythagoras to Plato. This notion was the historical vision underlying their synthesis of Christianity and Platonism. [125] Traversari's scholarship helped make Lactantius' works available to Florentine humanists, yet as we have seen in examining the Diogenes Laertius and Aeneas Gazeus translations, Traversari himself was reluctant to press the syncretism of Christianity and pagan philosophy.

This reluctance had its counterpart in Traversari's enthusiastic study of Tertullian, the early Latin Father who had asked,

"What indeed has Athens to do with Jerusalem?" In the winter of 1423-24 Niccoli acquired for Traversari a manuscript of Tertullian's *Apologeticus,* the African Father's defense of Christianity against Roman persecution, and the principal source for knowledge of second century Christianity and its reception in the Roman world. When after eager anticipation, Traversari received the manuscript, he wrote to Niccoli:

> With the greatest ardor and zeal I began immediately to read it, and the opinion held by many about this man happens to be true. His language is obscure. I would willingly accept this obscurity, however, if this book had been written more free from scribal errors. Great power of judgment and knowledge of all things thrive there. I will read it more carefully and diligently, or I will transcribe it or have someone else do so. [126]

Several months later, when Niccoli asked whether a transcription had yet been made, Traversari replied that he had not done so, for he hoped to obtain a less faulty copy of the text from a monastery whose new abbot was friendly with Cosimo de' Medici. [127] In early 1431 Traversari was still seeking a good text of the *Apologeticus* since Niccoli included a specific request for this work, as well as for Tertullian's *Adversus Marcionem* and *Adversus Iudaeos* in the list of manuscripts to be sought by Cardinals Cesarini and Albergati on their diplomatic missions to Germany and France. This list, the so-called *Commentarium*, named the manuscripts which Niccoli believed to be present in trans-Alpine monasteries and which he wished to be procured. At Fulda, which Poggio had visited during the Council of Constance, the Cardinals were to seek the Tertullian works. [128] Traversari applauded Niccoli's project, and remarked that he could expect good results since both Cardinals were "studiosi et humanissimi." [129] Several months later, in July 1431, Traversari observed to Niccoli that even if Alpine frost had cooled the Cardinals' ardor for seeking manuscripts, their humanist secretaries, Luca da Spoleto and Parentucelli, would keep Niccoli's hopes kindled. [130] The press of affairs, however, apparently did in fact prevent leisure for manuscript hunting. Fulda was not searched until twenty years later, when Parentucelli, then Pope Nicholas V, directed it to be examined. [131]

Parentucelli's trans-Alpine journeys, however, were not fruitless for Traversari's Tertullian scholarship: in 1433 he brought to the Council of Basel a manuscript containing all of Tertullian's works, including the *Apologeticus.* Aurispa, then at Basel, wrote Niccoli of the find, and by early 1434 the manuscript had made its way into Niccoli's library. [132] In the meantime, in June 1431, Traversari had obtained through Lorenzo de' Medici's efforts Cardinal Orsini's large Tertullian manuscript. This codex did not include the *Apologeticus,* but it did comprise a total of twenty-two works, including *Adversus Iudaeos* and *Adversus Marcionem,* Tertullian's defense of the humanity of Christ and of the prophetic importance of the Old Testament. Traversari was overjoyed to receive this volume, which had been discovered by Cusanus at Pforzheim in 1426, and which Orsini had ordered copied, [133] but found it written in "barbaric" letters and full of errors, which he judged to be the fault of the copyist rather than of the original manuscript. Nonetheless he intended to transcribe it immediately and to emend the text diligently. As for Tertullian's learning and genius: "Lactantius, Cyprian, and Jerome judged correctly. They admired his ardent nature, but they did not approve his difficult manner of speaking." [134] In 1432 Orsini asked for the return of the Tertullian, but a year later Traversari requested Orsini's permission to keep it and emend it according to Parentucelli's recent find, which he expected to receive shortly. [135] Orsini's manuscript was never returned and eventually entered San Marco, along with the transcription Niccoli had made of it. [136]

Tertullian, as Traversari had observed, did write in a highly original Latin style. He coined many new Latin words, and he wrote with a staccato terseness which doubtless offended the Ciceronian sensibilities of Lactantius and Jerome, as well as of the Quattrocento humanists. The medieval neglect of Tertullian, however, had stemmed largely from his conversion to a subsequently condemned Montanist sect. [137] Traversari knew of Tertullian's adherence to those "mad prophets," but so admired the penetrating quality of his mind that his enthusiasm was undaunted. [138]   And Tertullian's sharply anti-philosophical stance probably appealed to Traversari, who so strongly condemned the "inflata scientia" of scholastic theology.

Of all the Latin Fathers, Traversari, like Erasmus, favored Jerome. While still a youth he had studied Jerome's *Epistolae* so intently that he knew many by heart, "for it seemed to me that no teaching aroused such a powerful impulse to the *studia virtutum*." [139]   Frequently in his letters of spiritual counsel, Traversari advised the reading of these letters, [140] and in his mature years he also brought humanist critical scholarship to bear on the Jerome epistolary. In 1430 Poggio informed Niccoli that he was compiling a volume of Jerome's letters, and had already written out a hundred of the nearly one hundred and forty he had collected from a number of sources. He believed that in Montecassino there was a volume, written in Lombard letters, containing two hundred and twenty-five letters (more than he had ever heard reported), which he hoped to obtain through the help of Cardinal Branda Castiglione. [141] In January 1431, Poggio wrote again to Niccoli that the Abbot of Montecassino had refused to send the epistolary, alleging that the volume was too large. A monk of the monastery had informed him that the volume contained one hundred forty-five letters, but he had one hundred and seventy in his possession, which he promised to send when Niccoli returned to Florence. If he discovered more he would add them to his now anticipated two-volume edition. [142]   When Niccoli wrote Traversari of Poggio's work, he replied that he was in no way amazed at Poggio's claim to have so many Jerome letters, for doubtless many were spurious. [143] At length Poggio sent an index of his Jerome epistolary to Traversari, who remarked caustically to Niccoli that his suspicions were confirmed. It contained nothing that they did not already know, and he would send the index so that Niccoli could perceive the levity of Poggio's assertion that he had discovered so many unknown letters. [144] Traversari was correct in his judgment: the Jerome epistolary contains only one hundred and fifty letters, with one hundred and seventeen by Jerome, and the remainder written to Jerome or related documents. [145]

In January 1434, Traversari, while in Venice, copied and sent to Niccoli two Jerome letters which he had discovered in an epistolary belonging to Francesco Barbaro. [146] It is unclear whether these were previously unknown to Traversari, or simply alternate readings of letters he already knew, but, certainly, this is an example of Traversari's continued scholarly interest in the *Epistolae.*

Traversari's Latin patristic scholarship reveals characteristic humanist scholarly and intellectual concerns. He diligently sought ancient manuscripts of patristic writings, emended the Latin reading of the texts, and restored the Greek words and phrases. He admired most, and was most deeply read in, Lactantius and Jerome, the most eloquent of the Latin Fathers. He devoted particular attention to the letters of the Latin Fathers. Not only Jerome's, but also Ambrose's, Cyprian's, and Augustine's were objects of his scholarship. He also clearly admired the apologetic works of Tertullian and Lactantius, and displayed a preference for the scriptural exegesis of Hilary, Augustine, Ambrose, and Gregory the Great. In sum, what can be detected in Traversari's Latin patristic scholarship is the ascendency of the personal, the pastoral, and the historical over the dogmatic and metaphysical: a persistence in the humanist religious tradition of Petrarch. More striking, undoubtedly, than any originality in Traversari's approach is the scope of his knowledge of early Latin Christianity. His diligent acquisition of manuscripts and his wide familiarity with much of the patrimony of the Latin Fathers made their description of Christianity in late Roman antiquity and of the development and growth of the Church in the Roman world accessible to humanists.

Greek Patristics 1416-24:
The Greek Fathers and Monasticism

The early period of Traversari's Greek patristic scholarship was focused on works which related directly to the monastic life. His deep attachment to monastic spirituality and his respect for Prior Matteo Guidone's spiritual authority are probably the underlying reasons for this emphasis. Only in the mid-1420's, after Matteo's death and when Traversari had achieved prominence in Florentine humanist circles, did his studies encompass a broader scope.

Traversari's first translation in Greek patristics is most probably the letter which St. Basil sent to Gregory Nazianzen shortly after his retirement to Pontus, where he began a life of solitude following a two-year journey to Egypt, Palestine, Syria, and Mesopotamia to visit the famous ascetics. The letter, entitled "De fuga saeculi et de vita monastica" in a number of fifteenth century manuscripts of Traversari's translation, describes the aim and nature of ascetic solitude, by which Basil hoped to induce Gregory to join him in the monastic life. He depicts the ascetic life as the withdrawal from the cares of city, home, business, friends, and pursuit of human knowledge in order to arrive at a state of tranquillity and freedom where the passions can be purged from the soul. The letter gives practical advice on the desirable simplicity of food, clothing, and speech, which would free the mind for prayer and contemplation of God; and in it Basil especially urges meditation on Scripture and recommends the imitation of Joseph, Job, David, and Moses as exemplars of virtue. [147] This eloquent and personal appeal by the Greek Father who had founded Greek monasticism, and whose culture and holiness had just been celebrated by Bruni in the preface to his translation of Basil's treatise on education, must have proved particularly attractive to Traversari. [148] No prefatory letter accompanies Traversari's translation, but his admiration for Basil is evident in the gratitude he expressed to Francesco Barbaro for sending him a Greek manuscript of Basil's epistolary in 1417.

> I still desire your letter, but I judged it my duty to thank you for that volume of Basil's letters which you recently sent me and which brought me so much pleasure it is difficult to express. I am delighted with this man's learned utterance and his genius which approaches the ancients, as well as with the great age of this volume. As in other things, so especially in books, I esteem, heed, and respect antiquity. [149]

Traversari turned next to the translation of Chrysostom's *Adversus vituperatores vitae monasticae,* an apology for the monastic life. In his preface, Traversari indicates that he chose the work as one particularly appropriate to his vocation, and that he intended his translation both to inspire young monks and refute contemporary opposition to the monastic life. [150]

Shortly afterwards, around 1419, Traversari undertook the translation of the *Scala Paradisi* of the early Byzantine ascetic Johannes Climacus, Abbot of a monastery on Mt. Sinai. Written towards the end of the sixth century, this was the most influential work on asceticism in the Byzantine tradition. The title refers to the celestial ladder of Jacob's dream (Gen. 28: 12), and the division into thirty chapters alludes to the thirty "hidden" years of Christ's life prior to his active ministry. In effect a manual to the ascetic life, Climacus' work describes a step by step advance, first struggling against vice, then acquiring virtue, towards the ultimate goal of union with God through meditation. [151]   In the dedicatory letter to Prior Matteo, Traversari describes the *Scala Paradisi* as "this illustrious work, which teaches the precepts for the whole of monastic perfection," [152]   and he seems himself to have adopted Climacus' precepts of ascetic spirituality. From Rome in 1432 he wrote to his brother, "Nothing in life is sweeter to me, nothing dearer, than to recall to mind my beloved brothers advancing from virtue to virtue, ascending Jacob's ladder, and intent upon continual advance in divine servitude." [153]

In January 1424 Traversari had completed the first draft of yet another patristic treatise on monastic spirituality. This was the *De vera integritate virginitatis,* long preserved among the works of Basil the Great, but now attributed to Basil of Ancyra († c. 364). [154]   In the dedicatory letter to Gabriel Condulmer, Cardinal Protector of the Camaldulensians and later Pope Engenius IV, Traversari states that the delightful appearance of the work and its most honorable title impelled him first to read it, then to make the translation.

> With such diligence does this defender set forth, depict and praise the glory of virgin chastity, with such care does he safeguard, arm, and fortify it, and in short with such vigilance does he reveal and lay bare all snares and guard against them that in my judgment no one has ever dealt more diligently with this matter. Although very many, indeed nearly all

the Doctors of the Church, both Latin and Greek, extol the honor of virginity with the highest praise, and in many celebrated works have exhorted its preservation, yet no , one has pursued it so completely. [155]

At the same time that Traversari was working on the Ps.-Basil treatise, he was translating a Greek manuscript belonging to a different genre of monastic literature — the hagiography of the Eastern ascetics. His Latin version, the *Vitae Patrum,* consists of several works of spiritual edification and numerous lives of the desert Fathers, and it follows the precise order of his Greek source. [156] The first item, the anonymous *Paradisus animae* is a short allegory on the virtues of the soul. Then follows the important *Pratum spirituale,* written by the monk Johannes Eucratus, or Moschus (c. 550-619). This recounts nearly three hundred deeds and miracles performed by the ascetics of Egypt, Sinai, and Antioch — Moschus' contemporaries for the most part. It is similar in format and style to earlier edifying biographies of the desert Fathers, such as Palladius' *Historia Lausiaca,* composed 419/20 and quickly translated into Latin, and the *Historia monachorum in Aegypto,* also written in the fifth century and subsequently rendered into Latin by Rufinus. [157] In Traversari's Greek source, nine chapters of the lives or sayings of the desert Fathers were added and he translated these as well. During the winter of 1424, he wished to include this among the translations he planned to send at the request of the Archbishop of Genoa. But final revisions were held up first by Lenten devotions, then by an illness which forced him to postpone all scholarly activity, and only years later did he decide to publish it. [158] On 6 August 1431 he sent the translation to Eugenius IV with a short covering note.

I am pleased to send to your Holiness my translation of the *Vitae Sanctorum Patrum,* a work which, even if not weighty or worthy of the holiest man or one with the greatest power of judgment, might however by its novelty bring some pleasure. . . . If this work is confirmed by your authority, I will publish it, for until now it has lain hidden away in my desk. [159]

After Eugenius returned the translation, presumably with his approval, Traversari added a portion of the *Life of St. Daniel Stylite* and an account of the martyr saints Eugenia, Protus, and Hyacinth. The latter was Traversari's literary tribute to the relics of Protus, Hyacinth, and Nemesius which he had had transferred to S. Maria degli Angeli, and for which Ghiberti sculpted a classicizing bronze reliquary.[160] Why Traversari translated the *Life of St. Daniel Stylite* is unclear. The source for this work was a Greek manuscript of Simeon Metaphrastes' *Martyrum gesta,* an eleventh-century, ten volume collection of saints' lives drawn from earlier compilations and arranged for the Greek Orthodox liturgical year. Traversari requested it from Aurispa in 1430, apparently as a source for a planned translation of the *Passion of Cosmas and Damian,* the Medici patron saints. Aurispa sent one volume of the six which he had obtained in Constantinople and dispatched to Sicily, and the only one of the six he had managed to recover. This volume did not contain the *Passion,* and though Aurispa promised to give Cosimo the other five should he manage to recover them, there is no evidence that he did. Nor did Traversari ever translate an account of Cosmas and Damian.[161]

Traversari's abandonment of the *Vitae Patrum* for some seven years from 1424 to 1431, and the somewhat disparaging terms in which he described it to Eugenius, suggest that his ardor for this kind of hagiographic literature had cooled. True, he was preoccupied in the mid and late 1420's with his translation of Diogenes Laertius; but it was precisely in 1424, as will be seen, that Traversari's patristic scholarship shifted from a narrow preoccupation with the monastic life to a wide-ranging study of Christian antiquity. Rather than the ascetic heroism of the desert Fathers, he came to admire more the lives of Gregory Nazianzen, Chrysostom, and Athanasius, who had joined learning to piety, and who defended Scripture and the Church against heresy and persecution.

Traversari did not, however, completely neglect his former preoccupation with monasticism. In 1426, for instance, he sought from Niccoli a manuscript of the *Institutes* and *Collationes Patrum* of John Cassian, the great apostle of Eastern monasticism to the Latin West. The *Institutes* describes the organization and rules of monasteries in Palestine and Egypt, while the *Collationes* are conversations with the anchorites of Egypt. Both works had made accessible to Latin audiences the ascetic spirituality of the desert Fathers, and the *Collationes* especially were much admired for their edifying contents in the Middle Ages. [162] Moreover, when in the summer of 1433 Traversari came across a manuscript containing seven letters of St. Antony (251-356), the Egyptian desert Father and founder of Christian eremitic monasticism, he was greatly excited and arranged to have them transcribed. He described the letters as beautiful and full of sober doctrine, especially one to the monks of Arsinoë, a letter which Jerome, too, had especially admired. [163]

Traversari also worked to discover the historical roots of Benedictine monasticism in the Latin West. In the winter of 1423-24 Niccoli and Cosimo de' Medici were in Rome. Since they were quite near to Montecassino, Traversari entreated them to obtain from there the *Life of St. Benedict,* "which I have long wished for in vain," and the *Dialogue* of Desiderius, who as Abbot of Montecassino in 1058-87 had promoted the revival of classical learning at the monastery. [164] After repeated reminders Niccoli eventually sent an index of the library of Montecassino, but inexplicably the *Life of St. Benedict* was not included. Traversari suggested that it might have been catalogued under another title, and he repeated his great desire to have this and the *Dialogue* of Desiderius, which Niccoli had listed in the index. [165] It is uncertain when Traversari acquired copies of these works, perhaps not until 1429 when Poggio went to Montecassino, where he acquired a manuscript of Frontinus which he later sent to Florence. [166] At any rate Traversari possessed both by at least June 1433 when he arranged to have them copied for the Camaldulensian monastery of S. Michele di Murano in Venice whose Abbot, his great friend, had requested them. [167] The colophon of a manuscript of the *History of Montecassino,* now in the Vatican, indicates that Traversari did more than simply study the early history of the monastery; he actually edited and revised the work. Indeed the term used – *expolite* (polished, refined) – suggests that he may have brought certain of the humanists' conceptions of eloquence to bear on the medieval chronicle. [168]

Traversari studied as well the foundations of his own Order, the Camaldulensians, for he possessed a manuscript of Peter Damian's *Vita Romualdi.* [169] Moreover, in October 1433 while visiting monasteries in the Romagna, he made a special point of visiting the tomb of Peter Damian in the cathedral of Faenza. This cathedral preserved an ancient manuscript of Damian's writings, reputedly autograph, which Traversari took to his lodgings to examine carefully. [170]

Through his study of the *Vitae Patrum,* John Cassian, and the letters of St. Antony the Hermit, Traversari was acquainted with a number of the principal historical sources for the origins of Christian monasticism in Egypt. His work with Basil, Chrysostom, and Climacus enabled him to perceive the development of monasticism in the Greek East, and his knowledge of the lives of Benedict, Desiderius, and Romuald did the same for the Latin West. This sense of the historical tradition of monasticism in the Church is a prominent element in the encyclical letters of reform which Traversari wrote as General, attempting to inspire his fellow monks with the fervent asceticism and devout meditation he perceived in the patristic and early medieval founders of the monastic life. The revival of Christian antiquity meant, for Traversari, not only the recovery of patristic writings, but the resuscitation of pristine monastic spirituality as well.

Greek Patristics 1424-39:
The Study of Christian Antiquity

At the close of the preface to his translation of Chrysostom's *Adversus vituperatores,* Traversari promised Prior Matteo that if this pleased him he would translate other works of Chrysostom and dedicate them to his name. [171]   In the early 1420's Traversari did in fact translate a number of such treatises and collections of homilies: the first undertaken, and the only one formally published, was Chrysostom's *De providentia ad Stagirium.* Traversari completed the translation in 1420 and in 1428 dedicated it to Don Pedro, Duke of Coimbra, who in that year had visited Florence. [172] In this treatise, written in the last year of his life (407), Chrysostom reflects on two fundamental problems, God's providence and human suffering. He begins by stressing the limits of human reason and the transcendence of God; the mystery of God, however, can lead men to despair. To this the only antidote is recognition of God's love for man, revealed not only in the bounty of His creation, but also in the Incarnation. How then can one account for human suffering? Rather than providing a theoretical answer, Chrysostom describes the suffering of exemplary men of faith – Noah, Job, John the Baptist, and finally Christ on the Cross. Moreover, for himself, suffering has been the occasion for spiritual progress, indeed its cause. These themes – the incomprehensibility of God, His love for man, and the value of suffering – had been prominent in Chrysostom's thought from his early preaching in Antioch. Here they are eloquently summed up in a work distilled through his own recent experience of persecution and exile. [173]

The rhetorical power of the *De providentia* suggests its attractiveness to Traversari, but just as important are Chrysostom's central themes. In the dedicatory letter, where Traversari describes the consolation which the Greek Father had brought to his fellow monk Stagirius and his resolution of the demonic temptations which had led to his despair at God's judgment, he argues that the work offered to its readers great nourishment in *pietas.* [174] It is notable as well that the concerns prominent in the treatise – the remedy of despair, the absurdity of trying to fathom the divine mind with human reason, the importance of the Incarnation as a sign of God's love and man's dignity, the experiential quest for faith, the persuasiveness of historical exemplars – correspond to important elements in early humanist moral philosophy, such as Petrarch's *Secretum* and *De otio religioso,* Salutati's *De fato et fortuna,* and Valla's *De libero arbitrio.* [175] The popularity of Traversari's translation, attested to by nearly twenty extant fifteenth-century manuscripts, suggests that, like the treatises of Petrarch, Salutati, and Valla, it was responding to a major spiritual concern and a felt need for religious remedy.

In the winter of 1423-24 Traversari was bringing to completion his translations of Chrysostom's *On the Incomprehensible Nature of God,* the *Homilies against the Jews* and the dialogue *De sacerdotio.* [176] No dedicatory letters for these are extant, and indeed there is no certainty that Traversari ever composed any. But it seems likely that both the rhetorical power of the works and the subject matter appealed to him. Chrysostom preached the five homilies *On the Incomprehensible Nature of God* in Antioch in 386-87. Their defense of the ineffable, inconceivable, and incomprehensible nature of God was directed against the rationalistic tendencies of a radical Arian sect. Chrysostom castigates the Arians for daring to confine God to the limits of human reason, an attitude he regards as blasphemous arrogance. [177] The homilies are an exellent example of the author's eloquence, and his condemnation of philosophical speculation on the divine mysteries clearly corresponds to Traversari's admiration for Tertullian and his rejection of the inflated pretensions of scholastic theology. Chrysostom's *De sacerdotio,* written in the dialogue form so admired by the humanists and so widely adopted for their own writings, is a discussion of the proper understanding of the priestly vocation. It defends the priest's dignity and authority, argues for the importance of preaching to propagate the faith and to combat the attacks of Greeks, Jews, and heretics (St. Paul is described as the great exemplar of Christian eloquence), and stresses the necessity for each priest to seek virtue and holiness, concluding with a theme much loved by Quattrocento humanists, the comparative merits of the active and contemplative lives. [178] Though *De sacerdotio* is a defense of priestly authority, its concern for seeking moral virtue fits neatly once more with a central theme of humanist moral philosophy. Less apparent are the reasons for Traversari's translation of the *Homilies against the Jews,* where Chrysostom opposed the Christians frequenting Jewish synagogues and celebrating Jewish festivals, and argued as well that the Jews had been rightly punished for their treatment of Christ. [179] The rhetorical nature of the homilies again seems the most plausible reason for Traversari's decision to translate them, but Renaissance humanism was not marked by an end of animosity towards Judaism. Even those deeply immersed in Hebraic studies, such as Giannozzo Manetti and Giovanni Pico della Mirandola, distinguished between the Old Testament Hebrews and the Jews who lived after the birth of Christ. The prophetic utterances of Moses and the Old Testament prophets (including, for Pico, the mystical tradition of the Cabala) were to be accommodated to Christian belief, but Jewish ritual and religious practices were to be rejected and contemporary Jews converted to Christianity. [180]

Traversari's translation of another remarkable example of Chrysostom's oratory, the first of his twenty-one homilies *On the Statues*, probably dates from this same period of the early 1420's. The homilies were preached in Antioch in 387, during a period in which the populace was fearful that Emperor Theodosius would fulfill his threat to destroy the city in retribution for the mutilation of statues of himself and the imperial family. Chrysostom consoles the anguished crowds, but also castigates them for their vices which had brought divine wrath upon them. [181]

Apart from the opportunity to display his powers of translating effectively superb examples of patristic oratory, these works permitted Traversari to enlarge his scholarship beyond patristics in the service of the monastic vocation. The *De providentia,* in particular, seems to respond to the needs of lay piety. Traversari's translation from the mid 1420's of the twenty sermons of St. Ephraem (c. 306-73), the most celebrated of the Syrian Fathers, is directed to the same end. Much of Ephraem's Scriptural exegesis, oratory, and poetry had been rendered into Greek in the patristic age, and it was from Greek texts that Traversari made his translations. A number of these sermons concerned monastic life − meditation, spiritual exercises, the virtue of chastity, but the bulk provide spiritual counsel on penance, the passion of Christ, the Second Coming, and the Last Judgment. And it is these aspects of Ephraem's teachings that Traversari stresses in his dedication to Cosimo de' Medici, where he states that the study of Ephraem provides the means to a diligent examination of conscience. [182]

The enlarged scope of Traversari's patristic scholarship is doubtless attributable to Niccoli, who, after Prior Matteo's death in 1421, became the most decisive intellectual influence on his thought. The spreading fame of Traversari's Greek scholarship was important, too. We have seen that a number of

humanists and humanist patrons entreated him to direct his
attention to works of classical Greek philosophy, entreaties
which eventually resulted in his reluctant agreement to translate
Diogenes Laertius. Contributing also to the expanded
dimensions of Traversari's scholarship was papal support. Martin
V possessed the tenacity, the martial prowess, and· the
diplomatic shrewdness of an Italian prince — he was after all a
Colonna — rather than the enthusiasm for humanist intellectual
and cultural ideas of such scholar Popes as Nicholas V and Pius
II, and his impact on the humanist movement has usually been
dismissed as inconsequential. But in 1423 he sent two letters,
one to the Prior of S. Maria degli Angeli, and one to Traversari
himself, expressing support for Traversari's patristic scholarship.
In the letter to the Prior, Martin observed that it was the
opinion of Jerome that holy rusticity profits only itself, whereas
those who pursue the light of learning profit others by directing
them into the path of God's will. The Faith had spread through
all the world and defeated the perversity of heretics only
through men of learning, who are the burning candelabra of the
temple of the Lord, whose splendor enables others to walk in
the true light. All effort should be made to help and encourage
such men. He had heard that many in S. Maria degli Angeli were
pursuing the study of sacred letters. The prior should support
this. Above all "we do not wish you to impede in any way from
his resolute endeavor our beloved son, that learned man, Fra
Ambrogio, whom we have ascertained is engaged in translations
of sacred books. Rather you should encourage him in this
virtuous enterprise, for his labor is laudable and of great utility
to many." [183] In the letter to Traversari Martin focused more
specifically on the importance of translating the Greek Fathers.

> Your industry can offer no richer fruit to men than
> to render into Latin those most excellent Greek
> doctors, of whose knowledge we are ignorant, so that
> their teaching, through which we are exhorted to the
> celestial kingdom, may be made known to us. Known
> they can profit us; unknown they are of no use. We
> wish therefore, and we command by the authority of
> this letter, that just as you have laudably begun, you
> proceed forward daily, persevering in your ac-

> customed studies. Do not allow the grace given you
> by God to cool, but rather arouse it and exalt it,
> imparting your diligence to others. This would be
> most pleasing both to us and the Most High. [184]

Martin V's support for Traversari's Greek patristic scholarship
was probably in part the reflection of his own efforts for Greek
union with the Latin Church. Although Antonio da Massa,
whom he sent to Constantinople in 1422-23 to discuss the
question of unification, found the Greeks less receptive than
expected, Martin continued to work for a council of union for
the test of his pontificate. Antonio brought with him a number
of Greek manuscripts from Constantinople: among them was
the Diogenes Laertius, which Traversari used for his translation;
and a polemical work, the *Adversus errores Graecorum de
Processione Spiritus Sancti,* written by the Byzantine
theologian, Manuel Kalekas (d.1410). A student of Demetrius
Cydones, who translated Thomas Aquinas into Greek, Kalekas
converted to Latin Christianity, became a Dominican, and
partisan of the unification of the Churches. Kalekas was known
in Florentine humanist circles, for Jacopo Angeli da Scarperia
had become friends with him in Constantinople, and later after
his return to Florence sought manuscripts from him. Moreover,
when Chrysoloras left Florence in 1400, Kalekas hinted to
Angeli that he would welcome the vacated chair of Greek
studies at the Florentine studio. [185] Kalekas' treatise, however,
belongs not to the study of antiquity but rather to a popular
late medieval genre . In the thirteenth and fourteenth centuries
many polemical treatises on the error of the Greeks were
written, including one by Aquinas. Most centered on criticism
of the Greek position on the Procession of the Holy Spirit, a
subject of theological controversy between Greek East and
Latin West since the Photian schism of the ninth century. This
was also the principal matter of theological dispute at the
Council of Ferrara-Florence 1438-39. [186] When Antonio da
Massa returned with the Kalekas treatise, Marvin V, according
to the dedicatory letter, XXIII:3, commissioned Traversari to
translate the work. He completed the task hurriedly, in a
month's time, sometime in the summer or fall of 1424. [187]

In the dedicatory letter Traversari reveals for the first time his attitude towards the Greek Orthodox Church. He had no doubts that the Greeks were in error regarding the Procession of the Holy Spirit. Moreover, echoing medieval prejudices, he argued that whereas once the Greeks had excelled nearly all mortals in wisdom and eloquence, and in faith, religion, and other virtues, their innate fondness for contention had entangled them in subtleties and ensnared them in errors, with the result that they were so consumed by calamities that scarcely any vestige of their former glory and dignity remained. The Pope should imitate Christ, the eternal Shepherd, and if not restore the lost sheep to pristine sanctity, at least return them to the sacred sheepfold, thereby freeing them from destruction at the hand of the Turks, who would utterly destroy Christianity in the lands where it first arose. Nothing could be more glorious now that the schism within the Western church had been healed than that the still older schism between the Eastern and Western churches be ended, and the body of the Church be reunited again under one head. Nothing could be more meritorious than that the man who was rebuilding the collapsed sacred buildings in Rome should also apply himself wholeheartedly to renewing the Universal Church. [188]

Papal recognition, then, as well as the encouragement of his lay and clerical patrons and Niccoli's intellectual leadership began to direct Traversari to broader concerns in Christian antiquity. But the shift to a more historical study of early Christianity seems not to have been so much a conscious intellectual decision as the consequence of fortuitous circumstances. In late 1423 Niccoli sent Traversari an ancient volume which contained the Apostolic Canons, the decrees of the seven Ecumenical Councils and of other early synods, and numerous letters of the Fathers, including those of Cyril of Alexandria, Basil, Gregory of Nyssa, Gregory Nazianzen, and Athanasius, which dealt with the Councils or with ecclesiastical discipline. "I admit I was so moved by reading this, that I considered interrupting my work of translation, for the whole thing is worthy of esteem. I came upon nothing not full of dignity." [189] Excited by his reading, Traversari related an incident described in the volume which occurred at the Synod of Carthage (411), at which Augustine played a principal role in overcoming the Donatists. The incident, Traversari wrote, will cause Niccoli to hold the recent Council of Constance in greater veneration. During the course of the Synod it became necessary to consult the decrees of the Council of Nicaea, but because the Greek text was not available in Carthage, letters were sent to the Patriarchs of Constantinople, Alexandria, and Antioch, and to the Pope asking for the text of the decrees. And indeed the text was sent, and the letters which testified to the Eastern prelates' ardent faith were preserved, including one from Cyril of Alexandria.

> Oh to encounter such diligence, to be compared to these sordid times! But one must refrain from tears – though a pious man can neither read nor hear this without tears. This book seized me in a marvelous way, and it aroused me to read over as many matters of this kind as I could. . . . I had the desire to see if my slight talent could translate the Latin works into Greek. I quickly took up that lengthy letter of singular learning which Gregory the Great wrote to the priests of Constantinople, Alexandria, Antioch, and Jerusalem, and I translated the whole thing. . . . Behold, here I am. This is what I have devoted myself to.[190]

That Gregory had communicated with the clergy of the Eastern sees and that the Eastern Patriarchs had sent the decrees of Nicaea to Carthage signified for Traversari the close collaboration in support of the faith which had existed between Greek East and Latin West in the Early Church. Moreover it was in the conciliar activity of the Early Church that the sanctifying action of the Holy Spirit seemed most manifest. Just as the patristic Church presented itself to Traversari as a Church of Councils, so, Traversari seems to imply, the revival of conciliar activity in the present age was the resuscitation of action which most exemplified the Early Church.

In studying the activities of the Councils, Traversari confronted the Fathers not just as authorities, or as exemplars of virtue, but as men acting in a particular historical context.

His historical sense of Early Christianity was further enlarged as he turned almost immediately to reading intently the Greek text of Eusebius' *Ecclesiastical History.* In February 1424 he wrote to Niccoli, apologizing for his recent silence, caused by his intense reading of Eusebius for the past ten days:

> It is hardly possible to believe how struck I have been with this work. Though I had seen it previously in Latin it brought less pleasure to me than now when I have read it in the original language. In many places the author appears to have followed the Arian heresy, but I am delighted in the greatest way both with the majesty of his words and the charm of his eloquence. Above all ecclesiastical authors, at least the ones I have read, he is the greatest innovator in use of language. He displays great erudition in all the liberal disciplines. I was struck by many, indeed nearly all, the men whom history judged worthy, but especially Justin Martyr, Malchion, Clement of Alexandria, Pierius, Origen, and his followers Dionysius of Alexandria and Pamphilus who loved him greatly. [191]

With his increased knowledge of Christian antiquity derived from studying the history of the Councils and Eusebius, Traversari was prepared to understand the historical importance of Athanasius, whose works, with the exception of the *Life of St. Antony,* were virtually unknown to the medieval Latin West. Directly inspired by reading Eusebius, Traversari turned to studying the Greek text of Athanasius' most important works. He became so rapt with the beauty of language and doctrine of this "incomparable" Father that he could not tear himself away. He read first the *Oratio contra Gentiles* and the *Oratio incarnatione Verbi,* then the three *Orationes contra Arianos,* and was so impressed with the author's refutation of heretical ideas, and especially his stress on scriptural exegesis in the explication of theological doctrine, that he decided to translate his works. [192] Athanasius, who formulated the basic Trinitarian and Christological doctrines of the Church, was, as Traversari observed, firmly rooted in a scriptural theology: exegesis of the Gospels and the Pauline Epistles was the basis of his thought. In the *Oration against the Heathen* he argued that both philosophic pantheism and pagan polytheism were rife with immorality and superstition; then in the *Oration on the Incarnation of the Word* he demonstrated against Jewish and pagan objections the reasons for the Incarnation, Death, and Resurrection of Christ. The *Discourses against the Arians,* his chief dogmatic work, defended the doctrine of the Council of Nicaea on the eternal and uncreated nature of the Son, and like the *Orations* demonstrated that the central mysteries of Christian faith had been articulated in the Early Church not by dialectical disputation but through the power of sacred eloquence. [193]

Traversari's inspiration to translate Athanasius had to await fruition until earlier porjects, such as the *Vitae Patrum* and Diogenes Laertius, were finished. Two years later, in the summer of 1426, he was only about to begin the Athanasius. In the end he completed the *Orations* but made only a partial translation of the *Discourses.* In 1436 he dedicated the *Orations* to Pietro Donato, the Bishop whom he had met in Padua in 1433. Granted, Traversari remarks in the dedicatory letter, that Tertullian, Arnobius, Lactantius, Augustine, and a number of others had written copiously and with great elegance in Latin against pagan vainglory and superstition, so that it would seem nothing further could be said; yet Athanasius' extraordinary *pietas,* clearly manifested in his writings, suggested that a translation would not be unwelcome. Moreover, "He embraces the ignominy of the Cross so gloriously and defends it with such dignity that none of the faithful exists but that he would be affected most delightfully by reading this." [194] That he should dedicate the translation to Pietro was particularly appropriate, he asserted, for as defender of Catholic faith and the unity of the Church at Basel he was imitating the great achievements of the Greek Father. In addition Pietro's dedication to the recovery and restoration of antiquity, his benevolence, and his *pietas* and *humanitas* deserved recognition and commendation.

Traversari's translation was not widely diffused in the fifteenth century, but in the early sixteenth century it was published numerous times together with Tortelli's version of the *Life of Athanasius,* based on Greek and Latin sources, which he dedicated to Eugenius IV in 1440, and with Poliziano's partial translation c.1492 of Athanasius' *Epistola ad Marcellinum,* a letter which stressed the importance of Psalms for Christian meditation and prayer. [195] Traversari himself came to know the Greek text of the *Life of Athanasius,* for this was among the volumes which Lorenzo de' Medici brought back with him from Rome in 1431. [196]

His increased awareness of the whole of Christian antiquity caused Traversari, with Niccoli's collaboration, to intensify the search for patristic manuscripts. Works of the Latin Fathers could be procured from the ancient Benedictine monasteries, such as Nonantola and Pomposa; but Latin Christendom, with the exception of the Basilian monasteries of south Italy, possessed few Greek manuscripts. Traversari did study a Greek manuscript of Chrysostom and Ephraem the Syrian which had been present in the Florentine Franciscan monastery of S. Croce, before it entered Niccoli's library; but this is the only identified instance of his use of a Greek patristic manuscript whose original provenance was a Florentine monastic library. [197] Instead his principal sources of Greek texts were Niccoli's superb library, and, to a lesser extent, the Greek collection left to the Badia Fiorentina on his death in 1425 by Antonio Corbinelli, who had studied Greek under Chrysoloras in Florence. Most of these eighty or so Greek manuscripts, of which fifteen were patristic texts, were probably transcriptions of codices belonging to Chrysoloras, or to Guarino, who lived in Corbinelli's house during his Florentine sojourn, 1410-14. [198] Traversari was close friends with the reforming Abbot of the Badia, Gomes Ferreira da Silva – they conducted a joint reform visitation to the monasteries of the Vallombrosan Order in 1433 [199] – and in an undated note he thanked the Abbot for the loan of a Greek codex of Gregory Nazianzen, and for the general privilege he had extended to make free use of the Badia's library. To facilitate this use Traversari requested that the Abbot send an index of the Greek manuscripts. [200]

Niccoli's library was a far richer source, for he possessed the remarkable total of some fifty Greek patristic manuscripts. These included four or five of Basil, five of Gregory Nazianzen, one each of Athanasius and Gregory of Nyssa, and, astoundingly, seventeen or eighteen Chrysostom. Niccoli owned also at least four Greek texts of Scripture, and numerous manuscripts of old Latin translations of Origen, Gregory Nazianzen, and other Greek Fathers.[201] When Niccoli went to Rome in 1423, he left his Greek library with Traversari in S. Maria degli Angeli; and in the process of cataloging the collection, Traversari came upon the Athanasius, as well as Gregory of Nyssa's *Homilies on the Canticles,* which he read with great admiration for Nyssa's eloquence and lofty erudition.[202]

But Traversari was eager for new acquisitions, and he exploited every opportunity his humanist contacts presented in the search for Greek patristic texts. In January 1424 Giustiniani wrote that certain books belonging to Chrysoloras and Demetrio Scarano had become available in Venice, and that he was trying to arrange to have them come into Palla Strozzi's possession so that they would be accessible to Traversari in Florence. Traversari replied urging Giustiniani to acquire them instead for Niccoli, especially Demetrio's volume of Chrysostom's *Homilies on Matthew.* It was Strozzi, however, who acquired the manuscript. More disheartening was the news that two friars, to whom Giustiniani had entrusted a Greek volume to take to Traversari, had been caught in a squall while sailing from Venice to Padua, and fearing shipwreck threw everything overboard, including the manuscript.[203] Traversari did manage to obtain a few patristic manuscripts from Aurispa and Filelfo, but, as we have seen, their large collections of Greek manuscripts proved disappointing as sources of patristic texts. So also did the Greek library of Cardinal Giordano Orsini, an index of which Traversari obtained while in Rome in 1432.[204] While in Rome Traversari also examined carefully the Greek volumes in the Papal library, but found nothing new except the *De perfectione vitae religiosae* of the seventh century Nestorian ascetic and mystic Isaac of Ninevah.[205] Traversari also discovered, to his dismay, that much of Grottaferrata was in ruins, the Greek volumes scattered about, and of the manuscripts he examined none were unfamiliar.[206] He did, however, discover Jerome's translation of Origen's *Homilies on Luke* in S. Cecilia, and in 1433 while in Venice Francesco

Barbaro gave him a Greek manuscript of Gregory Nazianzen's orations. [207] Traversari also sought Greek patristic texts directly from the Greek East through Italian humanists, clerics, and merchants who had contacts there. It was Cristoforo Buondelmonti, a Florentine cleric and traveler in the Aegean, who obtained on Rhodes in 1415 the Nyssa manuscript Traversari was reading so avidly in 1424. [208] Antonio da Massa brought back from the conciliar negotiations at Constantinople, besides the Kalekas and Diogenes Laertius, a "gigantic" Chrysostom which came into Niccoli's possession. [209] Also in 1424 Traversari wrote to Niccoli praising a certain Salomone for sending from afar, apparently the Greek East, nothing but the most beautiful manuscripts, including a volume of Chrysostom's *Homilies on John.* [210] And in 1431 Traversari received from the Bishop of Corfu a gift of a Greek manuscript which included Palladius' *Life of Chrysostom,* a work he translated shortly thereafter. [211] As early as 1421-22 Traversari had been alerted to the importance of Crete as a source of Greek texts. It was reported that Homer, the Gospels, and other sacred texts could be purchased there for low prices. [212] Perhaps to take advantage of this, Traversari pinned his hopes on a Florentine merchant named Pietro, a man who seemed enthusiastic for the *studia humanitatis*, who set sail with the Florentine galleys for Alexandria in 1423. But Traversari's expectations were crushed by Pietro's sudden death en route. [213]

The most spectacular of Traversari's and Niccoli's quests for Greek texts was the journey of the Franciscan Francesco da Pistoia. In 1429 Francesco wished to make a pilgrimage to the Holy Sepulchre. Niccoli recommended him to Poggio, then Apostolic Secretary, who obtained from Martin V a license for the pilgrimage, including a plenary indulgence and a two-year safe-conduct, provided Francesco convey papal letters to the Sultan of Egypt. Poggio also stipulated that Francesco acquire sculpture for him en route. In November 1430 Traversari wrote Niccoli that he had learned that Francesco had visited Andreolo Giustiniani, the Genoese patrician resident on Chios, and that Andreolo promised to send gifts, apparently both manuscripts and ancient artifacts, to Niccoli and himself. Andreolo had amassed an impressive Greek library — though his grandson's claim of two thousand volumes is certainly exaggerated – much of it obtained from Greek monasteries in the wake of Turkish conquests. In the summer of 1435 Francesco finally came back from his lengthy pilgrimage, which had taken him through much of the Near East. The return journey brought him again through Chios, and Andreolo there gave him a letter to take to Traversari in which he announced he was sending him five Greek manuscripts. In July Traversari wrote Andreolo that he had received from him one very precious Greek manuscript (unnamed, but probably from Traversari's description, Photius' *Bibliotheca*, an important source of what classical and patristic texts had existed in antiquity), and that he eagerly anticipated receiving the others. To Andreolo he was sending his translation of Aeneas Gazeus. [214] Unfortunately Traversari does not identify the anticipated manuscripts, nor do we know if he eventually received them. But the episode suggests the range of contacts Traversari and Niccoli were able to influence in their search for Greek texts.

After reading the history of the Councils and Eusebius, Traversari was particularly anxious to acquire texts of the Apostolic Fathers, especially the *Epistolae* of Ignatius († c.110), and the *Adversus haereses* of Irenaeus († c.200), Ignatius' letters, written between Syria and Rome where he suffered martyrdom, are important early statements of Church doctrine. They were translated into Latin in the seventh century and again by Robert Grosseteste in the thirteenth, but manuscripts of the letters remained rare. [215] In June 1424 Traversari asked Cosimo de' Medici to enlist the help of Niccolò Albergati, Bishop of Bologna, to obtain a manuscript of the letters from Nonantola, but it is uncertain whether he met with any success. [216] In 1427-28, however, Parentucelli, while accompanying Albergati on diplomatic missions in Lombardy, acquired from the Certosa of Pavia the long recension of Ignatius' *Epistolae,* and Polycarp's *Epistle to the Philippians,* written shortly after Ignatius' death. Although uncertain, it seems likely that Traversari obtained this manuscript, for Parentucelli was diligent in sending his other patristic manuscript finds to Florence, and in 1428 he informed Niccoli of the discovery of these letters. [217] It was Parentucelli who did indeed procure for Traversari a manuscript of Irenaeus' *Adversus haereses*, perhaps the most important second-century theological work. In his attacks on the Gnostics, Irenaeus sets forth early Christian doctrine on the Trinity, Christology, the Scriptural canon, ecclesiology, and the primacy of Rome. Although translated into Latin in the patristic age, like works of the other Apostolic Fathers, it remained rare in the Middle Ages.[218]   Parentucelli came across the manuscript at the Chartreuse of Grenoble in 1431, while again accompanying Albergati on another diplomatic mission. He sent it, together with Jerome's translation of Theophilus of Alexandria's *Epistolae de Pascha contra Origenem,* to Traversari, who retained them until 1438.[219] During the pontificate of Sixtus IV, Giovanni Andrea Bussi, librarian of the Vatican Library, made preparations for an edition of Irenaeus, but it never appeared. Erasmus, who published the first edition of Irenaeus in 1526, used as one of his sources a copy of the Grenoble manuscript which Parentucelli had discovered.[220]

It was Niccoli himself who found in the Veneto in 1431, transcribed, and sent to Traversari the important *Shepherd* of Hermas († c.150), an apocalyptic treatise which stresses the importance of penance and provides a vivid account of the Christian community in Rome during the difficult period of the persecutions of Trajan.[221] Traversari was pleased to learn of Niccoli's discovery, for he thought the work had been lost; and although his ardor cooled when Niccoli expressed reservations about the quality of the *Shepherd*, he nevertheless looked forward to reading it.[222]

At the same time Traversari was seeking works of the Apostolic Fathers, his knowledge of the historical roots of Christianity was deepened through study of two important non-patristic sources, Josephus and Philo. Josephus (first century A.D.), the Jewish Pharisee, lived in Palestine until the fall of Jerusalem to Titus, then settled in Rome where he wrote *De bello Judaico* (75-79), an account of Titus' conquest, and *Antiquitates Judaicae* (completed in 93-94), a history of the Jewish people from Creation to A.D. 66. Josephus' works are a key non-Biblical source for Christ's trial and execution. Both works had been translated into Latin before the end of antiquity and were well-known in the Middle Ages, but Niccoli owned a tenth century Greek manuscript of the *Antiquitates*, and probably Greek texts of the *De bello Judaico*, as well. [223] In 1430 Traversari wrote Niccoli that he had received his volume of Josephus (no title specified), and that the manuscript could be easily restored under his direction at S. Maria degli Angeli. [224]   Philo   Judaeus   (c.30B.C.-A.D.45),   was   the Alexandrian Jew whose efforts to synthesize Greek philosophy and Jewish religion set such important precedents for the Alexandrian Fathers, Origen especially. In 1431 Traversari acquired from Filelfo a large Greek manuscript of Philo, which contained large parts of his allegorical commentary on Genesis, and much of the collection of treatises which expound Mosaic Law to Gentiles. One of these is the *De vita Moysis*, which Filelfo started to translate in 1428, but abandoned. [225] Some of Philo had been available in the Latin Middle Ages, but he was not widely known. During the 1470's and early 1480's Lilius Tifernas translated the complete works of Philo for Sixtus IV. [226]

In the nearly eight years from his initial reading of the Acts of the Ecumenical Councils in the winter of 1424 to his election as General in the fall of 1431, Traversari had acquired knowledge of many of the key works for understanding the historical development of Christianity in the ancient world. Philo and Josephus, Ignatius and Irenaeus, Tertullian, Athanasius, Eusebius, the history of the Councils – all concerned him. In no sense does Traversari's scholarship represent a systematic historical inquiry into the early centuries of Christianity, but his study of the Fathers' attacks on the Gnostic, Arian, and Nestorian heresies permitted him to see doctrine as formulated historically, in response to particular challenges. Moreover, through his study of patristic epistolaries, and the biographical accounts in Eusebius, and in Jerome's *De viris illustribus*, he became conscious of the Fathers, not as abstract doctrinal authorities, but as concrete historical personages. There is, for example, his lengthy discussion of whether Augustine and Jerome ever met in person, a discussion based on an exhaustive examination and sophisticated assessment of the available evidence in Augustine's letters and

Confessions, in Jerome's letters, and in the writings of such contemporaries as Rufinus. [227] Christian antiquity for Traversari was both historically real and personal, and the model to be emulated in the present. His approach corresponded to his humanist contemporaries' enthusiasm for Plutarch and Xenophon. But instead of finding the model of virtue in Cicero or Socrates, as the civic humanists did, Traversari upheld the outsized heroic qualities of such Fathers as Gregory Nazianzen and John Chrysostom; and in the early 1430's he translated lives of these two Greek Fathers.

First he tried his hand at the *Life of Gregory Nazianzen* written in the seventh century by Gregory the Presbyter. He had just acquired the Greek text from Giuliano Cesarini, who had detached and sent to Florence the pages containing the *Vita* from a manuscript of Gregory Nazianzen which the papal secretary Cencio de' Rustici had procured from Grottaferrata. Traversari immediately decided to translate it, and to dedicate it to Cesarini. He completed his task early in November 1430, in time to present it to Cesarini on the occasion of his elevation to the position of Cardinal. [228] In the dedicatory letter, Traversari describes Gregory Nazianzen as "that great man, extremely learned, and celebrated for his declaration of the doctrines of our faith, so esteemed that none of his statements have ever come into question. All that he wrote is Catholic. He speaks of God with so much gravity, and he has so set forth the highest mysteries of our faith, that he has earned the name of the Theologian." Yet it was not so much as a great doctrinal authority, but as a model of Christian virtue that Traversari admired him.

> You will observe his singular sanctity, his admirable wisdom, and his unconquered constancy amidst all adversity. It will gratify you, as it did me, to recognize this golden vessel, first prepared in the house of the Lord and equipped by divine favor with a capacity for all good work, then by the merits of his labors, his industry, and his perpetual vigils deserving that he become the sanctuary of the Holy Spirit. Nor do I doubt that your soul, attracted to piety, will burn with ardent desire to imitate his holy life and

purpose. But, why do I say, it will burn with ardent desire, since in your disdain of glory, your endurance of labor, and your love of Christ and the heavenly fatherland, you at present are eagerly imitating him? What is written of him, you will recognize in yourself, rather than read as something new. In this I hope and trust, dearest Giuliano. [229]

Gregory Nazianzen, called by Byzantines the "Christian Demosthenes" for his remarkable command of the rhetorical resources of Hellenistic Greek, was famed principally for his forty-five orations, though he also wrote numerous poems and letters. Except for one manuscript, this Cappadocian Father was known to the Latin Middle Ages only through the nine orations translated by Rufinus. [230] In the Renaissance, however, Gregory's stylistic excellence and his preference for a combination of ascetic piety and literary culture proved particularly attractive to humanists, and numerous translations appeared in the fifteenth and sixteenth centuries. Traversari was the first Renaissance scholar to devote attention to Gregory's works. [231] Prior to translating Gregory the Presbyter's *Vita*, Traversari had studied Nazianzen's letters from the one patristic text in the huge collection of Greek manuscripts which Aurispa had brought with him from Constantinople. In 1428 Parentucelli wrote to Niccoli that he had received from Aurispa that volume of Gregory Nazianzen, "about which you have insistently importuned me for information," and he promised to send it as soon as possible. [232]

In the 1430's Traversari devoted considerable scholarly attention to Gregory Nazianzen. In 1432 he mentions borrowing a volume of Greek poetry from Marco Lippomano in order to transcribe a poem written by Gregory; [233] and in 1433 Francesco Barbaro gave him a Greek manuscript containing thirty orations. [234] When Traversari resumed his work in patristics in the spring of 1436 after the lengthy six months' journey to Basel and Hungary, he turned first to translating four orations of Gregory. One of these, the *De obitu patris* [No. 18], he intended to dedicate to Alonzo de Cartagena, the critic of Bruni's translation of the *Nicomachean Ethics,* whom Traversari had met at Basel and found to be an adherent to the papal cause. During Traversari's stay at Basel, Alonzo's father had died, and to console him Traversari promised to send a translation of Gregory Nazianzen's oration on the subject. The other three were the orations *De pace* [Nos. 6, 23, 22], which Traversari planned to dedicate to Francesco Pizolpasso (c.1370-1443), the Archbishop of Milan, and an important humanist patron, whose large personal library included more than fifty patristic manuscripts. Among these were several of Traversari's translations of Chrysostom and a copy of his *Life of Gregory Nazianzen* dated 1432. Traversari had come to know Pizolpasso also at Basel, where he reported that the Archbishop, though tied to Viscontean anti-papal policy, had covertly favored the papal cause. During their colloquies there Pizolpasso had entreated Traversari to translate the *De pace*; and he promised to do so, provided Pizolpasso sent to Niccoli whatever rare Greek works he had in his library. Traversari completed his version of the four orations in July 1436, and sent them to Niccoli in Florence to read and to arrange for their transcription as dedication copies. Fra Michele, Traversari's humanist scribe, copied two of the orations *De pace* and returned them to Traversari; but, despite repeated inquiries, Traversari had received by late spring 1437 neither the final copy of *De obitu patris* nor the complete text of the orations *De pace*. [235] No further mention of the translations appears in Traversari's correspondence. Niccoli's death in January 1437 is a likely cause for the confusion surrounding the transcription. There is no evidence that the copies were ever sent to Alonzo or Pizolpasso, and only recently has Sister Agnes Clare Way identified as Traversari's an anonymous fifteenth century rendering of two of the orations *De pace* [Nos. 6 and 23]. [236]

In June 1431 Lorenzo de' Medici returned from Rome with the Greek text of Palladius' *Dialogus de vita S. Joannis*, a gift to Traversari from the Bishop of Corfu. Palladius (363/64—c.430) was a close friend of Chrysostom and a staunch supporter of the embattled Patriarch of Constantinople in his confrontation with imperial authority. In 405 he went to Rome to plead the deposed and exiled Patriarch's case before the Pope, and upon his return to the East, he was himself exiled for his support of his friend. The *Dialogus* composed during his exile in Syene in the year following the Patriarch's death, is the oldest and best account of Chrysostom's life. After the model of Plato's *Phaedo* an Eastern bishop and a Roman deacon converse in Rome about Chrysostom, shortly after his death. Palladius' principal intent was to defend the Patriarch against the charges of Theophilus of Alexandria, Chrysostom's most embittered foe, and the narrative of the last years of Chrysostom's life, when Palladius knew him personally, is especially vivid. [237]

As soon as Traversari received the *Dialogus*, he began to read it, was greatly excited by the work, and indicated to Niccoli his ardent desire to render it into Latin, if Niccoli approved. [238] Before he could begin, he was elected General. It then occurred to him that it would be especially appropriate "to translate this work in Rome where it was written, if I can find the leisure." [239] In February 1432 he wrote that he was determined to make the translation, and to dedicate it to the Pope, in hopes he might thus free his Order from the usual fiscal obligations involved in his promotion to the office of General. [240] The hope proved ultimately unfounded; but Traversari did finish this project in March, and before leaving Rome he presented Eugenius IV with the dedication copy. He found the Pope pleased with his gift — indeed Eugenius ordered it to be read at his table. [241]

In the dedicatory letter Traversari wrote that he had translated Palladius' life of Chrysostom so that "his life might be conspicuous to everyone and be set forth to be imitated, and that I might by such an exercise lift up the enfeebled soul suffering from cares; that by it I might expel from the soul whatever darkness it had brought down on itself, as much as the Lord might permit." Indeed it had been his own experience that when he perceived the life, mores, and virtues of this holiest man he gained much solace and increased strength.

> For who indeed is so made of iron that, as he wonders at the loftiness of his mind and his unconquered constancy amidst such severe and continuous persecutions, he does not love him ardently, does not long for, is not aroused to the grace of remorse? Who indeed is able not to wonder

most properly that so illustrious, so renowned a
bishop of so great a city could have been banished
from his episcopal seat, when he, however, was not in
the least concerned with the injustices done to him,
but in the midst of his own troubles took into
account only what would preserve the peace and
teaching of the Church? Indeed even after having
been driven into exile he still endeavored assidously
to comfort through letters the faithful who could not
endure the absence of their most skillful shepherd.
Happy is he certainly, by his constancy blessed, and
worthy to be admitted into the choir of the martyrs
whose sufferings for love of justice he imitated.

Traversari urged Eugenius to read the work carefully. "You will
discover many things worthy of thought which can delight and
instruct the well-prepared mind. As formerly Basil by his
miraculous teaching strengthened you, a celibate, in the vow of
angelic purity, so likewise Chrysostom by his example will teach
you as a pope to preserve the dignity of the Apostolic Chair
with praise and glory." [242]

A year and a half later, in September 1433, Traversari sought
from the Holy Roman Emperor Sigismund confirmation of the
imperial privileges which had accrued to the Camaldulensians.
In the audience before the Emperor in Ferrara, Traversari
noted that while on such occasions it was customary to give
gifts of gold and silver, in emulation of the Apostles he had
vowed a life of poverty. Therefore from the "treasure of the
slight intellect given me by God" he would present instead his
translation of the life of Chrysostom. [243] The translation was
much sought after in Traversari's lifetime: Francesco Barbaro,
Leonardo Giustiniani, and other Venetian and Bolognese
humanists all asked him for copies. [244]

In his translations of the lives of Gregory Nazianzen and John
Chrysostom, Traversari, then, provided patristic models of
Christian virtue — Gregory of the true theologian's ardent
wisdom, Chrysostom of the true bishop's unconquered devotion
to his flock. These men were not simply to be admired but
rather to be emulated, to be the inspiration to the clergy to
renew the fervent faith of Christian antiquity.

One major achievement of Traversari's patristic scholarship was the historical recovery of Christian antiquity; another was his understanding of patristic theology as essentially the exegesis of Holy Scripture. Even before concentrating on the Greek Fathers, he had become immersed in the Greek and Latin text of Psalms and the New Testament, for that was how he learned Greek. Meditation on Scripture was also central to the *studia pietatis* which he advocated. In 1424 he wrote to Giovanni Corvini, who was anguished by the death of his son and had sought Traversari's spiritual counsel:

> Your study strengthens this hope in me, for you write that you are devoting particular attention to sacred letters. Acutely perceptive is that statement of Jerome's: "Love knowledge of the Scriptures and you will not love sins of the flesh" [*Ep. ad Rusticum*]. Great affection for piety is imbibed through familiarity with, perpetual meditation on, and remembrance of sacred things. Through this we cast off the old man, and our soul is renewed in the image of Him who created us. [245]

There are indications that in the 1420's and '30's Traversari continued his study of the Greek text of the Bible. In late 1423 he was reading the Book of Job, the Wisdom of Solomon, and Ecclesiasticus, along with an anonymous Greek commentary on the Wisdom of Solomon which cited numerous Fathers including Origen, Basil, and Chrysostom. [246] Francesco Barbaro presented him with the Greek text of sixteen Old Testament prophetic books in 1433. [247] Moreover, shortly after 1430 Traversari began to study the Hebrew text of the Old Testament. [248] In the 1420's he grew familiar with such major Latin patristic exegetical works as Augustine's *Super Genesim ad literam* and Hilary's *Super aliquot Psalmos,* and he was studying the exegetical works of some of the Greek Fathers as well. In 1423-24 he was reading intently the Greek text of Gregory of Nyssa's highly mystical and speculative *Homilies on the Canticles* which followed Plotinus in their treatment of the union of love between God and the soul. Traversari admired the eloquence of the work and the grandeur of its thought, which were in no way inferior, he asserted, to Origen, whom Nyssa professed to follow. [249] Traversari knew some of the enormous body of Origen's exegetical homilies on the Old and New Testament, which, though not available in Greek (they had disappeared in the Origenist controversies of the fourth to sixth centuries), were accessible in the Latin translations made by Jerome and Rufinus. Niccoli's library contained a number of volumes of Origen's exegesis on the Heptateuch in addition to his *Commentary on the Canticles* and by the mid-1420's Traversari had read his *Commentary on Romans* as well. [250] We have noted Traversari's elation at finding Origen's *Homilies on Luke* in Rome. While there he also acquired from the Abbot of Montecassino an ancient manuscript which contained his twelve *Homilies on Isaiah.* Traversari asked Niccoli whether he owned a copy, and stated his plan to return with it to Florence if he could not find the leisure to transcribe it. [251] The Renaissance witnessed a remarkable revival of Origen, whose Platonism was especially admired by the Florentine Platonic Academy, and whose allegorical profundity in the elucidation of Scripture led Erasmus to regard him as the greatest of exegetes. [252]

Traversari was impressed with Origen, but he admired less the philosophical profundities of the Alexandrian school than the ethical and devotional emphasis of Chrysostom, whose Scriptural homilies, celebrated for their rhetorical quality, were in the tradition of the Antiochene school of literal exegesis. Indeed Traversari so admired these works of Chrysostom that in 1429 he decided to translate his homilies on the Pauline Epistles. Clearly this was to be a major project, for he wrote to Niccoli, "I ask also that you send to me the remaining three volumes of Chrysostom on the Epistles of Paul, for I wish to know for certain what of this work we are lacking, so that we can diligently seek it, and indicate it to friends on whom I have imposed this task." [253] Among the friends Traversari turned to for texts was Leonardo Giustiniani, but the Venetian reported that he did not own any volumes of Chrysostom's Pauline homilies. When Traversari learned this, he responded, "God will, I hope, heed my prayers, so that these books will come to us from somewhere. [254]

Chrysostom preached on the entire Pauline epistolary, and

his exposition of Paul's Epistles comprise nearly half of his extant homilies. Chrysostom's comments on Matthew, John, and Acts had been available to the Latin Middle Ages in Burgundio's translations, but of the huge corpus of Chrysostom's works on Paul only the thirty-four *Homilies on Hebrews,* translated by Mutianus at Vivarium in the sixth century, were known to the Latin West. [255]

Traversari's letters provide no indication as to which of Chrysostom's homilies on Paul he translated first. Perhaps it was the ten *Homilies on II Timothy*, completed, according to the colophon of the autograph manuscript, on 18 July 1429. Then it seems likely he turned to the six *Homilies on Titus*, followed by the eighteen *Homilies on I Timothy*, of which he had completed the first thirteen before his election as General of the Camaldulensians in the fall of 1431. Homilies VII-XIII of the autograph manuscript were written in Niccoli's hand, indicating his close collaboration on the project, and confirming Vespasiano's anecdote that he wrote at Traversari's dictation. [256] Traversari's initial tasks as General interrupted his scholarly work, but in the fall of 1432 he returned to the Homilies on I Timothy, and had completed three of the remaining five when he received Niccoli's letter admonishing him that his preoccupation with monastic reform was causing him to neglect patristic scholarship. Traversari promised to devote whatever free time he had to these studies, and remarked that he anticipated finishing the last two *Homilies on I Timothy* before Niccoli received his letter. Then he intended to turn to the *Homilies on Thessalonians.* [257] When, in early November, he sent the five completed homilies to his brother, Girolamo, asking him to add them to the ones previously translated, he wrote, "pray that the Lord will deign to grant me greater repose and tranquillity of mind so that I will have the strength to translate others." [258] Such was not to be. In mid-November Pope Eugenius imposed on him the task of reforming the Vallombrosan Order. [259] Traversari objected that he had just returned to patristic scholarship and had begun to translate again Chrysostom's homilies on the Pauline Epistles, "a work certainly of the greatest utility," and he asked to be relieved of this new responsibility for monastic reform. But the Pope insisted, and he postponed his plans while he made a visitation to the Vallombrosan monasteries. [260] He did eventually complete the three *Homilies on Philemon*, and the first two of the twenty-four *Homilies on Ephesians*, but he never returned to the *Homilies on Thessalonians*. [261] Traversari never formally published any of his translations of these Chrysostom homilies, but the autograph manuscript passed into the Library of San Marco, and from there the works were diffused to Rome, Urbino, and other humanistic centers in the fifteenth century. [262]

In the latter 1430's Traversari planned an even more ambitious project--a new translation of all ninety of Chrysostom's *Homilies on Matthew*. In the early summer of 1436, when he had returned to patristic scholarship after the arduous trans-Alpine journey as Papal Nuncio, he was contemplating the translation, but wished to confer with Pope Eugenius before actually committing himself to the project. Pending the forthcoming discussion with the Pope, he wanted to check the availability of the Greek text of the work. He noted that Fra Michele had affirmed that he held in S. Maria degli Angeli the Greek text of the first forty-five homilies in a manuscript which Cencio de' Rustici had brought from Grottaferrata, but he wondered why Cencio had not brought the second part, which they needed. [263] In November 1436, Traversari wrote to Cosimo de' Medici that the Pope intended him to be free to translate Greek sacred letters, and to this end had allotted the annual sum of two hundred gold scudi with which he was to hire four scribes. Of this allotment, hardly enough he asserts, the Pope had already given him one hundred, and had ordered him to proceed with the *Homilies on Matthew*, "since only twenty-five homilies are to be found translated by that extremely skilled translator Anianus." The whole College of Cardinals had urged the project as well; and he intended, as far as his powers permitted, to fulfill their demand. To Cosimo's burdensome cares Traversari wished to add two more. First he asked Cosimo to secure for him a number of Florentine scribes "who are extremely rapid, experienced, skilled in taking down and transcribing what is dictated, and who can succeed one another in turn, so that I will not have the labor of writing." He had need of a number of scribes for he intended to complete his translation of Ps.-Dionysius as well. "I mean to dedicate myself entirely to my former studies and prior delights, dividing the cares of our Order among others." The second request was that Cosimo procure and send to him a volume containing the first fifty *Homilies on Matthew* which he recalled having seen among Palla Strozzi's Greek books. He concluded by reminding Cosimo, "I would well-nigh say that your devotion to sacred matters will bring more benefit than any work in public or private business no matter how zealously undertaken." [264] Traversari knew that Strozzi had purchased a volume of the *Homilies on Matthew* in Venice in 1424 from a collection of manuscripts which had belonged to Demetrio Scarano. He must have thought that it had been sequestered when Strozzi was exiled to Padua on the return of the Medici to Florence in 1434, but in fact Strozzi took it with him. It is no wonder that Traversari wished to use this manuscript as a textual source, for it is dated 992. [265]

In early January 1437 Traversari anticipated the imminent completion of his Dionysius translation and he intended to turn immediately to the *Homilies on Matthew*, but he had heard no word· from Cosimo or Niccoli regarding the Strozzi manuscript or the procuring of the scribes he had requested, and he urged Fra Michele to ask them to respond to his requests. Meanwhile he had moved from Fonte Buona to the monastery at Soci in order to extricate himself more completely from the affairs of the Order and to devote himself more fully to scholarship. [266]

Traversari's hopes for returning to the peace of patristic scholarship were rudely jarred. In that very month the smoldering resistance of the Camaldulensian Hermits to his efforts at reform flared into open revolt. Almost all of 1437 he spent embroiled in this controversy. [267] Not until April 1438 during the Council with the Greeks at Ferrara, did he write to Fra Michele that amidst the negotiations at the Council he was thinking about bringing the translation to completion. A close friend had made accessible to him the Greek text of the second part of the *Homilies*; and he· hoped to find the first part among the Greek contingent at Ferrara, but Michele should be prepared to send the Grottaferrata volume of the first forty-five

homilies in case he could not discover it. [268] A week later, on
13 April, he wrote to the Pope that he intended to finish his
translation of the *Homilies on Matthew*, [269] but this is the last
reference to it. Traversari soon became completely involved in
scholarship directly related to the conciliar debates. When in the
fall of 1439 he at last returned to Fonte Buona, where he
anticipated taking up patristics again, he had but a few months
to live. Judging from Traversari's correspondence, it seems
unlikely that he completed translating any significant part of
the *Homilies on Matthew*, nor has any such manuscript been
discovered. But a decade later Parentucelli, then Pope Nicholas
V, commissioned George of Trebizond to translate this along
with other Greek patristic works. The Byzantine scholar left
unaltered Anianus' version of the first twenty-five homilies, but
he did translate all the remainder. [270]

It is intriguing that Pope Eugenius IV should have charged
Traversari with the translation of Chrysostom's *Homilies on
Matthew*, for in the twelfth century Eugenius III had
commissioned Burgundio of Pisa to render these homilies into
Latin. In many ways Eugenius IV sought to emulate his
predecessor, an endeavor Traversari had encouraged from the
outset by sending to him Bernard's *De consideratione*, which
had been originally addressed to Eugenius III. [271] Although
Traversari makes no mention of Burgundio's translation, he was
doubtless familiar, at least indirectly, with Burgundio as a
translator, since Poggio had complained to Niccoli of his too
literal versions of Chrysostom's *Homilies on John* and *Homilies
on Acts*. Burgundio's *Homilies on Matthew* were not widely
disseminated, but a copy was present in the library of the
Franciscan monastery of S. Croce in Florence, a collection
Traversari had utilized as a source of Greek texts. [72]

Although Traversari's translations of Chrysostom's homilies
were but a partial accomplishment of his intended projects and
never formally published, they were nonetheless an important
development in his patristic scholarship. They made evident to
the humanist audience that Chrysostom's theology centered on
the elucidation of Scripture in the service of preaching, and
thereby helped restore to western consciousness the patristic
view that the fundamental task of theology was Biblical

exegesis. Moreover, the homilies gave impetus to a major emphasis of mid Quattrocento patristic scholarship. In addition to George of Trebizond's numerous translations of patristic exegesis including Cyril of Alexandria's commentaries on Leviticus and John as well as Chrysostom's *Homilies on Matthew*, Lilius Tifernas translated and dedicated to Nicholas V Chrysostom's sixteen *Sermones de patientia Job,* and Francesco di Mariotto Aretino translated and dedicated to Cosimo de' Medici Chrysostom's *Homilies on John* (c.1459) and *Homilies on I Corinthians* (1457). [273] Chrysostom's homilies on the Pauline Epistles provide a vivid picture of late fourth century Christianity in Antioch, for they are filled with topical allusions — to rites, ecclesiastical discipline, the moral life of Christians in the city, the devotion of the solitaries in the surrounding countryside. As such they would have enlarged Traversari's historical comprehension of Christian antiquity, but his main interest was in using them as pastoral and ethical works. Indeed he translated first the homilies on the "Pastoral Epistles — Titus, and I and II Timothy. In the midst of completing the *Homilies on I Timothy* he wrote to Niccoli:

> I cannot have enough of the miraculous and most delightful teaching of this man. Indeed, in my judgment, no one, among the Greeks or the Latins, has seized more usefully upon this kind of discourse. These fiery exhortations to the highest moral conduct and to the *studia pietatis* cannot be praised as highly as they deserve. With what care does he sow into the hearts of his audience love of virtue, affection for God, hatred of sins, and contempt for the world! But I will not run on longwindedly about obvious things. [274]

The ethico-spiritual concern which dominated Traversari's religious outlook was also the emphasis of his Scriptural study. He did not, like Manetti in the 1450's, examine the historico-critical question of the textual traditions of Scripture. [275] Nor did he, like Valla, turn the methods of humanist critical philology on the Latin text of Scripture as the basis for assessing the validity of scholastic formulations of such

central doctrines as the Trinity, the sacraments, and grace. [276]
And yet by emphasizing the spiritual power of patristic sources,
especially the Greek Fathers, he helped undermine the
dominance of scholastic theology and thus prepare the way for
these more revolutionary developments of humanist theological
studies.

Traversari's final published translation was a new Latin
version of the writings of Ps.-Dionysius the Areopagite. The
Ps.-Dionysius corpus consists of four treatises: *De caelesti
hierarchia*, which explains how the nine angelic orders, divided
into three triads, mediate God to man; *De ecclesiastica
hierarchia*, which describes the clerical orders of bishop, priest,
and deacon as the image of the heavenly world; *De divinis
nominibus*, which discusses the being and attributes of God; and
De mystica theologia, which sets forth the *via negativa* ascent of
the soul to mystic union with the divine. Also included in the
corpus are ten letters as supplements to the teachings in the
treatises. The author of these works clearly wished to be
identified with Dionysius, the member of the Athenian
Areopagus, who was converted by St. Paul (Acts. 17: 34). Not
only does he dedicate the treatises to Paul's disciple, Timothy,
and address the letters to the Apostle John, and Bishops Titus
and Polycarp, among other early Church leaders, but he also
asserts that he witnessed at Heliopolis the eclipse of the sun
which occurred at Christ's death, and that he was present with
Peter and James at the funeral of the Virgin Mary. While
authorship is still a matter of dispute, it is clear that the writings
could not have originated before the end of the fifth century,
for their neo-Platonism produces the thought, at times
verbatim, of both Plotinus (d. 270) and Proclus (d. 485). Both
the Latin Middle Ages and Byzantium, however, regarded them
as the works of Paul's disciple. Accorded apostolic authority
they exerted enormous influence in both Western and Eastern
Christianity, especially in the promotion of mysticism. [277]

There are four medieval Latin versions of the Ps.-Dionysius
corpus. It was first translated in the early ninth century by
Hilduin, Abbot of St-Denis, who not only accepted Dionysius as
Paul's disciple, but identified him as well with the martyr saint
Dionysius of Paris, patron saint of France. In the 860's John

Scotus Eriugena, the Carolingian Greek scholar, produced a new and improved adaptation, which was widely diffused in the Middle Ages. In the latter twelfth century John Sarrazin, who had traveled widely in the Greek East, rendered the Ps.-Dionysius corpus anew into Latin. And, finally, Robert Grosseteste made a translation in the first half of the thirteenth century. In addition, numerous medieval theologians made commentaries on all or parts of the Dionysius corpus, including Scotus Eriugena, Hugh of St-Victor, Albertus Magnus, and Thomas Aquinas. [278]

As early as 1424 Traversari had access to two Greek manuscripts of Ps.-Dionysius' works from Niccoli's library. [279] But it was not until about 1430 that he contemplated making a translation, and in March 1431 he wrote to Niccoli, then in the Veneto:

> Of Dionysius I see what you feel. Dearest Niccolò, it was the entreaties of many which forced me to undertake the translation of Dionysius, for the extreme difficulty of the work made me very hesitant to enter upon it. Nor was it ever my thought to exclude my translation from your judgment. But I never presented it to you because I regarded it as unworthy of your reading. Abandoning all that I had previously done, I began again after your departure to render Dionysius into Latin. And by now perhaps I might have finished it entirely, except that I was diverted by the burden of cares imposed on me. I had completed *De caelesti hierarchia* and much of *De ecclesiastica hierarchia* when I was charged with this burden. I showed my translation to Tommaso [Parentucelli] not so that he might turn my head with flattery, as you seem to feel − how rightly you discern this in a monk and friend who has now spent thirty years in the work of God you may judge yourself! − but that he might give his frank judgment about it. [280]

During this same period, probably before January 1431 when Traversari assumed the position of Sub- Prior of S.Maria degli

Angeli, he also completed the translation of the Ps.-Dionysius letters. In May 1431, Cardinal Orsini, apparently one of the "many" who had urged Traversari to make a new Latin version of the Dionysius corpus, entreated Traversari to send, as soon as his taks permitted, the emended transcription of the letters. [281]

Traversari was awestruck by the Dionysius writings, and believed that a special state of religious tranquillity was essential to the task of translating them. In November 1432 when he returned to the Chrysostom homilies on the Pauline Epistles, he wrote to his brother:

> I dare not yet touch Dionysius at all, since truly many disturbances stand in the way. Nor am I fit to shake them off. If, the Lord willing and aroused by our prayers, the turbulence subsides and tranquillity returns, I will dare to enter with Moses into that darkness more full of grace than any light, so that from there I may hear the voice of the Lord. Nor will I hesitate to apply myself wholeheartedly also to the translation of this divine work. [282]

Not until April 1436 did enough tranquillity return for Traversari to return to his task. By early January 1437, having devoted himself "insatiably to these studies, desiring to make up for lost time," he had completed most of *De divinis nominibus*, and he sent letters to four Cardinals, including Orsini, announcing his progress and seeking funds to supplement the Pope's insufficient subsidy for the cost of parchment and scribes. Finally, on 18 March, he finished the treatises; and he then asked Michele to send him the previously translated letters of Dionysius so that he could add them to the manuscript. He remarked, however, that some revisions were still necessary before he could return the whole to Michele for final transcription. The last reference to the matter is in a letter of 27 September 1437 where he acknowledged receipt of Michele's finished copy in Bologna, and there had given it to Parentucelli to read over. In the spring of 1437 he had contemplated dedicating the work to Niccolò Albergati, the Cardinal Bishop of Bologna and Parentucelli's patron, but the published translation has no dedicatory letter. Was this omission the consequence of Traversari's pique at Albergati's veto of the welcoming oration he had prepared for the arrival in Venice of the Greek contingent to the Council of Ferrara? Or was it simply that immersion in scholarly preparations for the Council forestalled formal publication? [283]

Traversari's Dionysius was probably the most widely read of all his translations, and it was one of the most highly praised as well. Vespasiano reports that he heard Pope Nicholas V (Parentucelli) say, regarding the Dionysius, "that his was so worthy, that it was better understood in this simple text than in the others with their infinite comments." [284] Manetti, as we have seen, cited it as an example of a humanist translation which had improved on medieval literal versions, and Cusanus also preferred Traversari's translation. [285] In 1492 Ficino made a new translation of Ps.-Dionysius' *De divinis nominibus* and *De mystica theologia*, as part of his vast project of producing Latin versions of all of Plato and the neo-Platonists. [286] Lefèvre d'Étaples, however, chose Traversari's version for his publication of the Dionysius corpus in Paris in 1499, and John Colet used it for the abstract of the Ps.-Dionysius *Hierarchies* which he made at Oxford, probably in the fall of 1498. [287]

Although Traversari was thoroughly read in the early Greek and Latin Fathers, he expressed no doubts regarding the authenticity of the Dionysius corpus. Indeed in the oration which he delivered to the Council of Basel in August 1436, shortly after his arrival as Papal Nuncio, he argued that the hierarchy of ecclesiastical orders corresponded to the celestial hierarchy, confirmation for which could be found in Dionysius. While some suppose, he remarked, and try to prove from the Pauline Epistles, that the Apostle Paul made no distinction between bishops and priests, "Dionysius teaches the necessity of distinction; he was the disciple of the Apostle, and the one to whom (we rightly believe), as in a pure and capacious vessel, Paul poured out the heavenly mysteries which he heard when rapt to the third heaven." [288] Within two decades of Traversari's translation, however, Lorenzo Valla questioned their authenticity. Commenting in his *Adnotationes in Novum Testamentum* (c. 1453-57) on Acts 17:34, he noted first that the Areopagus was a law court, not a place of philosophical disputation. Paul therefore converted one of the judges, not a philosophic sage. Then, citing Ambrose and Jerome, he concluded that the eclipse of the sun at Christ's death was only a regional phenomenon, and that no one of the ancients mentioned witnessing an eclipse in Athens at that time. Next, and most tellingly, he pointed out that none of the Greek or Latin Fathers before Gregory the Great (d.604) mentioned the works of Dionysius. Finally he noted the conclusion of the most erudite of contemporary Byzantine theologians that the author of the Dionysius corpus was Apollinaris of Laodicea (c.310-c.390). [289] Valla's doubts, though reiterated by some sixteenth-century scholars such as Grocyn, did not find general support until the nineteenth century. And, in the latter half of the Quattrocento, Ps.-Dionysius provided the best model and, more importantly, the apostolic authority, for the fusion of Christianity and Platonism which the Florentine neo-Platonists so ardently sought.

An overall assessment of the more than two decades Traversari dedicated to Greek patristic scholarship must emphasize primarily the remarkable range of his studies. If at first he focused on the rather parochial concern for the monastic vocation, from the mid-1420's his extensive reading and translating embraced many of the principal works of the leading Greek Fathers, and the entire course of historical development in Greek Christianity from the Apostolic Age to the great Ecumenical Councils of the fourth to sixth centuries. Preoccupation with ecclesiastical affairs in the 1430's curtailed his scholarly activity and left incomplete his planned translations of Chrysostom's New Testament homilies. Nevertheless the total output of some two dozen versions of patristic treatises, saints' lives, and Biblical homilies compares favorably to the achievements of Bruni and others in classical Greek scholarship.

As we have seen, Traversari's translations were frequently prompted by occasional considerations — the availability of a text, the stimulation of current reading, the suggestion of a learned patron. No rigorous theological principle guided his selection, and indeed at first glance his choices seem merely to be isolated examples of patristic "monuments." Yet his understanding of the significance of Greek patristic literature emerges. The Greek Fathers were less admired as profound thinkers on the central mysteries of Christian truth than as the heroic architects of the Church, who, inflamed by the Holy Spirit, inspired fervent adherence to the Faith as much by the exemplary nature of their lives as by the eloquence of their works. He stressed their articulate and perceptive treatment of the moral and psychological dimensions of faith, not their metaphysical speculation. Hence, he translated Gregory Nazianzen's orations *De obitu patris* and *De pace* rather than the celebrated five "Theological Orations" which were the fruit of Gregory's long study and meditation on the Trinity. These were subsequently translated in the Quattrocento, c.1462, by Pietro Balbo, the close friend of Cusanus, who was indeed concerned with speculative theology. [290] The absence in Chrysostom of speculative and abstract theological thought, the rhetorical quality of his writings, his prominence as a great preacher, ecclesiastical reformer, and pastor of souls, above all his emphasis on the union of the *studia virtutis* and *studia pietatis* were all congenial to Traversari's humanist mentality. In Chrysostom's treatises and Biblical homilies Traversari found not the "arid" dialectical analysis of doctrinal propositions which he rejected as meaningless in scholastic theological inquiry, but rather an involvement with the Scriptural text and a fervent, charismatic exhortation to the life of faith.

The clearest expression of Traversari's ethico-spiritual approach to the Fathers is to be found in the dedicatory letter of his translation of the *Sermons* of St. Ephraem to Cosimo de' Medici, where he describes his contact with the writings of St. Ephraem as a personal encounter.

Recently I came upon a pilgrim from Syria (so they said) of advanced years, tall in stature, but bent over with age, with mild and decorous features presenting an appearance of holiness, and his eyes filled with tears. But these traits detracted nothing from his dignity, and indeed seemed to add to his authority and grace. This perpetual profusion of tears did not make his face seem hideous or wretched, but

> rather more serene and beautiful. He aroused
> affection in all who saw him.

Attracted by so much grace and dignity, Traversari longed to
speak with him, "hoping . . . I might perceive much pleasure
and utility from his conversation." When he greeted the
stranger, he found he knew Greek. He embraced him joyfully,
kissed his holy lips, and invited him to his cell.

> When we sat down, I perceived from his first words
> that he was a man knowledgeable in divine matters,
> aglow with exceptional piety, burning with the ardor
> of divine charity, solicitous, attentive, vigilant,
> stirring with his speech any torpor or idleness,
> inclined to pangs of conscience (which his tears
> clearly manifested), inimical to slacking and the
> harmful sense of security, gentle, mild, kindly, always
> reproving sins and praising virtue, powerfully inciting
> us with fear-inspiring supplication to love of God,
> contempt for the world, and to seeking eternal
> rewards. Good God, what joy, what comfort, how
> much profit I obtained from his worthy lips, when
> for many nights and days he conversed continually
> with me! Nothing can be conceived or expressed
> more graceful in appearance, more health-giving in
> doctrine, more precious, delightful, and welcome in
> companionship. In the midst of this joy, which
> affected me for many days, you, in whom I delight so
> much and to whom I owe everything, often came into
> mind. I wished you could participate in my joy and
> pleasure, and if possible have a taste of this guest. But
> it seemed extremely difficult, for he was wholly
> ignorant of our language. For your consolation and
> convenience, however, I persuaded him to learn Latin
> . . and with me teaching in a few days he learned our
> language. Indeed in my judgment he spoke better and
> with more erudition in Latin than in Greek.

Cosimo should receive this venerable guest with all honor,
veneration, and reverence, setting aside all public and private
business in order to confer with him, unencumbered with
worldly matters.

This you can always do with profit, but I think that in this period of sacred and solemn fasting it is necessary for you to do so. One ought to appropriate holy days not only for the usual devotion to good works, but also for the diligent examination of conscience. We can hardly satisfy this unless we set aside for a while our mortal occupations, cares, and thoughts. For how, when our eyes are confused with the dust of these cares so that we cannot even grasp and judge what is before our eyes, can we penetrate into our hearts and lay bare what is hidden within?

For this the sermons of St. Ephraem are particularly useful, since

all of his discourse is on God, divine things, penitence, future judgment, eternal life, the joy of the just, the pain of the reprobate, the perfecting of virtue, and the rooting out of sins. He approves that laudible judgment of Plato, that the highest philosophy is meditation on death, for his whole work seems to aim at this. [291]

Recognition of one's spiritual condition, examination of conscience, striving for virtue – these were the moral and psychological elements of lay piety which Traversari encouraged in his Florentine and Venetian humanist audience.

Just as Bruni, Guarino, Valla, and other humanist Greek scholars recovered to the Latin West the patrimony of Greek classical thought on politics, ethics for civic life, and history, so Traversari's scholarship made available the Greek Fathers' spiritual counsel regarding the monastic vocation, moral virtue, and Christian piety. In so doing he not only revealed the patristic adherence to the rhetorical culture so admired by the humanists, and the importance they attributed to eloquence as the exhortation to sincere belief and to the pursuit of virtue, but he also revealed Christian antiquity as the age of the Church most animated by spiritual energy, fervent faith, and heroic leadership. Just as Bruni saw in Republican Rome and Periclean Athens the intellectual creativity and moral energy which were being reborn in the Florentine *polis*, so Traversari hoped that the rediscovery of the pristine fervor of Christian antiquity would inspire the reform and renewal of the contemporary Church and religion. In his career as monastic reformer, involvement in the papal-conciliar struggle, and work for reunion of the Greek and Latin Churches he brought these hopes to bear on the pressing ecclesiastical issues of his day.

CHAPTER IV
PATRISTICS AND REFORM

On 3 March 1431 Gabriel Condulmer, Cardinal of Siena and Protector of the Camaldulensian Order, was elected Pope Eugenius IV. Born in 1383 of a Venetian patrician family, Condulmer as a youth had embraced the religious life. He collaborated in founding a chapter of reformed canons at S. Giorgio d'Alba in Venice, and he gave his entire fortune of 20,000 florins to the poor. After serving a year as Bishop of Siena, he was named Cardinal by his uncle Pope Gregory XII in 1408. In a career filled with diplomatic missions, governorships in the papal states, and other ecclesiastical posts, he continued an active interest in promoting monastic reform.[1]

Traversari had known and admired Condulmer from the early 1420's. In dedicating his translation of Ps.-Basil's *De vera integritate virginitatis* to the Cardinal Protector in 1424, he expressed gratitude for the exceptional affection the prelate had shown him, and urged the Cardinal to read the treatise intently, for he anticipated he would take great delight in it. No work better celebrated virginity, a virtue well-known to Condulmer for he adhered to this in his own life.[2]

Traversari also supported and encouraged the Cardinal Protector's efforts to reform the Camaldulensians. In August 1430 he wrote to him approving his convocation of a General Chapter of the Order to work for reform. Traversari expected that through the Cardinal's leadership the Chapter would lead "to the praise of God, the propagation of holy religion, and the observance of the Rule."[3] Hence Traversari was especially elated at the announcement of Condulmer's election as Pope. He wrote to Giustiniani:

> We were marvelously moved when we heard the joyous news that your fellow citizen Gabriel, a man of the highest reverence, had become Roman Pontiff. Great hope has arisen that not only Italy, long

> agitated by war, will enjoy repose, but also that all
> things will turn for the better and the whole world
> return to ancient holiness. God be with us and heed
> our prayers![4]

Traversari expressed himself in even more exultant terms to Niccoli. "Our city manifests the greatest delight. A new dawn seems to shine forth."[5]

Traversari wasted no time in attempting to realize favorable results from the Eugenius' unexpected election. In a long letter to the new Pope dated 10 March 1431, he charted a vast program of reform intended to regenerate the spiritual fervor of the apostolic and patristic Church. Bemoaning the fallen state of the contemporary Church, Traversari begins by contrasting the limited sphere of Christendom, reduced to but part of Europe by the Turkish expansion, with the universal sway of Christianity in the patristic age.

> Nearly the whole domain in which the dignity of the
> Christian name gloriously flourished, where there
> were so many lights of holiness, so many temples of
> divine wisdom, so many instruments of the Holy
> Spirit, has fallen — what a calamity! — to the heathen
> and the enemies of Christ. Africa — where first under
> that glorious martyr Cyprian, then under Augustine,
> gathered celebrated Councils attended by so many
> Fathers to defend the purity of the Faith against the
> perfidious, and in which the Novatians, Donatists,
> Pelagians, Manichaeans, and Arians were vanquished
> by the most powerful reasons, and so much condu-
> cive to moral discipline was instituted — all has been
> surrendered to the heathen. All Asia, and not a little
> of Europe, where universal synods were gathered
> from the whole globe, are likewise under the domin-
> ion of the heathen. All Greece, where there were so
> many heralds of the divine word, so many Philoso-
> phers of Christ, languishes in inveterate schism, and
> for its perfidy is pressed hard by the barbarians.

Moreover the whole West "where nearly alone the religion of Christ remains inviolate" is disturbed by the din of war, and

Italy itself exhausted by long-persisting devastation. Eugenius, however, should not despair of the seeming difficulties of restoring the Church to its former state. The Apostles, though poor and simple, and despite the greatest difficulties which gave no ground for human hope, did not shrink from the task of preaching. "Trusting in the word of God and in the promises of the Lord, these spirited men traversed the whole world. Without worldly power they overcame the kingdoms of the heathen. Though simple, they confuted the subtle wisdom of the philosophers." Quoting Isaiah (L.2), Traversari rhetorically asks, " 'Is the hand of the Lord shortened,' so that he cannot redeem, and what he once worked is not able to perform again? It is our sins in short which are at fault. For indeed if through resolute faith and unfaltering devotion we depended on God alone, . . . who does not know that what he did in the past for his saints will be done in the same way for us?" In the task of reform, therefore, Eugenius must have recourse to prayer, and in this effort ascend to the loftiest levels of his mind. There should be nothing modest or humble in his thoughts. As Pope he is vice-gerent of God on earth. "What do you fear? Our King, the Son of God, descended here so that he might make men gods. For if the Word of God is given to all who receive him, how much more perfectly do we consider it given to you, who have undertaken the vindication of others?"

Eugenius' first priority must be reform of the secular clergy, "who from former virtue and holiness have turned aside, and neglecting former strictness have become dissipated in licentiousness." Likewise he should restrengthen the lax religious orders so that they might once again "walk in the way of the Gospels." Once the clergy begin to adhere to God's commandments, the populace will eagerly follow, "for faith thrives where signs of holiness shine forth." The schismatics, whether recent (i.e. the Hussites) or long-standing (i.e. the Greeks), should be overcome by reason, not force of arms, and thus one catholic flock be gathered.

To make clearly evident to Eugenius what was fitting to the high office of the papacy, Traversari promised to send as "the gift of my poverty" Bernard's *De consideratione*. He promised also to answer Eugenius' request of the previous year and provide him with an emended text of the *Registrum Gregorii*, the large body of official letters written by Pope Gregory the Great during his pontificate.

In closing, Traversari commended the Camaldulensian Order to the Pontiff's protection, "and especially our monastery, where the monastic life has been preserved whole and inviolate for one hundred and thirty-five years."[6]

A month later Traversari fulfilled his pledge to send Eugenius the *De consideratione ad Eugenium*. This treatise, Bernard's last work, addressed to Pope Eugenius III (1145-53), a fellow Cistercian monk before his election to the papacy, was a complete exposition of the principles which should guide the new Pope. In particular, he admonished Eugenius to avoid ecclesiastical abuses and exhorted him to persist in the monastic virtues. The last book stresses the need for contemplation in order to know God's will.[7] Traversari asserted that this treatise, which set forth the proper norms for administering the pontificate, was particularly suitable for Eugenius IV, since the new Pope, like his namesake, had ascended to the papacy after early spiritual training in the monastery. Doubtless had Bernard been alive in their era, he would have sent the *De consideratione* to the new Eugenius. There is evident throughout Bernard's burning zeal for "the restoration of ancient holiness and decorum into the body of the Church. ... I beseech you, Blessed Eugenius, to read and reread this work, so that with your heart full of piety, you will be aroused to deeds of action."[8]

Traversari's general notion of reform, evident in these two letters to Eugenius IV, derives from the central concerns of his patristic scholarship and reflects the assumptions of humanist thought. It is the ancient Church, the Church of the patristic age and the Ecumenical Councils, which is held up as the model. The present age is deplored for its decadence, particularly the worldliness of the clergy. But there is no specific analysis of the ecclesiastical reasons for clerical abuses. All that is needed is the opening of the mind and the conversion of the heart. Sincere conviction, followed by resolute action — both inspired by the power of oratory — will bring change. Trust in God and pursuit of spiritual virtue will be decisive in restoring the Church to ancient holiness. Like Chrysostom, Traversari believed that "one man who burns with zeal is sufficient to set straight a whole people."[9] If that one man is also Pope, then all is possible.

In certain respects Eugenius IV seems to have shared Traversari's ideas of reform. He did strive to emulate his namesake: he was personally abstemious during his pontificate, recited daily the prayers of the monastic office, and requested burial in St. Peter's next to Eugenius III.[10] Moreover he began his reign with auspicious signs of reform measures regarding the clergy: before the end of March 1431 he issued a severe prohibition of clerical concubinage; and before the end of his first year as Pope he made efforts to curtail mishandling of the collation of benefices, forbade penitentiaries from demanding any but established fees, and worked to eradicate expectative favors (i.e. promise of appointment to a benefice on the death of the incumbent). All were abuses in which the investment value of a benefice threatened the exercise of spiritual office. In February 1432 he issued a long instruction governing the conduct of the Roman clergy, which was directly under his authority. Later in the decade he attempted to curtail the number of Curial officials.[11]

Significantly, also, monastic reform drew Eugenius' particular attention. By authorizing the foundation of Observant houses and the appointment of Observant visitors with broad powers to exercise discipline, Eugenius gave papal sanction and encouragement to a movement which from the latter fourteenth century had attracted proponents in both the mendicant and the older orders. In Traversari's lifetime it was the Franciscan San Bernardino of Siena, and the Dominican Sant' Antonino, Prior of San Marco in Florence, who were the most prominent promoters of mendicant reform. Leadership among the Benedictines was exerted by Ludovico Barbo (1381-1443), Abbot of S. Giustina in Padua. Named commendatory Abbot of this collapsed Cluniac abbey in 1408, Barbo became an authentic spiritual leader. He promoted strict adherence to the Benedictine Rule, and his monastery became the mother-house for a congregation of reformed abbeys throughout Italy. From one of these, Subiaco, Observant reform spread to Austria (Melk,

1419) and thence to Germany. By the end of the fifteenth century Barbo's movement had touched Spain where the reformed congregation of Valladolid was created; and from one of these monasteries, Montserrat, came the celebrated Spanish Biblical scholar Ximenes.[12] In the period 1432-35 Eugenius IV issued a series of papal bulls which systematized the new constitutional arrangements of Barbo's reform – the abolition of the abbot for life, the prohibition of the commendatory abbot, and the vesting of authority in an annual general chapter and visitors.[13] Characteristic of Barbo's reform was a renewed emphasis on the Benedictine vocation for study and learning, and the Benedictine abbeys again acquired excellent libraries, in large part as the result of bequests of humanist scholars and patrons. Palla Strozzi, for instance, left much of his library to S. Giustina; and Antonio Corbinelli, as we have seen, left his excellent Greek and Latin classical and patristic library to the Badia Fiorentina.[14] The Benedictine abbeys thus came to share in the scholarship of the humanist movement.[15]

Barbo himself was entrusted with the task of reforming the Badia Fiorentina. His brief visit to Florence c. 1418 allowed him to assess the collapsed state of the monastery, and to appoint Gomes Ferreira to carry out the work of Observant reform.[16] It seems to be this visit to which Traversari refers in a letter to Francesco Barbaro, where he expressed singular admiration for the Abbot and praised him as an extraordinary man of religion.[17] Since in 1420 Traversari excused his inability to furnish Barbaro with a copy of his Climacus translation by explaining that he had sent it to S. Giustina of Padua,[18] he must have been familiar with the Observant Benedictine reform which Barbo promoted.

Before the end of 1431 Traversari found himself suddenly thrust from the *vita contemplativa* of S. Maria degli Angeli and engaged in the *vita activa* of Observant monastic reform. In October of that year the Cardinal Protector of the Camaldulensians, John Cervantes, acting according to the wishes of Eugenius IV, convened a General Chapter of the Order at Bertinoro in the Romagna in order to work for reform. There the General of the Order, Benedetto Lanci da Forli, because of fiscal malfeasance and lax administration of discipline was

Fig. 1a. Hermits' cells at the Eremo, Camaldoli. *La Scala New York/ Florence.*

santa maria degliagnioli

Fig. 1b. Mid-fifteenth-century depiction of S. Maria degli Angeli, from codex of Marco di Bartolommeo Rustici (d. 1457). *Gabinetto Fotografico – Sopr. Gallerie – Florence.*

Fig. 2. Lorenzo Monaco, "L'Incoronazione della Vergine," Uffizi Gallery, Florence. *La Scala New York/Florence.*

Fig. 3a. Lorenzo Ghiberti, Reliquary for Sts. Protus, Hyacinth, and Nemesius, Bargello, Florence. *La Scala New York/Florence.*

Fig. 3b. Miniature portrait of Traversari, from preface to his translation of Diogenes Laertius, Biblioteca Laurenziana, Florence, Plut. 65, 22, f. 1ʳ, s. XV.

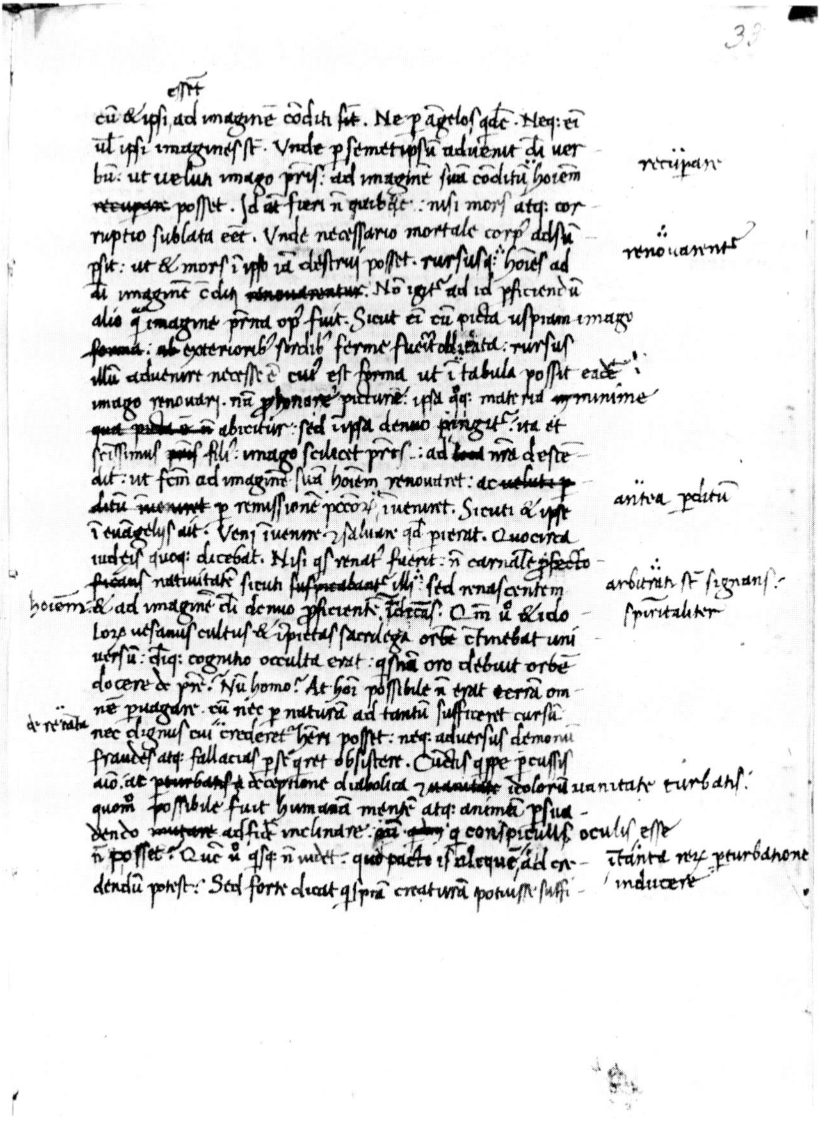

cū & ipsi ad imagine coditū sit. Ne p̄ agtios q̄dc . Neq̄: ei
ut ipsi imagine [e]st. Vnde p̄ semetipsū aduenit dī uer-
bū: ut ueluti imago pris: ad imagine suā coditū hoiem
recupare posset. Sd at fieri n̄ quibāt: nisi mors atq̄: cor-
ruptio sublata eet. Vnde necessario mortale corp̄ assū-
psit: ut & mors i ipso iā destrui posset. rursusq̄: hoies ad
dī imagine c diū renouarentur. No igit ad iā pficiendū ū
alio q̄ imagine primā op̄ fuit. Sicut ei cū picta usp̄iam imago
forma: ab exterorib̄ sordib̄ ferme fuit obliterata: rursus
illū aduenire necesse e cui est forma ut i tabula posset eade
imago renouari. nā pp̄t[er] picturē: ipsā qā: malit iā minime
q[uo]d abicitur: sed ipsa denuo pingit[ur]. ita et
s[anct]issimus p[at]ris fil[ius] imago scilicet pris: ad i[ma] na d[e]stē
ad: ut fcm ad imagine suā hoiem renouaret: de uolens p-
ditū re[ddere] p remissione p[e]c[cat]orū uenerunt. Sicut & ipse
i euāgelys ait. Venj iuenire q̄ saluari qd perut. Quocirca
iustis quoq̄: dicebat. Nisi q̄s renat[us] fuerit: n̄ carnale p̄fecto
ficiuns natiuitate sicut suspicabant illi. Sed n̄ nascentem
hoiem: & ad imagine dī demuo pficientē. Idcirc̄. Cū ū & ido
lorū ueesanus cultus & i pietas sacrilega orbe c̄tinebat uni
uersū: atq̄: cognito occulta erat: q̄snā oro debuit orbe
docere & p̄n. Nū homo? At hoc possibile n̄ erat: cerra omne puidgdn. cū nec p natura ad tantū sufficerent cursu
nec dignus cui crederet fieri posset: neq̄: aduersus demoni
fraudes atq̄: fallacias p̄ staret obsistere. Cuidus q̄ppe pcussis
aio: at plūbans a diuinitate diabolica uanitate icolorū uanitate turbatus:
quom possibile fuit humaā mēte atq̄: anima p̄suad
dendo ad sui i clinare: q̄ conspicuillig oculis este
n̄ posset: Que ū q̄se n̄ uidet: quo pacto i aleque ad cr[e]-
dendū pot[e]st: Sed forte dicat q̄ p̄ra creaturā potuisse suffi-

Figure 4. Rough draft, in Traversari's hand, of his translation of
Athanasius' *De incarnatione Verbi*, Biblioteca Nazionale Centrale, Florence, Conv. Soppr. J. VIII. 8, f. 33r.

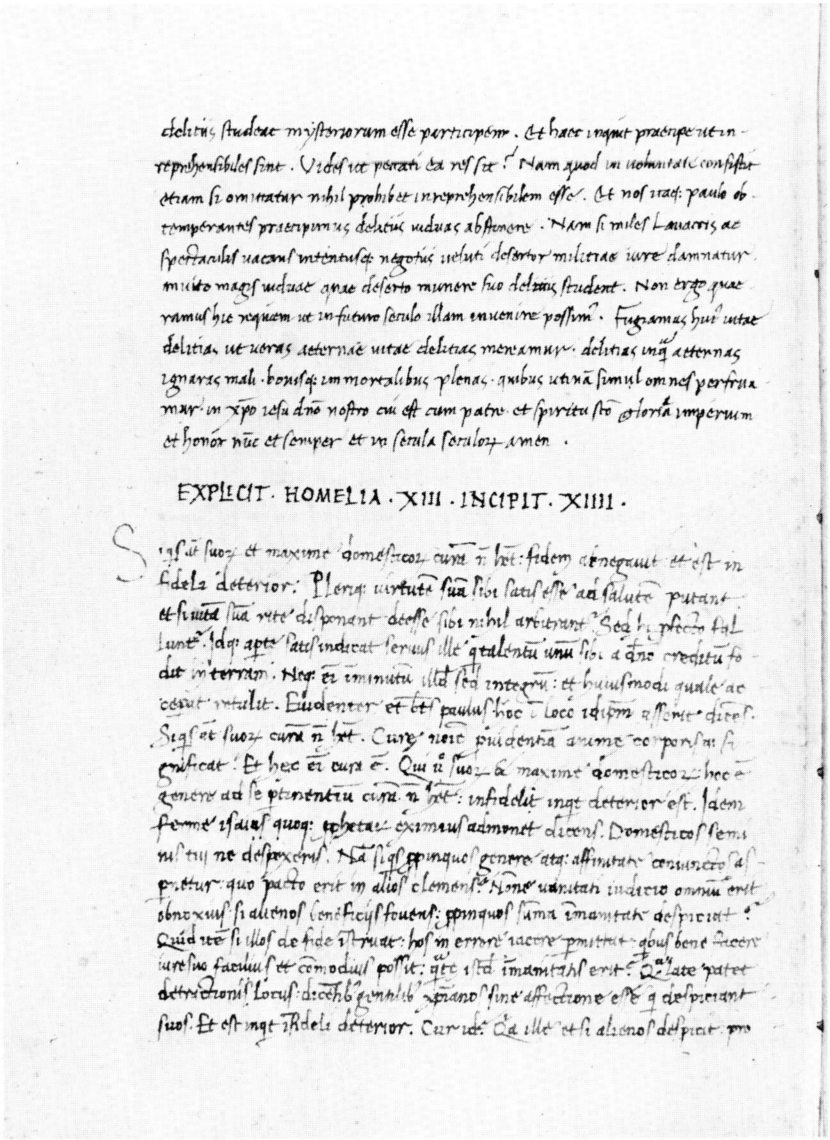

EXPLICIT. HOMELIA. XIIII. INCIPIT. XIIII.

Fig. 5. The autograph ms. of Traversari's translation of Chrysostom's *Homilies on I Timothy,* Biblioteca Nazionale Centrale, Florence, Conv. Soppr. J. VI. 6, f. 88ᵛ. The handwriting of the upper part of the page is Niccoli's; that of the lower is Traversari's.

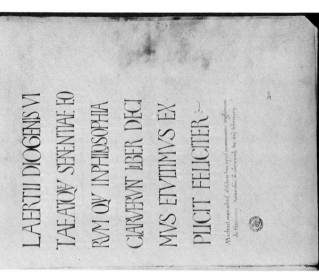
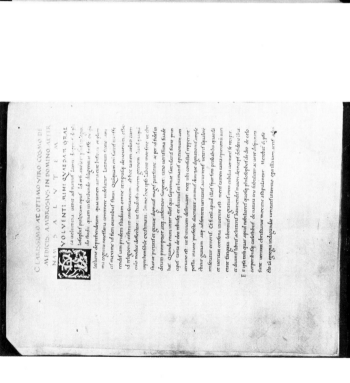

Figs. 6a and b. A fine example of the humanistic script produced at S. Maria degli Angeli, these are the first and last pages of the presentation copy (to Cosimo de' Medici) of Traversari's translation of Diogenes Laertius, written by Fra Michele. Biblioteca Laurenziana, Florence, Plut. 65, 21, ff. 1v and 210r.

Fig. 7. Bessarion (l.) and Cesarini (r.) reading the Decree of Union at the Council of Florence. Detail of Filarete's Porta Argentea (1445), St. Peter's, Rome. *Musei Vaticani, Archivio Fotografico, XXXII. 127. 57.*

Fig. 8. Lorenzo Ghiberti, detail of the "Gates of Paradise" to the Baptistry, Florence. The meeting of Solomon and Sheba depicted in the scene is a figural reference to the union of the Latin and Greek Churches at the Council of Florence. *La Scala New York/Florence.*

forced to resign; and on 26 October Traversari was elected in his stead, probably a reflection of the Pope's express intentions.[19]

The change in Traversari's life was dramatic. When he attended the General Chapter, it was the first time he had left S. Maria degli Angeli in thirty years. With the conclusion of the General Chapter at the end of October, he immediately began the effort to return the Camaldulensians to strict observance of the Benedictine Rule. For the next two and a half years he was almost constantly traveling, making visitations to each monastery of the Order. It was a serious, zealous, intensive effort to bring reform by direct, personal intervention in the spiritual life of each house. This effort is vividly recounted in his *Hodoeporicon*, a virtual day-by-day record of his travels from October 1431 to June 1434. In it Traversari gives careful attention to each visitation – the formal reception, solemn mass, collective and private interrogation, rebukes for lapses, exhortations to follow the strictness of the Rule – but here and there the repetitive accounts of each day's work are interrupted by dramatic episodes such as the imprisonment of Cosimo and Eugenius' flight from Rome. Moreover a sense of immediacy is conveyed by vivid descriptions of the difficulties of travel – winter blizzards in the Apennines, spring floods in the Romagna – and by his own emotional responses to seeing Lake Trasimene for the first time, to exploring the Roman ruins, to beholding the mosaics of Ravenna.

Traversari's initial assessment of the spiritual state of the Order entrusted to his care was that it had nearly collapsed in ruin.[20] Only a few monasteries earned his praise, notably S. Michele di Murano near Venice, which had been reformed by Paolo Venier, a friend of Barbo, and Abbot from 1392 to 1448.[21] Traversari wrote Venier that S. Michele possessed "the antiquae sanctitatis ac religionis decor."[22] Most others had serious shortcomings. One of his principal criticisms was the laxity of morals, particularly the failure to preserve the vow of chastity. Discovering that the nuns of a convent near Florence had engaged in surreptitious sexual activity, Traversari, incensed against these "prostitutes," threatened to burn their convent to the ground if word reached his ears of any further admission of men to their cloister. [23] More disturbing to the foundations of the monastic life was the failure to maintain cloister and the collapse of communal existence. A repeated refrain in the *Hodoeporicon* is admonition against wandering monks.

It is difficult to judge how advanced was the spiritual and material decay of the Order. A number of the more remote monasteries were depopulated, the buildings in disrepair. Others had been ravaged by war, such as S. Michele near Bologna about which Traversari corresponded with Vittorino da Feltre.[24] Traversari frequently speaks of the fiscal penury of the Order — indeed he was forced to borrow funds from Cosimo to pay for his trip to Rome.[25] Yet Camaldoli itself seems to have kept pace with the new techniques of agricultural management, consolidating its vast holdings into large *poderi* either worked directly by the monastery or rented. The 1427 *catasto* indicates that Camaldoli also earned considerable revenue from large flocks of sheep and the sale of timber from the substantial forests which surrounded the monastery. In 1382 Camaldoli came under Florentine control, and it ceded its seigneurial rights to communal legal jurisdiction. But this did not lead to lay fiscal exploitation of the monastic patrimony.[26] Undoubtedly other houses were less well-endowed than this head monastery of the Order, but there is no evidence of wholesale material collapse.

The most serious threat to the material and spiritual well-being of the monastic life was the widespread appointment of abbots *in commendam*. This meant that the office was bestowed on someone, usually a high ecclesiastical official or a powerful local lay lord, who did not possess the canonical qualifications for abbot. Originally the practice emerged in response to the desire for protection and favor, but in the thirteenth and fourteenth centuries it became a means of ecclesiastical, especially papal, patronage and a source of lay revenue. Even if the commendatory abbot did not unscrupulously exploit the fiscal resources of the monastery for his own benefit — at times they made generous endowments to the material fabric of the monastery under their control — the absence of a resident abbot effectively deprived the monastery of the *pater* and *magister* intended by the Benedictine Rule.[27] The commendatory abbot, as we have seen, was a primary target of the reform of Barbo and the Congregation of S. Giustina, and Traversari recognized the need for change in this area as well. While in Rome in the winter and spring of 1432, he attempted to persuade the Cardinals to relinquish to the Order the monasteries they held *in commendam,* but except from Cardinal Orsini, his efforts met with rebuff. [28]

Initially Traversari was highly optimistic about chances for real reform. In a letter written to his brother Girolamo in December 1431, a little over a month after his election and the beginning of his visitations, Traversari stated:

> I have great hope, my brother, of divine compassion
> for me; indeed I am practically certain that I am not
> devoid of His grace, but rather that through me as an
> instrument, however, useless, He is working what is
> pleasing to His eyes, both for my health and for those
> who are entrusted to my care. [29]

This initial optimism, however, was severely daunted by his lengthy stay in Rome awaiting Curial confirmation of his authority as General. For four months he bided his time while the administrative machinery of the Curia proceeded through its usual course. His stay was not entirely useless – he traversed the ruins with Poggio, examined papal and monastic libraries, completed his translation of the *Life of Chrysostom*, received Mariano Porcari's gift of the Hebrew text of the Old Testament – but, except for colloquies with the Pope, and more significantly with Ludovico Barbo, about the Observant reform, his effort to restore pristine spirituality to the Camaldulensians came to a halt. [30] Eventually he received Curial confirmation of his election, and verbal confirmation of the accrued privileges of his office and the Order, including exemption from certain taxes and a plenary indulgence for those who died while monks in good standing. Without the necessary funds, he was unable to obtain the actual bulls of confirmation before his departure. He was quickly disillusioned that the dedication of his translation of Chrysostom to the Pope would be accepted in lieu of the usual fees. Moreover, despite strong personal backing by Eugenius for his Observant reform efforts, Traversari failed to obtain powers he judged crucial to reform –

> The Pope was benign bowards me, but because of the
> prevailing malice of the times, he yielded nothing
> which seemed to prejudice the accustomed preroga-
> tives of the Curia. I sought, according to ancient
> practice, the right to reprove or even deprive from
> office (if such a penalty was merited) any Abbot or
> Prior of the Order. Thus, like the prophet, I could
> tear out the noxious shoots and plant what was
> useful, that is substitute for them men who were
> suitable. Henceforth, I desired the monasteries to be
> free from the Roman Curia, except in the case of the
> death of an abbot, and I requested the right of
> confirming abbots on the condition of paying the
> usual Curial taxes. Nothing of these things could I
> obtain openly, and this last least of all. [31]

Failure to obtain control over appointments was obviously a
devastating blow to Traversari's authority to initiate reform.
This, combined with the fiscal exactions of the Curia and the
failure of the Cardinals to give up their commendatory rights,
added as they were to the frustrations of waiting, led Traversari
to cry in anguish to his brother, "commend me to all the
brothers so that through their prayers I can be quickly liberated
from this western Babylon." [32]

Traversari's inability to acquire the powers essential for
reform, despite the benevolence of the Pope, indicates how
entrenched the bureaucratic apparatus of the centralized papal
monarchy was. From the Avignon period onwards, the Roman
Curia had derived revenues essential to its functioning from the
power over ecclesiastical preferment. To deprive an incumbent
from office as Traversari wished, or to make appointments
outside the Curial apparatus, threatened both political power
and financial investment. Neither was to be lightly given up.
Later, in September 1433, Traversari asked and received from
Emperor Sigismund in a personal audience in Ferrara confirmation of the imperial privileges granted to the Camaldulensians
by Sigismund's predecessors. [33] These may have had a certain
prestige value, but their practical usefulness must have been
dubious.

In the absence of institutional powers, Traversari relied primarily on force of character, on power of exhortation, and on prayer as the means to restore to his crumbling Order the "antiquae sanctitatis effigiem."

> I see my whole effort as this — that by divine power and my perpetual labor these dead members may be revived by word and example and at length become ashamed to have lain submerged so long in wretched torpor. I trust above all in the most eager hope in the Lord and in perpetual prayer that the Father may deign "to raise up from these stones children of Abraham" [Matt. 3:9] . . . . Pray therefore . . .that the Lord will illumine my heart with the light of his piety and kindle it with the flame of divine love. May He "protect me from the strife of men and the contradiction of tongues" [Psalms 30:21].[34]

Two long encyclical letters, one addressed to the Benedictines, the other to the Camaldulensians, reveal most clearly Traversari's exhortation to reform. The one to the Benedictines, written from Rome by order of Eugenius IV in 1432, begins by stressing the dignity of the monastic vocation. The monks are indeed the flower of the Church and the most illustrious of the Christian flock, since contemptuous of the allurements and pleasures of this life, they put on the yoke of Christ and take up His burden with their whole soul. Abandoning the tumults of worldly phantasms they ascend with Moses to the heights. Clinging to the Lord they enter the dazzling mists, and from there through perpetual prayer defend the whole Christian people. But the monks, by relaxing ancient vigor, have languished, and have no strength to wield their spiritual arms. Essential to their task is the conquest of carnal desire. When attacked by the venom of that ancient enemy, Satan, the monk should, imitating St. Benedict, focus his mind on Christ hung on the Cross and extinguish the fire of concupiscence with the more ardent flames of divine love. Christ, who conquered the world, will conquer the devil within once the soul is aroused to pristine fervor. Repenting past idleness and negligence, the monks should again turn their souls to the ancient spiritual delights, and by meditating day and night strive to reclaim their former dignity. "Free yourselves for prayer, silence, reading, and other spiritual exercises. Celebrate the Sabbath delights. Embrace sacred repose. Be seated with Mary at the feet of the Lord ... and strive with attentive ears to capture his celestial words. Acting thus you will be worthy of your vocation."[35]

The themes of returning to the pristine holiness of the early centuries of Christian monasticism and of turning from idleness and concupiscence to an inner devotion to Christ are present also in Traversari's missive to all the monks of the Camaldulensian Order, dated 26 March 1433. Using a prominent Scriptural metaphor, he asserts that the vineyard of which he had become guardian at the Lord's command had nearly died out: but a few of the monks wish to follow in the footsteps of the Holy Fathers by emulating their virtuous observance of the Rule. Admonishing them to contemplate the vineyard run wild with the thorns of carnal pleasures, Traversari urges them to cultivate the neglected field, uprooting the thorns and planting fruitful vines so that they might be transformed into "antiquam gratiam, atque ubertatem, et primae sanctitatis faciem." It is shameful not to imitate the example of so many noble Ancients. Indeed the foundations of the cenobitic life are to be found in the activities of the Apostles as described in Acts. Antony, Hilary, Pachomius, Basil, and Benedict, who committed the rules of monastic life to writing, all promoted it. Romuald made celebrated the monastic profession, as did Bernard and innumerable others who emulated his holiness. The glory, fame, purity, and holiness of the Camaldulensians is attested by the privileges accorded them by both Popes and Emperors. Before their eyes there stood so many examples of holiness worthy of imitation. The monks should therefore repudiate their torpor, and having compunction for their negligence return with their whole heart to the Lord. "Let us with determination seize upon the precepts of sacred instruction — let us rise up to punish our former desires. Nothing will be difficult, nothing hard, nothing bitter if the grace of compunction inflames our hearts and the love of virtue consumes the thorns of cupidity. ... What He showed forth to the saints whom we admire, He can show forth to us if we have

faith." But the monks must rid their lives of luxury and return
to frugality. Indeed, at present nothing distinguishes those who
profess a monastic vocation from those in secular life, for the
monks surpass the laity in their devotion to the delights of
meat, linen shirts, and soft mattresses, to say nothing of those
who invite the fires of perdition by violating the rule of
chastity. Especially blameworthy are the abbots, who instead of
giving examples of devotion to piety and the arduous struggle
for virtue lead monks to pleasures. Moreover, they treat other
monks as their servants, not as brothers, and act more like lords,
than fathers, in violation of all the rules of religion. Concluding,
Traversari exhorts them:

> Let us vindicate our dignity, and devote ourselves to
> being numbered among the children of God. In
> comparison to this inestimable reward all else is to be
> considered the least of concern. As St. Paul says, "I
> hold that the sufferings of this present time are not
> worthy to be compared with the glory which shall be
> revealed in us" [Romans 8: 18]. With our eyes raised
> to the heavens let us allow no honey-sweet allure-
> ments and deceptive pleasures to bring us earthward.
> In comparison to the acquisition of this most
> profound beauty, let all perceivable things be as filth
> to us. Only in God should the mind find repose. Let
> us, as John the Baptist said, "bring forth fruits
> worthy of penitence" [Luke 3: 8].... We have said
> these things as an endeavour of exhortation and
> admonition. It would be a great consolation indeed to
> us if through this exhortation your souls would yield
> and we perceive better fruit come forth. If, on the
> other hand, you persist without a sense of compunc-
> tion and refuse to change for the better, we, because
> we understand it to be our obligation, will presume to
> punish you, to the extent permitted by him who
> brought us to this office. We desire to accomplish this
> rather by exhortation than severe censuring. But for
> whoever chooses to persist in evil and not accede to
> warning, we know the words "compel them to enter"
> [Luke 14: 23]. We will exert our authority where

necessary, for what we are teaching and intending to preserve is not our own, but existed before us, above all with our Blessed Father Benedict, then as transmitted in the written Constitutions of our Order, in the General Chapter at Borgo [San Sepolcro], and then renewed in the celebrated General Chapter at Bertinoro. . . .[36]

These two encyclical letters are perhaps the best representatives of the hundreds Traversari wrote to individual monasteries, abbots, and monks in an effort to exhort, persuade, inspire, and convince his brothers of the imperative to awake from present sloth and to emulate the virtues of the Holy Fathers.[37] This massive effort was based on Traversari's optimistic trust that through the power of eloquence men's wills would be inflamed to seek the path of virtue and holiness. Another feature of his reform effort reflects the assumptions of the *studia humanitatis* as well. This was the emphasis he placed on establishing monastery schools to provide young monks with instruction both in the "fear of God" and in "letters." The curriculum of the *studia humanitatis* formed the basis of education in the schools Traversari established at Fonte Buona and at S. Maria della Rosa in Siena. This is noteworthy, for although renewed stress on education was part of Observant reform in general, the school which S. Bernardino founded emphasized not knowledge of letters, but rather command of scholastic theology and canon law.[38] Since reading, meditation, and emulation of the ancient Fathers nourished the inner spirituality, which Traversari regarded as the essence of Christian piety, education in the *studia humanitatis* was essential to the accomplishment of this. On occasions indeed Traversari felt the only real hope for reform of his Order lay with the "new progeny of Christ" being instructed in the monastery schools.[39]

In the course of the mid and latter 1430's Traversari's hope for reform changed to discouragement and finally disillusion. As early as the fall of 1432, he began to doubt there was any real desire for a return to spiritual grace; and he found himself accused of depriving the monks of their liberties. Enraged, he caustically remarked that they failed to recognize that "vera libertas in vera subiectione consistit."[40] Other obligations interfered as well with exclusive concentration on changing the Camaldulensians. In November 1432 Eugenius IV ordered Traversari, along with Gomes Ferreira, Abbot of the reformed Badia Fiorentina, to make a reform visitation to the monasteries of the Vallombrosan Order. This Order, like that of the Camaldulensians, had its origins in the monastic reform movements of the late tenth and early eleventh centuries. Its founder, Giovanni Gualberto of Florence (990-1073), favored the eremitic life, as did Romuald. In the high Middle Ages the Vallombrosans were a wealthy, powerful, and influential Tuscan Order, but by the late Middle Ages they were in decay. Traversari appealed to Eugenius to be released from this onerous additional burden, but he was unsuccessful; and so the early months of 1433 were spent traveling with Gomes to the Vallombrosan monasteries.[41] Then in 1435-36 came the journey to Basel and Vienna as Papal Nuncio.

By early 1437 Traversari had decided to extricate himself from administrative responsibilities and retire to a life of scholarship.[42] But he was almost immediately met with an open revolt of the Camaldulensian Hermits against his authority as General. Traversari had been particularly concerned with the reform of the Hermits at Camaldoli, the birth-place of the Order; and he was dismayed that his attempts to restore the life of solitary meditation there had met with resistance.[43] Exasperated by the Hermits' charges against him, and with their schemes to force his dismissal as General, Traversari wrote to Cosimo de' Medici in May 1437 that except for his reluctance to be dismissed while falsely accused, he would welcome release from the "useless burden" of his office and would delight in the opportunity to return to the life of contemplation and letters.[44] Eventually the controversy with the Hermits blew over, but for the last two years of his life Traversari was deeply involved with the council for Greek union and had little time to continue the work of monastic reform. In 1439 he wrote to Agostino da Portico, a monk of S. Maria degli Angeli whom he had named Prior of S. Maria della Rosa in Siena, that reform would be accomplished not by exhortation and persuasion but only by severe censuring.[45]

On the whole, Traversari's effort to return his Order to

Observant rule must be judged a failure. In certain monasteries where he succeeded in appointing leaders who shared his convictions there seems to have been a resurgence of austerity and spiritual piety. But no movement of real reform took hold of the Order in general. It is apparent that few of the monks shared Traversari's zeal to return to the spirituality of early Christian monasticism. His early studies of the first centuries of monasticism in both the Greek East and Latin West had inspired him with the desire to emulate their pristine fervor. But he did not succeed in making this ideal, which was so firmly rooted in the historical-spiritual assumptions of his patristic scholarship, one which could serve to inspire other monks. As Traversari himself came to realize, he was overly optimistic in trusting in the power of eloquence to convert the minds of men. The monasteries had been immersed too long in the social and economic fabric of medieval secular life to be extricated by persuasion, however forceful and eloquent. The administration of vast wealth accumulated over centuries inextricably involved the monasteries with lay society and assimilated them to a whole pattern of privilege, patronage, and favor. Traversari's reform, by insisting on rigid cloister, threatened the easy intercourse of lay patron and spiritual counselor, and all the mutual expectations this involved. Traversari's failure to obtain from the Curia clear-cut authority to appoint and dismiss priors and abbots was doubtless a decisive blow against his plans. In contrast, the new constitutional arrangements of the Congregation of S. Giustina, which abolished the abbot for life (and therefore the abuse of the commendatory abbot) and which vested executive power in visitors responsible to an annual general chapter, seem largely responsible for its success at reform. A similar measure was adopted by the Camaldulensians in 1476, when a number of cenobitic monasteries joined to form a congregation under the leadership of S. Michele di Murano. Pervasive reform of the eremitic life had to wait the charismatic asceticism of the Venetian Paolo Giustiniani (d. 1528).[46]

It is a further question whether the monastic vocation with its stress on ascetic austerity, isolated contemplation, and vicarious prayer and penance for lay society really served the pressing religious, spiritual, and moral needs of the urban, commercial society of Renaissance Italy. It was the mark of much of early Quattrocento humanist thought, notably that of Salutati and Bruni, to espouse the more activist ethos of the citizen, legitimating the quest for wealth and power, the value of human industry, and service to the state. Valla's denial that a superior spiritual status belonged *ipso facto* to the religious vocation was based, as was characteristic of so much of his thought, on his probings of the basic assumptions of much of medieval thought. He questioned whether poverty in itself was a sign of humility, denied that sexual abstinence was an inherent good, and argued that a religious life based on fear was inferior to lay charity based on love. Stress on the internal, subjective, and psychological aspects of faith – the dominant characteristic of humanist religious thought – tended also to undercut the corporate and external piety at the root of the monastic vocation.[47] Recent studies have indicated that the laity also questioned the value of the spiritual service of the monasteries. Herlihy's study of Pistoia provides evidence that piety, as measured by bequests and gifts, shifted markedly from the end of the thirteenth to the beginning of the fifteenth century. In the earlier period the long-established Benedictine monasteries were the principal beneficiaries of lay charity. By 1428 the great urban hospitals had largely supplanted them as the recipients of donations. Organized charity – care for the sick and elderly, poor relief, and dowries for indigent girls – replaced corporate prayer as the institutional expression of religious practice. Moreover, many of the important occasions of public worship took on the character of civic festivals. Herlihy uses the term "civic Christianity" to describe this phenomenon.[48] Becker's suggestive essay, "The Quest for Identity in the Early Italian Renaissance," is in substantial agreement. He concludes, "the character of early Renaissance Christianity is imbued with a feeling for community; the ascetic, contemplative, and penitential are in recession as the values of an activist Christianity become more apparent."[49]

An incident which occurred while Traversari was General seems to bear out the conflict between the newer, more practical modes of organized charity and the older spiritual values of the monastic life. In 1436, the Arte della Lana of Florence requested S. Maria degli Angeli to cede to the guild a garden belonging to the monastery for the construction of a textile mill. The monks objected to the project, arguing that the noise and the lascivious speech of the workers would disturb the religious peace of the monastery which, until then, had been located in the quiet outskirts of the city. Traversari shared their objections and wrote to the Medici brothers asking them to intercede with the Arte della Lana, "lest the construction of this building destroy that most ancient and noble ornament of the city." [50] At the same time the Florentine Signoria urged Traversari to approve the proposed structure since it would be conducive to "public utility" by providing employment, and "it is laudable to feed the poor."[51] Despite this request, Traversari denied permission. Indignant at his refusal, the Arte della Lana decided instead to build the mill in the adjacent garden belonging to the Hospital of S. Maria Nuova. Traversari was greatly provoked at the "perversity of these men," who rather than building the structure at further remove, as he had suggested, seemed intent on disturbing the peace of the monastery. [52]

There is additional evidence that promotion of the monastic life was not uppermost in the minds of the Florentine polity. In 1435 the Signoria asked Traversari to request from Eugenius both financial and spiritual support for the Ospedale degli Innocenti, the foundling hospital in close proximity to S. Maria degli Angeli. This project, begun in the late 1410's, was a major civic enterprise, and Brunelleschi's architecture made it a model of Quattrocento style. The Signoria hoped that through Traversari's intercession the Pope would transfer additional ecclesiastical income to the project and grant indulgences to donors.[53] By way of contrast, the Pippo Spano bequest made to S. Maria degli Angeli to build an oratory, the design for which was also commissioned from Brunelleschi, was sequestered in 1337 for the military budget and the proposed structure left uncompleted.[54]

The growth of lay piety and concern for social charity to alleviate the material needs of the poor and unfortunate should not, however, be over-stressed. The early Quattrocento also witnessed considerable patrician support, both for Observant reform of the ancient Benedictine abbeys and for material restoration of the buildings and fabric of the monasteries. Palla Strozzi and Rinaldo degli Albizzi contributed financially to the Badia Fiorentina, reformed by Gomes Ferreira after long decline.[55] Cosimo de' Medici sponsored the rebuilding of the Badia Fiesolana, as well as the more prominent project of restoring the monastery of S. Marco where Observant Dominicans under Sant' Antonino had replaced the lax Silvestrines. The patronage of such projects served also, of course, to underscore the wealth and prestige of the donor, but it is significant that Cosimo chose to contribute to these monasteries as well as to the family church of S. Lorenzo.

In addition to their support of monastery reconstruction, Florentine patricians respected the contemplative life, the pursuit of which was a prominent strain in humanist thought, though not, of course, identified exclusively with the monastic vocation. Cosimo kept a cell at S. Marco for retreat from public life, a cell where Fra Angelico appropriately frescoed the Adoration of the Magi for Cosimo's meditation. What better image was there of wealth used to honor the Faith and the Church? The solitude of Camaldoli, surrounded by the silence of pine forests, provided the setting for the *Disputationes Camaldulenses*, a dialogue on the relative merits of the active and contemplative lives, written by Cristoforo Landino, a member of Ficino's Platonic Academy. The principal speakers in it are Lorenzo the Magnificent, his brother Giuliano, Leon Battista Alberti, Donato Acciauoli, Ficino, and other Florentine patricians.[56] In this connection it should be recalled that Sto. Spirito, and later S. Maria degli Angeli, were the meeting places for daily humanist colloquies; hence the Florentine monasteries continued to be involved in the intellectual, as well as the spiritual, life of the city. Finally, Valla may have denied the superior status of the religious, but Salutati, who contributed so much to the development of civic humanism, wrote a treatise defending the superior perfection of the monastic life.

In July 1435 Traversari's attention was suddenly shifted from the effort of monastic reform to the major ecclesiastical issue of the day — the conflict between Pope and Council for authority in the Church. On the fourteenth of the month Eugenius IV named Traversari, along with Antonio da S. Vito, Auditor of the Rota, Papal Nuncio to the Council of Basel.[57] They were charged with conveying to the Council the papal response to the decision of the Council, reached in the twenty-first session on 9 June, to abolish all taxes on the confirmation of election to any ecclesiastical office, including annates, the principal papal tax on the Church at large. This decision was the latest in a series of conciliar actions which were directed at traditional papal prerogatives. The Council had previously acted on its own authority to send embassies, intervene in local ecclesiastical disputes, receive appeals from adverse judgment in papal courts, and to give dispensation for marriage impediments. At the same time, this body proclaimed an indulgence to contribute to the expenses of the projected council of union with the Greek Church.[58] It was at this point, when the Pontiff's authority seemed to have reached its nadir, that Traversari became Papal Nuncio. The appointment must have been completely unexpected, since Traversari had never previously served in a diplomatic capacity. In a hurried letter sent just before his departure, Traversari wrote, "We are sent to Basel, where matters are in a desperate strait, to see if a remedy can be discovered."[59] En route to Basel, he stopped briefly to visit Vittorino da Feltre in Mantua, saw Francesco Barbaro, then a magistrate in Verona, spent several days in Constance celebrating the feast of the Assumption and examining the libraries, and reached the seat of the Council on 20 August.[60]

By the summer of 1435 the Council had already been sitting in Basel for four years. It had been convoked in 1431 by Pope Martin V in fulfillment of the decree *Frequens* of the Council of Constance, which stipulated the convening of a General Church Council every seven years. Eugenius' initial policy had been either to prorogue the Council or to translate it to Italian soil where it would be more amenable to papal desires. But the depth of conviction for reform, and his deteriorating political and military power resulting from loss of control of the Papal

States, forced the Pontiff to be more conciliatory.[61] In June 1434, confronted by a revolt of the Roman populace which was provoked by a new papal tax to defray the cost of mercenary troops, Eugenius was forced to flee Rome in a rowboat, disguised as a monk. Barely escaping the stones flung at him from the banks of the Tiber, Eugenius managed to flee to Ostia, and thence to Civitavecchia where a Florentine galley brought him to Livorno and safety. At the same time Bologna, the most populous city of the Papal States, again revolted. Florence, however, where Eugenius resided for six of the next nine years, provided a generous welcome for the refugee Pope – Traversari in the *Hodoeporicon* describes the pageantry of the papal process from Pisa to Florence[62] – but deprived of political independence, Eugenius was hardly able to bargain with the Council from a position of strength.[63]

Traversari and Antonio da S. Vito, his fellow envoy, were sent to Basel without a precise reply to the recent conciliar action. More detailed instructions were to follow. In the meantime they were to defend papal prerogatives as best they could and attempt to persuade the principal leaders of the Council to be less recalcitrant. On 26 August Traversari and S. Vito· both addressed the Council, Traversari in defense of papal supremacy, S. Vito on the necessity of annates. Cesarini, the President of the Council, replied in refutation of both, but promised that the Council would deliberate on the advisability of granting the Pope some compensation for the loss of revenue. Traversari then endured a suspenseful and often agonizing five weeks awaiting further instructions, parrying as best he could the charges of papal obstinacy and misconduct. Despite his repeated, and increasingly anxious, pleas for instructions, the reply was not sent until 12 September, and it did not reach Basel until 4 October.[64] It is probable, as Traversari supposed, that communications were intercepted by agents of Filippo Maria Visconti, the Pope's inveterate enemy.[65] But it seems likely as well that Eugenius realized the precariousness of his situation and was stalling for time, hoping that his political position would improve and that Traversari and S. Vito could prepare the ground for some form of compromise. And indeed events did turn to the Pope's advantage. On 10 August peace was signed between Milan and the league of Florence, Venice, and the Papacy. This enabled Eugenius to reacquire Bologna and remove Visconti forces from Papal Romagna.[66]

Traversari did report some progress in private discussions at Basel. He seems in particular to have cultivated relations with prelates who supported humanist studies. Among these were Alonzo de Cartagena, Bishop of Burgos, and Francesco Pizolpasso, Archbishop of Milan. As we have seen Traversari intended to dedicate to them translations of Gregory Nazianen's orations.[67] He also established contact by letter with Nicolaus Cusanus, then absent from the Council, and he commended Papal confirmation of Cusanus' recent preferment.[68] But Traversari worked hardest to convert Cesarini to the papal cause. He had known the Cardinal from 1430, when he dedicated to him his translation of the *Life of Gregory Nazianzen*, and he had since been in contact with him by letter.[69] While at Basel Traversari dined frequently with Cesarini; humanist studies were a principal subject of their conversations, and the Cardinal expressed an eagerness to learn Greek. Traversari promised to provide instruction, and even sent to Florence for a Greek-Latin Boethius intended for Cesarini's use.[70] He expressed admiration for Cesarini's character and religious sincerity, but despite the friendly nature of their colloquies he was unsuccessful in persuading him away from the conciliar camp. Indeed not until March 1438, when the Greeks had already arrived in Venice for the council of union, did Cesarini leave Basel. He did not, however, subscribe to the extreme conciliarist views, and he resisted the efforts to dispose of Eugenius.[71]

Aside from a few prelates Traversari was dismayed with the situation at Basel. He reported tumult, division, and confusion, which he compared to the prideful building of the tower of Babel, and suspected that the French cardinals were fomenting schism in order to return the Papacy to Avignon.[72] While Traversari's position as Papal Nuncio hardly qualifies him as an objective observer, his characterization of the papal-conciliar conflict as a struggle for power rather than a real effort for reform has a considerable element of truth. The Council found that revenues from the Church at large were essential to its functioning: on 8 August, despite the abolition decree enacted two months previously, the Council ordered all who owed annates to pay them in full to the Council. At the same time it ordered all papal collectors to send all tax revenues to the Council and to render an account of them. Clearly what was at stake was control of the fiscal apparatus of the Church.[73]

On 7 October Eugenius' long-delayed reply to the Council's action of 9 June was read. Though couched in conciliatory terms he protested that the sudden abolition of annates without provision for alternate sources of income made impossible the functioning of the Curia, which was essential to the peace and well-being of the Church. He did, however, assent to the Council's decree of 7 September 1434 which made preliminary arrangements for the site and financing of the council with the Greeks, but cautioned that the proclamation of an indulgence to this end was unwise until the Greeks had agreed to come. Traversari reported that the response to the papal reply was tumultuous. There were shouts of anger and demands that the Pope be deposed.[74] Nevertheless the Council delayed a month before making a formal reply.

In the increasingly antagonistic atmosphere present at Basel during the remainder of his stay, Traversari repeatedly suggested two methods of solution to what he regarded as impending schism. First the Pope should address all the Christian princes, Emperor Sigismund in particular, explaining the scandalous situation at Basel and the gravity of the danger, and he should suggest that the princes withdraw their delegations from the Council. Secondly, lest schism occur, Eugenius should agree to all the decrees of the Council, even the one abolishing annates. Then with the Council dismissed the Pope should convene a new council, composed only of bishops and other prelates,

> in which the peace and unity of the Church can be preserved, and the actions of the Councils of Constance and Basel diligently scrutinized. Free from disturbances and with tranquil minds, what is conducive to true reform can be treated. This is what Saint Leo [Pope Leo I] did, who after that Council of Ephesus, not dissimilar from this present one,

> convened another Council ... in which what had
> been done was abrogated and salutary decisions
> enacted.[75]

It is instructive at this point to return to Traversari's oration
in defense of papal authority, delivered to the Council of Basel
on 26 August, for in it examples of Christian antiquity figure
prominently as the criterion by which to judge the relations
which should prevail between pope and council. Moreover it
reveals Traversari's characteristic historico-rhetorical approach
to theological and ecclesiological issues. Traversari begins his
argument by noting that while powers of binding and loosing
had been given to all the Apostles, Christ had declared Peter his
successor as governor of the Church. This is stated clearly in
Matthew 16: 18-19, "Tu es Petrus et super hanc petram
aedificabo Ecclesiam meam ..." Christ had appointed one
Vicar over his Church in order to preserve peace and unity and
to avoid schism. The establishment of one head in the Church
to whom the faithful are subject corresponds to the structure of
the physical universe, for the philosophers assert that the
heavens and the earth are governed by one God. The correspondence of the ecclesiastical with the celestial hierarchy is
manifest in the writings of Dionysius the Areopagite; and since
Dionysius revealed the secret teachings of St. Paul, the
Apostolic Church therefore maintained a hierarchical order of
authority, and did not consist merely of a government of
bishops and priests. In the patristic age the Roman See was
always venerated and respected. Whenever it was necessary to
refute heresy or expel schismatics, this was always effected
through the authority of the Bishop of Rome. Thus Athanasius
found support from the Pope against Arius, and St. John
Chrysostom had appealed to Pope Innocent to restore discipline
to the Church of Constantinople after his forced exile. Likewise
Thomas à Becket had found refuge in Rome after Henry II's
cruel attacks on ecclesiastical liberties. The sacred councils and
the Holy Fathers had always honored the papacy. The councils
had looked to the popes to preserve the faith or the discipline
of the Church, and the popes in turn had responded by enacting
and preserving the decrees of the councils. Gregory the Great,
for instance, asserted that he venerated the decisions of the first

four Ecumenical Councils like the four Gospels. Reminding the members of the Council that matters of sacred doctrine and institutions should never be governed by human passions but only through meditation on God, Traversari asserted that during the patristic age when all the East, Egypt, and Africa were Christian, and when so many saints glorified the Church, the annual provincial synods never acted with levity against the dignity and authority of the Roman See. If it was necessary to reproach or rebuke individual popes as Cyprian had done, or Bernard, this was always managed with the spirit of charity which had marked the relations between Peter and Paul. Turning to the specific question of papal revenues, Traversari declared that the papacy had always been particularly concerned with succoring the needs of the poor. Gregory the Great, for example, had spent large sums to support remote monasteries in the service of God. It would therefore be unjust to deprive the pope of funds for such charity. It was the will of God that the See of Rome should be dignified with worldly wealth, for "omitting that well known Donation of Constantine, we read in more authoritative history" that Constantine and many other kings, notably Charlemagne and Pippin, had given to the papacy not only gifts of gold and silver, but also landed wealth. Funds were also essential to the defense of the Roman Church, for it had been subjected in numerous wars to threats of destruction. Both Innocent III and Alexander III had been forced to flee Rome, as had more recently John XXIII before the troops of Ladislaus of Naples. Eugenius IV himself had just escaped danger. In conclusion, Traversari exhorted the Council to preserve peace and charity in the Church. The seamless garment should not be torn by dissension. Abuses in the Church should be abolished, but the honor and authority of the Apostolic See must be preserved whole and unimpaired.[76]

Traversari's argument that funds were essential to the Pope in order to provide for charity must rank among the more facile of apologies for papal taxation, since he himself had inveighed against the pomp and wealth of the "western Babylon."[77] Moreover, he had rebuked the Pope for the unnecessarily repressive papal regime in Bologna, which had been a principal cause of revolt there. The Angel of Peace ought not to be the fomenter of war, he remarked, and Eugenius should have used prudent counsel and a policy of clemency instead of resorting to force of arms.[78] Nevertheless Traversari's support for papal authority is unquestionably genuine. He longed for reform, but he feared schism more. He looked for the signs of charity which marked the pristine state of the patristic Church when East and West alike had respected the Apostolic See of Rome, founded on the blood of the martyrs. Significantly, Traversari did not uphold pontifical authority by legal arguments drawn from the medieval canon law tradition. It is not the medieval papal monarchy, exalted by the decretalists, which Traversari defended, but rather the See, venerated by the Fathers, which had preserved the faith from heresy and maintained the spiritual discipline of the Church.[79]

In retrospect Traversari's appeal to papal universalism seems ironic, for the Papacy was in the process of becoming a Renaissance state. It had been the policy of the thirteenth-century popes beginning with Innocent III to create an enlarged papal dominion in central Italy, but even by the end of that century, when the threatening presence of the Hohenstaufen had ended, the revenues of the papal state probably accounted for only ten percent of the total papal income.[80] Under Gregory XI (1370-78), the last pope before the schism, those revenues had increased to about twenty-five percent of the total. But it was the papacy of Martin V (1417-31) which marked the decisive change. The schism had dried up resources from the Church at large, but this was partially offset by Martin's reconquest of papal territory in central Italy. By 1426-27 the Papal States were contributing about forty-five percent of total revenues, and by the time of Sixtus IV (1471-84) this had increased to about sixty-three percent. Moreover "spiritual" income from the Church at large consisted increasingly of indulgences, dispensations, and the venal offices of the curial bureaucracy, rather than annates and other ecclesiastical taxes. Corresponding to the increased reliance on funds from the Papal States were the increased expenditures for mercenary armies to maintain control, militarily and politically, over the papal dominion in Italy.[81] Eugenius IV, who by 1434 had lost virtually all political authority in the Papal States,

doubtless experienced genuine penury. The abolition of annates, despite their decline as a source of income, would have
had a drastic effect on the remaining vestiges of papal income.

On 5 November, in its reply to the papal statement presented
the previous month, the Council determined that no compelling
reason had been presented to alter their original legislation of 9
June. Concluding that nothing more could be done at Basel,
Traversari left the following day, bound for an encounter with
Emperor Sigismund. He thus intended to fulfill part of the
mission to the Christian Princes which he had advocated to
Eugenius. Traversari was confident the princes would react
strongly against any threat of schism, and that it was clear that
justice and moderation belonged to the Pope, iniquity to the
Council. [82] The nearly one month journey to Hungary must
have been arduous at the onset of winter, but Traversari was
sustained by his sense of mission, by the opportunity to visit
monastic libraries at Ratisbon, and by the magnificent views of
towns and castles while sailing down the Danube to Vienna.
After several days of admiring the sites there, he left for
Sigismund's hunting lodge at Villa Arata, where he was greeted
by the Emperor and a public audience was arranged in the
nearby royal villa at Alba Regalis (Stalveisenburg). [83]

Sigismund, who became King of the Romans in 1411, had
been a moving force behind the convening of the Council of
Constance in 1414. He also had staunchly supported the
Council of Basel in its early stages, opposing Eugenius' efforts
to prorogue it. He did so in part because it seemed to offer the
only way to resolve the Hussite question which embroiled
Bohemia and had caused a series of military defeats for imperial
forces. [84] After his coronation as Emperor by Eugenius on 31
May 1433, however, Sigismund urged the Council to a more
moderate course. [85]

Traversari spent nearly two months with Sigismund's court.
During this period he presented two orations, one on 26
December 1435 to a large public assembly, the other in January
1436 in a more private audience with Sigismund. [86] He opened
his public discourse with lavish praise of the Emperor, compar-
ing his physical attributes and his majestic dignity to that of
Augustus or Solomon, and his magnaminity to Julius Caesar.

His piety, his faith, his zeal for religion could only be likened to that of Constantine, or of Theodosius, who, when reproved by St. Ambrose, made public penitence. He praised his vigilance against the Turks and the heretics (i.e. the Hussites) and rejoiced in his labors for peace and unity in the Church (an oblique reference to Sigismund's presence at Constance). He then asserted that Eugenius had the greatest desire to restore ancient holiness to the clergy and freely supported all honorable and appropriate reformation. The abolition of annates, however, threatened the honor and dignity of the Apostolic See of the Vicar of Christ and the Successor of Peter. Annates had long sustained Pope, College of Cardinals, and Curia, and were absolutely essential during a time when Eugenius had been forced to flee Rome before the forces of impiety. The Pontiff sought the suspension of the decree against annates, not certainly from motives of personal avarice — as a youth he had given all his money to the poor — but to preserve the authority of the Church, the Bride of Christ. Eugenius asked not the absolute annulment of the abolition of annates, but merely the suspension of the decree until there could be more considered judgment. Actions against the head of the Church should not be taken precipitously or without reason. After long discussion, the Council of Constance had judged annates licit, and while acknowledging abuses had recognized the need for papal reservation as well. Eugenius therefore asked Sigismund to intervene in the considerations of the Council and to act to preserve the unity, peace, and piety of the Church.[87]

Traversari wrote Eugenius that he purposely restrained his criticisms of the Council of Basel in his public discourse, but that he spoke more frankly in the private audience. In this second oration Traversari warned of the clear danger of schism, because the men at Basel had protracted "this deadly and wicked Council" for years and wished to substitute their will for that of the Roman Pontiff. This was demonstrated by their imperious demand that Eugenius revoke the laborious negotiations with the Greeks about a means of ending the schism of the Eastern Church. The decree abolishing annates, enacted amidst attacks on the Pope and Cardinals as reprobate, proved the schismatic nature of this body. When in antiquity did a

General Council of the Holy Fathers act against the Roman
Pontiff? At Nicaea, at Constantinople, at Ephesus, and Chalcedon — all attended by hundreds of prelates — "the opinion of
the Roman Pontiff was awaited as a divine oracle, and was so
revered that no one presumed to resist it or disapprove it."[88]
Yet at Basel where there were few men (and not all bishops) the
Council tried to weaken and overthrow the authority of the
Roman See. What presumption! And it used an attack on
simony as a mere pretext for promoting schism. Concluding,
Traversari assured Sigismund that Eugenius was eager to replant
the seeds of virtue in the Church, and hoped merely to subject
such matters as the abolition of annates to dispassionate
inquiry. What the *sanior pars* decided was useful to the Church
should prevail.

After this second oration Traversari could report some
progress to Eugenius in his efforts to win Sigismund's support
of the papal cause. He wrote the Pope that Sigismund had
never intended the Council of Basel to be the cause of schism,
but only to work for the public good. After the forthcoming
Diet, the Emperor promised to direct all his powers and his
whole mind to dissolve the Council.[89]

Traversari next accompanied Sigismund to his palace in
Budapest, which he compared in magnificence to that of
Xerxes, then returned to Vienna. From there, on 28 January
1436, he wrote Sigismund, denouncing in even sharper terms
the Council of Basel as a source of scandal and even of heresy.
Again Traversari stressed the Ecumenical Councils of the
Patristic Age as the models by which to judge this one:

> In the ancient, holy Councils it was customary that
> only bishops speak their opinions, and the affairs of
> the Church were treated with fear of God, zeal of
> religion, and fervor of faith. Now these matters are
> entrusted to the mob. As I witnessed myself, only
> twenty out of five hundred there are bishops. The
> rest are clergy of the lower orders or laity. All consult
> their private desires rather than what is proper to the
> common good of the Church. . . . The voice of a
> single cook. . . is regarded as of as much moment as

that of a Legate, or Archbishop or Bishop. What the multitude concludes is held as valid, and what this maddened crowd declares is ascribed to the Holy Spirit. They do not fear to blaspheme against the dignity of the Holy Spirit, making the one who inspires our hearts with peace and is always remote from schism the author of scandals and the leader of a seditious multitude. . . . Our Holy Fathers hardly ever extended a Council beyond as many months as this Synod protracts its business in years. The Fathers acted against the most pernicious heresies and re-formed the customs of the Church within a few months. These, our men − but indeed they are not ours but aliens − consume many years and do nothing except oppress the supreme Pontiff. Nothing fruitful, nothing for the propagation of religion, nothing for the praise of God has ensued, but only schism is sought.

Traversari then cites the Council's creation of a court to try cases, its conferral of the Archbishop's pallium, and its granting of indulgences. Clearly the intention is the permanence of the Council. "When from the erection of a new tribunal what is sought is the perpetuity of the Council, then the way is cleared to abrogate the existence of the Pope and the Apostolic See." Finally Traversari repeated his assertion that the French Cardinals' real intention was to remove the Papacy again to Avignon.[90]

Traversari certainly underestimated, or misrepresented, the extent of the disagreement and conflict present in the ancient Ecumenical Councils. But what is notable in his orations and letter to Sigismund, as well as in his oration to the Council, is his persistent use of Christian antiquity as the historical exemplar by which to measure the standard of the present Church. The patristic Church, as revealed to Traversari in the lives of the Fathers and in their works, was the model of faith and holiness and the inspiration to reform, just as the Roman Republic, in Livy's history, was for civic humanists the model of and the stimulus to civic virtue.

Traversari's embassy to Sigismund did not result in any striking change in the Emperor's policy towards the Council. In the remaining two years of his life he was largely involved with Bohemia and maintained a distracted neutrality in the growing struggle between Pope and Council. He made no effort to dissolve the Council – indeed he opposed the Pope's translation of it to Ferrara – but he objected to its declaration that Eugenius was contumacious. On 9 December 1437 he died. [91]

When Traversari returned to Italy, he resumed the burden of monastic reform and made sporadic efforts to return to patristic scholarship. Until he joined Eugenius in Bologna in August 1437, he seems to have followed the Papal-Conciliar struggle only at a distance. In the meantime Eugenius had shifted from conciliation to open opposition to the Council. The Pope exploited two developments which worked to his favor. First, the papal condottiere Giovanni Vitelleschi in a series of savage attacks in the summer of 1436 reconquered the Papal States. Second, the Greeks favored an Italian site for the Council of Union and insisted on papal presence. This insistence led to an irreparable split between the parties at Basel. The more extreme conciliarists, who were in the majority, held out for Basel, Avignon, or Savoy as the site for the council with the Greeks. The moderate conciliarists, declaring themselves the *sanior pars*, acquiesced, in the interests of resolving the schism with the Greeks, to a translation of the Council to an Italian site. In a stormy session on 7 May 1437 both parties read their rival decrees simultaneously. After this the majority party continued an ever more extreme attack on the Pope, first suspending his spiritual and temporal powers (24 January 1438), then depriving him of the papacy (25 June 1439), and finally electing the Duke of Savoy as the new pope (5 November 1439). The minority party gradually slipped away from Basel, especially after the opening of the Council with the Greeks in Ferrara in 1438. [92]

Eugenius accepted the minority decree of 7 May, and on 18 September 1437 translated the Council to Ferrara. It is noteworthy that less than two weeks previously, on 6 September, Traversari, then in Bologna with the Pope, had sent a long memorandum to Eugenius outlining the policies to be followed regarding both Basel and the forthcoming negotiations with the Greeks. Central to his case for the dissolution of the Council of Basel was again Pope Leo's action in dissolving the Council at Ephesus in 449, an argument that must have made some impression for in 1441 when Eugenius sent letters to the universities justifying papal action against the Council of Basel, he cited this precedent of Pope Leo.[93] The memorandum, however, makes clear that the dissolution of the Council should not mean retrenchment in papal action for reform.

> I have confidence in the Lord, that if your Holiness, together with fellow priests who are faithful adherents of Christ, proceeded vigorously to press for reformation of Church discipline, on the model of the venerable assemblies of the ancients, within fewer months than they [those at Basel] have required years you will accomplish everything. You will restore to the Church its splendor, and its image of pristine holiness, with the greatest praise of God and the exultation of the whole mystical body [of the Church]. You must depend on God, Holy Father, and implore his help in doubtful matters.[94]

The basic assumption of Traversari's work for reform was that personal spiritual renewal would lead to the restoration of purity to the Church. If men examined their hearts, if they recognized their existence before God, if they truly sought the life of faith and moral virtue, then peace, unity, charity would again flourish in Christendom as they did in antiquity. He paid no need to institutional reform. Insensitive to the inertia of institutional forces and the vested interests they involved, he was naive also about the necessity of power and its implications. But blindness to these issues and confidence in the persuasive power of eloquence to change men's wills were characteristic of much of early Quattrocento humanist moral philosophy. It took the acumen of Machiavelli to analyse the Papacy as a Renaissance state and to perceive the incongruency of ethics and politics.

In contrast to his naivete about politics, Traversari' exhortations to personal spiritual renewal reveal a realistic perception of the conflicting passions in men's souls. His letters of spiritual advice are expressed with a visual concreteness, often based on Biblical imagery, which gives them compelling power. A typical one urges Niccoli to receive Easter communion, which he had long neglected:

> . . . .if you have esteem for me, in these days sacred to Christian piety prepare yourself to take up and feed upon the flesh of the celestial lamb, so that from you and from your doorposts signed with the blood of the Lamb, be kept the destroyer of Egypt; and that crossing the Red Sea and traversing with great labor the desert of this world you may enter the Land of Promise; putting to flight the hereditary Amorite [i.e. the Devil] may you be deemed worthy to possess by hereditary right the heavenly Jerusalem. It is impossible to say how much I desire this of you. I implore this by the most ancient right of friendship. I will not endure that a man so close in friendship, grave in years, dedicated to sacred letters and erudite in them, did not for several years taste sacred nourishment. Unless our faith is often sustained and strengthened amidst the temptations of the world, it will grow weak and expire. [95]

Much of humanist religious thought, notably Salutati's and Valla's, attempted to include an enlarged vision of men's human aspirations and to justify lay existence as affording possibilities for a genuinely religious life. Traversari, however, despite his involvement in the humanist movement and his knowledge of classical antiquity, insisted on the sharp divorce of the secular and spiritual worlds. In this world man's condition is one of misery and misfortune, carnality and lust, and ultimately death. [96] In a moment of spiritual anguish in the midst of the struggle for monastic reform, Traversari described his own spiritual existence as dead:

> We are dead, not because as the Apostle said, "Our life is hidden with Christ in God" [Coloss. 3:3] (this, indeed, is the happiest death to be desired that we be dead to the world so that we may live our true life with Christ), but fully, wretchedly dead. Impelled by

> our sins, we are driven from the face of the Lord,
> flung here and there, like Cain a wanderer and
> fugitive, never at rest. Why not? As Augustine truly
> said, "Out heart is restless until it finds rest in God"
> [*Confessions,* Bk. I].[97]

To be purged from wickedness, to die to the world and its
concupiscence, one must embrace the Cross, and in response to
Christ's love for us, die with him in order to rise after the third
day into true and eternal life. [98] The ignominy of the Cross, the
saving act of redemption that frees men from the world, is the
focus of Traversari's thoughts, not the Incarnation with its
exaltation of man's creation in the image of God and its
promise of man's ultimate deification.

The *studia pietatis* — reading, meditation, prayer — are the
means to detach oneself from the world. [99] In describing the
silence, the introspection essential to prayer, Traversari frequently uses the term *ruminare*. In urging Eugenius to give
serious thought to Bernard's *De consideratione*, Traversari
wrote: "These things are to be ruminated upon with delight in
the secret inner chamber of our hearts, from where arises the
burnt offering, the welcome fat-sacrifice of prayer to God." [100]
The works Traversari favored for study and meditation were
Augustine's *Confessions,* Jerome's *Letters,* and especially St.
Bernard's *Commentary on the Canticles.* [101] Indeed Traversari's
description of the coming of Christ to the soul owes much to
the affective mysticism of this twelfth-century Father.

> On account of us and for our benefit, our bride-
> groom, the Son of the eternal King, has entered
> the virginal nuptial chamber. He is the One who
> "has placed His tabernacle in the sun," so that
> from there, "He may go forth as a strong man."
> [Psalms 19: 5-6], and vanguish the powers of
> the air, and for us and in us overcome the cun-
> ning of the ancient enemy. "Prepare your heart
> for Him" [I Samuel 7: 3] sons, so that in it He
> may recline as in a most pleasing lodging. "My
> delights," He says, "are with the sons of men" [Prov.
> 8:3]. He comes to us. He comes for us. He comes in

us. Remember the three-fold coming of the bride-
groom into the Church: for us He comes to us, so
that He may dwell in us. Run to meet His coming.
Receive him and do not desert yourselves, so that you
may set forth to meet Him. Otherwise you will be
unable to find Him. The Word of God "is not far
from anyone" [Acts 17:27], but is in our mouth and
in our heart. From yourself, therefore, run to
yourself, so that you may find Him, and that through
Him you may be deemed worthy to come to Him.[102]

But feeding on the "verdant, ever-flowering fields of Scripture,"
and "ruminating on the food of eternal life" [103] does not
suffice. The Christian, and especially the monk, the *miles
Christi,* must always be prepared to labor in the army of the
Lord as a co-helper of God's grace (*cooperator gratiae Dei*). [104]
Patience and humility are the key Christian virtues, for despite
prayer and meditation, despite preparing to receive Christ and
laboring with him, our spiritual life remains one of fear and
trembling. "I have ascertained sufficiently both from the
authority of divine revelation and from my own experience that
he 'who always fears is blessed' [Prov. 28: 14] and can lapse
only with difficulty." [105] At a time when many of Traversari's
humanist contemporaries were enunciating a new activist vision
of man which exalted his earthly possibilities for achievement –
a vision for which they found support in patristic exegesis –
Traversari instead felt most keenly the fragility, the misery, and
the sin of man's existence.

Traversari's stress on personal renewal, and on the inten-
sification of monastic spirituality, as the means to reform is
characteristic of many such movements throughout the Middle
Ages. St. Bernard comes immediately to mind, as do the
Brethren of the Common Life, who, like Traversari, stressed
ruminare and drew inspiration from the letters of the Latin
Fathers and the works of the twelfth-century spiritual
writers. [106] Traversari's spirituality also has much in common
with the piety of S. Bernardino, whom he knew, and with
popular Franciscan preaching in general. Moreover, his emphasis
on affective piety, on penitential mysticism, and on a semi-

pelagian exercise of the will to attain a state of grace has an affinity with the theological concerns of late nominalism, as exemplified in Gabriel Biel, though Traversari eschewed the logical categories of nominalist inquiry. [107]

What is striking about Traversari's ideas of reform is not their originality, but rather the intensity of his desire to restore the spirituality of the Early Church, and the consistency of his efforts to apply patristic precedents regarding monastic piety and conciliar action to the Church of the fifteenth century. Unlike Valla — or Luther — Traversari did not perceive in the recovery of Christian antiquity the necessity to challenge medieval formulations of the central tenets of faith. His was not an essentially theological renewal, nor did his image of reform partake of the semi-apocalyptic expectation which became increasingly prominent in late medieval thought, and which in the form of a myth of civic destiny was an undercurrent of popular religiosity in Florence in the late Trecento and Quattrocento, surfacing with stunning impact in the preaching of Savonarola. [108] Reform for Traversari stemmed from the vividness with which the writings of the Fathers presented to him early Christianity and his fervent hope that its historical recovery could provide the stimulus to, and the model for, contemporary renewal.

CHAPTER V

PATRISTICS AND UNION
OF THE GREEK AND LATIN CHURCHES

The Council of Ferrara-Florence 1438-39 failed ultimately to end the centuries-long breach between eastern and western Christians. Antagonism between Latin West and Byzantine East had been present from the ninth century, and an open schism had persisted from 1054. Rancor between the two great branches of Christendom had been exacerbated by the destructive passage of the Frankish armies of the First and Second Crusades through Byzantium. Then came the mutual atrocities of the Byzantine massacre of the Venetians in Constantinople in 1182 and the retaliatory Norman sack of Thessalonica in 1185. The Fourth Crusade of 1204 brought Latin conquest of Constantinople and the establishment of a Latin Empire, which, until its defeat in 1261, attempted to force Greek submission to the Roman Church, In 1274 a Council convened in Lyons to end the schism. The major impetus to this effort to end the separation, however, stemmed not from religious impulse but rather from the political and military exigencies of the Byzantine Empire. Michael VIII Palaeologus acquiesced to Latin theological positions in hopes of forestalling Charles of Anjou's impending campaign against Byzantium, but it was the Sicilian Vespers of 1282 which dashed Charles' grandiose schemes of conquest. Reprieved from immediate threat from the West, Michael's son and successor Andronicus II repudiated the union and deposed the pro-union Patriarch John Beccus.

The fourteenth century brought certain signs of intellectual and theological rapprochment between Latins and Greeks. Greek theologians came increasingly to admire the systematic theology of such Latin scholastics as Thomas Aquinas. At the same time Italian humanists had a reawakened interest in classical Greek studies and a revived admiration for Greek culture. The renewed efforts to end the schism in the early fifteenth century, however, again stemmed from the precarious military situation of the Byzantine Empire. This time it was the Ottoman Turks which threatened the Empire's existence. In the wake of the disastrous defeat at Nicopolis at the hands of Sultan Bajezid, Manuel II Palaeologus traveled to Italy, France, and England (1399-1403) in a futile search for military aid. His visit did prompt, however, a number of Latin theologians, notably Jean Gerson, to urge the convening of a general council to resolve not only the western schism, but also the longer-lasting split between the Latin and Greek Churches. Discussions for such a meeting took place at the Council of Constance 1414-18; negotiations to this end were protracted throughout the pontificate of Martin V (1417-31); and quarrels over its projected site and terms were a major source of the rancorous conflict between Eugenius IV and the Council of Basel. At length in July 1437 the Papal Nuncios, the representatives (including Nicolaus Cusanus) of the pro-papal minority faction at Basel, and the Greek envoys set sail for Constantinople to conclude final arrangements. The following February the Greek contingent, including the Emperor John VIII Palaeologus, the Patriarch of Constantinople, and the leading ecclesiastical and theological figures of the Byzantine clergy, reached Venice. The Council convened in Ferrara, then was transferred to Florence, where in July 1439 a Decree of Union was affirmed by both Churches. The major theological differences were resolved, including the central issue of the Procession of the Holy Spirit, but the Greek clergy with but few exceptions were unen-thusiastic about the union. Indeed two leading Byzantine prelates, Mark Eugenicus, Metropolitan of Ephesus, and George Scholarius, who became the first Patriarch under Turkish rule, worked actively against it. Since the impetus for union from both sides was in large part political, conditions were hardly propitious for a genuine ecumenical reconciliation between East and West. Through ecclesiastical union the Greeks, especially the Emperor, hoped to elicit western military aid against the Turks; while Eugenius expected that resolution of the Greek schism would undergird papal authority against the conciliar encroachments of Basel. There was little to inspire the Greek populace to union with the Latin Church, and there was an immediate and deeply felt spiritual resistance to any changes in the Greek liturgy or rites. Eugenius vigorously tried to fulfill the military obligations to the Byzantine Empire. But after initial successes, the Latin army, composed principally of Hungarians, was destroyed on the shores of the Black Sea near Varna in November 1444, and the Papal Legate Cesarini was killed. The Turkish conquest of Constantinople in 1453 brought a final end to the effort of union.[1]

Despite the ultimate failure to resolve the schism, the Council of Ferrara-Florence was an historical event of the first order. By meeting under papal aegis, rather than under the Council of Basel, the Council of Florence confirmed the primacy of papal over conciliar authority in the west. More significant perhaps were the intellectual repercussions. Virtually all the leading Italian humanists were present at the Council, especially during the later sessions in Florence. It was there that Latin scholars conversed with Bessarion, the brilliant young Metropolitan of Nicaea, and later Roman Cardinal, who became the foremost promoter of Platonism in the middle decades of the fifteenth century. It was in Florence also that the enigmatic Gemistos Plethon disputed the Platonic mysteries with the Italian humanists. In a treatise addressed to them he argued for the Platonic theories of creation and immortality and defended the Platonic doctrine of forms against the objections of Aristotle. In these sessions with Plethon Cosimo de' Medici (according to Ficino) was inspired with the idea to renew the Platonic Academy. Finally, the dogmatic discussions themselves, especially the conflicting Latin and Greek formulation of the doctrine of the Procession of the Holy Spirit, convinced Lorenzo Valla of the intellectual crisis of scholastic theology and confirmed for him the necessity to re-establish an exegetical theology, based on philological and rhetorical analysis of the text of Scripture, drawing, like the Greek arguments, from patristic commentary.[2]

Since Traversari was the foremost Latin expert on Greek patristic theology, he had a prominent role in the dogmatic disputations at the Council. His knowledge of Greek and his long years of study of the Fathers and the early Ecumenical Councils proved invaluable both for the theological discussions and in establishing personal rapport with members of the Greek contingent.

From the mid-1420's Traversari had been an advocate of union between the Latin and Greek Churches. The resuscitation of patristic antiquity implied for him the re-establishment of the ecumenical unity which animated the first centuries of Christianity. He stressed union as a principal goal for papal policy, first in the dedication of Kalekas to Martin V, then in the letter sent to Eugenius IV just after his election.[3] It is clear, however, that Traversari regarded the Greeks as schismatic. He dedicated years of scholarship to the Greek Fathers, and he hoped through translation to make some of the principal monuments of Greek patristic theology accessible to the Latin West, but he was convinced that it was Latin Christendom which had preserved inviolate the Christian faith.

On 6 September 1437, while the Latin envoys were en route to Constantinople, Traversari sent a letter to Eugenius in which he charted the policy which should be followed with the Greeks. "I have no doubt at all that they will acquiesce to us, since the authority of the Fathers, Greek as well as Latin, and indisputable reasons will conquer them."[4] The real problem was how to preserve the union. The Greeks should be generously and honorably received. With the conclusion of the reunion, Eugenius should send a permanent legate *a latere* to Constantinople. He should be a sincere, religious. and prudent man. Further, a hundred Greek youths should be brought to the West, where, while still young, they could learn the customs and rites of the Latin Church and be educated both in Greek and Latin letters. As adults they would be faithful and devoted adherents to the Roman See. Eugenius should not hesitate to confer authority on Greeks devoted to the Roman See, for Benedict XIII had not refused to ordain as bishops converted Jews, whom he judged suitable to the office. Afterwards they proved to be zealous promoters of the Catholic faith.

In the fall of 1437 Traversari also began scholarly preparations for the forthcoming Council. In September he wrote to Fra Michele in Florence, asking him to send a volume containing Gregory Nazianzen's orations on the Holy Spirit, "because in this business of the Greeks, which it is hoped will

take place shortly, it will be necessary."[5] At the same time
Eugenius charged Traversari with composing a welcoming
oration in Greek, which he was to deliver to the Greek
contingent on their arrival in Venice. Although the Pope read
and approved the oration, which Traversari composed along
with a Latin translation, it was never delivered. In letters to the
Pope and to Cristoforo da S. Marcello, Traversari displayed
some disappointment, saying simply that the leading members
of the Latin contingent decided against his giving this speech,
on what basis he did not know, but if it suited them to do
otherwise, he did not object.[6] Traversari gave careful thought
and attention to the oration, being particularly anxious that it
display eloquence in Greek.[7] He apparently fulfilled the
expectations of his fellow humanists, for when he later sent it
to Giustiniani for scrutiny, the Venetian replied that for
"elegance of thought, distinction of verbal expression, and
purity of discourse," he had never seen its equal among Latins.[8]
Therefore, despite the fact that it was never delivered, it
provides a useful touchstone of Traversari's thoughts on union
on the eve of the impending council.

How joyful an occasion it is, remarks Traversari, to perceive
the members of the sacred, mystical body of Christ hastening to
embrace each other in love and peace, so that with Christ as
corner-stone they might be joined in grace, faith, and piety.
What a testimony to constant faith is the Greeks' willingness to
undertake such a long journey in the face of so many dangers.
Their great faith is also testified by their persistent work for
union, despite the strife in the Roman Church, where under the
pretext of religion scandal had ensued. But nothing could
induce the Greeks to consider the convening of an ecumenical
council without the presence of the Pope. "You have rightly
comprehended that those ancient universal councils derived
their authority chiefly from this See, nor was anything ratified
without the approval of the Roman Church, which the Apostle
[i.e. St. Paul] maintained never erred in the cause of faith." In
matters of faith the Fathers always found refuge with the
Roman See.

St. Athanasius, Patriarch of Alexandria, first con-
sulted with the Roman Pontiff by letter on a matter
of faith, then turned again to the Roman Church
supplicating help from the plots of the Arian emperor. Likewise John Chrysostom of holy memory,
Bishop of Constantinople, when he had been driven a
second time into exile by the faction of the Egyptian
bishops, in the midst of turmoil and confusion,
entreated Pope Innocent by letter to assist immediately to prevent the discipline of the Church from
collapsing. Saint Cyril, Archbishop of Alexandria,
endured steadfastly those insidious artifices during
the First Council of Ephesus, and overcame them
chiefly through the solace and authority of Pope
Celestine. St. Leo, Bishop of Rome, with marvelous
devotion and vigilant care became aroused against the
Second Council of Ephesus and immediately condemned it. Incited, he put an end to those ecclesiastical issues himself in the letter to Flavianus,
Archbishop of Constantinople, in which he confuted
the errors of Eutyches and with the clearest proofs
brought to light Catholic Faith. Aroused by these and
similar examples of this kind (for many exist), you
have determined faithfully to seek the Holy Apostolic
See. You thus clearly confirm that you are not
unaware of the ancient deeds of the Fathers and that
you are striving with all your powers to imitate
them. [9]

Traversari then praises the devotion of the Greeks to the cause
of union, singling out the Emperor and the Patriarch for their
efforts. He assured the Greeks of Eugenius' benevolent support
for union and his desire to embrace them with charity.
Moreover, he concludes, the Pope eagerly desired to free the
whole of Byzantium from the Barbarians and at last remove the
infidel from the Holy Land.

Even after the Greeks reached Venice there was some
indecision whether to choose Basel or Ferrara. [10] This may in
part explain Traversari's concern to demonstrate the authority
of the papacy by citing previous occasions when the Greek

Church encouraged the intervention of Roman Pontiffs to resolve theological or ecclesiastical controversy. But the historical examples he cited were all drawn from the patristic age — another illustration of his notion of Christian Antiquity as the exemplary precedent for the contemporary Church. It is noteworthy also that Traversari makes no mention of the theological differences which divided the two Churches. He evidently hoped that mutual charity and desire for peace and unity would provide the momentum to overcome doctrinal divergences. Yet the Council was not, for Traversari, the meeting of two Churches equal in Apostolic authority and precedence. The Roman Church, which had never strayed, was preeminent.

Traversari reached Venice on 9 February, the day after the arrival of the Greeks. He quickly entered into conversations with the Greek Patriarch, who, he reported to Eugenius, was a man of great humanity and benevolence, anxious to meet and embrace the Pope, and whose sincere zeal for union was testified to by his willingness to expose himself to the dangers of a long journey despite his eighty years. Traversari entreated Eugenius to receive the Greeks with all honor and affection. Nor should he be offended if the Patriarch called him brother. The Church of Constantinople was second only to Rome, and minor questions of precedence should be overlooked with a spirit of toleration.[11]

In early March the Greek contingent left Venice for Ferrara, where, after the resolution of procedural difficulties, the Council opened on 9 April. Immediately after this, however, both delegations agreed to a four months' recess. The Pope and the Latin contingent were anxious to resolve quickly the matter of union, but only a few representatives of the western princes had arrived, and John VIII insisted on obtaining firm western commitments to military aid before unification. Minor theological differences might be discussed in the interim, it was agreed; but none of the major theological difficulties, particularly the Procession of the Holy Spirit, were to be disputed. Traversari took advantage of this interlude to scrutinize the Greek manuscripts which the Greeks had brought with them. He wrote to Pieruzzi in Florence that he had seen three exceptional volumes owned by the Emperor. These were the complete works of Plato; all of Plutarch including the *Symposium*, as yet unknown to Florentine humanists; and the complete Aristotle, with the commentary of Simplicius. He had also become friends with Bessarion, "a man of singular erudition and merit." The Archbishop of Nicaea had left much of his library behind at the Venetian naval base of Modon in the Morea, including two volumes of Strabo's *Geography*; but Traversari hoped to persuade him to have the books conveyed to the Council. Bessarion had brought with him, however, numerous mathematical texts, including works of Euclid, and an illustrated Ptolemy, which would be of interest to Pieruzzi. Traversari himself was most interested in the manuscript Bessarion had brought of Cyril of Alexandria's *Contra Julianum Apostatam*, which he desired to transcribe if Pieruzzi would send him the parchment. [12] He was also, as we have seen, looking for the Greek text of Chrysostom's *Homilies on Matthew*, so that he could resume the planned work of translation. At the same time he continued to make scholarly preparations for the impending dogmatic discussions. He asked Fra Michele to send from Niccoli's library the manuscripts of Athanasius and of Cyril's *Thesaurus*, the latter, like Athanasius' works, an important Greek patristic formulation of Trinitarian doctrine, and he inquired of Piero del Monte, then in England, whether the Acts of the Fifth Ecumenical Council could be obtained there. [13]

In May, the Greeks, bowing to papal pressure for some discussion to begin, agreed to meet informally to explore doctrinal issues. Each contingent appointed a committee of ten. It is highly probable that, Traversari was a member of the Latin committee, for it was agreed that each side should furnish the other with written statements of the arguments propounded in each meeting, and in a letter of 10 July he wrote, "I am handling nearly all the negotiations with the Greeks, translating from Greek into Latin and from Latin into Greek all that is said or written." [14] It was decided that the discussions should focus on the doctrine of purgatory, and since much of the argumentation depended on citation of Latin and Greek patristic authority, Traversari's knowledge of the Fathers must have proved particularly useful. For example, Torquemada's discourse made a careful examination of a passage of Chrysostom's *Homilies on I Corinthians,* a work which had not previously been translated into Latin.[15] In mid-July the discussions on Purgatory came to an abrupt end, probably because of an outbreak of the plague. On 16 July Traversari informed Cosimo of this problem and that he was making every effort to have the Council transferred to Pisa or elsewhere in Florentine territory.[16] The Pope considered transferring the Council, but not as yet to Florence, for the Greeks were reluctant to move still further from Byzantium. Padua and Treviso were possibilities, but at length on 6 September it was decided that the Council should remain in Ferrara. A leave of absence, however, was granted to all who wished to depart temporarily, and Traversari left immediately to attend to his mother, then gravely ill.[17]

The Pope gave Traversari permission to be absent for two weeks, but he did not in fact return to the Council until November. Besides his mother's health, the continuing work of monastic reform seems to have demanded his attention. Moreover, he seems to have been discouraged by the very slow progress towards union.[18] During his absence, however, the pace of activity at the Council increased: in mid-September an agreement was reached to open formal theological disputation, and the issue decided upon was the legitimacy of the Latin addition of *Filioque* to the Creed. This was first inserted at the Synod of Toledo in 589 and subsequently remained as part of the Latin Creed. The Greek Church had never accepted the theological doctrine of the Procession of the Holy Spirit from both the Father and the Son. Moreover it was the Greek position, as argued at Ferrara, that any addition to the Nicene Creed was forbidden. The Council of Ephesus (431) had prohibited "writing or composing another faith," an injunction repeated by subsequent Ecumenical Councils. To the Greeks this meant that the actual text of the Nicene Creed was inviolate. The Latins responded that *Filioque* was not an addition to the faith, but rather an exposition or development implicit in the credal formula itself. The only real issue therefore was the truth of the doctrine.[19]

The disputations in the fourteen sessions held in Ferrara from 8 October to 13 December depended heavily on close textual analysis of the actual decrees of the Ecumenical Councils and of relevant Greek patristic commentary. In the third session on 16 October the Greek spokesman Mark Eugenicus read excerpts from the Acts of the Councils and the commentary of Cyril of Alexandria. In response Cesarini displayed an ancient Latin codex of the Seventh Ecumenical Council (Nicaea, 787) which contained the words *et ex Filio*. The next day Cesarini wrote to Traversari, then in Florence, insisting that he return without delay to the Council. Theological disputations had begun with the Greeks declaring that the Latin addition of *Filioque* was a scandal and the cause of schism. He described the Greek exposition of manuscripts of the *Acta* of the Ecumenical Councils, and his own presentation of a Latin volume of the Seventh Council. He thought Traversari had seen the volume, which had come from the Dominican library in Rimini. He was chagrined, however, that he did not have in his possession a Greek codex of the Sixth, Seventh, and Eighth Councils which he was certain contained a badly erased *Filioque* such that the vestiges of the Greek words could still be read. This volume had belonged to Nicolaus Cusanus, for it was among the ones he had bought in Constantinople. Cesarini believed that Traversari had seen the passage in question, and moreover a receipt showed that he had borrowed the book. Did Traversari still have it? Cesarini would have given a hundred ducats if he could have been able to display it during the previous day's discussion. He continued:

> I ask by your honor and duty that you come here immediately, because in truth your presence is absolutely essential. I fear that these matters will suffer great prejudice unless you are present. See if you can obtain in Florence another codex of the Seventh Council, because if there is agreement with our book it would lend great strength to our side. Bring with you all your Greek volumes and those of Niccoli's and others' as well which touch on these points of dispute, especially the other ones Kalekas mentions, which you have described in a note. Bring also Cyril's *Thesaurus*. The transport will cost you

nothing, because it has been arranged with the Medici
Bank to send here immediately whatever books you
consign to them. Forget Camaldoli and the whole
Order, and come. Make haste for the faith of
Christ. [20]

Cesarini's letter is eloquent testimony of the esteem with
which Traversari's expertise in Greek patristic scholarship was
regarded by at least some members of the Latin contingent at
Ferrara. Nevertheless he did not return until some time in
November, and then only after a peremptory note from the
Pope himself. [21] When the disputations on the question of the
addition broke off in December, no agreement had been
reached. The Latins, however, with Cesarini as chief spokesman,
had presented weighty enough patristic testimony to shake the
belief of some of the Greek contingent that verbal divergence
from the creed of Nicaea was itself anathema. [22] The Latin
prelates, including Traversari, persistently pressed the Greeks to
shift the debate to the doctrinal validity of the Procession itself.
At length, near the end of December, they acquiesed, and on 2
January 1439 they agreed as well to the translation of the
Council to Florence. [23]

The decision to transfer to Florence was prompted by both
financial and military considerations. By the latter half of 1438
Eugenius was near bankruptcy. Maintenance costs for the Greek
guests had drained the papal budget already straitened by the
reduced flow of taxes produced by the rival demands of the
Council of Basel. In addition, the Milanese condottiere Niccolò
Piccinino was ravaging the Romagna and had already entered
Bologna. To remain in Ferrara invited capture. Florence offered
a military haven, and a fiscal solution as well. Eugenius had
already been borrowing substantial sums from Cosimo de'
Medici as early as April 1438; and the Florentine Signoria,
through its representative Lorenzo de' Medici, in December
offered to provide free accommodation for the Greeks and
agreed to advance a monthly subsidy. The Pope had earlier
favored Florence as a site for the council: now it seemed a
logical solution. As we have seen, Traversari had promoted the
move to Florence in the summer of 1438, but it is uncertain if

he was a moving force behind the transfer agreed to in January.[24]

In scattered groups the Latins and Greeks left Ferrara in late January and early February 1439. The Greeks were received in Florence with great ceremony, which included welcoming orations delivered in Greek by the Chancellor, Leonardo Bruni, for both the arrival of the Patriarch on 11 February and the entry of the Emperor on 15 February. Traversari himself reached Florence by 4 February.[25]

On 26 February the Council reconvened in S. Maria Novella. In eight lengthy public sessions held from 2 to 24 March the Latin and Greek delegations debated the doctrine of the Procession of the Holy Spirit, the central theological issue which divided the two Churches. The rival theological expositions of this question involved metaphysical assumptions and implications, the philosophical subtleties of which cannot be examined here. Much of the difficulty, as Valla acutely observed, involved the linguistic-semantic incongruencies of the respective Greek and Latin theological terminologies. Of course, by the fifteenth century the rival traditions on the Procession had hardened into formality, for over the centuries both sides had produced tracts attacking the other for errors on this point. The crux of the Latin argument advanced in the March sessions was to demonstrate that certain of the Greek Fathers had spoken of the Holy Spirit proceeding from both the Father and the Son. As at Ferrara much of the disputation was based on close textual analysis of patristic sources. The first five sessions focused principally on three texts – Epiphanius' *Ancoratus,* and Basil's *Adversus Eunomium* and *Homily on the Holy Spirit.* For each Traversari's scholarship was crucial to the Latin argument.[26]

When Giovanni Montenero O.P.. the Latin spokesman, opened his case in the first dogmatic session of 2 March, he cited a passage from Epiphanius:

> That the Holy Spirit receives being from the Son is proved by a statement of Epiphanius in that volume entitled *Ancoratus,* translated from an ancient Greek codex by Ambrogio [Traversari]. He says, "I call him

Son who is from Him [i.e. the Father], but Holy Spirit him who alone is from both." [27]

Mark Eugenicus immediately challenged Montenero's interpretation, stating that the Latin manuscript must be corrupt for there was no "is" in the passage corresponding to the "being" Montenero asserted was present. Later in the same session the Latins produced the Epiphanius text in question, and again Eugenicus asserted that the Greek contained no "is." [28] During the fourth dogmatic session of 10 March, Montenero returned to the disputed Epiphanius passage.

> When you replied to me, you said it was my habit to gather testimony from many places, as I did in that previous session with certain arguments produced from St. Epiphanius, in which the verb "is" does not belong. I will therefore return to these texts. Since there are present here many translators, many extremely expert, including above all the Emperor, I call upon all these to testify whether in these places which I cited "is" is understood. I did not put the word there, but rather Ambrogio [Traversari] who asserted it was necessary that it be understood. . . . I have learned from many of Ambrogio's translations that it was the usual practice of the Greek doctors not to express the word in propositions in which it is necessarily understood. . . . [29]

It was Traversari's authority as a Greek patristic scholar which Montenero was placing on the line. Gill comments that there is no doubt that "is" must be understood in the Epiphanius passage, though it is questionable whether it states "exists" as strongly as Montenero asserted. [30]

A subject of greater controversy was textual variations in a passage of Basil's *Adversus Eunomium*. In the first dogmatic session Montenero cited a statement from Book III which spoke of the Holy Spirit "having his being from the Son." In the third session Eugenicus replied that the Latin's Greek manuscript had clearly been tampered with, for the Greeks' texts contained no such statement. Montenero retorted that the Latins' manuscript had been just purchased in Constantinople by Cusanus, so that it had not been in Latin hands long enough to be tampered with. More likely it was the Greeks who had expunged the passage. There then ensued a debate on which reading was more consonant with Basil's thought. Eugenicus cited a letter of Basil's to his brother Gregory of Nyssa, which, he asserted, made plain that the Latins' text contained an interpolation foreign to Basil's mind. Montenero questioned Eugenicus' interpretation of the passage, which led to further debate before the session concluded as to whether Basil held that the Holy Spirit was third in order and dignity. [31]

The Latin contingent was disturbed by the variant readings of Basil's *Adversus Eunomium*, for their manuscript provided the clearest and most authoritative Greek patristic statement in support of the Latin doctrine. It was essential to demonstrate that theirs was the authentic text, and that Eugenicus' source was erroneous. To prove this, they could either consult other codices of the *Adversus Eunomium*, or they could explore Basil's meaning in this and in other of his relevant writings. It was Traversari who took a decisive part in the latter pursuit. Cesarini wrote to him:

> Father Ambrogio, you see now how necessary your work is to the Church. If you were to live to the age of Methusaleh, you could not in that whole lifetime be of more use to the faith than in these few days in which this disputation is being contended. Therefore drop all other business and devote all your attention to translating Greek books day and night. It would be especially useful if we could have translated in its entirety Basil's *Adversus Eunomium.* You know well how essential and pious this work is. You need no one to admonish you in divine matters, for from your youth you have been dedicated to God. Wherefore, noble father, translate this work of Basil without delay. . . . This morning Giovanni d'Arezzo [Tortelli] consigned to you a great many Basil treatises. See if there is anything among the things he brought which is useful to our cause. Tomorrow go to the Florentine monastery where you said today the *Epistolae* of Basil are, and see if they contain what the Archbishop

of Rhodes spoke to the Council regarding the Holy
Spirit as third in order and dignity. [32]

Traversari did in fact accomplish what Cesarini hoped he
would do. In the course of the fifth dogmatic session on 14
March, Montenero stated that he had wished to determine
which version of Basil's *Adversus Eunomium* had greater
fidelity and truth. He therefore had examined word for word
the similarities and differences in the respective readings of the
third book, "with Ambrogio translating." [33] Montenero went
on to argue that it was clear that certain passages in Eugenicus'
text must have been expunged, for his made Basil seem hesitant
where he should have been forthright and was counter to the
whole line of argument which Basil had enunciated at the
beginning of the book. [34] In the fourth session the Latin
contingent had displayed another Greek manuscript of Basil's
work which had the same reading as the text Montenero had
previously cited. When Bessarion returned to Constantinople
after the conclusion of the Council, he carefully examined all
the manuscripts of this work which he could find in monastery
libraries. He discovered that the more ancient codices supported
the. Latin reading, while more recent ones followed Eugenicus'
reading. More significantly, he found two manuscripts which
contained the passages Montenero had cited either badly erased
or inked over. [35] Traversari's scholarship was thus proved
correct.

The effects of Traversari's learning were not limited to the
close textual comparison of the two versions of *Adversus
Eunomium*. During the fourth dogmatic session on Tuesday, 10
March, Montenero stated:

Two days ago, that is Sunday, I was in the house of
the Cardinal of S. Sabina [Cesarini]. Fra Ambrogio,
who is here present and who excels in the great gift of
translating, was also there. A very ancient Greek
codex in parchment was brought by that erudite
translator of Greek literature, Leonardo d'Arezzo
[Bruni], Chancellor of this city. While he had the
book in his hands and as we were searching for a
certain letter, a homily of St. Basil on the Holy Spirit

appeared. I immediately said to this reverend father to read the whole homily to me, for I hoped this to be, as it was without doubt, a miracle brought about by the Holy Spirit. For if Basil, who was filled with the Holy Spirit, thought it necessary to say something firm and solid regarding faith in the Holy Spirit, he must have said it in this homily. I listened to the whole work, and at the conclusion I gave great thanksgiving to the Holy Spirit.[36]

Montenero went on to say that the homily proved that Basil believed the Holy Spirit proceeded from both the Father and the Son, and he quoted passages from the homily.[37] Eugenicus' response was again to challenge the Latin reading of the Homily, and later to dismiss it as a recondite work, of little significance in comparison to the major works of the Fathers and the Acts of the Councils.[38]

In the sixth session on 17 March, Eugenicus departed from the debate format and presented a complete exposition of the Greek position on the Procession. He cited Scripture, proceeded to the Acts of the early Ecumenical Councils, then quoted at length from the Greek Fathers, particularly Gregory Nazianzen and Cyril of Alexandria. In the seventh and eighth sessions on 21 and 24 March, Montenero replied with a complete exposition of the Latin position. He also began with Scripture, then devoted the remainder of the seventh session to the testimony of the Latin Fathers. In each case he was careful either to stress the authority accorded the Latin Father by the early Greek Church (e.g. Pope Leo I's decisive role in the Council of Chalcedon), or to note that Latin Father's proximity to Greek patristic thought (e.g. Jerome's study under Gregory Nazianzen). The force of the argument was to show that the Latin Fathers did not diverge from the Greek patristic tradition. Besides Leo I and Jerome, he also cited Hilary, Ambrose, Augustine, Gregory the Great, Isidore, and the *Acta* of the Synods of Toledo which preceded the Seventh Ecumenical Council (787). Montenero thus intended to reveal the full scope of the Latin patristic tradition on the issue of the Procession. In the eighth session he turned to the Greek Fathers. He began with passages from Basil and Epiphanius not previously cited, proceeded to Didymus, then quoted numerous passages from both Athanasius and Cyril. Finally he rebutted Eugenicus' citations from Gregory Nazianzen. At each instance, after he quoted the patristic source and concluded his exposition, Traversari read the Greek text of the Greek Father quoted. At the conclusion of the eighth session, the Greeks asked for a transcript of Montenero's speeches, including in particular the Latin patristic citations, so that the references could be checked. Replying for the Latin side, Cesarini stated that the Latin codices would be displayed two days later in the sacristy of S. Croce, and that he would have copies made of the relevant parts. On Thursday, 26 March, the Greek and Latin representatives met in the sacristy to examine the codices. Montenero's speeches and the presentation of the manuscript sources had a powerful effect on the Greek contingent, especially on Bessarion. Although the Greeks had not studied the Latin Fathers, they knew the names of the principal ones quoted. But the precise citation of Greek patristic sources in the original Greek was even more persuasive. In mid-April Bessarion declared openly to the Greeks his support for the doctrine of *Filioque.* Since all the Fathers of the Church, Latin as well as Greek, were inspired by the same Holy Spirit, they must be in fundamental agreement on matters of faith. With the Latin Fathers unanimously in support of the doctrine of *Filioque,* the Greek Fathers must be also; and the texts used by Montenero proved it.

For the next month and a half, while sessions were suspended, the Latins and Greeks worked for a dogmatic formula of *Filioque* agreeable to both sides. Bessarion, Isidore of Kiev, and Scholarius – all of whom had been persuaded by the strength of Montenero's patristic sources – gradually convinced most of their fellow Greeks. Only Eugenicus, who in the end did not sign the Decree of Union, adamantly resisted. In early June agreement was reached.[39]

Clearly the patristic sources cited by Montenero in the seventh and eighth sessions were the decisive arguments which led to Greek acceptance of the doctrine of *Filioque,* and it is virtually certain that Traversari was responsible for compiling them. Montenero took his quotes from a collection of Latin and

Greek patristic texts and excerpts from the *Acta* of early Councils, which is the present Laurenziana C.S. 603.[40] This volume must be the source of the speeches, and not later cullings from them, for though Montenero followed the general order of the compilation, he did not follow it exactly. Although this manuscript does not bear Traversari's name, and Montenero did not credit him as compiler, he was doubtless responsible. As early as the autumn of 1437 he had begun examining works of the Greek Fathers on the doctrine of the Holy Spirit, and in April 1438 he asked to have manuscripts of Athanasius and Cyril's *Thesaurus* sent him in Ferrara. Citations from both Fathers, including the *Thesaurus,* figure prominently both in the manuscript and in Montenero's speeches. In October 1438 Cesarini asked Traversari to return to Ferrara immediately, and to bring with him Cyril's *Thesaurus* and other texts which Traversari had described in a note to him.[41] In his letter of March 1439, Cesarini again refers to Traversari's continued scholarship. "I have procured that book of Authorities, which I am sending to you, so that after you finish Basil you can translate this, as you so worthily promised me."[42] It is uncertain what this "book of Authorities" is, but it may well be the patristic citations compiled on the issue of the Procession by John Beccus, the pro-union Patriarch at the Council of Lyons. Traversari knew Beccus' work, noting its presence in a Greek manuscript of orations of Gregory Nazianzen which belonged to the Badia Fiorentina.[43] Moreover, Beccus' citations are included in the Laurenziana compilation. Traversari, of course, also knew the patristic references on the issue of the Procession present in Kalekas, since he had translated Kalekas' work for Martin V.

Given Traversari's authority as a patristic scholar (attested to both in Cesarini's letters and in Montenero's public speeches to the Council), given his scholarly involvement with the Basil and Epiphanius texts which were the focus of debate in the immediately preceding sessions in Florence, and given the fact that it was he who actually read to the Council the Greek quotations cited by Montenero, it seems indisputable that he was responsible for the compilation. It was a remarkable work of scholarship. Kalekas and Beccus were probably the basic sources, but many other Greek patristic and conciliar citations were included which were not present in the compilations of either writer. Moreover, twenty-seven of the fifty-two Latin patristic and conciliar citations had not previously appeared in such a study on the doctrine of the Holy Spirit. [44]

Once the key doctrinal issue of the Procession had been resolved, the other theological issues — Purgatory, the Eucharist, and papal primacy — were rapidly settled, principally to the Latin advantage. In late June Traversari and Bessarion worked out the final wording of the Decree of Union, and this was signed on 6 July. [45]

Traversari was gratified that the cause in which he had labored so long had reached such a felicitous conclusion. He remarked how great a delight it was to witness both Churches joined in union as the Pope celebrated mass in the Florentine Duomo. [46] So overjoyed was he with these results that when the Armenians arrived in September "prepared to submit to the Roman Church," he reported also that news had reached Florence of the expected conversion of the Turks. [47]

Towards the end of September Traversari left Florence for Camaldoli, where he intended to retire to the *vita solitaria et contemplativa*. From there he wrote to Lorenzo de' Medici, asking him to send some glass for windows, so that he could keep out the chill winter blasts from his remodeled quarters. Reflecting on his return to solitude and meditation, he wrote:

> I admit, dearest Lorenzo, that this tranquillity pleases me. I seem almost to have navigated into port, whereas until now I was in danger, being tossed around by stormy waves. I labored with a ready will in that business with the Greeks (indeed, I believe however much knowledge of the Greek language I have was allotted me by divine gift for this time and this affair), but I was forced to exhaust both eyes and ears daily in that work, which was excrutiating to my mind so long nurtured on far different studies. And now, notwithstanding the presence of various daily tasks, these occupations are calmer and gentler than that abyss and labyrinth of inextricable cares. I find it

more pleasing and agreeable to mingle with peasants than with Cardinals and the Supreme Pontiff. . . . . I have dedicated myself, my life, and all my time to solitary quiet. . . . I promise you, God grant and direct, that this desert will bear forth sweet, rich, and delightful fruit — here where, with laziness and all torpor dissipated, I will give myself to these most pious studies, and in these delights find repose with perpetual pleasure.[48]

But Traversari did not long enjoy the rustic solitude of Camaldoli. In October he was called back to Florence on monastic business, and stricken again with the stomach ailment which for years had bothered him he died there on the 21st.[49]

CONCLUSION

The disputations on the Procession of the Holy Spirit at the Council of Florence served to underscore for the world of Italian humanism the authoritative character of patristic theology. Since the philological, rhetorical, and historical analysis of Greek patristic texts was central to the arguments presented there, these Conciliar debates highlighted precisely the humanistic intellectual concerns which Traversari had brought to his patristic scholarship. His prominence in preparing arguments which undergirded the Latin position must have focused attention as well on his translations of the Greek Fathers, the fruit of more than two decades of study.

The Council of Florence seems to have been decisive in confirming Valla's commitment to restructuring theology on a philologico-rhetorical basis. In the 1440's and early '50's he made an intensive study of the Greek New Testament and of Greek patristic exegesis. His increasing criticism of the theology of Aquinas, and his growing awareness of the inadequacies of the Vulgate culminated in a rancorous controversy with Poggio in 1452-53. Ironically, it was the elderly Poggio who upheld the traditional medieval formulation of Christian doctrine against Valla's criticisms. The dispute, which engaged humanist communities in Florence and Venice, as well as Rome, served, as the Council of Florence had a decade before, to make evident the nature of patristic theology, and the implications of its revival in a humanistic intellectual context. [1]

The middle decades of the fifteenth century saw as well continuing humanist Latin translations of the Greek Fathers. Pope Nicholas V (Parentucelli), who while secretary to Cardinal Albergati had procured numerous patristic texts for Traversari, and who had read and criticized Traversari's version of Dionysius the Areopagite, was the foremost promoter of Latin translations of the Greek Fathers. Under commission to Nicholas, George of Trebizond translated a number of Greek patristic works, including Chrysostom's *Homilies on Matthew,* which Traversari intended to do but never completed, Basil's *Adversus Eunomium,* large parts of which Traversari had translated during the Council of Florence, and Cyril's *Thesaurus,* which Traversari had studied in preparing the Latin arguments at the Council. Trapezuntius also turned into Latin Cyril's commentaries on Leviticus and on the Gospel of John, Eusebius' *Praeparatio Evangelica,* and Gregory of Nazianzen's orations "In laudem Athanasii" [21] and "Funebris in Basilium" [43].[2] We have noted previously the translations of Guarino da Verona (Basil's homilies *De ieiunio* and *De mutua parentum ac filiorum caritate,* completed 1438), Lilius Tifernas (Chrysostom's *Sermones de patientia Job,* dedicated to Nicholas V, and the *opera omnia* of Philo, dedicated to Sixtus IV), Francesco di Mariotto Aretino (Chrysostom's *Homilies on I Corinthians,* 1457, and *Homilies on John,* 1459), and Pietro Balbo (Chrysostom's *Homilies on the Statues,* dedicated to Pius II, and Gregory Nazianzen's five "Theological Orations", completed c. 1462). The patristic scholarship undertaken by Italian humanists in the middle decades of the Quattrocento needs further study, but it is clear that Traversari's concern for Christian antiquity persisted.

In the latter fifteenth century, Florentine intellectual energies centered on the revival of Platonic and neo- Platonic thought. Ficino's return to metaphysics, and the stress he and Pico placed on the esoteric *prisci theologi* — Hermes Trismegistos, Zoroaster, and Orpheus — went beyond Traversari's conception of sacred letters. The Florentine neo-Platonists sought the prophetic, poetic, mystical, and mythic origins of religion in the mysteries of the Egyptian and Persian sages rather than the evangelical piety of the Greek Fathers. Giles of Viterbo (1469-1532), the neo-Platonist General of the Augustinians, supported observant monastic reform and the eremitic ideal; and, like Traversari, regarded the first three centuries of the Christian era as a golden age. But his notion of reform is permeated with eschatological expectations derived from his study of the Cabala. His belief that the Church had degenerated spiritually because it became immersed in material things derives less from historical inquiry into Christian antiquity than from the meta-historical perspective of neo-Platonist eman-ationist metaphysics.[3]

Study of the Greek Fathers in the latter Quattrocento, however, was by no means neglected. Poliziano translated a substantial part of Athanasius' *Epistola ad Marcellinum,* a work which stressed the Psalms as a source for Christian prayer and inspiration, and published it in 1492 with the title *Opusculum in psalmos.* During the early 1490's Poliziano seems also to have given considerable attention to other Greek and Latin Fathers, especially works of Scriptural exegesis.[4] In the first decade of the sixteenth century Aldus Manutius published in Venice four volumes of *Poetae Christiani,* with one comprised of sixty-six poems of Gregory Nazianzen; in the same period, a certain Matthias Monachus translated thirty orations, three letters, and one poem of Gregory Nazianzen.[5] In the later fifteenth and early sixteenth centuries, many of Traversari's translations were printed, and so diffused all over Europe.[6]

Patristic scholarship was of course a principal interest of the northern humanists. Nothing in Italian Renaissance scholarship can match Erasmus' achievement: he translated and edited a vast amount of patristic literature – the *opera omnia* of Jerome (1516), of Cyprian (1520), of Athanasius and Hilary (1522-23), of Irenaeus (1526), the *Homilies* of Chrysostom (1527), a huge Augustine (1528-29), and finally Origen (1536). Besides these great editions which rolled off Froben's Basel press, he collaborated with Oecolampadius and Capito on an enlarged Chrysostom (1530), and wrote a preface to Pirckheimer's Gregory Nazianzen (1531).[7] How extensively Erasmus drew on previous Italian humanist patristic scholarship is a matter yet to be explored, but he seems to have been aware of the Quattrocento translations, and their precedent-setting, that is, humanist approach to the Fathers.[8] It is evident also that Lefèvre d'Étaples and his circle relied heavily on earlier Italian patristic scholarship for their editions of the Fathers published from 1499 to 1520. In addition to Traversari's translation of Dionysius the Areopagite, the Lefèvre circle published George of Trebizond's translations of Cyril's *Thesaurus,* Cyril's *Commentary on John,* and Basil's *Adversus Eunomium* as well as Basil's *Hexaemeron* in the translation which Argyropoulos made for Sixtus IV.[9] Both Erasmus and Lefèvre made use of the rhetorical-historical interpretation of the Fathers which had marked Traversari's patristic scholarship, and both stressed the humanist religious ideal of the union of *eruditio* and *pietas* and the opposition to the irrelevant intricacies of scholastic disputation.

The Protestant Reformers, who shared the humanists' antipathy to the scholastic synthesis of Christian doctrine and Aristotelian metaphysics, also found the Church Fathers' stress on Scriptural exegesis congenial to their insistence on *sola scriptura*. Melanchthon, in particular, regarded the Lutheran reform as essentially the return to patristic Scriptural theology and to the decisions of the early Councils, with the Pauline justification by faith alone as the criterion for judging the relative validity of patristic interpretation.[10]

Patristic theology was a central concern also of a group of humanist Catholic reformers in the first half of the sixteenth century. Giberti published numerous works of the Greek Fathers, holding that reform could only originate by returning to them. Cardinal Pole directed intensive scholarship towards Biblical and patristic studies in the 1520's, and in 1534 he joined Contarini and Sadoleto in a program for Church reform centered on the renewal of Biblical studies. Strongly influenced by the austere asceticism of the Camaldulensian eremitic reformer Paolo Giustiniani, Contarini turned from humanist studies to patristic and Biblical scholarship; and in the Ratisbon colloquies with Melanchthon in 1541, he rejected scholastic definitions of grace and justification, and relied instead on patristic exegesis of Scripture. His *Annotations* of 1542 are committed wholly to a Biblical theology, drawing heavily on Greek patristic exegesis.

For a fleeting moment, it appeared that some accommodation between Catholic and Protestant could be made on the basis of patristic theology; but this hope was shattered by Pope Paul III's insistence that the Protestants acquiesce to papal supremacy.[11] The Council of Trent, which refused to admit corrections to the Vulgate, and which under Jesuit leadership decreed Aquinas as the authoritative expositor of Catholic doctrine, proved a crippling blow to Italian humanist patristic studies in the service of reform. Banished from the authoritative mode of theological study, patristics instead became the refuge of men like the Venetian Paolo Sarpi who defended the pluralistic nature of the Venetian Church against papal hierocratic formulations.[12] Ironically, too, by the end of the sixteenth century many Protestant theologians began to return to dialectics to analyze the orthodox credal formulations of the Augsburg Confession and Heidelberg Catechism.[13] In the recriminatory passions of Catholic and Protestant polemics, the humanist quest for the historical experience of the Early Church, initiated by Traversari, came to an end.

NOTES

Preface

1 Marvin B. Becker, "An Essay on the Quest for Identity in the Early Italian Renaissance," in *Florilegium Historiale: Essays Presented to Wallace K. Ferguson,* eds. J.G. Rowe and W.H. Stockdale (Toronto, 1971), pp. 294-312; *id.,* "Individualism in the Early Italian Renaissance: Burden and Blessing," *Studies in the Renaissance,* XIX (1972), pp. 273-97; *id.,* "Aspects of Lay Piety in Early Renaissance Florence," in *The Pursuit of Holiness in Late Medieval and Renaissance Religion: Papers from the University of Michigan Conference,* eds. Charles Trinkaus and Heiko A. Oberman, *Studies in Medieval and Reformation Thought,* X (Leiden, 1974), pp. 177-99; Richard C. Trexler, "Death and Testament in the Episcopal Constitutions of Florence (1327)," in *Renaissance Studies in Honor of Hans Baron,* eds. Anthony Molho and John A. Tedeschi (Dekalb, Ill., 1971), pp. 29-74; *id.,* "Florentine Religious Experience: The Sacred Image," *Studies in the Renaissance,* XIX (1972), pp. 7-41; *id.,* "Ritual in Florence: Adolescence and Salvation in the Renaissance," in *The Pursuit of Holiness,* pp. 200-64; *id., The Spiritual Power: Republican Florence under the Interdict, Studies in Medieval and Reformation Thought,* IX (Leiden, 1974); Donald Weinstein, "The Myth of Florence," in *Florentine Studies: Politics and Society in Renaissance Florence,* ed. Nicolai Rubinstein (London, 1968), pp. 15-44; *id., Savonarola and Florence: Prophecy and Patriotism in the Renaissance* (Princeton, 1970); *id.,* "Critical Issues in the study of Civic Religion in Renaissance Florence," in *The Pursuit of Holiness,* pp. 265-70.

2 Paul Oskar Kristeller, "Studies on Renaissance Humanism during the Last Twenty Years," *Studies in the Renaissance,* IX (1962), p. 20.

3 Paul Oskar Kristeller, "Paganism and Christianity," in his *Renaissance Thought: The Classic, Scholastic, and Humanist Strains* (New York, 1961), p. 80; note also *id., Le Thomisme et la pensée italienne de la Renaissance* (Montreal, 1967), p. 66.

4 III: 20 (20, 22 November 1434); III: 21 (21, 1 December 1434); III: 22 (22, 3 December 1434); and III: 23 (23,4 December 1434). N.B. The Roman numeral and the number immediately after the colon refer to the book of letters and the individual number of the letter as it appears in the Mehus edition (see n. 15 below). The number in parenthesis and the date are those assigned to the letter by Luiso (see n. 17 below).

5 III: 29 (29, 25 February 1435); III: 30 (30, 14 March 1435); IV:

27 (27, 29 June 1436); note Traversari's request to the Venetian humanist Leonardo Giustiniani for the return of his letters: VI: 38 (41, 15 February 1435).

6 IV: 26 (25, 24 June 1436).

7 XIII: 14 (23, April-August 1437).

8 XIII: 15 (27, 7-8 February 1438).

9 Giovanni Card. Mercati, *Ultimi contributi alla storia degli umanisti,* Fasc. I: *Traversariana, Studi e Testi,* 90 (Città del Vaticano, 1939), esp. pp. 34-36.

10 XXV: 17 (undated).

11 Mercati, p. 54; Angelo Maria Bandini, *Catalogus Codicum ... Bibliothecae Leopoldinae sive Supplementi ad Catalogum Codicum ... Bibliothecae Mediceae Laurentianae* (Florentiae, 1791-93), II, cols. 447-49; Paul Oskar Kristeller, *Iter Italicum* (Leiden, 1963-67), I, p. 255.

12 Kristeller, *Iter*, I, pp. 156, 159.

13 E.g. Bibl. Riccard. 779 [Kristeller, *Iter*, I, p. 201]; Ambrosiana, L. 69 sup. [ibid., p. 333]; Marciana, Lat. Classe XI, 66 (3967) [ibid., II, p. 239]; Ottob. lat. 1677 [Mercati, p. 54ff].

14 E. Martène et U. Durand, *Veterum scriptorum et monumentorum amplissima collectio*, Tom II, III (Paris, 1724).

15 *Ambrosii Traversarii Generalis Camaldulensium aliorumque ad ipsum, et ad alios de eodem Ambrosio latinae epistolae a Domino Petro Canneto Abbate Camaldulensi in libros XXV tributae variorum opera distinctae, et observationibus illustratae. Adcedit eiusdem Ambrosii vita in qua historia litteraria Florentina ab anno MCXCII usque ad annum MCCCCXL ex monumentis potissimum nodum editis deducta est a Laurentio Mehus* (Florentiae, 1759). These volumes have been re-issued in photostatic reprint by Forni: Bologna, 1968. The first volume of Mehus' edition, i.e. the *Historia litteraria florentina ...* , was re-published in Munich, 1968, along with Eckhard Kessler's discussion of Mehus' scholarship, and a detailed Table of Contents to Mehus' history. For Mehus, note also Eric Cochrane, *Florence in the Forgotten Centuries, 1527-1800* (Chicago, 1973), p. 389.

16 In addition to Mercati, Luiso, and Dini-Traversari, see Ludwig Bertalot, "Zwolf Briefe des Ambrogio Traversari," *Römische Quartalschrif,* XXIX (1915), pp. 91*-106*, and P. Enrico Bulletti, "Due lettere inedite di Ambrogio Traversari," *Bulletino senese di storia patria,* LI-LIV (1944-47), pp. 97-105.

17 F.P. Luiso, *Riordinamento dell' epistolario di A. Traversari con lettere inedite e note storico-cronologiche* (Firenze, 1898-1903).

18 XXV: 10 (1440?); XXV: 11 (dated 1440); XXV: 12 (dated 1441); XXV: 14 (dated 1441).

19 Vespasiano da Bistici, *Le vite*, Edizione critica di Aulo Greco (Firenze, 1970), I, pp. 449-61.

20 J.B. Mittarelli and A. Costadoni, *Annales Camaldulenses*, 9 vols. (Venice, 1755-73). Vol. VI pertains to Traversari.

Chapter I

1 Archivio di Stato, Firenze, Conv. Soppr. No 86 (S. Maria degli Angeli), filza 95, lxxxxii r°; filza 96, xliii.

2 See also John Larner, *The Lords of the Romagna: Romagnol Society and the Origins of the Signorie* (Ithaca, N.Y., 1965), pp. 23, 36-37, 66.

3 A.S.F., Conv. Soppr. No 86, filza 95, lxxxxiii r°; filza 96, xlv. Ambrogio also had two sisters, Agostina who married into the prominent Florentine house of the Morelli in 1426, and a second (name unknown), who married at Galeata. There apparently was also another brother, Antonio, who inherited the family property at Portico. For fuller discussion see Dini-Traversari, pp. 19-26 and appended genealogical tables.

4 Canto XXII, ll 46-51.

5 D.A. Pagnani, *Storia dei Benedettini Camaldolesi: Cenobiti, eremiti, monache, ed oblati* (Sassoferrato, 1949); Anselmo Giabbani, *L'eremo: Vita e spiritualità eremetica nel monachismo camaldolese primitivo* (Brescia, 1945); Giuseppe Cacciamani, "La reculsion dans l'ordre camaldule," *Revue d'ascétique et de mystique,* XXXVIII (1962), pp. 137-54, 273-87.

6 Cacciamani, p. 286.

7 Walther and Elisabeth Paatz, *Die Kirchen von Florenz: Ein kungstgeschichtliches Handbuch,* III (Frankfurt am Main, 1952), pp. 107-47. Virtually no trace of the original medieval state of the monastery remains as the buildings comprising S. Maria degli Angeli were greatly altered when rebuilt in baroque style in the late sixteenth and seventeenth centuries. In 1864 the monastery was suppressed, and it now serves as a veterans hospital and as part of the University of Florence.

8 A.S.F. Conv. Soppr. No 86, filza 67; filza 64.

9 "Ego, Clementissime Imperator, Christi protegente gratia, in celeberrimo illo Monasterio, quod Florentiae sub titulo Beatae Mariae Virginis, et Sanctorum Angelorum conditum est, a puero sum enutritus, ibique triginta, et unum annos sub regulari observantia, et perpetua clausura transegi. Verum, agentibus peccatis meis, illa quiete, illo otio frui ultra non merui: et divino iudicio ex alto quietis sinu, ex placidissimo littore in infestissimum cogitationum pelagus abii, iussu Romani Pontificis Beatissimi Eugenii evulsus ab illa tranquillitate, et Praesul Religioni nostrae datus." "Oratio I" in Mehus, II, 1141.

10 "Hanc profecto veteres illi, quos admiramur, in tantum adspernati non sunt, ut Socratem senio iam gravem fidibus cecinisse constet, eius rei eatenus rudem: Divus Pater Augustinus sex libros de Musica scripserit, qui etiam sunt apud nos, intenderitque de melo etiam totidem scribere, si plus nactus fuisset otii. Mitto vetustiores illos, David scilicet sanctissimum Regem, ac reliquos, qui mirifice amarunt Musicam piam." VI: 31 (26, 29 January 1429). Note also VI: 32 (27, 5 February 1429).

11 Raimond van Marle, *The Development of the Italian Schools of Painting,* IX, pp. 107-256; Miklòs Boskovits, "Su Don Silvestro, Don

Simone e la 'scuola degli Angeli' *Paragone*, 265 (March 1972), pp. 35-61.

12 Fuere semper in nostro Monasterio (nec modo quidem desunt) qui illo orandis voluminibus scitissime, et venustissime utantur. Est quippe id ministerium otio religioso non indignum." VI: 34 (29, 27 May 1429).

13 VI: 26 (30, 1 August 1429).

14 "Redit ecce in memoriam, fili, quies illa nostra, et deliciae antiquae perstrigunt aciem, neque possumus nisi flere tam laetis, lautisque destitui solatiis, quibus fruebamur in solitudine cordis nostri, quum celebraremus apud vos sabbatum delicatum, et cantaremus Domino canticum novum, atque illi psalleremus in iubilo, cogimurque cum Iob ex imo cordis clamare: 'Quis mihi det, sim iuxta dies antiquos, quando Deus omnipotens erat mecum.' " XII: 21 (20, 30 April 1434). Cf. XI: 32 (32, 2 May 1432).

15 "Equidem, Nicolae carissime, patientiam, et humilitatem, quam me sacramenta docuerunt, cuique a puero per gratiam Christi me devovi, ad finem usque tenere paratus sum, ac de me ipso humilia sentire; si quando fortasse merear et ipse inter filios Dei numerari. Ad quam profecto emerendam excellentiam, nullum aliud nobis patere iter ipse mecum recognosces, si ex religionis sacramento Dei Filium ex alto Patris sinu descendisse ad terras, ut salubriter nobis dictis, factis, exemplisque pararet ascensum, humilitatemque cordis sectandum imperaret, memineris." VIII: 15 (16, 1424?).

16 "Vides quanta rerum varietas, quanta inconstantia fortunae, quam apertis documentis moneat nihil in rebus humanis, secundisque successibus gloriandum; quando haec omnia, quae iucunda videntur, atque firmissima, protinus abvolant." VIII: 35 (35, 18 November 1430). Cf. VIII: 20 (23, 1426?); VIII: 34 (34, 27 October 1430); and Ludwig Bertatlot, "Zwölf Briefe des Ambrogio Traversari," *Romische Quartalschrift*, XXIX (1915), p. 97*. In light of Traversari's frequent citing of Job, it is noteworthy that there existed in S. Maria degli Angeli in his lifetime an altar panel which depicted the Madonna and Child with St. Gregory and Job with predella scenes from the life of Job. See Paatz, *Die Kirchen,* III, p. 126. The humanist movement by no means was characterized by a universal optimism concerning man's condition. For humanist debates on man's dignity and misery, see Trinkaus, *In Our Image,* pp. 171-321.

17 See Ch. II, p. 30; for Marsili, see Ugo Mariani, O.E.S.A., *Il Petrarca e gli Agostiniani,* 2nd ed. (Roma, 1959), pp. 50-79, and Rudolph Arbesmann, O.S.A., *Der Augustiner-Eremitenorden und der Beginn der humanistischen Bewegung* (Würzburg, 1965), pp. 73-119.

18 *Epistolario di Coluccio Salutati,* ed. Francesco Novati (Roma, 1891-1911), IV, pp. 138-39.

19 Note Poggio's remarks in his funeral oration for Niccolò Niccoli: Poggius Bracciolini, *Opera Omnia,* ed. Riccardo Fubini, I (Torino, 1964), p. 271.

20 Antonia Mazza, "L'inventario della 'parva libraria' di Santo Spirito e la biblioteca del Boccaccio," *Italia medioevale e umanistica,* IX (1966), pp. 1-74.

21 Vespasiano da Bisticci, *Vite di uomini illustri*, ed. Greco, I, pp. 487-88.

22 The text was published by Cesare Vasoli, "La 'Regola per ben confessari' di Luigi Marsili," *Rinascimento*, IV (1953), pp. 39-44, reprinted in Vasoli's *Studi sulla cultura del Rinascimento* (Manduria, 1968), pp. 40-44.

23 Hans Baron, *Humanistic and Political Literature in Florence and Venice at the Beginning of the Quattrocento* (Cambridge, Mass., 1955), pp. 13-33, has demonstrated that the *Paradiso* is an anachronistic fictional work and therefore must be used with considerable caution as evidence for late Trecento ideas. For instance, Giovanni's attribution to Marsili of the historical theory of the founding of Florence under the Roman Republic is clearly erroneous, for Salutati and Cino Rinuccini developed these ideas only after 1400.

24 D. Gutiérrez, "La biblioteca di Santo Spirito in Firenze nella prima metà del secolo XV," *Analecta Augustiniana*, XXV (1962), p. 47.

25 Mazza, *loc. cit.*

26 The involvement of the regular clergy in the humanist movement, often overlooked by scholars, was substantial. Note Paul Oskar Kristeller, "The Contribution of Religious Orders to Renaissance Thought and Learning," *American Benedictine Review*, XXI (1970), pp. 1-55; reprinted in *Medieval Aspects of Renaissance Learning* (Durham, North Carolina, 1974), pp. 95-158.

27 Berthold L. Ullman, *The Humanism of Coluccio Salutati* (Padova, 1963), pp. 51-70; Hans Baron, *The Crisis of the Early Italian Renaissance*, 2nd ed. (Princeton, 1966), pp. 297-99; George Holmes, *The Florentine Enlightenment, 1400-50* (New York, 1969), pp. 31-35; D.J.B. Robey, "Virgil's Statue at Mantua and the Defense of Poetry: An Unpublished Letter of 1397," *Rinascimento*, 2nd s., IX (1969), pp. 183-203; Mario Fois, S.I., *Il pensiero cristiano di Lorenzo Valla nel quadro storico-culturale del suo ambiente, Analecta Gregoriana vol. 174* (Roma, 1969) pp. 195-260.

28 *Epistolario*, I, pp. 298-307, 321-29. For medieval views of Virgil, see Ernst Robert Curtius, *European Literature and the Latin Middle Ages* (New York, 1963), pp. 206-07, and Jean Seznec, *The Survival of the Pagan Gods* (New York, 1961), pp. 16-17.

29 *Epistolario*, I, pp. 305-06.

30 *Epistolario*, III, pp. 285-308, esp. 291-92. The concept of the Bible as poetry had been elaborated by Jerome and Cassiodorus and had dominated the medieval view until eclipsed by the rise of scholasticism in the thirteenth century: Curtius, pp. 40-41, 215-21. For Petrarch's and Salutati's use of the medieval figural tradition in the interpretation of Scripture, see Trinkaus, *In Our Image*, pp. 563-71, 683-704.

31 "Nam quid tam stultum et tam anile cogitari potest, quam vane opinionis errore damnare poetas, quorum dictis crebro exundat Hieronymus, nitet Augustinus, floret Ambrosius, nec careant patres Gregorius et

Bernardus, et quibus ipsum vas electionis stultum non reputaverit se fulcire." *Epistolario,* III, p. 290.

32 For Giovanni's life and his relations with Salutati, see Ullman, 59-63; and esp. Georg Dufner, *Die 'Moralia' Gregors des Grossen in ihren Italienischen Volgarizzamenti* (Padova, 1958), pp. 33-50; and Theodore F. Rich, "Giovanni da Sanminiato and Coluccio Salutati," *Speculum,* XI (1936), pp. 386-90.

33 *Epistolario,* III, 539-43.

34 Trinkaus, pp. 662-73.

35 *Epistolario,* III, p. 541.

36 A central conclusion of Trinkaus' study; see pp. xviii-xix.

37 The text of Giovanni's letter was published by Ullman, "A Letter of Giovanni da San Miniato to Angelo Corbinelli," *Studies in the Italian Renaissance* (Roma, 1955), pp. 251-55.

38 "Vide, precor, Lactantium Firmianum, singularem et validum ethnice religionis impugnatorem, et detrahe sibi que fecit ex poetis, philosophis et oratoribus fundamenta; postque considera quid valeret efficax sua disputatio deficientibus testimoniis poetarum." *Epistolario*, IV, pp. 183-84.

39 *Ibid.*, pp. 184-86. For the circumstances of Bruni's translation, his first of a Greek text, and his only patristic translation, see Baron, *Humanistic and Political Literature,* pp. 117-18.

40 Werner Jaeger, *Early Christianity and Greek Paideia* (Cambridge, Mass., 1961), p. 84; R.R. Bolgar, *The Classical Heritage and Its Beneficiaries* (New York, 1964), pp. 45-58.

41 Atque ideo libentius id fecimus, quod auctoritate tanti viri ignaviam ac perversitatem eorum cupiebamus refringere, qui studia humanitatis vituperant atque ab his omnio abhorrendum censent." "Prologus in Basilii Epistolam ad nepotes de utilitate studii in libros gentilium traductam per L. Aretinum," in Leonardo Bruni Aretino, *Humanistisch-Philosophische Schriften,* ed. Hans Baron (Leipzig and Berlin, 1928), pp. 99-100. Note L. Schucan, *Das Nachleben von Basilius Magnus 'Ad adolescentes'* (Geneva, 1973).

42 Edmund Hunt, ed., *Iohannis Dominici Lucula Noctis* (Notre Dame, 1940); Ullman, "The Dedication Copy of Giovanni Dominici's *Lucula Noctis,"* in *Studies,* pp. 257-77.

43 "Connexa sunt humanitatis studia, connexa sunt et studia divinitatis, ut unius rei sine alia vera completaque scientia non possit haberi." *Epistolario,* IV, p. 216; English trans. from Trinkaus, p. 560.

44 Note esp. *Epistolario,* IV, pp. 214-15, and Trinkaus, pp. 55-6.

45 Trinkaus, pp. 51-102.

46 For the wide dissemination of Salutati's letter, see Ullman, *Humanism,* p. 69.

47 Dufner, *Die 'Moralia',* pp. 49-80. In the preface to his translation of Bernard's *Sermons,* Giovanni wrote that they were rendered into the "vulgare . . . a consolazione di quelli che non sanno gramatica."

48 XVIII: 1 (1, 9 September 1420).

49 Dufner, p. 50.

50 ". . . quum graecas ipsas, latinasque literas tuo potissimum bene-
ficio, et auxilio sim consequutus." XXIII: 6 (1417).

51 "Cordi vero est, si hoc exercitationis genus gratum tibi esse
cognovero, sique tua fuero auctoritate confirmatus, gratiusque ocio nostro
consulueris; nonnulla etiam eiusdem viri monumenta (sunt autem fere
innumerabilia) simili studio, ac labore convertere, tuoque dicare nomini; ut
hoc vel minimo officio incredibili in me amori tuo satisfaciam. . . ." *Ibid.*

52 XXIII: 7 (1419).

53 "Huius mihi obitus tantum moeroris iniecit, tantumque tenebrarum
offudit oculis meis, ut credi vix possit. Ea enim erat eius in me amoris vis,
tanta benignitas, tam grata praesentia, ut sine illo vivere vix possim, ex quo
vita, ut ita dixerim, pendebat mea. Nego ego ullum hominem cariorem,
gratioremque fuisse, quam me sibi . . . Fateor, Francisce carissime, tantum
me cepisse moeroris, ut delicias omnes meas priores, humanitatis videlicet
studia ex tunc fere missas fecerim, vixque me hactenus colligere, ac
recuperare possim." VI: 19 (21, 23 August 1421).

54 Giuseppe Cammelli, *I dotti bizantini e le origini dell'umanesimo,*
Vol. I: *Manuele Crisolora* (Firenze, 1941); Roberto Weiss, "Jacopo Angeli
da Scarperia (c. 1360-1410/11)," *Medioevo e Rinascimento: Studi in
onore di Bruno Nardi* (Firenze, 1955), pp. 801-27.

55 "Summus Vir Emanuel Chrysolora, quum se apud Ioannem Pont.
Max. contulisset, multa mecum de tuis clarissimis virtutibus periucunde
quidem memorare solitus erat: neque ambigere te inter nostrae aetatis
viros non solum natura, & sanctimonia vitae, verum & ingenio, studio,
doctrina cum latinis, tum etiam graecis literis esse praestantissimum,
talesque viros tantis virtutibus praeditos solos existimare solere esse
sapientes, quod nec in prosperis insolescant, et adversos fortunae casus
media virtute cum aequanimitate patiantur." XXIV: 9 (1, 20 January
1417).

56 Cammelli, pp. 180-82. The text of the letter appears in Salvatore
Cirillo, *Codices graeci mss. Regiae Bibliothecae Barbonicae,* 2 vols.
(Napoli, 1826-32), pp. 259 ff. In VI: 4 (1, 20 October 1415) Traversari
writes to Francesco Barbaro that he is sending copies of Chrysoloras'
letters "De amicitia" addressed to himself and "De Mensibus" addressed to
Palla Strozzi. He had produced both copies with his own hand.

57 ". . . .teque in illius humanitate, doctrina, atque sapientia adquies-
cere maximum in modum gratulor. Est enim revera ea ingenii facilitate
atque copia, ut solus propemodum post veteres illos, quos ingenti
admiratione admiramur, quorumque libris exercemur ad studia humanitatis, palmam doctrinae facile meo iudicio referat. . . . Idque me sibi debere,
cum pleraque reliqua, tum amor eius viri, atque observatio quaedam mei
singularis ac mirifica facit. . . ." VI: 5(2, 28 February 1416), to Francesco
Barbaro.

58 Cammelli, pp. 157-58, 165, 178-80.

59 "Ut enim factus sum certior ex nostro Chrysolora, splendet, in Graeco, nitore eloquii." VI: 7 (4, 11 March 1416).

60 Vespasiano is clearly wrong, then, in stating that Traversari learned Greek under Chrysoloras: *Vite di uomini illustri,* ed. Greco, pp. 449-61. For Traversari's possession of the *Erotemata,* see XIII: 19 (31, April 1438).

61 ". . . nihil enim eiuscemodi penes me est, quod habeat una et greca uerba et expositionem latinam, non modo ex Plutarcho aut ex gentilibus reliquis, uerum ne ex sacris quidem litteris. Quoniam uero compertum tibi dixisti me grecas litteras absque miniculo preceptoris adsecutum, atque adeo consilium atque opem in adulescentulo instituendo postulasti, ut meis scilicet ille uestigiis per ignota itinera nitatur, pandam tibi, quo pacto mediocrem huiusce lingue peritiam adeptus sum. Psalterium habui grecum mihi per religionis institutionem admodum familiare. Id igitur cum latino conferre incepi atque notare tum singula uerba, tum nomina et reliquas orationis partes, quidque singula significarent mandare memorie ac uim uerborum omnium tenere, quantum fas erat. Ibi profectus inicium sumpsi. Transiui deinceps ad euangelia, epistulas Pauli actusque apostolorum hisque familiariter obseruatus sum; habent enim satis magnam uerborum copiam suntque omnia translata fideliter ac diligenter nec inconcinne. Postmodum uero et gentilium libros uidere uolui, eosque haud facile intellexi. Mihi igitur factum optimum uidetur . . . solisque inhereat interpretationibus ueterum sacris dumtaxat, que, quod ad uerum traducte sint, et proprie faciliores atque illius accomodatiores profectibus sunt. Prestaret quidem doctore uti; sed is nisi egregie peritus sit et linguam probe calleat, proficiet nihil, imo oberit plurimum rudi animo ac per id satis censeo certis niti quam ambigua et incerta sectari; loquor enim que expertus ipse sum." Bertalot, "Zwölf Briefe," pp. 101*-02*. In teaching Greek, Traversari followed this same method. Note the conclusion to the letter cited above, and VI: 2 (22, 11 March 1425) where he asks Francesco Barbaro to give him a Greek Psalter for use in teaching. Mehus, p. ccclxv, mentions seeing a Greek-Latin lexicon, written in Traversari's hand, in the library of the Camaldulensian monastery at the Eremo.

62 The two "Profession Books" of S. Maria degli Angeli disagree as to the year Scarano entered the monastery. A.S.F. Conv. Soppr. No 86, filza 95, lxxxxxiiii r° gives 1416, while filza 96, xlvi v° gives 1406. The former is clearly wrong for Traversari mentions "Senex Demetrius" present in S. Maria degli Angeli in VI: 4 (1, 20 October 1415).

63 VI: 5 (2, 28 February 1416); VI: 17 (7, 28 March 1417); and VI: 12 (16, 1 November 1419).

64 VIII: 3(5, January 1424); VIII: 10 (9, 16 ? 1424).

65 VI: 4 (1).

66 VIII: 31 (26, 24 September 1426).

67 G. Zippel, *Niccolò Niccoli* (Firenze, 1890) remains fundamental; note also Holmes, *Florentine Enlightenment,* pp. 11-12, 88-93. For Niccoli's library, see now Berthold L. Ullman and Philip A. Stadter, *The*

Public Library of Renaissance Florence: Niccolò Niccoli, Cosimo de' Medici and the Library of San Marco. Medioevo e umanesimo, 10 (Padova, 1972). A new Niccoli letter has recently been discovered: Tino Foffano, "Niccoli, Cosimo e le ricerche di Poggio nelle biblioteche francesi," *Italia medioevale e umanistica,* XII (1969), pp. 113-28.

68 "Quod Sanctorum Patrum Vitas, sermonesque contra Iudaeos, & quod Deus incomprehensibilis sit, placuisse tibi adseris, maximum in modum gaudeo; eroque hoc iudicio tuo, quod plurimi facio, confirmatior, et audacior ad cetera." VIII: 1 (8, 16 March 1424).

69 "Uterer ad te Naeviano versiculo, si id mihi religio permitteret, eo scilicet, quo ad Catonem scribens usus est Cicero: 'Gaudeo laudari abs te, ' frater, 'laudato viro'." VIII: 9 (11, 21 June 1424).

70 "Studiosi praecipue omnes, et humanitati dediti parentem suum, promotoremque amisisse querebantur. Et merito sane; namque iudicio meo (quod libere fateri liceat) non habuit Latina lingua, neque nostra, neque Patrum nostrorum memoria, hominem, cui plus debeat honoris et laudis. Is enim profecto si quid eruditionis, si quid eloquentiae hodie habet Italia (habet autem tantum, ausim dicere, quantum ante sexcentos annos non habuit) auctor, et princeps fuit. Is, ut graecarum literarum iam ante multa saecula apud nos extincta studia reviviscerent, primus effecit. Is, ut sepulta Vetustatis monumenta in lucem venirent, mirabili diligentia, et infaticabili studio solus ferme curavit; quum plerique, et quidem magni Viri ad id negligentius adfecti viderentur." IX: 21 (21, 12 February 1437). Niccoli died 3 February 1437. This tribute to Niccoli should not be regarded as excessive retrospective praise in the wake of Niccoli's death. Note the similar remarks in VIII: 2 (39, 8 July 1431), to Niccoli.

71 "Quod tantopere gratularis studiis nostris, nihil tu quidem novum, aut a tua natura, atque instituto alienum facis. Mihi vero persuasum est iampridem te non secus provectibus nostris, quam tuis commodis & lucris gratulari. Ceterum id molestissime tuli; quod tu priscae dignitatis, atque consuetudinis oblitus, ita te deiicis, ut adseras te perbeatum putare, qui merueris in nostram familiaritatem venire. Ista ne, quaeso, Nicolai mei verba esse debuerunt? Ita ne me suffundendum censuisti? Ita de te merui? An putas me molestius quidquam audire potuisse? Ego vero contra penitus statuo, neque te consuetudine mea feliciorem, quam me tua illustriorem, eruditiorem, beatioremque & sentio, & prae me fero. An vero ego ullum, post memorabilis suavitatis seniorem Patrem expertus sum amantiorem mei, quam te? Tu studiorum meorum ab ipsis fere incunabulis, fautor, incentor, adiutorque fuisti. Si quid in nostra, si quid in peregrina lingua profeci, tibi in primis debeo, ut non velim esse (quod avertat Deus) ingratissimus tuae benevolentiae, eximaieque in me pietati, cui, si quid profectibus nostris adcessit, acceptum referre debeam." VIII: 1 (8, 16 March 1424).

72 VI: 5(2, 28 February 1416).

73 VIII: 7 (1, prior to November 1421); VIII: 2(39, 8 July 1431); Vespasiano, "Frate Ambruogio," *Vite*, ed. Greco, p. 451.

74 Ullman and Stadter, *The Public Library*, pp. 3-15, 292-99.

75 VIII: 39 (14, 2 September 1424).

76 In 1434, complaining that Niccoli never wrote, Traversari threatened, "At id silentium tuum ulcisci ferme institueram, et nihil ultra rescribere. . . ." VIII: 54 (55, 16 March 1434). For Niccoli's objection to Traversari's preoccupation with reform, see VIII: 41 (44, second half 1432).

77 "Nicolao Nicoli", *Vite,* eds. d'Ancona and Aeschlimann, pp. 443-44.

78 Albertus a Sarthiano, *Opera omnia* (Roma, 1688), p. 227.

79 Mercati, *Traversariana,* pp. 46-47.

80 ". . . qui neque inter occupationes perpetuas ut aliquid sacrum ex greco transferam exigere nunquam desistit. . . ." Remigio Sabbadini, *Le scoperte codici latini e greci ne' secoli XIV e XV,* II (Firenze, 1967; first publ. 1905), p. 20.

81 *Carteggio di Giovanni Aurispa,* ed. Remigio Sabbadini (Roma, 1931), p. 27.

82 Arbesmann, *Der Augustiner-Eremitenorden,* pp. 120-41; Baron, *Crisis,* 1st ed., II, pp. 450-51.

Chapter II

1 "Placuit medio ex itinere, veluti ex curriculo, deflectere paulisper, ut Francisci Petrarchae tumulum in villa Arqua cerneremus. Vir enim nobilis erat aetate nostra, et literis deditus a quo ferme sunt excitata studia humanitatis, ut Mausoleum suum visere cuperem, facile de me obtinuerat. Eo salutato, precibusque pro illius requie fusis, contendimus ad Monasterium." *Hodoeporicon,* pp. 71-72. Salutati and Bruni also attributed the revival of learning to Petrarch: Herbert Weisinger, "Who Began the Revival of Learning? The Renaissance Point of View," *Papers of the Michigan Academy of Science, Arts, and Letters,* XXX (1944), pp. 625-38. For the shift from the late Trecento view of Petrarch as the restorer of classical Latin poetry to the Quattrocento view of Petrarch as the initiator of the wider movement of the revival of the Ciceronian ideal of the *studia humanitatis,* see Baron, *Crisis,* 2nd ed., pp. 254-69.

2 VI: 6 (3, 2 March 1416); VI: 17 (7, 28 March 1417); VI: 10 (10, 15 May 1418); VI: 14 (13, 1418-19); VI: 12 (16, 1 November 1419). For Barbaro, see Remigio Sabbadini, *Centrotrenta lettere inedite di Francesco Barbaro* (Salerno, 1884); id., "La gita di Francesco Barbaro a Firenze nel 1415," *Miscellanea di studi in onore di Attilio Hortis* (Trieste, 1910), pp. 615-27, republ. in *id., Storia e critica di testi latini,* 2nd ed. (Padova, 1971), pp. 25-35; Percy Gothein, *Francesco Barbaro: Fruh-humanismus und Staatskunst in Venedig* (Berlin, 1932).

3 VI: 14.

4 VI: 16 (6, 31 January 1417).

5 VI: 22 (19, 23? October 1420).

6 Commentaria tua de re uxoria ad Laurentium optimum, tuique studiosissimum adolescentem legi, gratulatusque sum iudicio meo, quod tu unus profecto nostra aetate es, qui et vetustissimorum hominum summa, et excellentia ingenia facile adaequare, et nostri temporis superare etiam idoneus sis. Macte virtue; qui talia rudimenta praetefers, quale ingenii lumen exercitatus Orator exhibebis? Nequeo satis tuum laudare, atque admirari ingenium." VI: 15 (5, 1 June 1416).

7 ... simus tam vetusta inter nos /in dies/ confirmata familiaritate devincti animusque ubicunque simus praesens sit ... Amor enim noster ille integerrimus cuius 'iacta sunt' a virtute 'fundamenta', nec verbis augetur nec silentio comminuitur." *Epistolario di Guarino Veronese,* ed. Remigio Sabbadini, Vol. I (Venezia, 1915), Ep. 77, pp. 151-52 (dated 4 October 1417). Sabbadini notes that the phrase "fundamenta alicius rei iacere" appears frequently in Cicero.

8 Verum haec ipsa tua sententia ... etsi sapienter, ac magnifice dicitur, est tamen severior, quam ut mihi probari possit; magisque ea Catoniana, quam Ciceroniana est. Nosti enim sane quam fuerit illi viro molesta absentium amicorum taciturnitas; nec iniuria. Quid enim sane adeo exhorrescit amicitia, ut solitudinem? an vero illa solitudo dicenda non est, quum amicorum conspectu, et contubernio destituti sumus? At istud amicorum desiderium literarum tantum crebra vicissitudine lenire, ac consolari consuevimus. ... Te nosse admodum volo, Guarine suavissime, atque una tecum Barbarum nostrum nihil mihi gratius, nihil iucundius adferri posse, quam literas nobis quam creberrimas, et festivissimas." V: 33(1, 16 October 1417). This is the only extant Traversari letter to Guarino, but clearly their correspondence was more extensive. Traversari mentions writing to Guarino in VI: 8 (8, 3 October 1417) and VI: 20 (17, 24 February 1420). He mentions receiving letters from Guarino in VI: 11 (12, 26 September 1418) and VIII: 9 (11, 21 June 1424). Guarino refers to a letter received from Traversari in a letter of November 1423: *Epistolario,* I, Ep. 245, p. 382. In letters of 1426-27 to his student Mariotto Nori, then in Florence, and to Niccoli, Guarino sends his greetings to "sancto monacho fratri Ambrosio!" *Epistolario,* Epp. 373, 395, 397. For Guarino, see Remigio Sabbadini, *Vita di Guarino Veronese* (Genova, 1891) and *Id ., La scuola e gli studi di Guarino Guarini Veronese* (Catania, 1896); both works were reissued in one volume, *Guariniana* (Torino, 1964).

9 XXIV: 19 (3, 1 October 1422); VIII: 8 (10, 25 May 1424).

10 Traversari's earliest letter to Poggio appears to be the one published in Mercati, *Traversariana,* pp. 22-23, dated by Mercati to November-December 1423. The only other extant Traversari letter to Poggio is II: 32 (22, 24 October 1433). Undoubtedly some of their correspondence is lost, for Poggio's two letters to Traversari XXIV: 7 (33, June 1429) and XXIV: 8 (35, 15 March 1430), were written in reply to Traversari. Traversari's earliest letter to Giustiniani, also 1423, appears in *Traversariana,* pp.

23-24. Mehus published sixteen Traversari letters to Giustiniani (VI: 23-38), dating from 1425-35, and five from Giustiniani to Traversari (XXIV: 20-24), dated 1431-38. For Guistiniani, see Aldo Oberdorfer, "Di Leonardo Giustiniano umanista," *Giornale storico della letteratura italiana,* LVI (1910), pp. 107-20.

11 Vespasiano, *Le vite,* ed. Greco, p. 451. For the development of humanist academies, See A. Della Torre, *Storia dell'Accademia Platonica di Firenze* (Firenze, 1902).

12 VI: 5 (2, 28 February 1416).

13 "Ex quo noster Cosmus Decemviratu discessit, deteriore in loco sumus. Is enim perpetuo celebrandus, gratus civibus ita se gessit in eo magistratu, ut nihil praetulisse patriae, ne salutem quidem suam, lapides ipsi clamare videantur. Ea enim animi generositate est, ut adspectu ipso deiectos quosque, ac moerore tabescentes erigeret, melioreque spe esse iuberet. Porro tanta vigilantia in illo fuit, ut quidquid prosperum emersit, ipsius potissimum industriae fuerit. Atque utinam tales cives haberemus plures! Nulla unquam fuit Respublica beatior, ac felicior." VIII: 2 (39, 8 July 1431). Note Alison M. Brown, "The Humanist Portrait of Cosimo de' Medici, Pater Patriae," *Journal of the Warburg and Courtauld Institutes,* XXIV (1961), pp. 186-221.

14 "Ubi vero Cosmum ipsum vidimus ita servari, maximo quidem dolore commoti sumus, et praesentem rerum faciem, et praeteritam fortunam volventes animo. Temperavimus tamen a lachrymis quantum potuimus. Verum tantam illo offendimus magnitudinem animi, tantumque praeteritae fortunae suae totiusque mundanae gloriae contemptum, ut majorem certe non desideraverimus. Idem vultus, eadem oris dignitas, eadem gratia perseverabat, ut miserari potius afflictam Civitatem quam suas reputare injurias videretur. Denique, post longum nostrum sermonem, qui consolaturi adveneramus, consolationis plurimum cepimus; jamque magis miserati Civitatem sumus, quae hujusmodi homines tam fortes, adeo magnanimos et constantes, tantaeque in patriam pietatis, amitteret, a quibus servata saepius Civitas ipsa fuisset." *Hodoep.*, p. 88. Note Curt S. Gutkind, *Cosimo de' Medici, Pater Patriae, 1380-1464* (Oxford, 1938), pp. 62-105.

15 "Cum, paucis post diebus, Deo miserante, iv. ferme noctis hora dimissus est. Postridie vero, quam profectus ille fuerat, cometes in Coelo visus multorum animos sollicitavit. Egimus gratias Deo, qui et illum aperto periculo et nos perpetua cura sollicitudineque levavit." *Hodoep.* p. 90.

16 VIII: 9 (11, 21 June 1424).

17 VIII: 35 (35, 18 November 1430); VIII: 2; Sabbadini, *Le scoperte,* I, p. 111.

18 XII: 13 (12, 21 November 1433); XI: 24 (24, 31 March 1432); XXIV: 50 (9, 23 February 1425).

19 See pp. 154-55; 68.

20 F. Pintor, "La libreria di Cosimo de' Medici nel 1418," *Italia medioevale e umanistica*, III (1960), pp. 190-99.

21 Gutkind, p. 241.

22 See, pp. 71-76. 163-65.

23 "Gratissime accepi studium ardens Laurentii nostri ad sacras literas, Moraleque illud S. Gregorii avidissime legisse, et summe admiratum, boni gustus, et sani indicium censui. Ei commentum Origenis in Epistolam ad Romanos, ut iubes, non solum libenter, verum et gratissime mittam; ... magnumque mihi beneficium videbor consequutus, si per tuam diligentiam, atque operam, et adminiculum iuventus hisce studiis se dederit, quae sola vera esse, et salubria; utinam tandem animadvertant, qui hattenus horum fuere negligentes." VIII: 11 (6, 1 February 1424).

24 Vespasiano, *Le vite,* ed. Greco.

25 VII: 9 (8, 27 November 1436); VII: 7 (10, 29 May 1437); VII: 8 (11, 1 June 1437).

26 VII: 3 (6, 30 August 1435); VII: 4 (7, 6 December 1435); VII: 11 (13, 16 July 1438).

27 "Pueris nostris mirifice gratulor, qui Carolo preceptore non minus felices sunt quam dudum Alexander vel Leonide primum pedagogo vel postea magistro Aristotele." Bertalot, "Zwolf Briefe," p. 99*; first publ. by Luiso, *Riordinamento,* II, pp. 7-9, and dated August 1430. Marsuppini deserves a new study, but note Vespasiano's "Vita di Meser Carlo d'Arezo" and G. Zippel's still useful *Carlo Marsuppini d'Arezzo* (Trento, 1897).

28 See below, p. 73.

29 "Vtilius puto huic eum operi incumbere quam Homeri poema conuertere; licet enim elegantissimum habeat versibus componendis ingenium, promptaque illi ac parata sit rerum omnium uerborumque copia, multum tamen iudicio meo laborabit, antequam Homeri dignitatem latine queat seruare eumque ita latinum facere, ut non a se ipso degeneret." Bertalot, p. 99* Perhaps Marsuppini heeded Traversari's advice, for not until 1452, bowing to Pope Nicholas V's insistence demands, did he begin a translation of the *Iliad*. He completed only Book I and parts of Book IX before his death: Vespasiano, *Le vite*, ed. Greco, p. 594 n.1.

30 VIII: 5 (3, 18 December 1423; VIII: 6 (4, 27 December 1423); VIII: 3 (5, January 1424); VIII: 11 (6, 1 February 1424); VIII: 12 (7, 27 February 1424); VIII: 8 (10, 25 May 1424): VIII: 28 (12, 26 July 1424); *Carteggio di Giovanni Aurispa,* Ep. VII (27 August 1424), pp. 10-15, and Appendix II, pp. 160-63. For Rinuccio, see D.P. Lockwood, "De Rinucio Aretino graecarum litterarum interprete," *Harvard Studies in Classical Philology,* XXIV (1913), pp. 51-109.

31 *Carteggio,* Ep. XXXIII (1427), p. 51, and Sabbadini's note p. 13; Paul Lawrence Rose, "Humanist Culture and Renaissance Mathematics: The Italian Libraries of the Quattrocento," *Studies in the Renaissance,* XX (1973), pp. 46-105, esp. pp. 56-68.

32 Eugenio Garin, "Ritratto di Paolo dal Pozzo Toscanelli," in *La cultura filosofica del Rinascimento italiano* (Firenze, 1961), pp. 313-34; Rose, pp. 59-62.

33 *Carteggio,* Ep. LII (2 January 1430), LIII (15 March 1430), LIIII

(28 April 1430), LV (18 July 1430), pp. 66-72; *Lorenzo Ghibertis Denkwurdigkeiten,* ed. Julius von Schlosser (Berlin, 1912), II, pp. 11-13; Rose, 60-61.

34 Richard Krautheimer, *Lorenzo Ghiberti* (Princeton, 1956), pp. 159-88. For Traversari's role in another major Florentine artistic project, Brunelleschi's "Rotunda degli Angeli," see my "Ambrogio Traversari and the 'Tempio degli Scolari' at S. Maria degli Angeli in Florence" in the forthcoming *Festschrift* for Myron Gilmore by the Fellows of Villa I Tatti.

35 VI: 8 (8, 3 October 1417).

36 *Carteggio,* Ep. VII (27 August 1424); V (11 February 1424), X (13 September 1424), XI (26 October 1424), XII (1 December 1424), XVI (23 February 1425), XVII (May 1425), XVIII (11 June 1425), XVIIII (19 July 1425), XX (2 August 1425); Mehus, V: 34 (2, 1 September 1424), VIII: 39 (14, 2 September 1424).

37 *Carteggio,* XXXIII (1427).

38 VIII: 8 (10, 25 May 1424).

39 *Carteggio,* LV (18 July 1430).

40 "Ex Graecia nullum sacrum volumen attuli, praeter Gregorii Epistolas, credo, ducentas; qui liber etsi emendatus sit et ubique legi possit, eius pulchritudo tamen ad lectionem pigrum hominem non invitaret. miseram ex Constantinopoli electissima quaedam volumina sacra non pauca in Siciliam iam pridem; nam et ea mihi, verum fatear, minus cara erant et regi Graecorum nonnulli malivoli me saepissime accusarant, quod urbem illam libris expoliassem sacris; gentilibus enim non tam grande crimen videbatur." *Carteggio,* Ep. VII.

41 "Id abs te ego summis precibus postulo, ut libros illos sacros, quos ex Byzantio in Siciliam te transmisisse adseris, ad nos perduci quam commodius poteris facias. Eos, velim credas, avidissime exspecto. Neque enim fieri potest inter illos delitescant thesauri Babyloniis praeferendi." V: 34.

42 *Carteggio,* LII (2 January 1430), LIII (15 March 1430), LIIII (28 April 1430), LV (18 July 1430).

43 XXIV: 32 (18, 13 June 1428). For Filelfo, see Carlo de' Rosmini, *Vita di Francesco Filelfo da Tolentino* (Milano, 1808) and G. Zippel, *Il Filelfo a Firenze* (Roma, 1899).

44 XXIV: 29-41 (17 March 1428-26 March 1429). Note the fuller text of XXIV: 34 publ. as Ep. IV in Rosmini, Bk I, pp. 115-16.

45. *Carteggio di Giovanni Aurispa,* Ep. L (31 July 1429), p. 65.

46. VI: 34(29, 22 May 1429); VI: 26 (30, 1 August 1429).

47 "Traduxit quaedam ex graeco: quanto cum sudore nostro, fateor, explicari difficillime potest. Vincit illius improbitas propositum meum, quo illi aditum ad me prorsus obstruere decreveram, ne otium meum aliis intentum, et deditum studiis obtunderet; fregitque constantiam." VI: 30 (34, 14 October 1430). Traversari does not mention which translations he collaborated on with Filelfo. While in Florence Filelfo translated two orations of the Athenian Lysias, Xenophon's *Agesilaus* and *Polity of the*

Lacaedaemonians, and Plutarch's lives of Lycurgus and Numa: Rosmini, I, pp. 57-59, 130-32.

48 VIII: 36 (36, March 1431); cf. VI: 30. In XXIV: 32 (18, 13 June 1428) Filelfo had informed Traversari that he was undertaking a translation of "vitam Moysis ex Iudaeo Philone".

49 Rosmini, I, Ep. VI (29 May 1430), p. 117; Mehus, XXIV: 43 (52, 2 May 1433).

50 *Carteggio di Giovanni Aurispa,* Ep. LXV (early 1433).

51 "Venne in tanta fama et riputatione, sī per la sanctitā della vita congiunta colla dotrina, che in Firenze non veniva persona di conditione, che non andassi agli Agnoli a visitarlo, perchē nollo avendo fatto non gli pareva avere veduto nulla." "Frate Ambruogio," ed. Greco, p. 451.

52 VIII: 12 (7, 27 February 1424); VIII: 1 (8, 16 March 1424); VIII: 8 (10, 25 May 1424).

53 VIII: 16 (27, second half 1426); VIII: 5 (3, 18 December 1423); VIII: 11 (6, 1 February 1424); VIII: 12 (7, 27 February 1424); VIII: 8 (10, 25 May 1424).

54 Guido Battelli, "Una dedica inedita di Ambrogio Traversari all' Infante Don Pedro di Portogallo, Duca di Coimbra," *Rinascita,* II (1939), pp. 613-16; for the life of Don Pedro, see Frederick Hartt, Gino Corti, and Clarence Kennedy, *The Chapel of the Cardinal of Portugal (1434-1459) at San Miniato in Florence* (Philadelphia, 1964), pp. 27-64 *passim.*

55 "Non itaque improbo si quid contra philosophorum sentiamus inventa, si modo nostra probabilibus verisque rationibus muniamus." Remigio Sabbadini, "Cronologia documentata della vita di Lorenzo Valle, detto il Valla," in L. Barozzi and R. Sabbadini, *Studi sul Panormita e sul Valla* (Firenze, 1891), pp. 64-65; republ. in Laurentius Valla, *Opera omnia,* ed. Eugenio Garin (Torino, 1962), II, pp. 370-71. The date of the letter is 4 September 1433. Barozzi attributed a second letter to Valla regarding the *De vero falsoque bono* as Traversari's, but Sabbadini, pp. 66-67, 210-11, argued persuasively that this second letter was written by Marsuppini. In his *Antidota in Pogium* (*Opera omnia,* I, p. 343) Valla wrote that in addition to Decembrio, he had sent his dialogue to the "elegantes" humanists "Guarinum, Leonardum, Ambrosium, Carolum." For the reception of the dialogue, see the critical edition, Lorenzo Valla, *De vero falsoque bono,* ed. Maristella de Panizza Lorch (Bari, 1970), p. xlii. Among recent discussions of Valla's dialogue are Trinkaus, *In Our Image,* pp. 103-70, and Mario Fois, S.J., *Il pensiero cristiano di Lorenzo Valla nel quadro storico-culturale del suo ambiente (Roma, 1969), pp. 95-167.*

56 For Traversari's search for manuscripts, see pp. 116-17.

57 *Hodoep.,* p. 31, VIII: 42 (41, 3 March 1432); XI: 27 (27, 11 April 1432).

58 VIII: 45 (46, 30? May 1433); VIII: 46 (47, 6 June 1433); VIII: 47 (48, 20 June 1433); *Hodoep.,* pp. 61-69. For Ciriaco, see Edward W. Bodnar, S. J., *Cyriacus of Ancona and Athens* (Bruxelles, 1960), and

Charles Mitchell, "Archaeology and Romance in Renaissance Italy," in *Italian Renaissance Studies,* ed. E.F. Jacob (London, 1960), pp. 455-83.

59 *Hodoep.*, p. 74; VIII: 49 (50, 19 July 1433); VIII: 50 (51, 19 July 1433); VIII: 51 (20 July 1433). Niccoli had met Vittorino during a trip to Venice in 1430-31. In VIII: 2 (39, 8 July 1431), Traversari wrote that he was pleased to have had confirmed by Niccoli's personal experience the truth of Vittorino's widespread fame for virtue and erudition.

60 Traversari's letter, dated 19 January 1433, appears in Sabbadini, *Le scoperte,* II, pp. 19-20. Aratus (c. 315-240/239 B.C.) wrote a lengthy astronomical poem, the *Phaenomena,* which was widely disseminated in antiquity and translated into Latin by Cicero and Germanicus.

61 "Nicolaus Treverensis, homo studiosissimus, et librorum copia insignis, scripsit ad me, multumque oravit, ut te interpellarem. ... Et quoniam, ut audio, homo est multum eruditus, te oro haveas caussam istam suam commendatam; quia multum studiis nostris conferre potest eius, quam hic mihi literis comparavi, familiaritas." III: 48 (48, 24 October 1435). Note Edmond Vansteenberghe, *Le Cardinal Nicolas de Cues (1401-1464)* (Frankfurt-am-Main, 1963; first publ. Paris, 1920), pp. 24, 58-59; and Paul E. Sigmund, *Nicholas of Cusa and Medieval Political Thought* (Cambridge, Mass., 1963), pp. 219-21.

62 Sigmund, pp. 222-25.

63 "Dimisi apud generalem Cameldunensium [sic] Proculum de theologia Platonis, ut transferret. Supplico instantissime, quoniam nunc vacare liberius poterit. Solicita eum." Josef Koch, *Cusanus-Texte,* IV: *Briefswechsel des Nikolaus von Cues* in *Sitzungsberichte der Heidelberger Akademie der Wissenschaften* (1942-43), pp. 35-36.

64 See pp. 221-22.

65 Rudolf Haubst, "Die Thomas- und Proklos-Exzerpte des 'Nicolaus Treverensis' in Codicillus Strassburg 84," *Mitteilungen und Forschungensbeiträge der Cusanus-Gesellschaft,* I (1961), pp. 17-51. Note also Paul Oskar Kristeller, "A Latin Translation of Gemistos Plethon's *De fato by* Johannes Sophianos Dedicated to Nicholas of Cusa," in *Nicolò Cusano agli inizi del mondo moderno* (Firenze, 1970), pp. 183-84, and *Id.*, "Byzantine and Western Platonism in the Fifteenth Century," in *Renaissance Concepts of Man and Other Essays* (New York, 1972), pp. 103-04.

66 A note in Vat. Pal. lat. 149 f. 243^V states, "Ambrosius generalis Camaldulens, florentinus, hanc translationem fecit, quo 1440 [sic] decessit. Et magister Paulus magistri Dominici, physicus florentinus, magistro Niccolao de Cusza hos libros sic translatos 1443 transmisit." (see Vansteenberghe, p. 12). Cusanus was close to Toscanelli, dedicating his *De transmutationibus geometricis* (1450) to him, visiting him several times in Florence, and dictating to him his last will: Vansteenberghe, pp. 11-12. Cusanus' complete Ps.-Dionysius, the present ms. Kues 43, was copied by his secretary Peter Erkelenz. The Diogenes Laertius (ms. Harleian 1347) was copied in 1462 and contains numerous marginal notations in Cusanus' hand. See Vansteenberghe, p. 29.

67 Kristeller, "A Latin Translation," p. 192. For the place of Ps.-Dionysius in Cusanus' thought, see Vansteenberghe, pp. 410-16, and Morimichi Watanabe, *The Political Ideas of Nicolas of Cusa with Special Reference to his 'De Concordantia Catholica'* (Genève, 1963), pp. 31-32.

68 *Hodoep.*, pp. 60, 78.

69 Sabbadini, *La scuola,* pp. 138-45.

70 William H. Woodward, *Vittorino da Feltre and Other Humanist Educators* (Cambridge, 1897), pp. 67-82.

71 Trinkaus, *In Our Image,* pp. 230-58, 571-601.

72 VI: 31 (26, 29 January 1429), VI: 32 (27, 5 February 1429), VI: 33 (28, 8 May 1429), VI: 34 (29, 22 May 1429).

73 The text was published by Pier Giorgio Ricci, "Una Consolatoria inedita del Marsuppini," *La Rinascita,* III (1940), pp. 363-433. Note Holmes, *Florentine Enlightenment,* pp. 106-08.

74 See pp. 163-66.

75 XIII: 17 (29, 7 April 1438); XIII: 20 (31, 5 May 1438); Mercati, *Traversariana,* pp. 12-13.

76 Vespasiano, "Ser Filippo di Ser Ugolino," ed. d'Ancona and Aeschlimann, pp. 444-54; Ernesto Lasinio, "Della biblioteca di Settimo e di alcuni suoi manoscritti passati nella Mediceo-Laurenziana, *Rivista delle Biblioteche e degli Archivi,* XV (1904), pp. 169-77.

77 "Nihil ambigo fore, ut hominem transferas in sententiam tuam, quando ea oratoria virtute emines, ut possis vel inimicissimis etiam in caussa non aeque bona persuadere quae velis. Quanto magis trahendum, et quidem non reluctantem, putemus hominem amicum fortassis certe non inimicum, et ab humanitate, ut audio, non abhorrentem? Adde quod piis vires Deus semper subpetit." V: 35 (15, 17 November 1432).

78 "Doleo quidem, praestantissime vir, cum tuarum vero literarum causa, quas augere in dies et sacris praeceptis ornare destitisti nunquam, dum tibi per otium licuit, ut jam ex Graecis hausta Doctoribus complura abs te edita volumina legantur. Doleo, inquam, te tantis nunc negotiis premi ut ad ea obeunda honestissima studia nihil tibi quidquam temporis supersit. Sed est quod me consoler, teque pariter tua prudentia consoleris, quod egregie praeter caeteros magnos et excellentes viros gerendis in rebus plurimum de virtute mereris, cum et Rhetoris nostri nunc quidem sententia virtutis laus omnis in actione consistat." Woodward, *Vittorino,* p. 82.

79 VI: 8(8, 3 October 1417); Sabbadini, *Le scoperte,* I, pp. 77-83.

80 *Poggii Epistolae,* ed. Thomas de Tonellis (Florentine, 1832), [reprinted in Poggius Braccioloni, *Opera omnia,* ed. Riccardo Fubini (Torino, 1964), III], I, Bk. I, Ep. VI, VIII, XIII. An English translation of Poggio's letters to Niccoli has now appeared: Phyllis Walter Goodhart Gordan, *Two Renaissance Book Hunters: The Letters of Poggius Bracciolini to Nicolaus de Niccolis* (New York, 1974). For Poggio's stay in England, see Roberto Weiss, *Humanism in England during the Fifteenth Century,* 2nd ed. (Oxford, 1957), pp. 13-21.

81 ". . . caeterum illud officium, non libertatis initium est, sed officina servitutis. Intellige, quid dico: non ego illam quaero libertatem, quae vacet omni cura, ac molesta; . . . sed illam in qua paucioribus sim subjectus, quam Tullius ait, vivere ut velis. Prior sanctior esset, sed Spiritus ubi vult spirat, non volentis, neque currentis, sed miserentis est Dei, qui potens est facere cum voluerit non ex meritis, sed ex vocante. In hac vita Ambrosius est noster, quem ego judico felicissimum: reputat enim omnia ut stercus, ut Christum lucrifaciat. Nos quibus tantae non adsunt animi vires, hanc mediocritatem cupimus sectari, in qua Deum sequentes, non omnino mundo serviamus." *Poggii Epistolae,* I, Bk. I, Ep. XXII.

82 XXIV: 7(33, June 1429). The inventory of the ninety-five books Poggio owned at his death is published in Ernst Walser, *Poggius Florentinus: Leben und Werke* (Berlin, 1914), pp. 418-23. (I wish to express my thanks to Mr. Samuel Hough of Brown University for his kind permission to examine his unpublished study of Poggio's library.) For Poggio's anti-clerical polemics, see Walser, pp. 110-34; Riccardo Fubini, "Un'orazione di Poggio Bracciolini sui vizi del clero scritta al tempo del Concilio di Costanza," *Giornale storico della letteratura italiana,* CXLII (1965), pp. 24-33; *id., Introduzione alla lettura del 'Contra Hypocritas' di Poggio Bracciolini* (Torino, 1971).

83 "Nimium permagna est charitas multorum, qui communem utilitatem praeferunt privatae; animas enim suas perdunt, ac produnt, ut salvent alienas." XXIV: 8 (35, 15 March 1430).

84 V: 10 (27, 16 July 1434).

85 "Quid, Carolus, de nostro Ambrosio iudicatis, inquit? Recta ne an tortuosa philosophabatur via? Nunquid vobis Hypocrisim redolebat?

Nequaquam, Hieronymus inquit. Fuit enim vir optimus, meo iudicio, ac probatissimus; qui in suo coenobio literis deditus, multa scripsit magna cum laude & doctrina. Summa certe fuit praeditus humanitate ac virtute.

Laudo vitam illius, Carolus inquit, & existimo extra Hypocrisim fuisse, dum in Coenobio Florentiae Musis vacavit. Sed factus Abbas paulum divertit a priori vivendi cursu. Ambiebat enim paulum subocculte, ut aliquid altius videretur appetere. Recordimini, Nicolaum nostrum, virum in loquendo liberum & amicissimum illi, solitum saepius reprehendere supervacuas curas, quibus sponte implicabatur, & ad rubeum Pileum tendere retia, dictitabat." *Opera omnia,* II, p. 79.

86 Trinkaus, *In Our Image,* pp. 258-70.

87 Bruni's "Prologus in Phaedonem Platonis" (1404/05), dedicated to Pope Innocent VII, was published in *Humanistisch-Philosophische Schriften,* ed. Baron, pp. 3-4.

88 Note for instance in his treatise on education, the *De studiis et litteris liber* (1422-29), that Bruni distinguishes between studies that belong to religion and those that pertain "ad bene vivendum." It is the latter, involving the study of classical ethical thought, which most interest Bruni. The text appears in *Humanistisch-Philosophische Schriften,* p. 12.

For Bruni's Greek scholarship, see, in addition to Baron, *Crisis,* and *Humanistic and Political Literature,* Eugenio Garin, "La 'retorica' di Leonardo Bruni," *Dal Rinascimento all'Illuminismo: Studi e ricerche* (Pisa, 1970), pp. 21-42.

89 Trinkaus, 673-74.

90 As we have seen (Chap. I, pp. 28, 30.), Traversari kept up with Bruni's Greek scholarship [note also VIII: 5 (3, 18 December 1423)], and he was delighted that the long standing quarrel between Niccoli and Bruni was finally patched up: VIII: 16 (27, second half 1426). But he criticized severely Bruni's *Phaedrus* translation (see Ch. III, p. 113), and he regarded as inappropriate Ghiberti's consultation of Bruni in planning the narrative scenes of the "Gates of Paradise": VIII: 9 (11, 21 June 1424), and Krautheimer, *Ghiberti,* pp. 159-61.

91 ". . . si Grammaticus ille, quem in Indice notasti tibi videtur non indignus nostro usu (erit autem dignissimus, si sapiat vetustatem, atque antiquam illam latinitatem & diligentiam) mittas illum ad me . . ." VI: 6 (3, 2 March 1416). Vespasiano equated Traversari with Bruni as the renewer of the Latin language: "Frate Ambruogio," ed. Greco, pp. 455-56.

92 VIII: 3, 12, 8, 28 (January-July 1424); *Carteggio di Giovanni Aurispa,* V (11 February 1424), XVI, XVII, XVIII (February-June 1425).

93 XI: 16 (17, 18 February 1432), and *Hodoep.,* p. 30.

94 XI: 48 (48, 7 November 1432).

95 Dini-Traversari, Documento n⁰ 4. Undated, but likely written during the period when Traversari mentioned recuperating from an attack of stomach pains, XV: 33 (34, 4 January 1435).

96 ". . . dette opera alle lettere ebree, et di quelle ebe qualche notitia." "Frate Ambruogio," ed. Greco, p. 450.

97 Trinkaus, *In Our Image,* pp. 581-601.

98 Umberto Cassuto, *Gli Ebrei a Firenze nell' età del Rinascimento* (Firenze, 1918), pp. 274-75.

99 Trinkaus, 578-81.

100 Sabbadini, *Le scoperte,* I, pp. 211-12.

101 *Hodoep.,* p. 31; XI: 21 (21, 3 March 1432); VIII: 42 (41, 3 March 1432).

102 Note esp. his request to Barbaro: VI: 4 (1, 20 October 1415). Traversari also sought indices from Aurispa, Filelfo, Rinuccio da Castiglione, and Cardinal Giordano Orsini [VIII: 42 (41, 3 March 1432)]. When Niccoli left his library in S. Maria degli Angeli in 1423-24, Traversari made an index of the collection: VIII: 4 (2, 17 December 1423); VIII: 5 (3, 18 December 1423).

103 B.L. Ullman, *The Origin and Development of Humanistic Script* (Rome, 1969); Ernst H. Gombrich, "From the Revival of Letters to the Reform of the Arts: Niccolò Niccoli and Filippo Brunelleschi," *Essays in the History of Art Presented to Rudolf Wittkower,* eds. Douglas Fraser, Howard Hibbard, and Milton J. Lewine (London, 1967), pp. 71-82; Millard Meiss, "Towards a More Comprehensive Renaissance Palaeography," *The Art Bulletin,* XLII (1960), pp. 97 ff.

104 Sabbadini, *La scuola,* pp. 48-49, 107-08.

105 Ullman, *The Origin,* pp. 59-77.

106 XI: 19 (1, ?).

107 Ullman, *The Origin,* pp. 98-103.

108 XIII: 14 (23, April-August 1437).

109 VIII: 7 (1, prior to November 1421); VIII: 2 (39, 8 July 1431); VI: 5 (2, 28 Februaary 1416). Hans Baron, "Aulus Gellius in the Renaissance," in *From Petrarch to Leonardo Bruni: Studies in Humanistic and Political Literature* (Chicago, 1968), pp. 196-215, observes that Gellius' *Noctes Atticae* was one of the classical works which, though not unknown to the Middle Ages, became reasonably intelligible only through the critical efforts of the humanists.

110 V: 33 (1, 16 October 1417).

111 "Verum eius operis duo sunt exemplaria, neutrum perfectum; sed utrumque quantum coniicere possum, mendosum, atque interdum mutilatum . . . Nosti quantum sit traducenti necessaria boni exemplaris fides. Eam quia hactenus desidero in illis duobus voluminibus, peto abs te, ut si sit penes te, vel alium quempiam civium tuorum huiusmodi opus, mature ad nos perferendum cures, ut extrema manus labori nostro possit adponi. Fiet enim ex collatione trium exemplarium, ut multum opis, ac facilitatis in emendando, ac limando opere adcedat." VI: 23 (23, 27 May 1425).

112 VIII: 44 (43, 27 April 1432). Origen did write homilies on Isaiah. These were translated by Jerome: Berthold Altaner, *Patrology,* trans. Hilda Graef (New York, 1961), p. 227.

113 "Opusculum tamen quoddam Ciceronis titulo insigne transcripsit, ac detulit secum; quod meo quidem iudicio illius non est. Habet synonima primum, tum de verborum differentiis. Eruditum quidem non negarim virum; longe tamen a Tulliana dignitate." VIII: 44. The manuscript in question was one which Luca da Spoleto, secretary to Cardinal Cesarini, brought back from a lengthy diplomatic journey to France and Germany in 1431: Sabbadini, *Le scoperte,* I, p. 106, II, p. 214.

114 See Traversari's praise of Niccoli quoted Chap. I, p. 22.

115 The earliest inventory of the library at S. Maria degli Angeli was made in 1513. This was published by Serenella Baldelli Cherubini, "I manoscritti della biblioteca fiorentina di S. Maria degli Angeli attraverso i suoi inventari," *La Bibliofilia,* LXXIV (1972), pp. 9-47. There are documents of bequests of books dating from 1385, including missals, breviaries, a Bible, and "omnes libros teologales quod habebat in dicta civitate Florentie" which Cardinal Frias of Spain left in 1420. Some books were left to the monastery in 1385 by Francesco Bruni, Florentine notary, teacher of rhetoric at the Florentine Studio (1360-61), pontifical secretary in Avignon (1362-c. 1381/82), and correspondent of both Petrarch and Salutati. We are uninformed as to what volumes were in this bequest, but presumably there were some classical texts. For Francesco Bruni, see the brief sketch of his life in Novati, ed., *Epistolario di Coluccio Salutati,* I, pp. 42-43.

116 Sabbadini, *Storia e critica,* pp. 70-71.

117 VI: 6 (3, 2 March 1416).

118 VI: 8 (8, 3 October 1417); VI: 14 (13, 1418-19); Sabbadini, *Storia e critica,* pp. 35-39.

119 *Carteggio di Giovanni Aurispa,* Ep. XI (26 October 1424), pp. 18-19.

120 In his notes on the *Letters to Atticus,* Traversari demonstrates knowledge of Caesar's work. He was lent Curtius Rufus by Cosimo: VII: 1 (19, ?).

121 *Carteggio,* Ep. XXXIII (1427), p. 51. Sabbadini notes that this was probably a copy of the manuscript containing eight books which Guarino discovered in 1419; see also *Storia e critica,* pp. 263-73.

122 *Carteggio,* Ep. XVI (23 February 1425), pp. 23-25; VIII: 50 (51, 19 July 1433).

123 For Traversari's reading Bruni's, Barbaro's, and Filelfo's translation, see pp. 28, 38, 113. For the request for Leonardo Giustiniani's translations of Plutarch's Cimon and Lucullus, see VI: 16 (6, 31 January 1417). For Bernardo's translation, see *Hodoep.,* p. 75; XXIV: 25 (54, 12 October 1433); and Patricia H. Labalme, *Bernardo Giustiniani: A Venetian of the Quattrocento* (Roma, 1969), pp. 45-54.

124 IX: 7 (18, 1 December 1434).

125 See esp. Trinkaus, *In Our Image,* Pt. I. Note also Eugene F. Rice, *The Renaissance Idea of Wisdom* (Cambridge, Mass., 1958), Ch. I; Jerrold E. Seigel, *Rhetoric and Philosophy in Renaissance Humanism* (Princeton, 1968); and Hanna H. Gray, "Renaissance Humanism: The Pursuit of Eloquence," *Journal of the History of Ideas,* XXIV (1963), pp. 497-514.

126 "At qui ignarus eloquentiae est, hunc indignum prosus qui de theologia loquatur, existimo." Laurentius Valla, *Opera omnia,* I, pp. 117-20.

127 Hanna H. Gray, "Valla's 'Encomium of St. Thomas Aquinas' and the Humanist Conception of Christian Antiquity," in *Essays in History and Literature Presented by the Fellows of the Newberry Library to Stanley Pargellis,* ed. Heinz Bluhm (Chicago, 1965), pp. 37-51. Valla's *Encomium* is now in an English trans., Leonard A. Kennedy (ed.), *Renaissance Philosophy* (The Hague, 1973), pp. 17-26.

128 "Quem enim vel socordissimum non moveat vel orationis dignitas, vel argumentorum, quibus uteris, subtilis elegantia? Non est nobis ferreum pectus, et adamantina praecordia; non silvis natos Hircanae nutrivere tygrides." V: 33 (1, 16 October 1417). Cr. Vergil, *Aeneid,* IV, 11. 365-67.

129 "Converti me ad Athanasium legendum, tantaque summi, et eximii viri admiratio tenuit, ut ab eo divelli non possim. Legi duos eius libros adversus Gentiles; namque in primo Gentilem superstitionem arguit; in secundo Crucis, ac divinae Incarnationis tuetur ignominiam tanta argumentorum vi, sententiarumque gravitate, ut agi quidem ea caussa, ut est plerisque acta, et in primis a nostro Lactantio, dignius tamen, atque divinus non posse videatur. Legi ex ordine tres iam libros adversus Arium, nam quinque sunt, et magni quidem: tantaque fragrantia pietatis refectus

sum, ut nihil me legisse meminerim, quod huic operi conferri possit. Eminet in eis literis incomparabilis viri venustas quaedam tum sententiarum, tum verborum, digna profecto, quam omnes admirentur, venerentur, ament. Granditer enim eam caussam, ut dignum fuerat, agit cunctasque illius haeresis obiectiones ita aperit, arguit, refellit, tantaque Scripturarum sacramenta enodat, ut exsatiari eius lectione non possim. Quid plura? Statui apud me convertendo, igneo ac coelesti homini debitis meis me totum dedere; si quid otii suppeditare potuero; nihil enim illius doctrinae salubrius, nihil ignitius reperiri posse constanter adfirmaverim." VIII: 12 (7, 27 February 1424).

130 Woodward, *Vittorino*, p. 152.

131 XI: 17 (18, 23 February 1432); doubtless the "libros teologales" which Cardinal Frias bequeathed to S. Maria degli Angeli (see above, n. 115) were scholastic works.

132 Iris Origo, *The World of San Bernardino* (New York, 1962), p. 118; for the emblem and charges of heresy, see pp. 117-30.

133 ". . . sed tamen spero, volente Iesu Christo, suadentibus amicis, te multa bona hic reparando, reconciliandoque posse instaurare forsan spirituale aedificium, quod per Patrem nostrum fratrem B. aedificatum erat. . . . Meminisse enim volo hoc nomine Iesu duriora perpessos inter saevitiam crudelissimorum Gentilium, aliorumque nefandorum hominum insolentissimam rabiem, impulsore diabolo, Apostolos esse." II: 40 (1, February-April 1426).

134 ". . . immortale divinae eloquentiae flumen magnificentia quadam semper exscrescens in illo dulcissimo, et plenissimo ore divinissimi hominis fratris Bernardini, quo sanctarum scripturarum potenti eloquentia, ac omnipotentia gloriosissimi, et victoriosissmi Nominis Iesu universam curiam Romanam, et omnem populum ex inimicissimis sibi amicissimos fecit, et in cognitionem divinarum rerum, et viae Domini, devotionemque sanctissimi Nominis Domini nostri Iesu Christi a profundo pelago omnium vitiorum, ac perditissimis moribus, et tenebris eorum ignorantiae, desperataque salute traduxit. . . . Illud postremo ante oculos ita literis tuis effinge conflictum, confusionemque illarum elatarum mentium, quae livore superbissimo contabescunt, mentes inquam illorum, qui simulata iustitia, et inflata scientia primates in Ecclesia Dei novum fundamentum, deleto nomine Iesu, inducere conantur, qui malunt videri, quam esse, in literis, et in spiritu exspertes omnis sapientiae. Tu velim mihi enarres, quo vultu, quo ore, quibus recessibus festinis, qua verecundia, et rubore repulsi foveas, et latebras eorum requisierunt. Utinam adfuissem, et perspexissem triumphalem victoriam Iesu Domini nostri per fratrem Bernardinum, virum Dei bonum, verum, sanctum, ac iustum, vidissemque illos insolentissimos, nefariosque homines contradicentes viro sancto in contumeliam Iesu Domini nostri, sarcinulas literarum suae inflatae scientiae abditas sub pallio magnificentissimae Religionis reportantes rabie eorum solita in cavernas suas, contra quos Propheta decantat: 'Sepulchrum patens est guttur eorum, linguis suis dolose agebant, iudica illos Deus!' " II: 41 (2, April ?

1426). (Paul quotes this same verse in Romans 3: 13).

135 "Has breves non sine summis lacrymis, et ingenti cordis dolore ad Reverentiam tuam conscribo ... tamen interdum veror non coelitus hoc esse, quod tu Praedicator paupertatis in Christo Iesu, aedificator innumerabilium animarum, desiderator Evangelicae vitae, designatus, et pronunciatus sis Episcopus." II: 39 (3, June 1427).

136 Origo, pp. 223-25.

137 Barozzi and Sabbadini, *Studi sul ... Valla*, pp. 168-80.

138 "Iuri civili te dare operam ... sum factus certior. Probo id quidem; sed ea ratione ut potius Iurisconsultos veteres, quam Commentatores ignavos tibi hauriendos, atque imitandos moneam. Habent illi in se plurimum dignitatis, veteremque elegantiam praeferunt, quam novi isti interpretes in tantum abest, ut consequi potuerint, ut per imperitiam linquae saepenumero ne intelligant quidem. Alioquin hisce studiis nequaquam absque cultiorum detrimento studiorum vacare posses. Si enim antiqua illa, et limatiora ingenia professionem iuris licet claram, et oratori quoque, teste Cicerone, pernecessariam, non usquequaque praedicabant, multumque illi deesse ad gratiam orationis testabantur; quum tamen illi ipsi Iurisconsulti essent peritissimi; quid ipsi statuere possumus, quum vix reliquiae nudae, ac tenues supersint, illaeque tanta barbarie interpretum violentur. Triduo se iuris consultum fore, si navaret operam, Cicero iocatur in Servium Sulpitium, ut adpareat quanti eam exercitationem fecerint. Vides de hac re quid sentiam. Placet, ut iuri plane des operam; sed latinae linguae, et cultioris musae te damnum nolo perpeti." V: 18 (18, second half 1432). Note Mercati, *Traversariana,* pp. 62-64.

139 "Frate Ambruogio," ed. Greco, p. 452.

140 XIII: 8 (22, April-May 1437); XI: 22 (21, 14 May 1434); XIII: 3 (11, 17 May 1434).

141 VI: 2 (22, 11 March 1425).

142 The school was established some time between 17 December 1432 when Traversari wrote that Allegri had agreed to head the school, and 25 March 1433 when he wrote that Mariotto had begun instruction: XI: 53 (53); XI: 58 (58). In XV: 6 (6, 13 September 1432), Traversari asked Mariotto to head the school and described to him its purpose. For Traversari's early encouragement to Mariotto to pursue humanist studies, see XV: 1 (1). Note Mercati, *Traversariana,* p. 4 for the dating of this letter. From 1453-78 Allegri was General of the Camaldulensians: Cacciamani, "La réclusion," p. 151. Humanist studies also formed the curriculum of the school established under Traversari's direction at S. Maria della Rosa in Siena: I: 20 (13, 2? April 1435); and P. Enrico Bulletti, "Due lettere inedite di Ambrogio Traversari," *Bullettino senese di storia patria,* LI-LIV (1944-47), pp. 97-105 (letter to Priors of Siena dated 16 January 1437).

143 III: 31 (31, 21 March 1435); cf. Bulletti, "Due lettere."

144 III: 31.

145 Richard C. Trexler, "Ritual in Florence: Adolescence and Salva-

tion in the Renaissance," in *The Pursuit of Holiness,* pp. 200-64, esp pp. 209-10.

146 VIII: 50 (51, 19 July 1433) and *Hodoep.,* p. 74. For Guarino's and Vittorino's schools, see W.H. Woodward, *Studies in Education during the Age of the Renaissance* (New York, 1965; first publ. 1906), and Eugenio Garin, *L'educazione in Europa 1400-1600* (Bari, 1957), esp. pp. 122-32.

147 XV: 38 (39, 31 August 1435).

148 Note IV: 12 (11, 24 February 1435) where Traversari praises Allegri for the students' rapid progress in Latin. For conflict with the Prior of the Eremo over the school, see XV: 22 (22, 18 December 1433).

149 *Hodoep.,* pp. 138-39; XV: 33 (34, 4 January 1435); cf. III: 31.

150 XV: 33.

151 Dufner, *Die 'Moralia',* p. 40.

152 "Ego non lubenti animo, summaque cum aviditate perlegerem fratris amantissimi literas, eas praecipue, in quibus adeo flagranter humanitatis studia, tantaque cum aviditate complecteris . . . Tu velim, mi frater . . . adhibeas acrem, atque pervigilem operam studiis probitatis, atque virtutis; nec coepisse contentus, prosequare summa diligentia, nervisque omnibus praeclarum eruditionis, atque sanctitatis nomen. Nullum tibi tempus perire patiaris, quin aliquid agas de sacris literis; nullae tibi horae satis sint pro adfectu, atque desiderio ad prosequenda studia humanitatis. Cura tibi sit praecipua, atque vigilans peritissimorum, sanctissimorumque virorum, eorum scilicet, quos vetustas venerabilis commendat, praecepta, institutaque mandare memoriae. Placeant illorum tibi literae; eisque cura effici quam maxime familiaris. Nec nostrorum modo praecepta, atque libros revolvendos existima; verum externam quoque doctrinam pro copiosiore peritia, proque nitore linguae tibi ediscendam, iuxta veterum praecepta sentio. Fuere quippe plerique ex illis viris maxime studiosi sapientiae, ut ex ea re vocabulum acceperint, adeo virtutis amatores, honestique fautores, ut prope Religioni nostrae adcessisse videantur." XI: 19 (1, ?).

153 "Potest eim utrumque decentissime aptari, ut in spiritalibus studiis, et in eruditione proficias, evadasque in dies, et in sanctitate provectior, et in eruditione instructior. Immo ausim dicere ibi cumulatiorem doctrinae gratiam adfuturam, ubi divina magis abundaverit gratia. Est enim inter dona Spiritus Sancti scientia quoque adiuncta pietati, et quam Spiritus Sancti repleverit mentem, eam omni scientiae nitore collustrat." XII: 2 (2, 18 December 1431). Agostino, Traversari's fellow countryman from Portico di Romagna, made his profession at S. Maria degli Angeli in 1423 at the age of fourteen. In 1435 he left to become Prior of S. Maria della Rosa in Siena, one of the monasteries where Traversari promoted a humanist education for the young monks. For Agostino, see the *Registrum monachorum* of S. Maria degli Angeli, A.S.F. Conv. Soppr. No 86, filza 95, lxxxxiiii r⁰.

154 ". . . tu sepultam fere humanitatem excitasti; tu sopita hominum

corda ad haec honestissima studia prior evigilare fecisti, iuventutemque proclivem in vitia, ut sese ex coenoso voluptatum gurgite ad hoc placidissimum doctrinae littus reciperet, vi ignitae adhortationis effecisti." VIII: 2 (39, 8 July 1431).

155 *Ibid.*

156 VII: 2 (2, 1433).

157 VIII: 12 (7, 27 February 1424); VIII: 1 (8, 16 March 1424).

158 VIII: 8 (10, 25 May 1424); for Antonio da Massa's journey to Constantinople see M. Viller, "La question de l'union des Eglises entre Grecs et Latins depuis le Concile de Lyon jusqu'à celui de Florence, 1274-1438," *Revue d'histoire ecclesiastique,* XVII (1921), p. 292, and Joseph Gill, S.J., *The Council of Florence* (Cambridge, 1959). pp. 33-37.

159 VIII: 1.

160 "Vides quam incertus sit humanae conditionis status, atque fragilis vita nostra, et morti quotidie obnoxia. Patere, quaeso, me hoc praesertim tempore sacras haurire literas, sacrisque vacare rebus, quibus a puero me ipsum devovi. Parebo votis vestris, si vita comes fuerit." VIII: 8.

161 R.D. Hicks, trans., *Diogenes Laertius: Lives of Eminent Philosophers* (Cambridge, Mass., 1942), I, pp. xviii-xxii; Richard Hope, *The Book of Diogenes Laertius: Its Spirit and Method* (New York, 1930).

162 Eugenio Garin, "Ricerche sull'Epicureismo del Quattrocento," in *La cultura,* pp. 72-87.

163 Sabbadini, *Le scoperte,* II, pp. 9-10, 137-38; J.T. Muckle, C.S.B., "Greek Works Translated Directly into Latin before 1350," *Mediaeval Studies,* V (1943), p. 110; Valentin Rose, "Die Lucke im Diogenes Laertius und der alte Ubersetzer," *Hermes,* I (1866), pp. 367-97.

164 Erwin Panofsky, *Renaissance and Renascences in Western Art* (New York: Harper Torchbook ed., 1969; first publ. Stockholm, 1960), p. 84.

165 ". . . ut extrema manus labori nostro possit adponi." VI: 23 (23, 27 May 1425).

166 VI: 25 (24, 8 July 1425); note also VI: 27 (25, 5 August 1425), and VII: 2.

167 "Revertar postmodum ardentiore animo, et maiore siti ad sacras Literas, ut coeperam, exercitii caussa transferendas, magno meo gaudio dulciusque osculabor eas, quibus infans paene adsuetus eram." VI: 27.

168 VIII: 26 (19, 1425-26?). The volume Traversari sought was probably the present Laur. San Marco. 125 s. XII, which contains Boethius' *De syllogismis,* and the *De topicis differentiis,* plus Aristotle's works on logic. Before Niccoli owned it, it had been in the possession of Salutati: Ullman and Stadter, pp. 202-03.

169 VIII: 17 (20, 1426?).

170 XXIV: 38 (25, 10-20 September 1428), and above, p. 39; for Traversari's justification for omitting to translate the verses, see the dedicatory letter, XXIII: 10. Agostino Sottili, "Autografi e traduzioni di Ambrogio Traversari," *Rinascimento,* 2nd s., V (1965), p. 11, has

identified the presentation copy of Traversari's translation as the present
Laur. LXV 21. It was written by Fra Michele, and dated 8 February 1433.

171 "Nihil enim sanctae caritati postponendum quis non videat?
Verum, quum sit ordinata caritas, proximumque ut nos ipsos ex Legis
instituto diligere iubeamur; non tamen salutem propriam negligere
debemus. Medium itaque iter incedendum est, et sub Domini protectione
confugiendum. Adsit igitur divina clementia piis conatibus nostris, ut
amicorum votis videamur morem genere, et propriae saluti facere satis."
VII: 2.

172 "Proemium illud nostrum super Laertium probari tibi gratulor:
satisque me oblatrantium linguas armasse rationibus videor." VIII: 47 (48,
20 June 1433).

173 "Imo hoc ipso labore meo fore ut christianae pietatis, et gratiae
dignitas magis patesceret, ac per id fides in Deum promptior, ac ardentior
surgeret ratio verissima suadebat. Quando enim inter illos, qui sapientiae
saecularis fuere principes, tanta de Deo, rebusque et divinis, et humanis
opinionum concertatio est, ut se invicem destruant, neque ubi consistas
reperire possis; maiore profecto alacritate animus divinae dignitatis
amplectitur gratiam, atque ad fontem veritatis adcurrens veteris squalorem
miseratur erroris. Etsi enim apud illos sparsim probabilia quaedam, et
veritati consona invenire est; mens tamen tanta opinionum varietate
fatigata libentius, et gratius intra cubicula veritatis se recipit, et divinis
libris, et literis audiendis maiori deinceps desiderio inhiat. Et ipsa tamen,
quae apud nobiliores quosque Philosophos de Deo, de coelo, corpor-
ibusque coelestibus, de natura rerum subtiliter, ac vere disputata sunt,
veritati christianae maxime adstipulantur. Merebatur enim profecto tam
egregia indagandae veritatis intentio, opera illa tam acris ingenii, adeo
celebre studium sudoris sui fructu non usquequaque destitui, Deo id
permittente, ut illorum quoque testimonio Fides vera firmamentum, ac
robur acciperet. Multa in his et dicta graviter, et facta constanter invenias;
ut non modo ex eorum libris fidem inviolabilis veritas capiat, verum
exemplis quoque religionis nostrae incitamentum virtutis accedat. Quam
foedum enim, quamque plenum dedecoris est, si Christianum hominem, et
de Deo suo pendentem, et cui aeternae vitae spes certa sit, virtuti, et
continentiae dare operam pigeat; cum gentiles viros, et a veri Dei cultu, ac
religione longe alienos probitati, modestiae frugalitati, ceterisque id genus
animi humani ornamentis impensius studuisse compererit! Pleraque exem-
pla huiusce pene dixerim evangelicae perfectioni proxima sunt; ut
pudendum vehementer, et erubescendum sit, si id minus exhibeat Christi,
quam mundi Philosophus, plusque in pectore gentili possit amor gloriae
inanis, quam in animo christiano religiosae pietatis adfectus. His atque
huiusmodi rationibus facile mihi persuasum est, ut hoc traducendi munus
non modo ut inutile non adspernarer, seu ut noxium fugerem sed contra
penitus ut commodum, ac necessarium constanter adgrederer. Nempe si
quem forte plus aequo eiusce hominum admiratio rapiat, eorumque gesta
nostrati philosophiae praeferre, seu conferre etiam exemplis velit (id quod

solum ferme timemus) is leniter admonendus erit solidam potius virtutem, quam adumbratam virtutis imaginem admiretur." XXIII: 10.

174 For Salutati, see Ch. I, n. 28; the Bruni preface appears in *Humanistisch-philosophische Schriften,* ed. Baron, pp. 3-4. For Traversari's Lactantius scholarship see Ch. III, pp. 117-20; he had Augustine's *De doctrina Christiana* transcribed for Guarino, VI: 27 (25, 5 August 1425).

175 Corvinus' copy is the present cod. 817 of the Biblioteca Trivulziana of Milan: Kristeller, *Iter,* I, p. 363. The San Marco copy, a large volume with illuminated initials, dated 1455, is the present Laur. S.M. 323; Ullman and ·Stadter, p. 221. For other fifteenth century mss., see Kristeller, *Iter,* I, pp. 13, 72, 99, 187, 342, 349; II, 94, 95, 107, 226, 230, 417, 466, 476. The first printing was by Nicolas Jenson in Venice, 1475. Not until after 1500 was Traversari's translation printed outside Italy. For the printed editions, see James Hutton, *The Greek Anthology to the Year 1800* (Ithaca, N.Y., 1935), pp. 85-87.

176 E.g., Traversari eagerly examined Vittorino's Greek volume of Plato's *Laws, Epistles,* and *Republic:* VIII: 49 (50, 19 July 1433); and he tried to acquire from the Abbot of Grottaferrata a Greek volume of Aristotle's *Metaphysics* for Marsuppini: VIII: 42 (41, 3 March 1432), VIII: 44 (43, 27 April 1432).

177 "Praeterea postulavimus, ut Ethica ad Eudemium Aristotelis mitteret ad nos legendam, vel forsitan etiam transferendam." XIII: 9 (19, 8 January 1437).

178 Enea di Gaza, *Teofrasto,* Maria Elisabetta Colonna, trans. (Napoli, 1958), pp. vii-xviii; Basile Tatakis, *La philosophie byzantine* (2e Fascicule supplementaire to Emile Brehier, *Histoire de la philosophie*), 2nd ed. (Paris, 1959), pp. 27-34.

179 Traversari's letter to Andreolo appears in Mercati, *Traversariana,* pp. 26-29. Mercati suggests, p. 20, that Traversari's source for the Greek text of the. *Theophrastus* is the present Marcianus Gr. 496, s. X. In VI: 12 (16, 1 November 1419) Traversari wrote to Francesco Barbaro that he was *not* contemplating a translation of "Aeneas" (Gazeus?), since he could not find a complete text of it. It is possible he could have translated the *Theophrastus* as early as 1422-23, for no extant letters date from this period. Another possibility is the period 1427-31, when again direct evidence of Traversari's activity is slight. If it was completed in either of these earlier periods, why would he wait so long before "publication"? (However, if Traversari translated Chrysostom's *De providentia Dei* in 1419-20, as seems highly likely, he allowed eight years to elapse before dedicating it to the Duke of Coimbra: see Ch. III, p. 130.

180 "Opusculum Aeneae cuiusdam docti plane, et eruditi viri quum grece legerem, latinum facere placuit. Est enim ea vel doctrinae gratia, vel materiae dignitas, ut vel inertes quosque animos in admirationem sui exscitare possit. De Anima quippe illi omnis sermo est: agitque subtiliter ista viri disputatio ut docti quique, Gentiliumque disciplinis imbuti sensim, et per rationes ad fidei catholicae rudimenta, et pietatis penetralia ipsa

pertingant; dum Philosophorum vanas, et varias, atque inter se dissidentes de Anima opiniones verissimis rationibus, argumentisque confutat, veritatemque christianae fidei, et naviter, et grate, atque venuste subinferit. . . . Accipies igitur, Andreole vir Illustris, Aenaem nostrum iam plane pium. et per te Roma accipiat suae gentis auctorem; qui longe verius de se protestari possit 'Sum pius Aeneas' quam ille olim Anchisae filius." XXIII: 11.

181 Eugenio Garin, "Il problema dell'anima e dell'immortalità nella cultura del Quattrocento in Toscana," in *La cultura,* pp. 93-118.

182 Firenze Bibl. Riccardiana cod. 709 f. 190 "Hic liber est Marsilii Fecini Florentini et ab eo scriptus mense maii 1456." Traversari's translation of Aeneas Gazeus is written on f. 134-83. See Paul Oskar Kristeller, *Studies in Renaissance Thought and Letters* (Roma, 1956), pp. 164-65; *Iter,* I, p. 198. Traversari's translation was widely disseminated in the fifteenth century. In addition to the manuscripts listed by Colonna, p. xl, see Kristeller, *Iter,* I, pp. 146, 227, 261, 296, 353, II, pp. 4, 6, 174, 210, 317. It was first printed in 1513 (Venice), thus coinciding with the Fifth Lateran Council. One of the few enactments of the Council was a condemnation of the position of the Paduan Averroists who believed that the immortality of the soul could not be proved by reason. A second edition, published by Beatus Rhenanus, appeared in Basel in 1516. Incidentally it is Agostino Giustiniani, author of the preface to the 1513 edition and grandson of Andreolo, in whose library on Chios Agostino states he found Traversari's translation, who is responsible for the oft-repeated but erroneous information that Traversari visited Chios in person while on a trip to the East. Agostino's preface appears in Mehus, XXV: 34.

183 "Est enim ea Hesiodi quoque sententia Catholicae concinens veritati: 'durum esse, & arduum, ac perdifficilem virtutis adscensum, et confragosis anfractibus asperum; in quo primum multo conatu, multoque labore desudandum sit!" XV: 22 (22, 18 December 1433). Note, for a general discussion of humanist moral philosophy, Paul Oskar Kristeller, "The Moral Thought of Renaissance Humanism," *Renaissance Thought II* (New York, Harper Torchbook ed., 1965), pp. 20-68.

184 "An vero . . . quid sit pietas? Meministi profecto, uti Ciceronis sententia gravissimum id vocabulum fiet, cui neque benevolentia, neque studium valeat comparari. Sed enim ea vis vocabuli discutienda a nobis videtur. Atque, ut a sacris literis capiamus initium; scribit Apostolus Paulus discipulo, quem unice diligebat, Timotheo, dicens 'O Timothee exercete ad pietatem: corporalis enim exercitatio ad modicum utilis est; pietas ad omnia valet.' Id etiam vocabulum graece θεοσέβεια dicitur, latine 'Dei cultus' transferri potest. Et, Apolline teste, pietas nihil aliud est, quam 'Dei notio,' vel 'Dei cultus.' Vides nempe, ut pietatis nomen in se omnem virtutis, ac probitatis speciem habet reconditam. Quum enim illa ad patriam, et ad parentes ex Ciceronis sententia pertineat, imo et ad Deos ipsos, quos colebat plures, ac varios gentilis error; Pauli vero testimonio ad res divinas maxime referatur; id quod et oraculum Apollinis probat; nos

magistram sequentes veritatem, Apostoli quoque innitentes monitis, pietatem rem prope divinam intelligimus, ad quam exerceri discipulum singularis meriti hortatur Apostolus. Atque, ut paucis exsprimam ego quod sentio, 'Pietas' idipsum est quod 'munditia' cordis, sive 'puritas' cordis; de qua Salvator ait: 'Beati mundo corde, quoniam ipsi Deum videbant.' Nisi forte dicat aliquis pietatem esse viam, per quam ad cordis munditiam pervenitur, ut sit illa veluti instrumentum tantae rei. At qui ego omni constantia adseveraverim utrumque idem esse; licet in eo differre ista videantur, quod munditia cordis, veluit destinatio, vel σκοπὸς sit, ad quam pervenire curamus, ut omnia quaecumque gerimus, ad eum finem referantur; pietas vero actus, quo tantam rem inquirimus." V: 12 (31, 1436?). Cf. Traversari's discussion of *pietas* in the dedication of his translation of Chrysostom's *De providentia Dei* to Don Pedro, Duke of Coimbra: Battelli, "Una dedica inedita," p. 615.

185 XI: 19 (1, ?).

186 XV: 1 (1, 12 March 1423?), to Mariotto Allegri.

187 "Quid autem vera virtus est, nisi illa, quam Apostolus tradit, dicens, Christum 'Dei Virtutem,' et 'Dei Sapientiam'? Hunc virtutum omnium fontem, hunc totius perfectionis auctorem ut toto haurias pectore hortor, atque commoneo; ut iuxta illius pollicitationem, 'fiat in te fons aquae salientis in vitam aeternam!' Nihil tibi ex omni virtutis specie deesse poterit, si illius in te subscipias, et amplectaris parentem. Non sapientia: quo enim pacto quum ipse sit sapientia Patris? Non fortitudo: quippe quum ipse sit 'Dominus fortis, et potens in praelio; qui adligavit fortem armatum, eiusque abstulit spolia.' Non iustitia: ipse enim 'factus est nobis a Deo Patre iustitia et sanctificatio.' Non prudentia, non temperantia: quippe sine illo nullae istae sunt. Non gloria, 'quum sit ipse Rex Gloriae.' Non opes, quid enim eo opulentius, qui Regem saeculorum possidere meruit? Nihil denique clarum, et expetendum eximio huic possessori deesse satis constat. XV: 1.

Chapter III

1 ".... invenimus Origenis in Lucam triginta & novem Homilias ab Hieronymo traductas; tantoque gaudio elati sumus, ut Croesi opes vicisse putaremus; sola enim ex fama notae erant; caeterum, qui vidisset aut legisset, adhuc inveneram neminem. Ea res nuntiata Florentiae, magnum gaudium excitavit, & praecipue Nicolao meo amicissimo & studiossimo. Eas continuo transcribendas curavi; una & alias in tres Psalmos, Auctoris ejusdem: licet volumen ipsum adeo putre erat, ut vix pauca legi possent." *Hodoep.*, p. 29. Cf. XI: 16 (17, 18 February 1432) and VIII: 42 (41, 3 March 1432). In fact it was the original, not a transcription, which entered Niccoli's library. It is the present Laur. S.M. 610 s.IX: Ullman and Stadter, *The Public Library*, pp. 102,136.

2 "Exegisti a me iure tuo ... ut exercitii caussa aliquid sacrarum

literarum ex graeco converterem. Aiebas enim fore optimi auspicii, si huiusmodi monumentis primitias studiorum meorum consecrarem, facturumque rem convenientissimam & voto, & instituto meo, si non minus studii, operae, & diligentiae in transferendis nostratis philosophiae magistris ostenderem, quam fecissent aetate nostra hodieque facerent nonnulli clarissimi, atque doctissimi viri familiares nostri in convertendis externae sapientiae auctoribus." XXIII: 6.

3 A study of Greek patristic theology in the Latin Middle Ages remains a *desideratum.* Useful are: P. Albert Siegmund, O.S.B., *Die Überlieferung der Griechischen Christlichen Literatur in der Lateinischen Kirche bis zum Zwölften Jahrhundert* (München-Pasing, 1949); J. T. Muckle, C.S.B.. "Greek Works Translated Directly into Latin Before 1350." *Mediaeval Studies* IV (1942), pp. 33–42, and V (1943), pp. 102-14; and Kenneth M. Setton, "The Byzantine Background to the Italian Renaissance," *Proceedings of the American Philosophical Society*, C (1956), pp. 1-76.

4 Johannes Quasten, *Patrology* I (Utrecht, 1949), *passim*; Berthold Altaner, *Patrology* (New York, 1961; trans. from second German ed., Freiburg, 1961, by Hilda Graef), pp. 443-47, 459-62; Pierre Courcelle, *Late Latin Writers and their Greek Sources* (Cambridge, Mass., 1969; trans. from 2nd French ed. of *Les lettres grecques en Occident de Macrobe a Cassiodore*, Paris, 1948, by Harry E. Wedeck), pp. 48-127, 142-43.

5 Henri de Lubac, *Exégèse médiévale*, Premier partie, Tome I (Lyons, 1959), pp. 207-38.

6 Courcelle, pp. 146-47, 205-06; Chrysostome Baur, O.S.B., "L' entrée littéraire de Saint Chrysostome dans le monde latin," *Revue d'histoire ecclésiastique*, VIII (1907), pp. 249-65; Ernest Honigmann, "Anianus, Deacon of Celeda (415 A.D.)," *Patristic Studies, Studi e Testi* 173 (Città del Vaticano, 1953), pp. 54-58; André Wilmart, "La collection des 38 homélies latines de Saint Jean Chrysostome," *The Journal of Theological Studies*, XIX (1917), pp. 305-27.

7 Courcelle, pp. 149-208.

8 Courcelle, pp. 273-409.

9 Altaner, p. 253.

10 Setton, pp. 2-16.

11 Mäieul Cappuyns, O.S.B.. *Jean Scot Érigene: sa vie, son oeuvre, sa pensée* (Bruxelles, 1964).

12 Charles Homer Haskins, *Studies in the History of Mediaeval Science* (Cambridge, Mass., 1924), pp. 160-71. No Gregory Nazianzen attributable to Aristippus is extant, but in the preface of the *Meno*, he asserts that he has begun a translation of this Greek Father at the order of King William I.

13 Mario Flecchia, "La traduzione di Burgundio Pisano delle Omelie di S. Giovanni Crisostomo sopra Matteo," *Aevum* 26 (1952), pp. 113-30.

14 Haskins, pp. 206-09.

15 J. de Ghellinck, *Le mouvement théologique du XIIe siècle* 2nd ed. (Bruges, 1948) pp. 221-49.

16 D. A. Callus, ed., *Robert Grosseteste, Scholar and Bishop: Essays in*

Commemoration of the Seventh Centenary of His Death, (Oxford, 1955), pp. 1-97, 121-45.

17 Flecchia, p. 115.

18 Salvatore I. Camporeale, *Lorenzo Valla: Umanesimo e teologia* (Firenze, 1972), pp. 304-11.

19 Beryl Smalley, *The Study of the Bible in the Middle Ages,* 2nd. ed. (Oxford, 1952), pp. 304-11.

20 Berthold Altaner, "Die Kenntnis des Griechischen in den Missionsorden während des 13. und 14. Jahrhunderts," *Zeitschrift für Kirchengeschichte,* 53 (1934), pp. 479-80.

21 *Ibid.,* pp. 436-93.

22 Viller, "La question de l'union," pp. 294-95.

23 Setton, "Byzantine Background," pp. 9, 38-40.

24 Tatakis, *La philosophie byzantine,* p. 240.

25 VIII: 49 (50, 19 July 1433); a transcription of Planudes' translation was present in Niccoli's library: Ullman and Stadter, *The Public Library,* p. 253.

26 Giovanni Mercati, *Notizie di Procoro e Demetrio Cidone, Manuele Caleca e Teodoro Meliteniota ed altri appunti per la storia della letteratura bizantina del secolo XIV. Studi e Testi,* 56 (Città del Vaticano, 1931), pp. 28-40; Setton, "Byzantine Background," pp. 29-57.

27 Steven Runciman, *The Last Byzantine Renaissance* (Cambridge, 1970), p. 80.

28 Livarius Oliger, O.F.M., *Expositio Regulae Fratrum Minorum auctore Fr. Angelo Clareno* (Quaracchi, 1912); Altaner, "Die Kenntnis," pp. 482-86.

29 *Paradiso,* X: 94-138; XII: 127-45.

30 Runciman, pp. 19-23.

31 François Masai, *Pléthon et le platonisme de Mistra* (Paris, 1956).

32 See Guarino's account of Chrysoloras' methods in Sabbadini, *Epistolario di Guarino Veronese,* II, pp. 269-71; and the discussion in R. R. Bolgar, *The Classical Heritage and Its Beneficiaries from the Carolingian Age to the End of the Renaissance* (New York, Harper Torchbook ed., 1964; first publ. Cambridge, 1954), pp. 87-88.

33 A. Vacalopoulos, "The Exodus of Scholars from Byzantium in the Fifteenth Century", *Cahiers d'histoire mondiale,* X (1967), pp. 463-80; Deno John Geanakoplos, *Greek Scholars in Venice: Studies in the Dissemination of Greek Learning from Byzantium to Western Europe* (Cambridge, Mass., 1962).

34 Paul Oskar Kristeller, "Italian Humanism and Byzantium," in *Renaissance Concepts of Man and Other Essays* (New York, 1972), pp. 64-85 at pp. 74-75.

35 Viller, "La question," XVIII (1922), pp. 30-31.

36 Letter to Antony of Bergen, 16 March? 1501, quoted from Barbara Flower's English trans. in appended "Selected Letters" to Johan Huizinga, *Erasmus and the Age of the Reformation* (New York, Harper Torchbook ed., 1957), p. 202.

37 See Chap. I, p. 22; Bruni claimed that Greek letters had been dead in Italy for seven centuries: Holmes, *Florentine Enlightenment,* p. 10.

38 See pp. 7-12, 117.

39 *Poggii Epistolae* Bk. I, Ep. VI.

40 Smalley, *The Study of the Bible,* pp. 46-82.

41 de Ghellinck, *Le mouvement,* pp. 221-49.

42 Heiko Oberman, *The Harvest of Medieval Theology* (Cambridge, Mass., 1963), p. 202.

43 Dom Jean Leclercq, *Recueil d'études sur Saint Bernard et ses écrits* (Roma 1962-69), I, pp. 278-95, 298-319, II, pp. 373-85, III, pp. 213-66;R.P.J. Daniélou, S.J.. "S. Bernard et les Pères grecs," in *Saint Bernard théologien,* Actes du Congrès de Dijon 15-19 Septembre 1953, *Analecta Sacri Ordinis Cisterciensis,* IX (1953), Fasc. 3-4/Jul.-Dec., pp. 46-55; l'Abbé Jean Châtillon, "L'influence de S. Bernard sur la pensée scolastique au XIIe et au XIIIe siècle," *ibid.,* pp. 268-88; Dom Olivier Rousseau, "S. Bernard, 'Le dernier des Peres',", *ibid.,* pp. 300-308.

44 See pp. 169-70, 200.

45 Damasus Trapp, O.E.S.A., "Augustinian Theology of the 14th Century: Notes on Editions, Marginalia, Opinions, and Book-lore," *Augustiniana,* VI (1956), pp. 146-274.

46 Arbesmann, *Der Augustiner-Eremitenorden,* pp. 36-55; Bernard M. Peebles, "The Verse Embellishments of the 'Milleloquium Sancti Augustini'," *Traditio,* X (1954), pp. 555-66. Bartolomeo produced a similar *Milleloquium* for Ambrose.

47 Trapp, pp. 181-207; Gordon Leff, *Gregory of Rimini: Tradition and Innovation in Fourteenth Century Thought* (Manchester, Engl., 1961); Oberman, *Archbishop Thomas Bradwardine, A Fourteenth Century Augustinian: A Study of His Theology in Its Historical Context* (Utrecht, 1957), pp. 211-33; J. W. O'Malley, S.J., "A Note on Gregory of Rimini: Church, Scripture, Tradition," *Augustinianum* V (1965), pp. 365-78.

48 John Hiltalingen, probably the most historically concerned of the fourteenth century Augustinians, makes frequent citations of the Latin Fathers e.g. Ambrose (31), Gregory the Great (32), Jerome (20), but virtually none of the Greek Fathers (e.g. Athanasius 2, Basil 5), except for Chrysostom (12), Origen (61), and John of Damascus (65). Anselm (156), Bernard (31), and Hugh of St.-Victor (85) are among the many twelfth-century Doctors cited. The thrust of Hiltalingen's patrology, however, is overwhelmingly Augustinian for Augustine is cited 800-1000 times: see Trapp.

49 Trinkaus, *In Our Image,* p. 47; note also Paul Oskar Kristeller, "Augustine and the Early Renaissance," *Studies in Renaissance Thought and Letters* (Roma, 1956), pp. 355-72; and with a different emphasis, Riccardo Fubini, "Intendimenti umanistici e riferimenti patristici dal Petrarca al Valla, " *Giornale storico della letteratura italiana,* CLI (1974), pp. 520-78.

50 "The Ascent of Mont Ventoux," trans. Hans Nachod, in Ernst Cassirer, *et al., The Renaissance Philosophy of Man* (Phoenix PB ed.,

Chicago, 1956), p. 44: for discussion of the *Secretum*, see Trinkaus, *In Our Image*, pp. 5-17.

51 Peebles, "The Verse Embellishments."

52 Mariani, *Il Petrarca,* pp. 15-33; Arbesmann, *Der Augustiner-Eremitenorden,* pp. 16-36.

53 Trinkaus, *In Our Image,* pp. 28-41. 65-66.

54 *De otio religioso,* ed. Giuseppe Rotondi, *Studi e Testi,* 195 (Città del Vaticano, 1958), pp. 102ff.; and Trinkaus' discussion, *In Our Image,* pp. 565-68.

55 See pp. 8-14.

56 When completed, the principal source for humanist translations will be the *Catalogus translationum et commentariorum: Mediaeval and Renaissance Latin Translations and Commentaries* eds. Paul Oskar Kristeller and F. Edward Cranz (Washington, D.C.); the first two volumes have appeared (1960, 1971). See also Eugenio Garin "Ricerche sulle traduzioni di Platone nella prima metà del sec. XV," *Medioevo e Rinascimento: Studi in onore di Bruno Nardi* (Firenze, 1955), I, pp. 339-74; and *id., "Le traduzioni umanistiche di Aristotele nel secolo XV," Atti dell' Accademia Fiorentina di Scienze Morali 'La Colombaria',* XVI (n.s. II, 1947-50), pp. 55-104. For Nicholas V's patronage, see Cesare Vasoli, "Profilo di un Papa umanista: Tommaso Parentucelli," *Studi sulla cultura del Rinascimento* (Manduria, 1968), pp. 69-121.

57 Cammelli, *Manuele Crisolora* pp. 121-25; Garin, "Ricerche sulle traduzioni di Platone,", pp. 345-60; Roberto Weiss, "Jacopo Angeli da Scarperia", pp. 801-27.

58 Chrysoloras' ideas are presented in a letter of his student Cencio de' Rustici, published in R. Sabbadini, *Il metodo degli umanisti* (Firenze, 1920), pp. 23-24.

59 W. Schwarz, "The Meaning of 'Fidus Interpres' in Medieval Translation," *The Journal of Theological Studies,* XLV (1944), pp. 73-78; *id. Principles and Problems of Biblical Translation* (Cambridge, 1955). pp. 34-37; Courcelle, *Late Latin Writers* esp. 52 ff.

60 Such a comparison is made by Franz Blatt, "Remarques sur l'histoire des traductions latines," *Classica et Mediaevalia,* I (1938), pp. 223-26.

61 For Boethius, Cassiodorus, and Eriugena, see Blatt, pp. 233-42, and Schwarz, "The Meaning," pp. 73-78. Mario Flecchia, "La traduzione", provides a line by line comparison of Burgundio's and Anianus' translations of a part of Chrysostom's *Homilies on Matthew.* For the text of Burgundio's preface to his translation of this work, see Haskins, *Studies,* pp. 151-52.

62 Nec tamen est ab hominis greci professione requirendum latinum eloquium, hac presertim etate, qua vix supra puram grammaticam elevamur etiam nos Latini. Non sunt hoc tempore Cicerones, Hieronymi, Rufini, Ambrosii, vel Chalcidii, non Cassiodori, non Evagrii, non Boetii, quorum translationes tante sunt venustatis atque dulcedinis, quod nichil

possit ornatus vel perspicuitatis in his que transtulerunt desiderari. . . . Moleste ferens igitur nos vel hoc modicum sic habere Plutarchi, quod nec libenter legere nec facile possit percipi quid sentiret, cogitavi mecum opusculum illud de sue translationis obsuritate planiore dicendi genere in lucem intelligentis revocare; ut quanvis ita non possemus ad litteram legere Plutarchum, nichil tamen quo ad sententiam nos lateret." *Epistolario di Coluccio Salutati*, ed. Novati, II, pp. 480-83. For English translation, see Setton, "The Byzantine Background," pp. 50-51. Note also Jerrold Seigel, *Rhetoric and Philosophy in Renaissance Humanism: The Union of Eloquence and Wisdom, Petrarch to Valla* (Princeton, 1968), pp. 116-18; and Weiss, "Jacopo Angeli da Scarperia." p. 821.

63 "Ego antea Augustinum legebam, nunc est in manifus Jo. Chrysostomus. Legi nonulla ejus Opuscula, et Sermones omni cum venustate translata; nunc vero alia percurro longe inferioris eloquentiae, prout varii translatores fuere, ut sunt XXXV Homeliae super epistola Pauli ad Hebraeos, item VII Homeliae in laudem Pauli Apostoli, quarum interpres fuit Anianus quidam satis doctus. Praestant LXXXVIII Homeliae in Evangelium Joannis, quarum, si interpres fuisset eloquens, nil doctius, nil gravius, nil magnificentius legisses. Sed is fuit Pisanus quidam, qui se fatetur in prolego de verbo ad verbum transferre; nec tanta est translatoris inconcinnitas, quin mirum in modum elucest facundia auctoris." *Poggii Epistolae* ed. Tonellis, Bk. I, Ep. VI (Fubini, III. pp. 30-31.)

64 The text of Bruni's letter, *Epistolae*, ed. L. Mehus, 15ff., was republished by Garin, "Ricerche sulle traduzioni di Platone," pp. 361-63. For the circumstances of the translation, see Baron, *Humanistic and Political Literature,* pp.114-21.

65 The text appears in *Humanistisch-Philosophische Schriften* ed. Baron, pp. 102-04; note also Baron, *Crisis*, 2nd ed., pp. 284-85.

66 *Schriften,* pp. 81-96.

67 Baron, *Humanistic and Political Literature*, pp. 119-21.

68 Seigel, p. 119. Note also Bruni's procedure in producing a humanist Latin version of the Ps.-Aristotle *Economics* (Book III of the Greek text had been lost): Baron, *Humanistic and Political Literature* pp.166-72; Josef Soudek, "The Genesis and Tradition of Leonardo Bruni's Annotated Latin Version of the (Pseudo-) Aristotelian *Economics,"* *Scriptorium* XII (1958), pp. 260-68. Compare Aurispa's emendation in translating Lucian's *Comparatio:* David Cast, "Aurispa, Petrarch, and Lucian: An Aspect of Renaissance Translation," *Renaissance Quarterly*, XXVII (1974), pp. 157-73.

69 *Schriften*, pp. 76-81. The Latin medieval text which Bruni criticized is that of Robert Grosseteste, slightly revised and corrected by William of Moerbeke: Ezio Franceschini, "Leonardo Bruni e il 'Vetus interpres' dell 'Etica a Nicomaco'," *Medioevo e Rinascimento: Studi in onore di Bruno Nardi,* I, pp. 297-319.

70 Seigel, pp. 109-10.

71 *Ibid.,* pp. 123-33.

72 Eugenio Garin, "La 'retorica' di Leonardo Bruni," *Dal Rinascimento all'Illuminismo: Studi e ricerche* (Pisa, 1970), pp. 21-42; note also *id.*, "Ricerche sulle traduzioni di Platone," pp. 345-46, and *id.*, "La fortuna dell'etica aristotelica nel Quattrocento," in *La cultura* pp. 60-71.

73 Note esp. Nancy S. Struever, *The Language of History in the Renaissance: Rhetoric and Historical Consciousness in Florentine Humanism* (Princeton, 1970), pp. 63-82.

74 L. Minio-Paluello, "Iacobus Veneticus Grecus: Canonist and Translator of Aristotle," *Traditio*, VIII (1952), pp. 265-304.

75 Callus, *Robert Grosseteste* pp. 1-69.

76 Gerard Verbeke, "Guillaume de Moerbeke et sa methode de traduction," *Medioevo e Rinascimento: Studi in onore di Bruno Nardi*, II, pp. 779-800.

77 XXIII: 6 (1417); Battelli, "Una dedica inedita," p. 615

78 "Quo in opere summus ille vir philosophiam nostram contra vituperatores, et derogatores omnes ita magnifice, tantaque vel orationis dignitate, vel argumentorum vi, vel sententiarum ubertate tuetur; ut omnibus post hac maledicis ora perpetuo silentio obstruxisse videatur. Id igitur libentius convertere institui, quo nostris summae spei Adolescentibus, atque omnibus ubique Monachis summo et solatio, et usui fore arbitratus sum: quum illi caussam suam animadverterint a praestantissimo viro, ante mille annos tanta vel cura subsceptam, vel elegantia, et ubertate defensam. Praeterea plurimorum, qui vitae praesentis commodis, et voluptatibus addicti monasticae vitae instituta carpere non desinunt, hoc studio, et labore nostro vel reprimendam audaciam, vel instruendam ignorantiam putavimus. ... Quorum in manus libri isti si inciderint, non nihil de irrationabili furore, et inconsultissima indignatione remittent: et nisi fuerint penitus exscordes, manus etiam fortassis dabunt; quum viderint se tot, et tam variis doctissimi viri rationibus conclusos, et circumscriptos. ... In quibus si quid inconcinnius dictum offenderis (offendes autem plurima) imperitiae interpretis imputes velim. Neque enim tantum mihi adrogo, ut putem me eloquentissimum virum pari orationis luce transferre potuisse: imo vero non ambigo quin illum sese longe inferiorem in lingua nostra videri fecerim; quum in sua, hoc est in graeca incredibili facilitate, et ubertate fluat. Quibus ego in rebus illum, si, ut erat optimi officium interpretis imitari non potui; tibi in primis, Pater optime, imputare debebis, qui immemor virium nostrarum, easque amore potius, quam ratione metiens, rem doctissimorum hominum ab imperito requisisti. Ego enim, quum tuam istam iussionem mihi minime spernendam, seu detrectandam arbitrarer, malui in me eloquentiam desiderari, quam fidem." XXIII: 6.

79 Traversari himself sent copies to Francesco Barbaro, VI: 9 (9, 10 January 1418); and Eugenius IV, XI: 10 (11, 15 December 1431). Cosimo de' Medici had a copy written by Giovanni Aretino, an important early practitioner of humanistic script: Ullman, *Humanistic Script*, p. 94. Three ecclesiastics with humanist interests – Pietro Donato, Bishop of Padua;

Francesco Pizolpasso, Archbishop of Milan; and William Grey, Bishop of Ely – all possessed copies of it: Agostino Sottili, "Ambrogio Traversari, Francesco Pizolpasso, Giovanni Aurispa: Traduzioni e letture," *Romanische Forschungen* LXXVIII (1966), p. 49.

80 XXIV: 63 (dated convincingly to 1424 by Sabbadini, *Epistolario di Guarino Veronese*, III, p. 41); note Traversari's comments on Paolo in VII: 1 (c. 1429-30).

81 ". . . ita ut putem me id effecisse, quod Gregorius summopere postularat ab eo, qui scriptas abs se epistolas in graecam linguam convertat, ut scilicet non verbum de verbo, sed sensum transferret." VIII: 6 (4, 27 December 1423), to Niccoli.

82 See p. 19.

83 "Est quidem id opus in Latinum traductum, verum ita imperite, ut praeter syllabas, qui intelligat, fere sit nemo. Si illud accepero, fortassis illi reddam faciem suam, quam sibi quodammodo traductoris imperitia, atque perversitas abstulit." VI: 7 (4, 11 March 1416).

84 "Aiebas enim priorem illam interpretationem tibi parum satisfacere, viderique ad intelligendum difficillimam, difficultatis ipsius caussam prudentissime coniiciens, quod is scilicet, qui prior transtulit (quicumque tandem ille fuerit; nam temere definire non audeo) inhesisset literae, atque contra veterum eruditorum praecepta de verbo ad verbum transtulisset: exspetebasque a me ut sensum illius viri aptius, atque lucidius promerem. . . . ipsumque opus ex integro converti prioris illius Interpretis vestigia omnino deserens, sensumque eius lucide, quantum pro ingenii tenuitate licuit, exprimere conatus. . . . (Neque enim deerunt, qui me adrogantem, et temerarium insimulent, qui post priorem illum Interpretem, quem afflatum spiritu Sancto id opus transtulisse pertinacius, quam consideratius adseverabunt, denuo transferre ausus sim). . . . Praeterea traductionem illam esse obscurissimam ne ipsi quidem negabunt. Quod ergo crimen meum est, si quod ille obscurius transtulit, apertius ipse, et aliquanto etiam latinius convertere conatus sum? Porro quam fuerit ille Interpres eruditus quid adtinet dicere? Contendant isti peritissimum illum in utraque lingua exstitisse: Ego ab illis longe dissentiens, in neutra illum satis plenum fuisse veraciter adseverabo. Nam graeca pleraque non recte intellexisse cuilibet eius linguae vel mediocriter perito facile constabit: et latina erudite posuisse, qui adfirmat sese imperitissimum esse haud obscure significat. Sanctissimum illum fuisse virum si adseverant; facile, ac perlubenter consentiam: non tamen, quia sanctus fuerit, eruditum etiam fuisse sequitur, atque idoneum ad transferendum. Aliud enim sanctitas est, atque aliud eruditio. Imo vero si sanctus fuit; ne id quidem tentare debuit, quod commode implere non posset, neque id onus subire, quod virium suarum excederet modum. Facit enim iniuriam doctissimo viro, qui illum imperite, ac rustice loquentem reddit." XXIII: 7.

85 Oliger, *Expositio*, pp. xxxvi, li-lii.

86 VI: 21 (18, March-October 1420).

87 ". . . est quippe illud opus densum, arctum, facundiaeque minus

capax, et quod utilius, quam amoenius existimandum rectissime sit." VI: 22 (19, 23? October 1420).

88 Sane istud in primis mihi curae fuit, ut simplicitatem graece dictionis servaret latina translatio." XXIII: 2 (1431).

89 XXIII: 1 (1424).

90 See pp. 72-73.

91 VIII: 8 (10, 25 May 1424); VIII: 9 (11, 21 June 1424). Sabbadini, *La scuola* pp. 133-35, provides a useful comparison of the differing styles of translation of Plutarch made by nine different Quattrocento humanist translators, including Bruni, Guarino, Francesco Barbaro, and Filelfo.

92 For Traversari's remark on ancient translations of sacred texts, see Chap. I, pp. 19-20. For Manetti's discussion, see Trinkaus, *In Our Image* pp. 596-601. A line by comparison of Traversari's Ps.-Dionysius with the four preceding medieval literal translations can be made by examining P. Chevalier, O.S.B., *Dionysiaca: Recueil donnant l'ensemble des traductions latines des ouvrages attribués au Denys de l'Aréopage,* 2 vols. (Paris, 1937-50).

93 Ullman and Stadter, *The Public Library*, pp. 125-267.

94 See pp. 219-21.

95 Trinkaus, *In Our Image*, pp. 79-80.

96 VIII: 12 (7, 27 February 1424); VI: 27 (25, 5 August 1425).

97 XIII: 13 (26, 27 September 1437).

98 VIII: 6 (4, 27 December 1423). For Corvini, see Sabbadini, *Storia e critica,* 2nd ed., pp. 313-29.

99 See p. 24.

100 "Audeo dicere, maius opus est, quam Augustini super Genesim ad literam. Stilus ipse eruditi, et acutissimi viri." VIII: 5 (3, 18 December 1423).

101 *Ibid.* Also note K. W. Humphreys, *The Library of the Franciscans of the Convent of St. Antony, Padua, at the Beginning of the Fifteenth Century* (Amsterdam, 1966).

102 VIII: 8 (10, 25 May 1424).

103 Giuseppe Gullotta, *Gli antichi cataloghi e i codici della Abbazia di Nonantola, Studi e Testi,* 182 (Città del Vaticano, 1955); José Ruysschaert, *Les manuscrits de l'Abaye de Nonantola: Table de concordance annotée et Index des manuscrits, Studi e Testi,* 182 bis (Città del Vaticano, 1955).

104 VIII: 1 (8, 16 March 1424); Sabbadini, *Le scoperte,* I, p. 89.

105 VIII: 16 (27, second half 1426); XIII: 14 (23, April-August 1437); Sabbadini, *Le scoperte,* I, p. 90.

106 XXV: 3 (1428); VIII: 36 (36, March 1431); Sabbadini, *Le scoperte,* I, p. 91.

107 *Hodoep.,* pp. 31, 58-81; VIII: 43 (42, 12 April 1432); VIII: 44 (43, 27 April 1432); VIII: 47 (48, 20 June 1433); VIII: 48 (49, 3 July 1433); VIII: 49 (50, 19 July 1433).

108 VIII: 52 (53, 12 December 1433); *Hodoep.,* pp. 101-02. Note A.

Campana, "Il codice ravennate di S. Ambrogio," *Italia medioevale e umanistica* I (1958), pp. 15-64.

109 XIII: 4 (14, 16 September 1435).

110 VII. 4 (7, 6 December 1435); II: 18 (29, 28 January 1436).

111 C. Mazzi, "L'inventario quattrocentesco della Biblioteca di Santa Croce di Firenze," *Rivista delle Biblioteche e degli Archivi*, VIII (1897), pp. 16-31, 99-113, 129-47; P. Francesco Mattesini, O.F.M., "La Biblioteca di Santa Croce e Fra Tebaldo della Casa," *Studi Francescani*, LVII (1954), pp. 254-316; Charles T. Davis, "The Early Collection of Books of S. Croce in Florence," *Proceedings of the American Philosophical Society*, CVII (1963), pp. 399-414; S. Orlandi, *La Biblioteca di S. Maria Novella in Firenze dal secolo XIV al secolo XVI* (Florence, 1952); David Guiterrez, "La Biblioteca di Santo Spirito in Firenze," *Analecta Augustiniana*, XXV (1962), pp. 5-88; the patristic library at the Carmine was less extensive: K. W. Humphreys, *The Library of the Carmelites at Florence at the End of the Fourteenth Century* (Amsterdam, 1964), pp. 12-13. For Boccaccio's library, see Mazza, "L'inventario"; for Salutati's, Ullman, *The Humanism of Coluccio Salutati*, pp. 129-209.

112 Krautheimer, *Lorenzo Ghiberti*, pp. 159-88.

113 Note Salutati's discussion of the eloquence of various classical, patristic, and medieval authors in *Epistolario*, ed. Novati, III, pp. 82-85. For Salutati's knowledge of Lactantius, see Ullman, *Humanism*, pp. 102, 234, 258; for his criticism of Lactantius, see Trinkaus, *In Our Image*, p. 101.

114 Quasten, *Patrology*, II, pp. 392-410.

115 *Humanistisch-Philosophische Schriften*, p. 6; note also p. 19.

116 "Maxime vero inter omnes, qui de Christiana religione umquam scripserunt, eminet et excellit nitore quodam et copia Lactantius Firmianus, vir omnium Christianorum proculdubio eloquentissimus, cuius facundia et dicendi figura ingenium illud, de quo loquor, praeclare instituere atque alere potest. Probo autem huius maxime eos libros, quos *Adversus falsam religionem* conscripsit; item quos *De ira Dei* et *De opificio hominis*. Quos lege, quaeso, si litteras amas, eorumque suavitate quasi ambrosia et nectare imbuaris!" *Ibid*. p. 8.

117 This is the present Bibl. Naz. Cent. Firenze, C.S.B.4.2609: Sottili, "Autografi," p. 4; for the text of the colophon, see Mehus, I, p. ccclxxxvii.

118 "Nihil profecto fuit, quod vel abs te dignius, vel mihi suavius imperari possit; itaque eius emendationi totus incumbam, atque eo gratius, quo maxime viri delector ingenio, qui (constantissime dixerim) nemini veterum ne Ciceroni quidem ipsi aureo, atque immenso flumini eloquentiae meo iudicio unquam cederet." VI: 5 (2,28 February 1416).

119 "Miseratus sum sortem doctissimi viri, mecumque tacitus indignabar, aureum illud ingenium imperitorum violari manibus. Laudavi praeterea consilium tuum, quo tu virum illum hac iniuria liberare cogitasti, misistique ad nos, qui etsi minus eruditi, studiosi tamen satis, atque diligentes sumus. Itaque spondeo, ut antea iam feci, me acrem operam

daturum, ut is, quem to mendosissimum ad me misisti, quam emendatissimus ad te proficiscatur, atque de imperito, barbaro, et rustico, quantum fieri per nostrum laborem poterit, eruditus, latinus, et urbanus fiat." VI: 7 (4, 11 March 1416).

120 VI: 16(6, 31 January 1417); note also VI: 15(5, 1 June 1416).

121 VIII: 29 (13, 29 August 1424); VIII: 39 (14, 2 September 1424); VIII: 40 (15, 2 September 1424).

122 Sabbadini, *Le scoperte*, I, p. 90.

123 VIII: 27 (38, 1431); VIII: 2 (39, 8 July 1431). In 1427 Guarino wrote to Florence seeking information from Traversari regarding this Lactantius manuscript: *Epistolario*, ed. Sabbadini, I, p. 568.

124 VIII: 52 (53, 12 December 1433).

125 Eugenio Garin, "La 'dignitas hominis' e la letteratura patristica," *Rinascita*, I (1938), pp. 102-46; Trinkaus, *In Our Image*, pp. 183-84, 230-58.

126 "Cum ardore maximo, et studio continuo legere incoepi: occurritque vera de illo viro a maioribus lata sententia; quod scilicet obscurus in loquendo sit. Eam tamen obscuritatem haud ingrate admitterem, si emendatius is liber scriptus fuisset. Magna profecto vi sententiarum, scientiaque rerum omnium viget. Legam illum tritius, atque diligentius, vel ipse transcribam, vel transcribendum alteri iniungam." VIII: 10 (9,16? March 1424). Note also VIII: 5 (3, 18 December 1423).

127 VIII: 8 (10, 25 May 1424).

128 For the text of the *Commentarium*, see Rodney P. Robinson, "Thè Inventory of Niccolò Niccoli," *Classical Philology*, XVI (1921), pp. 251-55. Note discussion in Sabbadini, *Storia e critica*, 2nd ed,, pp. 5-9; and Nicolai Rubinstein, "An Unknown Letter by Jacopo di Poggio·Bracciolini on Discoveries of Classical Texts," *Italia medioevale e umanistica*, I (1958), pp. 383-400.

129 VIII: 36 (36, March 1431).

130 VIII: 2 (39, 8 July 1431).

131 Sabbadini, *Storia e critica*, 2nd ed., pp. 203-04.

132 Sabbadini, *Le scoperte*, I, pp. 115-16; *Storia e critica*, 2nd ed., pp. 159-60. *Carteggio di Giovanni Aurispa*, ed. Sabbadini, Ep. LXVI, pp. 81-82.

133 See Chap. I, pp. 32-33. Traversari lists the contents of the manuscript in VIII: 37 (37, 23 June 1431).

134 "Quid de illius ingenio, et doctrina sentiendum sit, ipse melius nosti. Verissime enim de illo senserunt Lactantius, Cyprianus, Hieronymus, qui illius ardens ingenium admirati loquendi genus parum facile non probaverunt." VIII: 37.

135 II: 9 (20, 23 October 1433).

146 Orsini's Tertullian is the present Bibl. Naz. Cent. Firenze, C.S. I, VI, 10 = S. Marco 528 s. XV; Niccoli's transcription is B.N.C. Firenze, C.S. I, VI, 11 = S. Marco 529 s. XV.

137 Quasten, *Patrology*, II, pp. 246-51.

138 VIII: 2 (39, 8 July 1431).

139 "Dum essem adolescentulus, et tuae ferme aetatis, nullius mihi doctrina ignitior, nullius efficacior visa est, potentiorque ad exscitandos actus ad virtutum studia, exsecrationemque vitiorum. Adeo autem illas ipsius epistolas mihi familiares effeceram, ut multa ex eis capita memoriter referre possem." V: 12 (31, 1436?), to Giovanni Lucido Gonzaga.

140 e.g. V: 31, to Corvini. This letter should be dated c. 1424; see VIII: 9 (11, 21 June 1424), and Sabbadini, *Storia e critica*, 2nd ed., pp. 313-29.

141 *Poggii Epistolae*, ed. Tonellis, I, Bk. IV, Ep. 11 (Fubini, III, pp. 320-21).

142 *Ibid.*, Bk. IV, Ep. 17.

143 VIII: 36 (36, March 1431).

144 VIII: 14 (45, 1432?).

145 Altaner, *Patrology*, p. 471.

146 *Hodoep.*, p. 117; VIII: 53 (54, 28 January 1434).

147 An English translation of this letter appears in the two volume edition of Saint Basil, *Letters*, trans. Sister Agnes Clare Way, C.D.P., *The Fathers of the Church*, Vol. 13 (Washington, D.C., 1951), I, pp. 5-11. For Basil's life and works, see Quasten, *Patrology*, III, pp. 204-36.

148 For the dating of the translation, see Sottili, "Ambrogio Traversari," pp. 44-47; to the lengthy list of fifteenth century manuscripts of Traversari's translation (incipit "Agnovi litteras") provided by Sottili can now be added Bibl. Municipale Reggio Emilia Turri E 18, and Vat. lat, 13860 (from S. Michele di Murano): *Kristeller*, Iter, II, pp. 84, 387. Filelfo later made a translation of this letter: Eugene F. Rice, Jr. *The Prefatory Epistles of Jacques Lefèvre d'Etaples and Related Texts* (New York, 1972), p. 139.

149 "Etsi tuas literas adhuc desidero; officii tamen mei interesse existimavi gratulari tibi pro volumine illo Epistolarum Basilii, quod nuper mihi abs te redditum tanta me voluptate adfecit, ut dici non facile possit. Delector enim cum erudito dicendi eius viri genere, ac veteribus illis proxime adcedente ingenio, tum eius voluminis antiquitate, quam cum in rebus ceteris, tum maxime in libris diligo, observo, et in honore habeo". VI: 17 (7,28 March 1417).

150 See above, pp. 83-84, 108-09. For the dating of the translation, see VI: 16 (6, 31 January 1417) and VI: 17 (7, 28 March 1417); note also Sottili, "Ambrogio Traversari," pp. 47-49. Besides the manuscripts listed by Sottili, p. 49, note Kristeller, *Iter*, I, p. 235, and II, pp. 97, 413.

151 Tatakis, *La philosophie byzantine*, pp. 53-58; John Rupert Martin, *The Illustration of the Heavenly Ladder of John Climacus, Studies in Manuscript Illumination*, No. 5 (Princeton, 1954).

152 ". . . opus illud egregium, in quo totius Monasticae perfectionis norma rectissime traditur . . ." XXIII: 7 (1419?). Traversari must have begun the translation after 11 March 1416 when he wrote Francesco Barbaro seeking the Greek text of the work: VI: 7(4). It was completed by

1 November 1419, when Traversari promised to send it to Barbaro as soon as a friend returned it: VI: 12 (16). Fifteenth century manuscripts of Traversari's translation include the one copied "ab originalibus exemplaribus" for William Grey, Bishop of Ely, by the humanist scribe Antonio di Mario in 1448; this is the present Balliol 78: Ullman, *Humanistic Script*, p. 103. Another early copy is Vat. lat. 522, written in 1436; Vat. lat. 523 also contains Traversari's Climacus. For other fifteenth century manuscripts, see Ullman and Stadter, *The Public Library*, p. 239; Kristeller *Iter*, I, pp. 74-75, 159, 272, 300, 403: II, 6, 25, 152, 163-64, 180, 282, 466.

153 "Nihil enim est mihi in hac vita dulcius, nihil carius, quam dilectissimos fratres meos proficere de virtute in virtutem, et ascendere Iacob scalam, perpetuisque successibus inhaerere famulatui divino recognoscere." XI: 14 (15, 9 February 1432).

154 Quasten, *Patrology*, III, pp. 201-03. Note VIII: 2 (5 January 1424).

155 "Prolixum satis librum S. Basilii Caesariensis Episcopi, viri profecto gravissimi, de vera integritate Virginitatis inscriptum ex graeco converti. Quippe amoena ipsius operis frons, atque honestissimus titulus ad perlegendum primo, tum etiam ad transferendum me facile impulerat. Neque vero ab inscriptionis gratia cetera dissentiebant; verum pulcherrimo vestibulo reliquae structurae partes respondebant. Tanta enim diligentia patronus ille pudicitiae adeo insignis Virginitatis decus componit, ornat, instruit, tanta cura tuetur, armat, munit, tanta denique vigilantia insidias omnes praecavet. detegit, aperit, ut meo quidem iudicio nemo unquam eam rem egerit diligentius. Licet enim permulti, imo fere omnes Ecclesiae Magistri cum Latini, tum Graeci Virginitatis insigne summis exstulerint laudibus, atque ad eam servandam plurimis ingenii sui, praeclarisque monumentis hortati sint; nullus tamen ex amussim cuncta prosequitur." XXIII: 4. Fifteenth century manuscripts of Traversari's translation include Brit. Mus. Add. 19057 which once belonged to S. Maria degli Angeli: Ullman and Stadter, p. 73. Note also *ibid.*, p. 139; Ullman, *Humanistic Script,* p. 101; Kristeller, *Iter,* I, pp. 54, 74-75, 151, 299, 371; II, 18, 412-413, 566.

156 For detailed discussion of the stages of Traversari's translation and their dating, see E. Mioni, "Le 'Vitae Patrum' nella traduzione di Ambrogio Traversari," *Aevum*, XXIV (1950), p. 319-31. Mioni has identified the autograph of Traversari's translation as the present Bibl. Naz. Cent. Firenze, C.S. G,4, 844 (formerly S. Maria degli Angeli), and Traversari's Greek source as the present Laur. Plut. X,3 (=F); this latter once belonged to Niccoli: Ullman and Stadter, p.255.

157 Altaner, *Patrology*, pp. 146, 254, 592-93.

158 Mioni notes, p. 322, that the revisions Traversari intended to make were never done. In VIII: 16 (27, second half 1426) Traversari wrote to Niccoli "Volumen item illud graecum, unde Vitas sanctorum Patrum transtuli, gratissimum feceris, si mittes." Perhaps he intended to complete the preparations of the text for publication at that time, but he did not in fact manage to do so.

159 "Volumen de Vitis Sanctorum Patrum a me traductum Sanctitati tuae mittere placuit, opus etsi non grave, dignumque sanctissimo, et gravissimi iudicii viro, novitate tamen sua aliquid voluptatis allaturum. . . . Id opusculum si fuerit auctoritate tua confirmatum, legendum edetur: namque adhuc prima scheda intra scrinia delitescit." XXIII: 2.

160 *Hodoep*. p. 39; I: 3 (3, 1 May 1431); VIII: 32 (30, c. 1425); Krautheimer, *Lorenzo Ghiberti*, pp. 138-39, 147, 286.

161 *Carteggio di Giovanni Aurispa*, ed. Sabbadini, Ep. LII (2 January 1430), LIII (15 March 1430), LIIII (28 April 1430), LV (18 July 1430). For Metaphrastes, see F. H. Marshall, "Byzantine Literature," in *Byzantium: An Introduction to East Roman Civilization*, ed. Norman H. Baynes and H. St. L. B. Moss (Oxford, 1948), p. 236. When Traversari visited Venice in 1433, Francesco Barbaro asked for a copy of the *Vitae Patrum*, and Traversari arranged to send him one: XI: 73 (73 June 1433), XII: 13 (12, 21 November 1433). Among extant fifteenth-century manuscripts are ones made for Cosimo de' Medici (Laur. Mediceo- Fiesolano, LXII) and Biagio Molino, Latin Patriarch of Jerusalem and Chancellor to Eugenius IV (Vat. lat. 1214, dated 1435): Mioni, pp. 325-26. In 1444 Feo Belcari made an Italian translation of Traversari's *Vitae Patrum*, the only one of Traversari's translations to be rendered into the vernacular in the fifteenth century: Mioni, pp. 326-27.

162 VIII: 16 (27, second half 1426); Altaner, *Patrology*, p. 538.

163 VIII: 48 (49, 3 July 1433); VIII: 49 (50, 19 July 1433); VIII: 52 (53, 12 December 1433). See Quasten, *Patrology*, III, pp. 148-53.

164 VIII: 11 (6, 1 February 1424). For Desiderius, see David C. Douglas, *The Norman Achievement 1050-1100* (Berkeley, 1969), pp. 194-97.

165 VIII: 10 (9, 16? March 1424); VIII: 8 (10, 25 May 1424); VIII: 9 (11, 21 June 1424).

166 This is Sabbadini's suggestion, *Le scoperte*, I, pp. 88-89.

167 XI: 75 (75, 19 June 1433); XIX: 21 (21, 15 March 1434).

168 The colophon reads, "Explicit liber quartus et ultimus hystorie Casinensis monasterii per fratrem Leonem Marsicanum et per Petrum Diaconum edite, expolite vero per fratrem Ambrosium generalem Camaldulensium quam ego Johannes scriba R. mi in Christo patris domini Mariocti de Aretio [i.e. Mariotto Allegri] Generalis Camaldulensium de eius mandato feliciter transcripsi anno domini MCCCCLXVI de mense Junii." Kristeller, *Iter*, II, pp. 476, 604. The ms. is the present Fondo Chigi J. VIII, 258. Professor Kristeller has kindly informed me that Traversari's revised history of Monte Cassino is also found in a ms. in Moscow, Lenin State Library, Shelf mark: Fond 218, N 389. The ms. is from S. Michele di Murano.

169 IV: 26 (25, 24 June 1436).

170 *Hodoep*. p. 100.

171 See Chap. I, p. 15.

172 In VI: 12 (16, November 1419) Traversari wrote to Francesco Barbaro, "Chrysostomi tres alios libellos, qui sunt apud me, traducere

instituti, pulchros sane, atque utiles." In VI: 21 (18, March-October 1420) Traversari wrote, "Chrysostomum meum necdum exspolivi." In VI: 18 (20, 19? October 1420) Traversari informed Barbaro that the Chrysostom translation had been completed some months before, and he would have sent it to him but that the tardiness of the scribe held up its transcription. Though no title of this Chrysostom translation is indicated, it must be *De providentia*, for the only other Chrysostom work in three books which Traversari translated was *Adversus vituperatores*, which was completed by March 1417 (see above, n. 150). In most fifteenth-century manuscripts, especially those with Florentine provenance, this translation is dedicated to Don Pedro, Duke of Coimbra: Laur. Plut. XIX, 25; Laur. Fies. 45; Bibl. Naz. Cent. Firenze, Conv. Soppr. B.2.2915 (formerly Badia Fiorentina); Oxford Balliol College 154 (copied for William Grey, Bishop of Ely, by Antonio di Mario 1447); Bibl. Naz. Torino E.II.11; but in other fifteenth-century manuscripts the translation is inscribed to René d'Anjou, King of Naples: Bibl. Com. Ferrara II 332; Vat. Ross. 141; Vat. Ottob. lat. 1677. Mercati, *Traversariana*, pp. 65-66, argues that Traversari probably did in fact dedicate the translation to both men, despite the fact that the text of the dedicatory letter is precisely the same in both cases, for there are other instances in Traversari's epistolary in which the text of one letter, in different manuscripts, appears directed to different persons. On the contrary, Sottili, "Ambrogio Traversari," p. 48, argues that the manuscript tradition is decisively in favor of the dedication to Don Pedro, and that while it is not impossible that Traversari would dedicate the translation to both men, it is highly unlikely he would use precisely the same text to do so. In my judgment the inscription to King René is spurious. The dedicatory letter indicates that the man in question had visited S. Maria degli Angeli where he and Traversari engaged in conversation: see the text as published by Battelli, "Una dedica inedita," p. 615. The archives of the Spedale degli Innocenti show that Don Pedro stayed there in 1428, but a stone's throw from S. Maria degli Angeli: Hartt, *et al., The Chapel of the Cardinal of Portugal*, p. 29. Since René d'Anjou did not visit Florence until June 1442, nearly three years after Traversari's death: A. Lecoy de la Marche, *Le Roi René*, I (Paris 1875), pp. 218-20, he and Traversari could not have conversed in S. Maria degli Angeli. The dedication to René probably entered the manuscript tradition in the 1450's. Jacopo Antonio Marcello, Venetian patrician, humanist, prominent captain in the Venetian military service, governor of Padua, and leading supporter of the Angevin claim to Naples, sent in the 1450's to René, who had acquired a large library of classical and patristic texts, a number of humanist translations of Greek works. Among these was the complete text of Guarino's translation of Strabo's *Geography*, which Guarino had dedicated to Marcello in 1458, and which Marcello in turn "dedicated" to René in 1459: Millard Meiss, *Andrea Mantegna as Illuminator* (Glückstadt-Hamburg, 1957), pp. 30-51; for René's library, see Lecoy de la Marche, II, pp. 182-97. Marcello also dedicated to René in

1453 a Latin translation of Chrysostom's first homily *On the Statues* (not Traversari's translation, for the texts differ), which he stated a learned friend had just discovered: Mercati, *Traversariana*, pp. 82-85. Given Marcello's propensity to rededicate translations to René, it seems likely he did the same with Traversari's translation of Chrysostom's *De providentia*. For additional fifteenth-century manuscripts of this translation, see Kristeller, *Iter*, I, pp. 9, 60, 273, 293, 299, 329; II, pp. 6, 204, 216, 388.

173 Note the useful introductory notes to Jean Chrysostome, *Sur la providence de Dieu*, ed. and trans. Anne-Marie Malingrey. No. 79 in *Sources Chrétiennes*, ed. H. de Lubac, S.J., J. Daniélou, S.J., and C. Mondésert, S.J. (Paris, 1961).

174 Battelli, "Una dedica inedita."

175 Trinkaus, *In Our Image*, Pt. 1.

176 In VII: 12 (7, 27 February 1424) Traversari wrote to Niccoli, "Sex illos Chrysostomi libellos librarius absolvit, Sermonesque: *Quod Deus sit incompraehensibilis. Contra Iudaeos* Sermones illi scribendi restant, qui apud te sunt." Though not identified by title it seems certain that "sex illos Chrysostomi libellos" refers to *De sacerdotio*, for it is the only work of Chrysostom in six books which Traversari translated. Francesco Pizolpasso, Archbishop of Milan, owned a copy of Traversari's rendering of *De sacerdotio*. It is the present Bibl. Ambros. Milano C 99 sup: Sottili, "Ambrogio Traversari," p. 49. Bibl. Com. Ariostea Ferrara II 333 also contains this translation: Kristeller, *Iter*, I, p. 60. An old Latin version of *De sacerdotio* was extant in the early Middle Ages: Siegmund, *Die Überlieferung*, p. 97. It was also translated again, in the late sixteenth century, by Pompilio Amaseo (d. 1585): note mss. in Kristeller, *Iter*, II, pp. 412, 423.

177 Quasten, *Patrology*, III, p. 451.

178 *Ibid.*, pp. 459-63.

179 *Ibid.*, pp. 452-53.

180 Trinkaus, *In Our Image*, pp. 722-60.

181 Quasten, *Patrology*, III, pp. 457-58. In VIII: 18 (21, 1426?) Traversari wrote to Niccoli, "Peto autem, ut volumen unum Chrysostomi ex his quae sunt Conventus sanctae Crucis, in quo, nisi fallor, quaedam opuscula Ephrem Syri habentur de laudibus Ioseph, ad me mittas." This can be identified with the present Vat. Barb. gr. 528 s. IX, the only Niccoli volume with works both of Ephraem and Chrysostom. Since it is the single version Niccoli possessed of the *Homilies on the Statues*: Ullman and Stadter, p. 251, it seems the likely Greek source for Traversari's translation. Because of Traversari's familiarity with the manuscript, and his reference to it as a Chrysostom, one might conjecture that he previously used it to translate the Chrysostom homily. Traversari's translation is present in Vat. lat. 411 ff. 1-21, and Vat. lat. 555: Mercati, *Traversariana*, p. 83; and was included in the compilation of Traversari's Chrysostom made for William Grey by Antonio di Mario: Sottili, "Autografi," pp. 7-8. In 1460 Pietro Balbo, Cusanus' friend, translated the whole of the homilies

On the Statues, dedicating them to Pope Pius II: Mercati, p. 83.

182 For Ephraem's life and works, see Altaner, *Patrology*, pp. 401-05. A Latin collection of six Ephraem sermons was disseminated widely in the Latin West from the early Middle Ages: Siegmund, *Die Überlieferung*, pp. 67-71. This miscellany was present at Nonantola (Gullotta, pp. 14-21), at the monastery of S. Maria del S. Sepolcro, the library of which was incorporated into the Badia Fiorentina in 1434 (Blum, pp. 181, 18-19), and eventually in the library of S. Marco (Laur. S.M. 503 s. XII), but it is uncertain whether this ms. had been in Niccoli's possession (Ullman and Stadter, p. 158). There is no evidence that Traversari knew the medieval translation, but clearly it was readily accessible to him. Four of the twenty sermons Traversari translated had been previously turned into Latin: "De poenitentia," "De iudicio et resurrectione," "De vita et exercitatione monastica," and "De compunctione." Traversari had translated nineteen Ephraem sermons before he asked Niccoli to send the S. Croce Greek ms. which contained Ephraem's "De laudibus Ioseph." (See note 181 above). Traversari did translate "De laudibus Ioseph", adding it to the other nineteen sermons, though a number of fifteenth century mss. contain only the nineteen. (Fifteenth century mss. include Vat. lat. 257 (dated 1453), and Vat. lat. 258 (dated Florence 1435). For other fifteenth-century mss., see Bandini, *Cat. Bibl. Leopold.*, II, col. 312-14, III, col. 9; *id.*, *Laur. lat.*, III, col. 9, 337; Kristeller, *Iter*, I, pp. 54, 149, 153, 178, 235, 315; II, pp. 41, 530. For the dedicatory letter to Cosimo, pp. 163-65.

183 "Dilectum vero filium fratrem Ambrosium virum utique doctum, quem sacrorum voluminum translationibus vacare intelleximus, nequaquam volumus per te ab hoc suo studio ac proposito modo aliquo impediri, sed adjuvari potius in hoc exercitio tam honesto. Est enim labor suus tum laudabilis, tum vero maxime utilis multis." Antoine Thomas, "Extraits de Archives du Vatican pour servir à l'histoire litteraire du moyen-âge," *Mélanges d'archéologie et d'histoire par l'École Francaise de Rome*, IV (1884), p. 51. Thomas dates both this and the following letter to 1423. The manuscript of the two letters is Arch. Vet. Ret. 359, fol. 14 vo and 15 ro. For Martin V's coolness toward intellectual interests, see Peter Partner, *The Papal States under Martin V: The Administration and Government of the Temporal Power in the Early Fifteenth Century* (London, 1958), p. 196; and Holmes, *Florentine Enlightenment*, p. 81.

184 "Neque enim uberiorem fructum afferre potest hominibus industria tua quam grecos excellentissimos doctores, quorum scientia nobis est ignota, latinos faciendo ex grecis, ut eorum doctrina, per quam ad celestia hortamur regna, nobis fiat nota. Utilia enim nobis cognita prodesse possunt, incognita nullam afferre possunt utilitatem. Volumus igitur et tibi presentium auctoritate mandamus quatenus, prout laudabiliter cepisti, in solitis studiis et exercitio perseverans proficias in diem et gratiam quam tibi a Deo data est non sinas tepescere sed eam excites atque extollas, faciens illam tuam diligentiam aliis quoque communem, quod et Altissimo gratissimum erit et gratissimum nobis." Thomas, p. 52.

185 Weiss, "Jacopo Angeli da Scarperia," pp. 810, 812; Setton, "The Buzantine Background," pp. 56-57.

186 Altaner, "Die Kenntnis," pp. 469-79.

187 The colophon to Traversari's translation in Vat. lat. 4064 reads, "Antonius Marius florentinus transcripsit II Kl. Decembr. MCCCCXXIIII Florentiae." See Sottili, "Autografi," p. 8. The translation had therefore been completed before 30 November 1424. In VIII: 8 (19, 25 May 1424) Traversari mentions that Antonio da Massa had visited S. Maria degli Angeli while enroute to Rome. It seems unlikely that Traversari could have had the Greek text of Kalekas before this time. Antonio di Mario also transcribed the work for Cardinal Albergati: ms. Bologna, Bibl. Universitaria 656 (dated 14 March 1427) (Ullman, *Humanistic Script*, p. 100). In an undated letter Traversari wrote to Condulmer that he was fulfilling the Cardinal's request for a copy of the Kalekas translation: Bertalot, "Zwölf Briefe," p. 103. For other fifteenth century manuscripts of the translation, see Kristeller, *Iter*, I, p. 294; II, pp. 211, 414.

188 XXIII: 1. For Martin V's modest efforts at restoration of Roman basilicas, see Torgil Magnuson, *Studies in Roman Quattrocento Architecture, Figura: Studies edited by the Institute of Art History University of Uppsala*, Vol. 9 (Stockholm, 1958), pp. 33-35, 184, 196.

189 "Fateor ita sum adfectus ea lectione, ut transferendi studium intermittendum putaverim; sunt omnia probabilia, imo probatissima, nihilque non plenum gravitatis offendi." VIII: 6 (4, 27 December 1423). Traversari describes in detail the contents of the manuscript in this letter and in VIII: 3 (5, January 1424).

190 "O miram diligentiam, et temporum istorum faeci conferendam! Sed lacrymis parcendum est, quamvis ista sine lacrymis pius animus nec legere, nec audire possit. Rapuit me mirifice is liber, atque ad evolvenda quanta possem eius generis, commovit acriter.... Natus est amor experiundi si quid valeret tenue ingeniolum in convertendis Latinis Monumentis in graecam linguam. Adripui mox synodicam epistolam ipsius Gregorii prolixam, et doctrinae singularis, quam scripsit ad Constantinopolitanum, Alexandrinum, Antiochenum, Hierosolymitanumque Sacerdotes, totamque transtuli... Ecce hic sum. Habes quibus me studiis dedam." VIII:6.

191 "Legi, ex quo ad te non scripsi, Eusebii Caesariensis Ecclesiasticam historiam Graece decem ferme diebus. Ea me ita rapuit, ut vix credi possit. Etsi enim eam alias Latine videram; minus tamen mihi voluptatis adtulerat, quam modo, quum in sua lingua illam legi. Quamvis enim in plerisque locis notetur Auctor Arianae haereseos fuisse; delectatus sum maxime tum maiestate verborum, tum eloquii maxima suavitate. Est praeter ceteros Ecclesiasticos, quos quidem legerim, maximus innovandorum verborum artifex, magnamque prae se liberalium omnium disciplinarum eruditionem ferens. Rapuerunt me plurimi, immo fere omnes viri illi, quos historia dignos iudicavit; sed isti, in primis Iustinus Philosophus ac Martyr, Malchion, Clemens Alexandrinus, Pierius, Origenes, suus Dionysius Alexandrinus, et Pamphylus omnium sibi, ut ipse testatur, amantissimus." VIII:

12 (7, 27 February 1424). In early 1424 Traversari was also seeking, from Aurispa, the Greek text of Eusebius' *Chronicon*: VIII: 3 (5, January 1424); VIII: 12. Both Rufinus' Latin translation of Eusebius' *Ecclesiastical History* and Jerome's of the *Chronicon* were widely disseminated in the Latin Middle Ages: Siegmund, *Die Überlieferung*, pp. 73-80; Quasten, *Patrology*, III, p. 315.

192 See Chap. II, pp. 60-61.

193 Quasten, *Patrology*, III, pp. 24-28.

194 "Iste complectitur ignominiam Crucis ita gloriose tantaque cum dignitate tuetur, ut nemo fidelium sit quin ex ea lectione suavissime afficiatur." Vat. lat. 259, f. 1ʳ. In XXV: 3 (1428) Parentucelli remarks that when he had visited Florence (in the summer of 1426), Traversari "in manibus habebat Athanasii Alexandrini plura, quae traducturus erat." For fuller discussion of this translation, see Sottili, "Autografi," pp. 4-6, 12-13.

195 Lucia Cesarini, "La versione del Poliziano di un opuscolo di S. Atanasio," *Rinascimento*, 2nd series, VIII (1968), pp. 311-21.

196 VIII: 37 (37, June 1431). Given Traversari's admiration for Athanasius, it is noteworthy that Niccoli owned the only extant manuscript of old Latin translations of Athanasius writings, the present Laur. S. M. 584 s. IX-X. The provenance of the manuscript was probably Bobbio. It contains the Ps.-Athanasius *Contra Apollinarium*, Athanasius' short treatise *De incarnatione Dei Verbi et contra Arianos* (not to be confused with the orations of similar title which Traversari translated), *Epistula ad Adelphium episcopum*, *Epistula ad Maximum philosophum*, the spurious *De incarnatione Dei Verbi*, *Epistula ad episcopum Persarum*, part of the spurious *De Trinitate*, as well as Latin translations of Gregory Nazianzen's orations, five letters of Basil, a letter of Gregory of Nyssa, a letter of Chrysostom, and five letters of Cyril of Alexandria. See Mercati, *Codici latini Pico Grimani Pio . . . e i codici greci Pio di Modena . . . Studi e Testi*, 75 (Città del Vaticano, 1938), pp. 186-91; and Altaner, "Altlateinische Übersetzungen von Schriften des Athanasios von Alexandreia," *Byzantinische Zeitschrift*, XLI (1941), pp. 45-59.

197 See above, n. 181.

198 Rudolf Blum, *La Biblioteca della Badia Fiorentina e i codici di Antonio Corbinelli*, *Studi e Testi*, 155 (Città del Vaticano, 1951).

199 Chap. IV, p. 181.

200 The note is published in Mercati, *Traversariana*, pp. 32-33.

201 Ullman and Stadter, *The Public Library*, *passim*.

202 VIII: 4 (2, 17 December 1423); VIII: 5 (3, 18 December 1423); VIII: 6 (4, 27 December 1423); VIII: 3 (5 January 1424).

203 VIII: 3 (5, January 1424), VIII: 10 (9, 16? March 1424).

204 VIII: 42 (41, 3 March 1432).

205 *Ibid.*

206 *Ibid.*, XI: 21 (21, 3 March 1432), *Hodoep.*, p. 31.

207 See pp. 41, 83.

208 Ullman and Stadter, *The Public Library*, p. 249.

209 VIII: 27 (38, 1431).

210 VIII: 40 (15, 2 September 1424).

211 XI: 8 (9, 10 December 1431).

212 XXIV: 46 (11 February 1422?); VIII: 7 (1, prior to November 1421).

213 VIII: 5 (3, 18 December 1423); Michael E. Mallett, *The Florentine Galleys in the Fifteenth Century* (Oxford, 1967).

214 VIII: 35 (35, 18 November 1430); VIII: 48 (49, 3 July 1433); Mercati, *Traversariana*, pp. 15-20, 26-29.

215 Quasten, *Patrology*, I, pp. 63-76; Siegmund, *Die Überlieferung*, pp. 89-90.

216 VIII: 9 (11, 21 June 1424).

217 XXV: 3 (1428); Sabbadini, *Le scoperte*, I, p. 91.

218 Quasten, *Patrology*, I, pp. 287-313; Siegmund, *Die Überlieferung*, pp. 90-91.

219 XIII: 18 (30, 11 April 1438); Sabbadini, *Le scoperte*, I, pp. 106-07.

220 José Ruysschaert, "Le manuscrit 'Romae descriptum' de l'édition erasmienne d'Irénée de Lyon," in *Scrinium Erasmianum*, ed. J. Coppens, I (Leiden, 1969), pp. 263-76.

221 Quasten, *Patrology*, I, pp. 92-105.

222 VIII: 2 (39, 8 July 1431).

223 Niccoli's manuscript of *Antiquitates Judaicae* is the present Laur. 69, 22, s. X: Ullman and Stadter, p. 81. For the medieval diffusion of Latin translations of Josephus, see Siegmund, pp. 102-07.

224 VIII: 34 (24, 27 October 1430).

225 See Chap. II, p. 39. Filefo's Philo entered Niccoli's library and is the present Laur. 69, 11, s. XIV: Ullman and Stadter, p. 261; note Bandini, *Catalogus codicum graecorum*, II, cols. 630-34.

226 Siegmund, pp. 127-28; L. D. Ettlinger, *The Sistine Chapel before Michelangelo: Religious Imagery and Papal Primacy* (Oxford, 1965), pp. 86, 116-17.

227 X: 13 (11, 24 April 1437); for Traversari's knowledge of Jerome's *De viris illustrious,* see VIII: 48 (49, 3 July 1433).

228 II: 30 (9, 2 November 1430); VIII: 36 (36, March 1431). Cesarini was formally elevated to the position of Cardinal 8 November 1430: see the sketch of his life in Joseph Gill, *Personalities of the Council of Florence* (Oxford, 1964), pp. 95-103. For Gregory the Presbyter, see Quasten, *Patrology*, III, p. 238. His *Life of Gregory Nazienzen* was translated by Ademarus Beneventanus at Beneventum in 903. Only three manuscripts of this translation, all from France, are extant. It is unlikely therefore that Traversari knew of its existence. The *Life* was translated twice again in the sixteenth century, in 1504-07 by Matthias, an Italian Benedictine monk of the Congregation of Montecassino or the Congregation of S. Giustina di Padova, and in 1530 by the German humanist

Pirchkheimer: Sister Agnes Clare Way, C.D.P., "Gregorius Nazianzenus," in *Catalogus translationum et commentariorum* II, 1971, pp. 173-77. To Way's list of eleven fifteenth century manuscripts of Traversari's translation of the *Vita* should be added Vat. Ross. lat. 50 (VII, 50): Kristeller, *Iter*, II, p. 468.

229 ". . . . Gregorius ille Nazianzenus, vir summus, atque scientissimus, et in nostri dogmatis adsertione celeberrimus, sicque probatus, ut nihil ex eius dictis unquam in quaestionem venerit. Adeo denique catholica sunt, quae ille scripsit omnia; tantaque gravitate de Deo loquitur, et altissima quaeque sacramenta edisserit, ut a Theologia nomen invenerit. . . . Animadvertes ex ea profecto singularia sanctitatis insignia, admirabilem sapientiam, atque invictam inter omnia adversa constantiam. Iuvabit mecum recognoscere vas illud aurem instructum in domo Domini, et praeparatum ad omne opus bonum divino primum munere, tum etiam laborum meritis, et industria, perpetuisque vigiliis id promeruisse, ut Sancti Spiritus evaderet templum. Neque ambigo, ardebit animus ad pietatem pronus sancti Viri vitam, propositumque imitari. Et quid dicam, ardebit? quum in praesentiarum quoque illum despectu gloriae, laborumque tolerantia, et amore Christi, patriaeque coelestis haud segnis imiteris, potiusque in te ipso, quae de illo scribuntur, recogniturus, quam novi aliquid lecturus videaris. Ea mihi de te spes est, ea fiducia, Iuliane carissime." XXIII: 5 (November 1430).

230 For Nazianzen's life and works, see Quasten, *Patrology*, III, pp. 236-54. For Rufinus' translation, see Way, " Gregorius Nazianzenus," pp. 127-34. Niccoli owned two manuscripts of Rufinus' translation: Laur. S. M. 579 s. XI, and Riccardiana 345 s. XIV. As indicated on the flyleaf, the latter was a gift to Niccoli by Fra Matteo da Viterbo, an acquaintance of Traversari: Ullman and Stadter, pp. 72, 137; VI: 19 (21, 23 August 1421?). and VIII: 8 (10, 25 May 1424). Ms. Laur. S. M. 584, owned by Niccoli, contains the Latin translation of Athanasius (see above, n. 196) and Latin translations of two Nazianzen orations not done by Rufinus, plus two Nazianzen letters and a poem; Mercati, *Codici latini Pico*, pp. 188-89; Way, pp. 134-35.

231 For Renaissance translations of Gregory Nazianzen, see Way, pp. 135-72.

232 "Gregorii Nazianzeni volumen egregium (quod a me scire instantissime flagitasti) et, mihi quantum datur intueri, diligenter, magnificeque conscriptum ab Aurispa accepi, ad te, quum opportune fieri poterit, Florentiae deferendum." XXV: 3 (4 June 1428). In Ep. LV, 18 July 1430, Aurispa asked for its return: *Carteggio di Giovanni Aurispa*.

233 XI: 24 (24, 31 March 1432).

234 XI: 73 (73, 5 June 1433).

235 XIII: 7 (18, 13 July 1436); III: 59 (59, 21 July 1436); IV: 31 (28, 22 July 1436); III: 60 (60, 27 July 1436); XII: 29 (24, 25 September 1436); XIII: 10 (20, 10 March 1437); XIII: 8 (22, April-May 1437). For Pizolpasso, see Riccardo Fubini, "Tra umanesimo e concili," *Studi*

medievali, ser. 3, VII, Pt. I (1966), and Angelo Paredi, *La biblioteca del Pizolpasso* (Milano, 1961) pp. 323-70; Sottili, "Ambrogio Traversari", pp. 49-52 discusses the Traversari translations owned by Pizolpasso. Niccoli owned four Greek manuscripts which contained Gregory Nazianzen orations: Ullman and Stadter, pp. 80, 249. Laur. Conv. Soppr. 118 (formerly S. Maria degli Angeli), s. X contains the Greek text of sixteen Gregory orations, but whether this was present in the monastery during Traversari's lifetime is unknown: see Rostagno and Festa, *Supplementa* to Bandini, *Catalogus*. The Greek manuscript of Gregory Nazianzen orations which Traversari borrowed from the Badia (see above, p. 140), was probably Laur. C.S. 138, which had belonged to Corbinelli: Blum, *La Biblioteca*, pp. 78, 114, 158.

236 "The Lost Translations Made by Ambrosius Traversarius of the Orations of Gregory Nazianzene," *Renaissance News*, XIV (1961), pp. 91-96. Note also *id., Catalogus translationum,* II, 1971, pp. 135-36.

237 VIII: 37 (37, 23 June 1431); XI: 8 (9, 10 December 1431). For Palladius, see Quasten, *Patrology*, III, pp. 176-80; Altaner, *Patrology*, p. 254.

238 VIII: 37.

239 "Vitam Chrysostomi cura ut mittas; eam enim cupio Romae, ubi scripta fuit primum, si quid otii consequi possim, transferre." XI: 9 (10, 12 December 1431). Note also the dedicatory letter, XXIII: 3 (March 1433). Traversari seems to have confused the setting of the dialogue with its place of composition.

240 XI: 15 (16, 13 February 1432).

241 VIII:42 (41, 3 March 1432); XI: 24 (24, 31 March 1432); XI: 31 (31, 28 April 1432); *Hodoep.* p. 30.

242 ". . . . eiusque quoque esset omnibus vita conspicua, atque proposita ad imitandum, et animum curis aegrum, et marcidum huiusmodi exercitatione relevarem; eaque caliginem omnem, quae se illi offuderat, quantum Dominus donaret, abstergerem. . . . Quis enim adeo ferreus sit, ut hunc non vehementer amet, non cupiat, non exscitetur ad compunctionis gratiam, dum animi illius celsitudinem, invictamque constantiam inter persecutiones acerrimas, atque perpetuas admiratur? Quis vero non dignissime queat admirari Vrbis tantae Pontificem tam clarum, tam illustrem pelli solio Episcopali potuisse? cum ille tamen nihil minus, quam iniurias curaret suas, soliusque Ecclesiasticae servandae pacis ac disciplinae inter pressuras quoque suas rationem habere videretur: adeo ut in exilium etiam actus fideles quoque, et peritissimi Pastoris absentiam ferre non valentes literis consolari studiose curaverit. Felix profecto, et ipsa sua constantia beatus, dignusque qui Martyrum inseratur choris, quorum et passiones pro iustitiae amore tolerando, est imitatus, ... Invenies profecto plura cognitione dignissima, quae oblectare, atque instruers bene instructum animum possint, ut quem olim Basilius noster coelibem in Angelicae puritatis instituto mirabili doctrina roboravit, Ioannes itidem noster exemplo suo Pontificem Apostolici solii dignitatem cum gloria, et

laude tenere doceat." XXIII: 3. In the 1430's, Traversari translated three of Chrysostom's seventeen letters written to the widow Olympias, one of his strongest supporters during his exile: Sottili, "Autografi," pp. 9-10. Note Quasten, *Patrology*, III, p. 469.

243 Oratio I. Note also V: 1 (25, 13 September 1433), and *Hodoep.* pp. 82-84.

244 XI: 75 (75, 19 June 1433); XII: 20 (19, 14 March 1434); XIII: 8 (22, April-May 1437). For fifteenth century manuscripts of this translation, see Bandini, *Bibl. Leopold.*, II, cols. 739-40; Kristeller, *Iter*, I, p. 153, II, pp. 128, 210, 312, 423.

245 "Ad haec spem auget mihi studium, quod sacris literis te impendere praecipuum scribis. Scitum quippe illud Hieronymi nostri est: 'Ama scientiam scripturarum, et carnis vitia non amabis.' Imbibitur animo ex ea sacrarum rerum familiaritate, perpetuaque meditatione, ac memoria pietatis adfectus ingens, per quem exuta vetustate, animus noster in dies renovatur ad imaginem eius, qui creavit eum." V: 31. On the basis of Traversari's comments on Corvini in VIII: 9 (11, 21 June 1424) and Sabbadini, *Storia e critica*, 2nd ed., pp. 313-29, this letter should be dated to the Spring of 1424. Note Antonio Corsano's discussion of the significance of Traversari's Scriptural studies in *Per la storia del Rinascimento religioso in Italia: dal Traversari a G. F. Pico* (Napoli, 1935), pp. 10-12.

246 VIII: 5 (3, 18 December 1423).

247 *Hodoep.*, p. 66; VIII: 46 (47, 6 June 1433).

248 See Chap. II, pp. 51-52.

249 VIII: 5; VIII: 3 (5,January 1424). Note Quasten, *Patrology*, III, p. 266.

250 For Niccoli's Origen holdings, see Ullman and Stadter, pp. 136, 146. For Traversari's knowledge of the *Commentary on Romans*, see Chap. I, p. 33. For the fate of Origen's work in Greek, see Quasten, II, pp. 37-101.

251 VIII: 44 (43, 27 April 1432).

252 Edgar Wind, "The Revival of Origen," *Studies in Art and Literature for Belle da Costa Greene*, ed. Dorothy Miner (Princeton, 1954), pp. 412-24. André Godin, "De Vitrier à Origene: Recherches sur la pastristique Érasmienne," *Colloquium Erasmianum: Actes du Colloque International réuni à Mons du 26 au 29 octobre 1967 à l'occasion du cinquième centenaire de la naissance d'Érasme* (Mons, 1968), pp. 47-57.

253 "Oro autem, ut reliqua tria Chrysostomi volumina in Epistolas Pauli ad me mittas. Cupio enim adhuc nosse certius quidnam ipsius operis nobis desit, ut inquirere id possimus diligentius, atque amicis, quibus id munus iniunxi, significare." VIII: 25 (29, 1429). As early as 1424 Niccoli owned at least two volumes of Chrysostom's homilies on the Pauline Epistles; for in that year, when Traversari was in charge of Niccoli's library, he lent two volumes to Jacopo Corbizzi: VIII: 12 (7, 27 February 1424). Corbizzi was the intimate friend of Antonio Corbinelli: see Blum,

La Biblioteca della Badia Fiorentina, pp. 51-55. Niccoli's library eventually contained Greek manuscripts of Chrysostom's *Homilies on Genesis, Homilies on Hebrews*, and *Homilies on First Corinthians*, and it is probable it contained as well Chrysostom's *Homilies on John, Homilies on Ephesians, Homilies on I and II Timothy, Homilies on Titus, Homilies on Philemon, Homilies on I and II Thessalonians, Homilies on Galatians*, and *Homilies on Philippians*. See Ullman and Stadter, p. 80.

254 "Aderit Deus, ut spero, votis nostris, ut hi libri ad nos undecumque deferantur." VI: 26 (30, 1 August 1429).

255 Quasten, *Patrology*, III, pp. 441-51; Siegmund, *Die Überlieferung*, pp. 91-101.

256 The autograph manuscript is Bibl. Naz. Cent. Firenze C.S. J.VI.6 (=S. Marco 574). The colophon to II Timothy is on f. 148. Note Vespasiano, "Frate Ambruogio," ed. Greco, p. 451, and Sottili, "Autografi," pp. 8-11, 14.

258 VIII: 41 (44, second half 1432).

258 ". . . . et ora, ut mihi Dominus et otium largius, et animum tranquilliorem largiri dignetur, ut cetera quoque convertere valeamus." XI: 48 (48, 7 November 1432). The colophon to the translation of the *Homilies on I Timothy*, written in Traversari's own hand, reads "Absolvi II Kalendas Novembris in nostro monasterio Fontis Boni. Anno Domini 1432." Bibl. Naz. Cent. C.S. J.VI.6, f. 102^r.

259 XI: 49 (49, 15 November 1432).

260 "Antiqua iam repetere studia inceperam, et Chrysostomi Commentarios in Epistolas Pauli, opus profecto utilissimum, ex Graeco traducere; quum adlatae a tua Sanctitate litterae me in alia longe diversa invitum quidem trahunt." I: 4 (4, 29 November 1432).

261 Ms. Pal. Capponi 187 (141) Bibl. Naz. Cent. Firenze contains the translation of the first two *Homilies on Ephesians*. Vespasiano, in the list of Traversari translations he appends to "Frate Ambruogio," (ed. Greco, p. 461) states, "Cominciò a tradurre Grisostimo sopra la pistola Ad Corinthios, tradussene omelie dua." It seems likely, as Sottili, "Autografi," p. 7, n. 12 suggests, that Vespasiano mistook Ephesians for Corinthians.

262 Vatican manuscripts include Vat. lat. 393, 394, 395, and 396 (written in Rome in 1454). For other fifteenth century manuscripts, see Bandini, *Cat. Leopold*, II, cols. 19-20, 308-09, 726-29; Kristeller, *Iter*, I, p. 137, II, pp. 6, 456, 556; Stornaiolo, *Codices Urbinates latini*, I, pp. 37-38. Vespasiano, "Frate Ambruogio," ed. Greco, p. 451, states, "Sono ancora di mano di Nicolaio queste sua tradutioni [of Chrysostom's Homilies on the Pauline Epistles] in Sancto Marco . . ."

263 XIII: 6 (17, 15 June 1436); XIII: 17 (29, 7 April 1438). Note Sottili, "Ambrogio Traversari," pp. 42-43.

264 "Iniunxit Pontifex, ut traducendis ex Graeco sacris literis vacem, atque ad hoc librarios quatuor conducam, ipso sumptuum ferente sollatia, licet tenuiter satis. Ducentos enim ad id annuos aureos constituit; ex quibus in praesentiarum centum tantummodo mihi dari iussit, mandans, ut

Commentarium Chrysostomi super Matthaeum transferam, quando Aniani peritissimi interpretis solae xxv Homiliae reperiuntur. Ad hoc totum Collegium Cardinalium adspirat satis, nullusque fuit, qui Pontificem ardenter non impulerit, instituique pro viribus parere iubentis imperio. Tuis curis ingentibus hanc adiectam velim, Cosme noster; primo, ut numerum librariorum adsequar nostratium, qui sint velocissimi, neque imperiti, excipiantque dictata commode, atque transcribant, et sibi succedant invicem, ne ipse in scribendo laborare habeam. Adde, quod, Deo miserante, Dionysium simul absolvere animus est, ut necessarium sit hic librariorum numerus; ut veteribus omnino studiis, antiquisque deliciis me dedicare valeam, Religionis curis in plures distributis. Pallas noster inter sua Graeca volumina L priores in Matthaeum Homilias habuit, easque Florentiae servari arbitror; maxime quum duplicatum id opus apud eum viderim. Te oro agas auctoritate, ut volumen illud ad nos perferatur; quo destinato operi manus admovere possimus. Plus enim ferme dixerim utilitatis adferet tuum istud in rebus sacris studium, quam acris quaevis opera rebus, aut publicis, aut privatis impensa. Partire, si placet, hoc onus, et Nicolao nostro seni optimo, et studiosissimo, vel librariorum inquisitionem, vel voluminis illius indaginem permitte." VII: 9 (8, 27 November 1436).

265 See above p. 141. Strozzi's manuscript is the present Vat. Urb. gr. 20: Aubrey Diller, "Greek Codices of Palla Strozzi and Guarino Veronese," *Journal of the Warburg and Courtauld Institutes*, XXIV (1961), p. 315.

266 XIII: 9 (10, 8 January 1437); IV: 29 (31, 11 January 1437).

267 Chap. IV, p. 181.

268 XIII: 17 (29, 7 April 1438).

269 I: 31 (31, 13 April 1438).

270 Bandini, *Catalogus cod. lat. Bibl. Med. Laur.*, IV, cols. 439-41; Vespasiano, "La vita di Nicolao P.P. V," ed. Greco, pp. 65-69; Vasoli, "Profilo di un Papa umanista: Tommaso Parentucelli," pp. 104-06; R. Klibansky, "Plato's *Parmenides* in the Middle Ages and the Renaissance," *Mediaeval and Renaissance Studies*, I (1941-43). pp. 296-98.

271 See pp. 87, 169-71.

272 Flecchia, "La traduzione di Burgundio Pisano," pp. 119-21.

273 For Lilius Tifernas' translation, see Kristeller, *Iter*, pp. 387, 469. For Francesco di Mariotto's translations, see Bandini, *Cat. cod. lat. Bibl. Med. Laur.*, IV, cols. 442-44; Bandini, *Cat. Leopold.* II, cols. 726-29; Kristeller, *Iter*, I, p. 162.

274 "Exsatiari non possum tanti viri mirabili, suavissimaque doctrina. Et profecto iudicio meo nullus unquam utilius dicendi genus, neque apud Graecos, neque apud nostros adripuit. Adhortationes illae ad mores optimos, et studia pietatis ignitae digne laudari pro merito nequeant. Quanta illi cura est, quam ingens studium amorem virtutis, adfectum in Deum, odium vitiorum, contemptu saeculi auditorum pectoribus prorsus inserere. Sed non ero prolixior in re aperta." VIII: 41 (44, second half 1432).

275 Trinkaus, *In Our Image,* pp. 578-601.

276 *Ibid.* pp. 571-78; Camporeale, *Lorenzo Valla,*, pp. 211-468.

277 Altaner, *Patrology*, pp. 604-09.

278 Chevalier, *Dionysiaca*, I, pp. xi-cxviii.

279 VIII: 12 (7, 27 February 1424).

280 "De Dionysio quid sentias video. Ego, Nicolae carissime, Dionysium ut traducere instituerem plurimorum extorserunt preces. Facit enim difficultas summa operis ipsius, ut cunctabundus admodum adgressus id sim. Nequa eam traductionem meam iudicio tuo subducere unquam animus fuit, sed illam nequaquam tibi obtuli; quia lectione tua indignam existamavi, totumque quod ceperam omittens, post protectionem tuam de novo Dionysium ipsum latinum facere incepi. Iamque fortasse totum exegissem nisi ab eo opere avocasset curarum moles imposita. De coelesti Hierarchia absolvi, magnamque partem Ecclesiasticae traduxeram; quando mihi hoc onus iniunctum est. Ostendi illum Thomae ipsi, non ut blanditiis deliniret caput meum (etsi tu secus sentire videaris: quod quam recte de Monacho, et amico facias, qui trigesimum iam annum in Dei opere exegit, tu videris) sed ut libere de eo iudicaret." VIII: 36 (36, March 1431).

281 XXIV: 4 (43, 20 May 1431). In VIII: 37 (37, 23 June 1431) Traversari asserted to Niccoli that his tasks at the monastery left him with virtually no leisure. For six months he had translated nothing at all, and he had hardly read anything either.

282 "Dionysium adhuc adtingere minime ausus sum; quod revera perturbationes obsistunt plurimae; nec idoneus sum eas exscutere. Si, Domino imperante, et precibus nostris exscitato, sedentur fluctus, et tranquillitas redeat; ingredi audebo cum Moyse caliginem omni luce gratiorem; ut inde audiam vocem Domini; nec ambigam illi quoque divino operi convertendo totus insistere." XI: 48 (48, 7 November 1432). Note the similar sentiment in VIII: 45 (46, 30? May 1433).

283 III: 53 (53, 21 April 1436); VII: 9 (8, 27 November 1436); XIII: 9 (19, 8 January 1437): "Dionysium de Divinis Nominibus iam magna ex parte transegimus, huiusmodi studiis inexsplebiliter dediti, et amissa tempora resarcire cupientes." II: 11 (30), 12 (31), 13 (32), 16 (35), all dated 11 January 1437. XIII: 11 (21, 2 April 1437); XIII: 8 (22, April-May 1437; XIII: 14 (23, April-August 1437); XIII: 12 (25, 13 September 1437); XIII: 13 (26, 27 September 1437). A number of fifteenth-century manuscripts of Traversari's Dionysius translation have the following colophon at the end of the text of *De mystica theologia*: "Absolvi Ambrosius peccator Dionysii Opuscula in Monasterio Fontisboni XV Kal. Aprilis Anno Dominicae Incarnationis MCCCCXXXVI [i.e. 18 March 1437] indictione XV. Emendavi, et cum Graeco contuli in Heremo III Idus Aprilis [i.e. 11 April]. Laus Deo sit semper." See Laur. Plut. XVII, 22 (Bandini, *Cat. Laur. lat.,* I, cols. 344-46); Laur. Gadd. LXXXV (Bandini, *Cat. Leopold.,* II, col. 84); Bibl. Naz. Cent. Firenze, Conv. Soppr. C 3, 2791 (Kristeller, *Iter,* I, p. 156); and Bibl. Palatina Parma Pal. 58 (*ibid.* II, p. 34). The Vatican Library in the fifteenth century possessed six manuscripts of Traversari's translation of the works of Ps.-Dionysius.

These are the present Vat. lat. 169-174. The colophon of Vat. lat. 169 indicates that it was copied for Pope Nicholas V in 1450. For other fifteenth-century manuscripts, see Bandini, *Leopold.* II, cols. 743-44; *id., Laur. lat.,* I, col. 346; Kristeller, *Iter,* I, pp. 30, 58, 371, 383, II, pp. 4, 93, 100, 128, 216, 413, 469. For Traversari's relations with Albergati, see Chap. V, n. 6.

284 "Opere sacre, l'opere di Dionisio Areopagita, libro mirabile, tradutto da frate Ambruoso. Eranvi prima più tradutioni tutte barbare. Udii da papa Nicola che questa traducione era così degna che la s'intendeva meglio questo testo simplice che non s'intendevano gli altri con infiniti comenti v'erano, ..." "Vita di Nicolao P.P. V;" ed. Greco, p. 68.

285 See pp. 44, 113.

286 Kristeller, *The Philosophy of Marsilio Ficino* (New York, 1943), Ch.2; Chevalier, *Dionysiaca,* I, pp. civ-cv.

287 Lefèvre published the *Epistolae* of Ignatius and Polycarp along with the Dionysius corpus, thus gathering in a single volume, which he entitled *Theologia vivificans: Cibus solidus,* what he believed were the earliest writings of the Apostolic Church. Lefèvre's preface to this work has been published in Eugene Rice, Jr.. *The Prefatory Epistles of Jacques Lefèvre d'Etaples and Related Texts* (New York, 1972), pp. 60-71. Note also *id.,* "The Humanist Idea of Christian Antiquity: Lefèvre d'Etaples and His Circle," *Studies in the Renaissance,* IX (1962), p. 142. For Colet's use of Traversari's Dionysius, see Sears Jayne, *John Colet and Marsilio Ficino* (Oxford, 1963), pp. 29, 37.

288 "Legant qui volunt Dionysium Areopagitam Scriptorem nobilissimum, et plenissime admonebuntur. Licet enim arbitrentur quidam Apostolum Paulum eosdem, et Episcopos, et Presbyteros dicere, idque ex dictis illius probare nitantur; Dionysius tamen Apostoli discipulus, in quem, veluti in vas mundum, et capacissimum refudisse arcana illa coelestia, qua raptus ad tertium coelum audivit, merito creditur, necessariam distinctionem docet." Oratio II.

289 Camporeale, *Lorenzo Valla,* pp. 428-30.

290 Way, *Catalogus translationum,* II, 1971, pp. 138-40.

291 "Peregrinum nuper offendi e Syria, ut aiebant, profectum ad nos aetate longaevum, statura procerum sed iam senio incurvum, vultu placidum, atque decorum, adspectu ipso denique, et habitu sanctitatis insignia praeseferentem, subfusum oculos lacrymis; sed ita ut ex eo et nihil dignitatis detractum, et plurimum auctoritatis, et gratiae videretur adiectum. Sicque ex ea perpetua fere profusione lacrymarum faciei nihil foeditatis, nihil squaloris insederat, sed evaserat tota serenior, nitidior, comptior, omniumque intuentium in se provocabat adfectum. . . . ardebam eum adloqui, eiusque familiari frui contubernio, sperans . . . ex eius colocutione me et utilitatis plurimum, et voluptatis percepturum. . . . Vbi consedimus, ab ipso statim sermonis exordio animadverti senem meum divinarum rerum peritissimum, flagrantem eximiae pietatis adfectu, ardore divinae charitatis incensum, solicitum, intentum, pervigilem, torporem,

atque desidiam omni sermone lacessentem, compunctionis amicissimum
(id illae eius adeo illustres lacrymae haud obscure signabant) remissionis,
ac noxiae securitatis inimicum, lenem, placidum, mitem, vitja ubique
resecantem, laudantemque virtutes, adfectus denique nostros ad amorem
Dei, saeculique contemptum, atque ad ambienda aeterna praemia, formid-
andaque supplicia potentissime moventem. Deus bone, quid gaudii, quid
solatii, quantumque emolumenti ex hospitis adeo insignis ore percepi;
quum me dies, ac noctes plurimas perpetua oratione adloqueretur! Nihil
eius vel adspectu gratius, vel doctrina salubrius, vel consuetudine carius,
iucundius, laetius dici, aut fingi potest. Verum inter haec gaudia nostra,
quibus plures dies incredibiliter adfectus sum, tu, quem maxime diligo,
cuique omnia debeo, saepe in mentem veniebas: cupiebamque te festivita-
tis nostrae, tantaeque laetitiae participem fieri, tantique hospitis, si fieri
ulla ratione posset, gustum aliquem capere. Sed quum perdifficile id
videretur, quia esset ille penitus nostri sermonis ignarus, induxi placidissimum senem, ut commodi tui, atque consolationis caussa latine quoque
loqui disceret. Neque sane adnuit senior sanctus, ut mihi, tibique morem
gereret, atque in primis sanctae charitati satisfaceret (est quippe mecum tui
amantissimus) praeter aetatis consuetudinem se mihi in disciplinam dare:
meque docente paucis diebus ita linguam nostram consequutus est; ut meo
quidem iudicio latine melius, et eruditius loquatur, quam graece. . . . Quod
quum alias semper utiliter facere; tamen hoc sacri, solemnisque ieiunii
tempore necessario tibi faciundum esse censeo. Debet hoc sibi non
immerito vindicare sanctorum reverentia dierum, ut solitis bonorum
operum studiis aliquid adiiciamus, nosque ipsos, atque conscientias nostras
diligentius discutiamus: Quod minime implere possumus, nisi mortalium
occupationum paulisper cura, et cogitatione postposita. Nam quo pacto
huiusmodi curarum pulvere turbatum oculum in cordis penitiora infigere
possumus, et subtilius abdita quaeque rimari; quum ne ea quidem, quae
sunt ante oculos, plane discernere, ac diiudicare valeamus? . . . . sed omnis
eius oratio de Deo est, rebusque divinis, de Poenitentia, de Iudicio futuro,
de Aeterna vita, de Gaudio Iustorum, de Reproborum poenis, de
acquirendis, consummandisque virtutibus, de evellendis radicitus vitiis. Iam
vero laudatissimam illam Platonis sententiam, qua summam philosophiam,
meditationem mortis esse definivit, ita probasse deprehenditur, ut omnis
ferme eius sermo in ea tuenda esse videatur." XXIII: 9 (1426?).

Chapter IV

1 Joseph Gill, S. J., *Eugenius IV: Pope of Christian Union* (Westminister, Md., 1961), pp. 15-37.

2 XXIII: 4.

3 "Comperi, mi Pater, . . . te Capitulum generale praedicti Ordinis
nostri mandasse celebrandum; quod optime, atque sanctissime abs te
factum laudo, ut ex eo conventu fiat aliquid, te praesente, et agente, quod

pertinet ad laudem Dei, atque ad propagationem sanctae Religionis, et observantiae regularis." II: 2 (6, 6 August 1430).

4 "Laetissimo nuntio adfecti mirifice sumus, quo civem vestrum summae reverentiae virum Gabrielem adsumptum Pontificem Romanum percepimus. Magnaque suborta spes est, fore ut non modo Italia a bellis, quibus iamdiu vexatur, conquiescat; verum omnia vertantur in melius, et in antiquam sanctitatem redeant universa. Adsit Deus, et adspiret votis nostris." VI: 36 (36, 10 March 1431).

5 "Maximam civitas nostra laetitiam ostendit, novaque sibi lux oriri visa est.' VIII: 36 (36, March 1431).

6 "Loca autem illa fere omnia, in quibus Christiani nominis dignitas gloriosissime floruit, ubi tot sanctitatis lumina, tot divinae sapientiae templa, tot Sancti Spiritus organa fuere (me miserum!) Gentilibus, atque hostibus Christi concessere. Africa illa, in qua sub Cypriano gloriosissimo martyre primum, postea sub Aurelio Augustino celeberrima Concilia tantorum Patrum, ob tuendam contra perfidos fidei puritatem, congregata sunt, in quibus Novatiani. et Donatistae, Schismatici, Pelagianique, et Manichaei, et Ariani potentissimis rationibus debellati sunt, tamque multa salubriter ad disciplinam morum fuerunt instituta, tota Gentilibus cessit. Asia item tota, et Europae pars haud exigua, ubi universales omnes synodi ex toto orbe collectae sunt, in ditionem itidem devenere Gentilium. Graecia omnis, in qua tot divini verbi praecones, tot fuere Christi Philosophi inveterato schismate languet, atque a Barbaris ob perfidiam premitur. ... occidens totus, ubi solum ferme inviolata Christi religio resedit, iam pridem bellorum fremitu quatiatur, Italiaque ipsa diutina clade fatiscat.... Meminerimus quantos in labores Apostoli missi sunt, cum undique difficultate summa cuncta plena essent, nullaque spes humano more considerantibus, sed desperatio ingens undique sese aperiret. Num ideo illi segnius exequuti sunt praedicationis munus? Nihil minus. Sed profecto in Dei verbo sperantes, ac de Domini sui promissionibus hilares percurrerunt orbem universum, regnaque gentium inopes, et Philosophorum argutam sapientiam simplices sub iugum miserunt. 'Numquid abbreviata est manus Domini,' ut salvare non possit, et quod tunc operatus est, modo quoque non queat operari? Peccata nostra prorsus in causa sunt. Nam profecto si fide certa, ac devotione nil nutante de Deo solo penderemus, si illum intra nostri cordis hospitium per summam munditiam exciperemus, qui nesciat eum, quae dudum per sanctos suos operatus est, modo quoque facturum? Atque ut, unde coepit, recurrat oratio, magna tibi mentis altitudine opus est, Eugeni Sanctissime. Nihil tibi humile, nihil mediocre cogitandum. Vice Dei fungeris. Deus in Terris sis necesse est. Quid reformidas? Ad hoc descendit Rex noster Dei filius, ut homines faceret Deos. Quod si cunctis donatum est Dei verbum in se recipientibus; quanta id excellentia tibi datum putemus, qui ceteros vindicandos accepisti? ... Cogitandum tibi summopere censeo de compondendo primum Clero, qui ab illa priore honestate, ac sanctitate plurimum se detorsit, atque, prisca severitate omissa, in lasciviam ferme resolutus est.

Piget inspicere quam omnes ferme ab honesto instituto deviarint. Itidem et de Religionibus ceteris te facere convenit; ut et quae bene vivunt, et recte ad evangelium gradiuntur, tua auctoritate firmentur, et solutiores quaeque auctoritatem item sentiant tuam . . . . Quid de populo Christiano dixerim? Audeo dicere, si adfuerit, qui ducat per semitas mandatorum Dei, illum tota alacritate sequuuturum. Viget in his maxime fides: et ubi indicium aliquod sanctitatis illuxit, facile, immo et libenter, ac desideranter, accurrunt. Schismatici, vel veteres, vel novelli, ratione potius, quam armis debellandi catholicoque gregi sunt inserendi. . . . Commendo Sanctitati tuae Ordinem nostrum, ut eius protectionem et ipse non deseras, et alteri, qui sit iuxta cor tuum, et prosequatur quae feliciter coeperas, eum commendes. Monasterium autem in primis nostrum, in quo Religio iam centum et triginta quinque annos integra, et inviolata servatur, ut sub speciali protectione subscipias vehementissime cupio." I: 1 (1). Traversari's statement "Ad hoc descendit Rex noster Dei filius, ut homines faceret Deos," resembles the phrase "Factus est Deus homo, ut homo fieret Deus, in a sermon the Middle Ages erroneously attributed to St. Augustine. The phrase was widely quoted in the Middle Ages and a paraphrase of it appears in Petrarch's *De remediis utriusque fortunae:* see John W. O'Malley, "Preaching for the Popes," in *The Pursuit of Holiness,* pp. 408-43.

7 Leclercq, *Recueil d' études sur Saint Bernard* III, pp. 117-35.

8 "Ardet animus pleraque subgerere Sanctitati tuae de restitutione, seu reparatione veteris sanctitatis, antiquique decoris in Ecclesiae corpore. . . . Te oro atque obsecro, Eugeni Beatissime, id opusculum relegas, inditumque sacro pectori pietatis adfectum in opus apertae actionis exsuscites." I: 2 (2, 7 April 1431). Note Traversari's repeated stress on the *De consideratione* in his admonition to Eugenius to persist in the work of reform: I: 32 (32, 19 July 1438). It is uncertain whether Traversari sent the *Registrum Gregorii* to Eugenius as well. In I: 3 (3, 1 May 1431) he reiterates his willingness to send an emended text to the Pope.

9 Chrysostom's statement appears in his first homily *De statuis.* Traversari translated this sermon: see Ch. III, p. 133. For a discussion of Chrysostom's statement and of his reform ideas in general, see Gerhart B. Ladner, *The Idea of Reform: Its Impact on Christian Thought and Action in the Age of the Fathers* (Cambridge, Mass., 1959). pp. 126-29. For a sketch of fifteenth century humanist ideas of reform, see Eugenio Garin, "Desideri di riforma nell'oratoria del Quattrocento," *La cultura filosofica del Rinascimento italiano,* pp. 166-82. Traversari's stress on *doctrina* and *pietas* as the means to reform of course characterizes as well the far better known reform notions of Northern Humanism: see Oberman, *Forerunners,* pp. 9-10. His admiration for the early Church was rooted in considerable knowledge of its history and literature, drawn from both Latin and Greek sources; but a nostalgia for the purity of the ancient Church was widespread during the Conciliar era: note E. Delaruelle, et. al., *L' Église au temps du Grand Schisme et de la crise conciliaire (1378-1449),* (Tournai,

1962-64), II, pp. 894-95.

10 Vespasiano, "Vita di Eugenio IV P.P.," ed. Greco, p. 26.

11 Gill, *Eugenius IV*, pp. 184-86.

12 David Knowles, *Christian Monasticism* (New York, 1969), pp. 137-39.

13 Gill, *Eugenius IV*, pp. 188-89.

14 For Corbinelli's bequest, see Ch. III, p. 140; for Strozzi's see Diller, "Greek Codices of Palla Strozzi and Guarino Veronese," pp. 314-15.

15 The general issue of the relation between humanism and monasticism in the Renaissance is one where much work needs to be done, as Kristeller noted in his suggestive "The Contribution of Religious Orders to Renaissance Thought and Learning," especially pp. 1-3. For the humanist collections in monastery libraries, see *ibid.*, pp. 3-9.

16 Blum, *La Biblioteca della Badia Fiorentina*, pp. 15-16.

17 "Optimus, atque in omni religione praestantissimus vir Ludovicus Abbas sanctae Iustinae, dum reverteretur ad vos, aliquantulum remoratus est nobiscum. Amavimus insignem virum, atque singulari quadam admiratione amplexati sumus." VI: 14 (13, 1418-19).

18 VI: 20 (17, 24 February 1420).

19 For Traversari's own account of his election, see *Hodoeporicon*, pp. 11-13. For Traversari's work of reform see Dini-Traversari, pp. 149-94; Gill, *Eugenius IV*, pp. 190-91; and Gene Brucker, *Renaissance Florence* (New York, 1969), pp. 197-99.

20 II: 4 (10, 12 December 1431).

21 For a brief notice on Venier, see J. B. Ross, "Gasparo Contarini and His Friends," *Studies in the Renaissance*, XVII (1970), pp. 202-203.

22 XIX: 4 (4, 15 September 1432).

23 *Hodoeporicon*, p. 18.

24 See Ch. II, pp. 46-47. Traversari proposed the union of depopulated monasteries, for two or three monks could neither preserve the rules of the Order, nor perform the required spiritual offices: see III: 21 (21, 1 December 1434).

25 *Hodoeporicon*, pp. 26-27.

26 P. J. Jones, "A Tuscan Monastic Lordship in the Later Middle Ages: Camaldoli," *Journal of Ecclesiastical History*, V (1954), pp. 168-83.

27 For the pervasive late medieval practice of appointing commendatory abbots, see Knowles, *Christian Monasticism*, pp. 120-21; and Gregorio Penco, O.S.B., *Storia del monachismo in Italia* (Roma, 1961), pp. 324-29. For the high value certain Florentine patrician contemporaries of Traversari placed on commendatory control of monasteries, see the intrigue engaged in by Buonaccorso Pitti as described in his diary: *Two Memoirs of Renaissance Florence*, ed. Gene Brucker (N.Y.: Harper T.B. ed., 1967) pp. 88-95.

28 *Hodoeporicon*, p. 30.

29 "Magna mihi spes suborta est, mi frater, divinae in me miserationis. Fore enim certum habeo, ut in me illius gratia vacua non sit, sed operetur

per me veluti instrumentum, inutile licet, quae placita sunt in oculis suis, in salutem meam, et eorum, quorum mihi cura credita est." XI: 6 (7, 4 December 1431).

30 "Contendimus summo studio, quae ad optimam reformationem Religionis nostrae pertinere videbantur, a Pontifice summo impetrare, per nos ipsos interpellantes saepe Pontificem, et per alios familiarius illi inhaerentes, praecipue per Venerabilem Patrem nostrum Abbatem Sanctae Iustinae, Prioremque Sancti Pauli.' *Hodoeporicon*, p. 29. While Cardinal, Eugenius IV had introduced the reforms of S. Giustina to S. Paolo fuori le mura by naming Barbo Prior in 1426; Gill, *Eugenius IV*, pp, 188-89.

31 "Erat in nos Pontificis animus benignissimus; sed temporis praevalente malitia, quaedam indulgere noluit, quae consuetudini Curiae praejudicium afferre videbantur. Petebamus, ut liceret nobis antiquo more, Praelatos Ordinis corripere ac privare etiam (si mererentur ea poena plecti), ut juxta Prophetam, evellere noxia germina, et utilia plantare possemus; eisque substituere, quos sciremus idoneos: porro Monasteria non nisi per mortem Praelatorum vacare in Curia Romana volebamus: confirmationesque Praelatorum ea lege poscebamus, ut solverent in Curia taxationem consuetam. Nihil horum, libere, impetrare potuimus; et hoc extremum, minime omnium." *Hodoeporicon*, p. 29. For the privileges confirmed by the Curia, see *Ibid.,* pp. 29-30. In XI: 32 (32, 2 May 1432) Traversari criticized openly to his brother the avarice of the Roman Curia.

32 "Commenda me quaeso fratribus omnibus, ut illorum praecibus occidua Babylone cito liberari possimus." XI: 17 (18, 23 February 1432).

33 For Traversari's meeting with Sigismund see *Hodoeporicon*, pp. 81-84. Traversari's address to Sigismund on this occasion is published as "Oratio I" in Mehus, II, cols. 1141-44. For Traversari's desire to have the ancient imperial privileges confirmed, see XIX: 12 (12, 9 September 1433), to Venier.

34 "Enitendum mihi potius video studio omni, ut quae mortua sunt, ope divina, et perpetuo labore nostro reviviscant exemplo, verbo, erubescantquę tandem se miserabili sopore tamdiu iacuisse demersos. Utendum mihi video remedio salubri ad eos excitandos, spe ante omnia in Dominum intentissima, et oratione perpetua, ut summus Pater familias dignetur 'de lapidibus istis subscitare filios Abrahae'. . . . Ora itaque . . . ut Dominus cor nostrum lumine suae pietatis illustret, et flamma divini amoris accendat nosque 'protegat a conturbatione hominum, et contradictione linguarum.' " XIX: 5 (5, 6 November 1432).

35 Vacate orationi, silentio, lectioni, et reliquis spiritalibus studiis; celebrate sabbatum delicatum, otiumque sacratum amplectimini, et cum Maria sedete ad pedes Domini . . . verbaque coelestia intenta aure captate, et ita vos agite, ut vocatione vestra digne ambulare videamini." IV: 6 (5, 1432?).

36 "Adripiamus magno animo sacrae institutionis normam, et in ultionem praeteritae desidiae consurgamus. Nil erit difficile, nil durum, nil adsperum; si corda nostra gratia compunctionis incenderit, spinasque

cupiditatum virtutis amore consumpserit.... Quod exhibuit illis sanctis viris, quos miramur, et nobis protest exhibere; si fides adsit. . . . Nostram nobis vindicemus dignitatem; atque inter filios Dei computari studeamus. Minima sunt, quae impendimus, comparatione inaestimabilis praemii, iuxta Pauli sententiam: 'Existimo' enim, inquit, 'quod non sunt condignae passiones ad futuram gloriam quae revelabitur in nobis.' Erectos in coelum oculos nullis patiamur mulcentibus, atque fallentibus in humum volup-tatibus deprimi. Sit nobis prae comparatione pulchritudinis intimae foedum omne, quod cernitur: soloque in Deo mens nostra adquiescat. Debemus iuxta Beati Ioannis Baptistae sententiam, 'dignos fructus poe-nitentiae facere;' ut qui nos per illicita defluxisse conspicimus, a licitis quoque abstineamus. Sed ista exhortandi, atque admonendi studio diximus. Multum certe consolationis capiemus, si vestros animos huius-modi adhortationibus cedere, atque ad meliorem frugem evadere videri-mus. Ceterum si absque compunctionis sensu perstiteritis, convertique ad meliora renueritis; nos quod officii nostri esse intelligimus, exsequi conabimur; quantum ipse permiserit, qui nos ad hoc ministerium provehi voluit. Cupimus quidem blanda potius adhortatione, quam severiore censura nos gerere. Sed si qui perstare in malitia sua maluerint, neque monitis cedere; scimus scriptum esse: 'compelle intrare:' auctoritatemque, ubi opus erit, exeremus. Neque enim nostra sunt, quae praecipimus, et servanda proponimus: sed ante nos a Beato Patre nostro Benedicto primum, deinde a Constitutionibus nostris in scriptis tradita, et postremo in generali Capitulo Burgi, ac deinde Britonori celebrato renovata. . ." XVIII: 3 (12, 26 March 1433).

37 These letters are collected in Mehus as Bks. XIV, XVI-XX, and parts of XII and XIII. Such a volume of correspondence must have demanded enormous time and energy. At one point Traversari complained that the daily task of writing had left him with aching arm and trembling fingers; unless the Pope provided a subsidy for scribes he could not possibly manage the additional task of producing translations: IV: 31 (28, 22 July 1436).

38 For the schools Traversari founded, see Chap. II, pp. 66-68; for Bernardino, see Origo, *World of San Bernardino*, pp. 217-18.

39 XV: 6 (6, 13 September 1432).

40 XI: 45 (45, 18 October 1432).

41 For a brief sketch of the foundation of the Vallombrosans and its place in contemporary reform movements, see David Knowles, *From Pachomius to Ignatius: A Study in the Constitutional History of the Religious Orders* (Oxford, 1966), pp. 17-19. For Traversari's role in the reform of the Vallombrosans, see *Hodoeporicon*, pp. 43, 47-50; I:4 (4, 29 November 1432), to Eugenius IV; XI: 49 (49, 15 November 1432) and XI: 52 (52, 15 December 1432), to Girolamo Traversari; II: 8 (18, 1 February 1433), to Cardinal Giordano Orsini; IV: 9 (7, 15 November 1432) to Ricciardo, General of the Vallombrosans. Gomes Ferreira seems to have been the moving force behind the project to•reform the Vallombrosans:

note IV: 7 (4, 14 February 1432), to Gomes, in which Traversari raises objections to his proposals for the Order: namely, the severe depopulation of many of the houses, strong resistance of the monks to emending their lives, the high cost (4000 gold scudi) of transacting new appointments of reforming abbots through the apparatus of the Roman Curia, and his own desire to concentrate on the Camaldulensians. Nevertheless Traversari had discussed the matter with Ludovico Barbo, who suggested that he accompany Gomes on a visitation to the Vallombrosans.

42 See Chap. III, p. 155.

43 XVII: 14 (16, 30 December 1433).

44 VII: 7 (10, 29 May 1437). Note also VII: 8 (11, 1 June 1437) and Dini-Traversari's discussion on pp. 188-93.

45 XII: 47 (46, 3 February 1439).

46 See the entry "Camaldules" in *Dictionaire de Théologie catholique*, II, cols. 1423-24.

47 Trinkaus, *In Our Image*, pp. 674-82.

48 David Herlihy, *Medieval and Renaissance Pistoia: The Social History of an Italian Town, 1200-1430* (New Haven, 1967), pp. 241-58.

49 Marvin B. Becker, "An Essay on the Quest for Identity in the Early Italian Renaissance," *Florilegium Historiale: Essays Presented to Wallace K. Ferguson*, J. G. Rowe and W. H. Stockdale, eds., (Toronto, 1971), p. 305. Note also *id.*, "Aspects of Lay Piety in Early Renaissance Florence," in *The Pursuit of Holiness*, pp. 177-99.

50 ". . .ne velint pro struenda mole illa Monasterium destrui antiquissimum, et nobilissimum, civitatisque ornamentum." XVII: 27 (30, 30 May 1436).

51 ". . . Paternitatem vestram hortamur, atque rogamus ut adnuere velit, et commoditatem istam Consulibus, atque Arti pro communi utilitate praestare. Etenim, si pascere pauperes laudabile est; commendata vobis haec Ars debet esse, quae plures semper in Civitate nostra pavit, et pascit; ut aliquid etiam insit petitioni nostrae, quod acceptum Deo esse videatur." XXIV: 17 (31 May 1436).

52 XVII: 28 (31, 5 June 1436); XVII: 29 (32, 13 June 1436).

53 I: 19 (12, 25 February 1435).

54 Arturo Linacher, "Il 'Tempio degli Scolari'," *Atti della Societa Colombaria* (1918-19/1919-20), pp. 47-65. Note also my "Ambrogio Traversari and the 'Tempio degli Scolari' at S. Maria degli Angeli in Florence" in the forthcoming Festschrift for Myron Gilmore by the Fellows of Villa I Tatti.

55 Blum, *La Biblioteca della Badia Fiorentina*, pp. 14-18.

56 For Landino, see most recently Pompeo Giannantonio, *Cristoforo Landino e l'umanesimo volgare* (Napoli, 1971).

57 The papal letter of appointment appears as XXV: 1 in Mehus. It bears the date "xiv Iuli MCCCCXXXV. Pontificatus nostri anno V."

58 Gill, *Council of Florence* pp. 60-63, 66; note also Charles-Joseph Hefele and Dom H. Leclercq, *Histoire des Conciles*, Vol. VII, Pt. 2 (Paris,

1916), pp. 885-87, and Johannes Haller, *Concilium Basiliense Studien und Dokumente*, Vol. I (Liechtenstein, 1971; first printed Basel, 1896), pp. 132-33.

59 "Basilean mittimur (quoniam ferme desperata sunt omnia) remedia rebus inventuri." XV: 37 (38, July 1435), to Mariotto Allegri. In 1433 Traversari had been considered for the post of Florentine legate to Basel, but he did not receive the appointment: XI: 57 (57, 19 March 1433),and *Hodoeporicon* pp. 50-51.

60 Traversari provides the fullest account of his journey in XVI: 47 (38, 23 August 1435), but note a condensed version of this letter sent 30 August 1435 to Cosimo de' Medici: VI: 3 (6).

61 Gill, *Eugenius IV*, pp. 39-97.

62 pp. 132-38. Traversari accompanied the Pope from Pisa to Florence, and expressed pride that Florence had been a refuge for two popes (John XXIII and Eugenius IV) and that Martin V had spent a year and a half in the city as well.

63 For details of Eugenius' political position, see Gill, *Eugenius IV*, pp. 39-68, *passim*.

64 III: 44 (44, 4 October 1435). Traversari's activity at Basel can be discerned in detail from the sixteen lengthy letters he wrote to Cristoforo da S. Marcello, Papal Referendary: III: 35-50 (35-50, 27 August-6 November 1435); as well as from his five letters to Eugenius IV: I: 11-15 (15-19, 23 August-25 September 1435). For discussions of Traversari's action, see Dini-Traversari, pp. 226-73; Hefele-Leclercq, pp. 887-95; and Haller, pp. 133-34.

65 III: 39 (39, 16 September 1435).

66 Gill, *Eugenius IV*, pp. 82-83.

67 See Chap. II, pp. 147-48.

68 See Chap. II, p. 43.

69 See pp. 42-43, 146-47.

70 XIII: 5 (15, 4 October 1435).

71 Gill, *Eugenius IV*, pp. 102-03.

72 III: 35 (35, 27 August 1435); II: 10 (28, 26 September 1435), to Cardinal Orsini.

73 Gill, *Council of Florence*, p. 67; Gill, *Eugenius IV*, pp. 78-79.

74 II: 46 (46, 8 October 1435).

75 "Sane, mi pater, illud erit faciendum ante omnia Pontifici nostro; quando fuerit absolutum Concilium hoc, ut quamprimum Synodum electam solis ex Episcopis omni ex parte collectis instituat, in qua caveatur Ecclesiae paci, atque unitati, examinenturque diligenter, et discutiantur Constantiensis, ac Basileensis gesta Concilii, fiatque reformatio vera, et congrua, quietis animis, atque omni perturbatione liberis. Quod fecit Leo Beatissimus, qui post Ephesinam Synodum in nullo huic dissimilem, Synodum ipse collegit, in qua abrogatis, quae instituta fuerant nequiter, salutaria ipse constituit." III: 50 (50, 6 November 1435). Cf. III: 39 (39, 16 September 1435), where Traversari first suggests this form of solution

(but without reference to Leo I). There he stresses above all that the decree *Frequens* of the Council of Constance should be annulled as "scandalorum omnium fomitem." Pope Leo I (440-61) attacked the monophysite tendencies of a Council meeting at Ephesus in 449. He declared the actions of this "Robber Council" null and void, and convened a new Council at Calcedon (451). There, under the presidency of a papal legate, the Christological doctrine ennunciated in Leo's letter *Ad Flavianum*, was declared the authoritative statement on the Incarnation: Altaner, *Patrology,* pp. 369-73; Quasten, *Patrology,* III, pp. 526, 537. It is probable that Traversari had studied the events of Chalcedon in considerable detail. In addition to his general familiarity with the early Councils (see Ch. III, pp. 136-37), in 1434 he sought an ancient volume of the *Acta* of the Council of Chalcedon, together with the commentary of Facundus (of Hermiane?), which he had learned was present in a monastic library in Bologna: IX:10 (8, July 1434) and IX: 11 (9, 26 July 1434).

76 "Ut enim Constantini donationem illam vulgatissimam omittam, hunc ipsum Principem in graviore historia legimus, et alios subinde Reges praeter auri, et argenti ingentem in vasis sacris summam, fundos egregios, et innumeros Romanae Ecclesiae dono dedisse . . ." Mehus, Oratio II. The text of this oration also appears in Joannes Dominicus Mansi, *Sacrorum Conciliorum nova et amplissima collectio,* Vol. 29 (Paris, 1904; reprinted Graz, 1961). cols. 1250-57. Traversari's reluctance to base his argument on the Donation of Constantine may reflect Cusanus' critique of the Donation in his *De concordantia catholica,* III, 2 (written 1433). Valla's more trenchant attack on the validity of the Donation, his *De falso credita et ementita Constantini donatione declamatio,* appeared in 1440. For details, see Fois, *Il pensiero cristiano di Lorenzo Valla,* pp. 324-32.

77 See above, p. 176.

78 I: 7 (7, 14 August 1434); Dini-Traversari, pp. 208-25.

79 Traversari's oration to the Council of Basel was "published," as also were his orations to Sigismund and that prepared for the arrival of the Greeks in Venice. The ideas expressed in them therefore received a wider diffusion than just the immediate audience which heard him speak. Among the fifteenth-century miscellanies of humanist oratory and epistolary which contain Traversari's orations are the following: Vat. Regin. lat. 1612 f. 81 (Kristeller, *Iter,* II, p. 409); Venezia, Marcianus latinus, Classe XIV, cod. 12 (4002) (from S. Giovanni in Verdara, Padova) (*ibid.,* II, p. 246); Venezia, Marcianus latinus, Classe XIV, cod. 127 (4332) (from S. Michele di Murano) (*ibid.,* II, p. 247); Vat. Ottob. lat. 1677 f. 397 (*ibid.,* II, p. 432). Note also Bartolomeo Vigliarana's request that Traversari send him copies of his orations: X: 7 (9, 6 February 1437). Traversari's stress on the exemplary nature of the Church of antiquity in his oration at Basel can instructively be compared to Pier Paolo Vergerio's speech to the conclave of Cardinals in 1406, where he urged the Cardinals to end the Western Schism, and argued that it would never have occurred if the spirit of the Early Church had still been present: Holmes, *Florentine Enlightenment,*

pp. 56-57.

80 Daniel Waley, *The Papal State in the Thirteenth Century* (London, 1961), p. 275.

81 Peter Partner, "The 'Budget' of the Roman Church in the Renaissance Period," in *Italian Renaissance Studies*, E. F. Jacob, ed. (London, 1960), pp. 256-78.

82 III: 46 (46, 8 October 1435).

83 VII: 4 (7, 6 December 1435), to Cosimo.

84 Mandell Creighton, *A History of the Papacy during the Period of the Reformation* (London, 1892). Vol. II, pp. 61-91.

85 Gill, *Council of Florence* pp. 48-50, 68-69.

86 Traversari describes the circumstances of these orations in a letter to Eugenius IV: I: 17 (21, January 1436).

87 Mehus, Oratio III.

88 "Semper enim, et ubique Romani Pontificis sententia, veluti oraculum divinum expectabatur, tantaque illi habebatur reverentia, ut nullus resistere, nullus non approbare praesumeret." Mehus, Oratio IV.

89 I: 17.

90 "Solebant in antiquis, sanctissimisque Conciliis soli Episcopi sententias dicere, et Ecclesiae tractare negocia cum timore Dei, et religionis zelo, fideique fervore. At nunc vulgo res tanta committitur. Vix enim (ut ipsi coram notavimus) ex quingentis hominibus viginti Episcopi sunt, ceteri vel inferioris ordinis clerici, vel in totum laici sunt, omnesque privatis passionibus, potius quam communibus Ecclesiae commodis consulunt.... tantumque habet momenti vox unius Coci ... quantum Legati, vel Archiepiscopi cuiusvis, aut Episcopi. Et quod multitudo concludit, id pro rato habetur, et quod deterrimum est, Spiritui Sancto adscribitur, quod furiosa multitudo dictarit. Ita non verentur Spiritus Sancti blasphemare maiestatem; quasi auctor ille sit scandalorum, et seditiosae multitudinis dux, qui pacem cordibus nostris inspirat, et a schismate semper remotissimus est. ... Sancti Patres nostri Concilia vix unquam tot produxere mensibus, quot isti annis hanc Synodum protrahunt. Agebant illi contra perniciosissimas haereses, reformabant Ecclesiae mores, idque perfecte, atque integre, et intra paucissimos menses. Nostri isti, imo non nostri, sed alieni annos plures consumunt, iam nihil agentes, nisi quo pacto summum Pontificem deprimant. Nullus fructus, nulla Religionis propagatio, nulla Dei laus hinc sequitur; sed sola Ecclesiae scissura quaeritur. ... dum perpetuatio Concilii ex novi erectione tribunalis inquiritur, dum ad nihil aliud, quam ad Pontificis nostri, et sanctae Sedis Apostolicae abrogationem vacatur." V: 3 (29, 28 January 1436).

91 Creighton, II, pp. 152-62.

92 Gill, *Eugenius IV*, pp. 83-145, *passim.*

93 *Ibid.*, p. 143.

94 "Ego confido in Domino, si Sanctitas tua cum fidelibus Christi tibi adhaerentibus Sacerdotibus reformationi Ecclesiasticae disciplinae insistere pergat, instar venerabilium illorum antiquorum conventuum, intra pau-

ciores menses, quam illi exergerunt annos, peraget omnia, et restituet Ecclesiae ornatum suum, ac priscae sanctitatis effigiem, maxima cum Dei laude, et exultatione totius corporis mystici. Pendendum de Deo est, Pater Beatissime, ipsiusque in rebus dubiis implorandum auxilium." I: 26 (29, 6 September 1437).

95 ". . . . si me diligis, sanctis diebus Christiana pietate suscipiendis vescendisque celestis Agni carnibus para, ut arceatur abs te et a postibus tuis signatis Agni sanguine exterminator Egypti, transitoque Mari Rubro et deserto seculi multo labore peragrato, terram repromissionis introeas celestemque Ierosoliman fugato Amoreo hereditario iure possidere merearis. Dici non potest quantum id de te et cupiam et iure antiquissime familiaritatis exposcam. Neque enim fero amicissimum hominem, aevi iam gravem sacris litteris apprime deditum et eruditum, plures iam annos sacrosanctam non attigisse alimoniam; quia nisi sepe suscitetur ac firmetur fides nostra inter seculi temptationes fatiscit et deficit." Mercati, *Traversariana*, pp. 46-47.

96 Writing to Poggio on the death of his brother Girolamo, Traversari stated, "Etsi enim illi gratulandum potius est, qui virgo purus, et Monachus integer de morte ad vitam, de tenebris ad lucem, de exilio transivit ad Patriam, saeculique huius evasit lubricum, carnis iam nexibus liber . . ." II: 32 (22, 24 October 1433). Note also XI: 17 (18, 23 February 1432).

97 "Sumus enim mortui; non quod iuxta Apostolum 'vita nostra abscondita sit cum Christo in Deo' (ea quippe, ut foelicissima optanda mors est, qua saeculo morimur, ut cum Christo vivamus veram vitam) sed morte plane miserabili, per quam, peccatis nostris agentibus, a facie Domini proiecti huc, atque illuc, in morem Caim 'vagi' ac 'profugi' feramur, neque usquam consistimus. Quidni? 'Est' enim iuxta Augustini verissimam omnino sententiam, 'inquietum cor nostrum donec in Deo requiescat.' XIII: 29 (8, 11 April 1433).

98 *Ibid.*

99 E.g. XIII: 32 (16, 22 December 1435): "Exercete vos, filii in Christo dulcissimi, ad studia pietatis. Vacate lectioni, meditationi insistite, et orationibus sacris perseveranter incumbite. Silentium pro viribus servare studete, quia 'cultus iustitiae silentium' [Isaiah 32: 17], et 'in multiloquio peccatum evitari non potest' [Prov. 10: 19].

100 "Ruminanda sunt ista suaviter in secreto cubiculo cordis nostri, unde evaporet orationis incensum, gratum, et pingue sacrificium Deo." I: 3 (3, 1 May 1431).

101 For advice to read Bernard, see XIII: 23 (5, 11 October 1432). For advice to read Augustine and Jerome, see above pp. 24, 81. Bernard enjoyed a great revival in the late Middle Ages, both in Italy and the North: see Giles Constable, "The Popularity of Twelfth-Century Spiritual Writers in the Late Middle Ages," *Renaissance Studies in Honor of Hans Baron*, eds. Anthony Molho and John A. Tedeschi (Dekalb, Illinois, 1971), pp. 13-22.

102 "Propter nos, et pro nobis, filii, sponsus noster aeterni Regis filius

virgineum ingressus est thalamum, qui 'in Sole posuit tabernaculum suum,' ut inde 'procedat ut gigas,' et debellet aereas potestates, et pro nobis, atque in nobis superet antiqui hostis astutias. 'Praeparate illi corda vestra,' filii, ut in eis, velut in diversorio gratissimo libentius accubet. 'Deliciae meae,' inquit, 'esse cum filiis hominum.' Ad nos venit: propter nos venit: et venit in nobis. Memento, fili, quod in Ecclesia de adventu sponsi triplici, propter nos venit ad nos, ut habitaret in nobis. Occurrite illi, filii advenienti. Subscipite illum, neque a vobis ipsis discedatis, ut obviam proficiscamini. Alioquin non illum invenire poteritis; quia verbum Dei 'non longe est ab unoquoque vestrum;' sed in ore nostro est, et in corde nostro. Abs te itaque ad to occurre, ut eum invenias, et per illum ad illum pervenire merearis." XIII: 32.

103 ". . . virentia sempiternis floribus scripturarum prata . . . ruminare aeternae vitae pabula . . ." *Ibid.*

104 XI: 27 (27, 11 April 1432).

105 "Satis enim exploratum habeo tum auctoritate divinarum literarum tum exsperimento proprio, eum 'qui semper sit pavidus beatum esse,' difficileque labi posse." V: 31 (1424).

106 R.R. Post, *The Modern Devotion: Confrontation with Reformation and Humanism* (Leiden, 1968), esp. pp. 98-108, 323-30.

107 For Biel, see Heiko Oberman, *The Harvest of Medieval Theology* (Cambridge, Mass., 1963).

108 A useful survey of the strands of late medieval reform thought is Oberman, "The Case of the Forerunner," in his *Forerunners of the Reformation: The Shape of Late Medieval Thought* (New York, 1966), pp. 1-49. For millenarianism in Florence, see Donald Weinstein, "The Myth of Florence," in *Florentine Studies: Politics and Society in Renaissance Florence,* ed. Nicolai Rubinstein (London, 1968), pp. 15-44; and *id., Savonarola and Florence: Prophecy and Patriotism in the Renaissance* (Princeton, 1970).

Chapter V

1 Joseph Gill, S. J.. *The Council of Florence* (Cambridge, 1959); Deno John Geanakoplos, "The Council of Florence (1438-39) and the Problem of Union between the Byzantine and Latin Churches." in *Byzantine East and Latin West: Two Worlds of Christendom in Middle Ages and Renaissance* (New York, Harper TB, 1966), pp. 84-111; M. Viller, "La question de l'union des Églises entre Grecs et Latins depuis le Concile de Lyons jusau'à celui de Florence (1274-1438)," *Revue d'histoire ecclesiastique,* XVII (1921), pp. 260-305, 515-32; and XVIII (1922), pp. 20-60.

2 For Plethon, see Holmes, *Florentine Enlightenment,* pp. 257-58; Masai, *Pléthon et le platonisme,* pp. 328-32. For the impact of the Council on Valla, see Camporeale, *Lorenzo Valla,* pp. 234-76.

3 See above, pp. 136, 168-70. For a detailed treatment of Traversari's

involvement in the work for Church reunion, see Costanzo Somigli, O. Camald., *Un amico dei Greci: Ambrogio Traversari* (Arezzo, 1964).

4 "Non ambigo equidem adquieturos nobis, quippe quos, et auctoritates sanctorum Patrum, non minus Graecorum quam Latinorum, et rationes ipsae revincunt omnino irrefragibiles," I: 26 (29, 6 September 1437).

5 "Praeterea quoniam sumus mature Bononiam redituri, volumus inspicias, an in alio volumine Gregorii Nazianzeni, quod est apud vos, sint de Spiritu Sancto sermones; ipsumque volumen mittas ad nos; quia in re Graecorum, qui proxime adfuturi exspectantur, erit necessarium." XIII: 13 (26, 27 September 1437). The Pope's residence from 1436 until the end of January 1438, when he departed for Ferrara, was Bologna. Traversari was present in Bologna throughout the autumn of 1437. His preparations for the Council were therefore made while in close contact with the papal court.

6 "Orationem, quam legerat Beatitudo tua, visum est maioribus nostris non esse recitandum, nescio qua intentione; bona tamen credo. Graece hanc scripseram ita pronunciandam; sed quia illis aliter placuit, mihi quoque non displicuit." I: 30 (30, 20 February 1438). Cf. III: 65 (65, 21 February 1438). It seems likely that Cardinal Albergati, in charge of the Latin welcome, vetoed Traversari's planned oration. Traversari had previously quarreled with Albergati, who had commendatory control of a Camaldulensian monastery which he was reluctant to give up: See I: 22 (23, April 1436); I: 24 (25, 25 May 1436); I: 25 (26, 3 August 1436).

7 "Graecam orationem scripsimus de mandato Pontificis; et ita, ut nihil graecitatis in ea desideratum sit. Latinum quoque eamdem fecimus." XIII: 16 (28, 11 March 1438).

8 "Orationem tuam graecam (quoniam iudicium scrutaris meum) ita lego, ut et sententiarum elegantiam, et ornamenta verborum, ac puritatem sermonis ex homine latino fluentem nunquam in illa non admirer pariter, et irascar improbitati, et malignitati eorum, qui ne illam recitares impedimento tibi fuerunt." XXIV: 24 (65, 26 April 1438).

9 "Tenetis enim probe Sanctis illis antiquissimis, universalibusque Conciliis auctoritatem ex ea potissimum Sede semper obvenisse, neque ratum unquam aliquid fuisse habitum, quod non Romanae Ecclesiae approbasset auctoritas, cuius numquam in causa fidei aberrasse iudicium constat Apostolo. ... Sic denique Athanasius beatissimus Alexandrinus Praesul et per litteras primum Pontificem Romanum de fidei ratione consuluit, et quum Ariani Imperatoris insidiis ad supplicium quaereretur, secundo Romanam Ecclesiam adiit. Sic sanctae memoriae Ioannes Chrysostomus Constantinopolitanus Episcopus, quum in exilium secundo Aegyptiorum Episcoporum factione ageretur, perturbatis, et confusis rebus Innocentii Romani Pontificis per litteras flagitavit auxilium orans, ut labenti iam iam succurreret Ecclesiasticae disciplinae. Cyrillus item beatissimus Alexandrinus Antistes, quas in prima Ephesina Synodo insidias perpessus est, Coelestini Romani Pontificis solatio in primis, et auctoritate

superavit. Secundam Ephesinam Synodum reprobavit simul, et seditiosam Leo Sanctissimus Romanus Antistes irritavit mirabili studio, et cura pervigili; atque hic ipse Flaviani Constantinopolitani Antistitis litteris excitus Ecclesiasticae quaestioni rescripto suo finem imposuit Eutychis confutatis erroribus, et Fidei Catholicae luce evidentissimis documentis ostensa. His, atque istiusmodi exemplis (nam plurima suppetunt) provocati Sanctam vobis Apostolicam Sedem expetendam fideliter constituistis aperte comprobantes, vos antiqua Patrum gesta et non ignorare, et imitari studere pro viribus." Mehus, *Oratio* V.

10 Gill, *Council of Florence*, p. 102.

11 I: 30 (30, 20 February 1438).

12 "Cum Niceno Archiepiscopo singularis eruditionis ac meriti viro magna mihi familiaritas est. Eum, quoniam ardet ingenio licet ceteris iunior, est enim tricenarius, de re libraria cum diligenter inquirerem, pauca secum detulisse deprehendi, sed magnam librorum molem Mothone reliquisse. . . . Cyrilli magnum volumen contra Iulianum Apostatam habet; quod et transcribendum curabimus. . . ." Mercati, *Traversariana*, pp. 24-26. Note also XIII: 17 (29, 7 April 1438); XIII: 19 (31, 24 April 1438); XIII: 21 (32, 31 May 1438).

13 "Thesauros Cyrilli in Papyro inter nostri Nicolai volumina perquiri diligentissime facias, et ad nos mittendos cures, Athanasii quoque chartaceum itidem volumen; quia sunt in futura disceptatione summe necessarii Scriptores isti." XIII: 18 (30, 11 April 1438). Piero del Monte replied to Traversari in October 1438 that he hoped to discover the Acts in the monastery of St. Albans: Johannes Haller, *Piero da Monte: Ein Gelehrter und Päpstlicher Beamter des 15 Jahrhunderts. Seine Briefsammlung. Bibliothek des Deutschen Historischen Instituts in Rom*, XIX (Rome, 1941), pp. 79-83.

14 "Negocia ista Graecorum omnia ferme ipsi conficimus, vel ex graeco in latinum, vel ex latino in graecum convertendo, quae dicuntur, ac scribuntur omnia." XIII: 34 (34, 10 July 1438). Note Gill, *Council of Florence*, pp. 114-15, 118.

15 For Torquemada's discourse, see Gill, pp. 122-23. Neither Siegmund nor Muckle list a medieval translation of Chrysostom's *Homilies on I Corinthians*, but Francesco di Mariotto Aretino translated it in 1457; see Ch. III, p. 157.

16 VII: 11 (13, 16 July 1438).

17 Gill, pp. 126-27. Traversari left Ferrara in such haste that he did not take formal leave of Cardinal Albergati. He apologized in a letter written from Bologna 7 September 1438: II: 20 (40).

18 In XII: 44 (42, 5 October 1438) Traversari mentions spending twenty consecutive days in one monastery working for reform. On 31 May 1438 he had written, "Lente res agitur cum Graecis, magnamque sive constantiam, sive pertinaciam dogmatum appellem ignoro, plurimumque difficultatis emensurum speramus, et certo coniicimus. Nos tamen, quantum Deus largitur, diligentiae nihil omittimus." XIII: 33 (33).

19 Gill, *Council of Florence*, pp. 131-69.

20 "Rogo pro honore tuo, et debito statim venias huc: quia in verbo· veritatis praeséntia tua est supra modum necessaria: et timeo quod res istae patientur magnùm praeiudicium, nisi adsis. Vide si posses habere Florentiae aliquam VII Synodum, quia, si concordaret cum libro nostro, esset nobis ad magnum robur. Ferte vobiscum omnia illa volumina graeca tam vestra, quam Nicolai, vel alterius, quae tangunt istos differentiarum articulos, et praesertim volumina illa, quae allegat ille Kaleka, quae alias descripsisti in una schedula. Portes inter alia librum Thesaurorum Cyrilli. Nihil tibi constabit vectura; quia ordinatum est cum Banco de Medicis quod libros per te ei assignandos statim huc mittat. Dimitte Camaldulum, et totum Ordinem, et veni: propera propter fidem Christi." XXIV: 5 (66, 17 October 1438).

21 XXIV: 3 (67, 3 November 1438).

22 Gill, *Council of Florence,* pp. 166-69.

23 *Ibid.,* pp. 169-74.

24 *Ibid.,* pp. 174-79.

25 *Ibid.,* pp. 182-83; VII: 12 (14), to Cosimo, dated Florence 4 February.

26 For detailed discussion of the rival theological positions on the issue of the Procession and of the arguments advanced in the sessions in Florence, see Gill, pp. 180-226. For Valla's observations, see Camporeale, esp. pp.242-49, 273-76.

27 "Spiritum Sanctum a Filio ipsum esse accipere probatur ex dicto s. Epiphanii qui in illo volumine, quod inscribitur *Ancoratus.* ex antiquo Graeco codice ab Ambrosio in Latinum converso, de persona Patris locutus: 'Filium illum dico,' inquit, 'qui ex ipso est; Spiritum vero Sanctum, qui solus ex ambobus est.' " *Quae supersunt Actorum Graecorum Concilii Florentini,* ed. Joseph Gill, S.J. (Roma, 1953), Pars II, p. 256.

28 Gill, *Council of Florence,* pp. 195-96.

29 "Quando vero tu mihi respondebas, dixisti mei moris esse ex multis locis colligere testimonia, ut feci sessione superiore prolatis quibusdam beati Epiphanii sententiis, quibus non est appositum verbum 'Est.' Ergo me ad illas referam. Quia hic praesentes sunt multi interpretes et peritissimi multi, et maxime imperator, hos omnes voco in testes utrum, in iis quae protuli, subintelligatur 'Est'; non ego apposui, sed Ambrosius, qui illud necessario intelligi asserit. . . . ex multis Ambrosii interpretationibus comperi, doctorum Graecorum videtur esse hic mos, ut in propositionibus, in quibus verbum necessario intelligitur, non soleant illud exprimere. . . ." *Actorum Graecorum,* pp. 336-37.

30 *Council of Florence,* p. 224.

31 Ibid., pp. 199-203.

32 "Pater Ambrosi, vides quantum opera tua nunc est Ecclesiae necessaria. Quamdiu vixeris, etiamsi aequares Mathusalem, non potes omni vitae tuae tempore tantum fidei prodesse, quantum his paucis diebus,

quibus hoc exercetur disputationis certamen. Quocirca opus est, ut cunctis aliis negotiis indicas ferias, et solum graecis transferendis voluminibus diebus, ac noctibus totus incumbas. Supra modum prodesset, si haberemus ex integro volumen Basilii contra Eunomium translatum. Nosti optime quam hoc sit necessarium, et pium opus. Non eges admonitore in rebus Dei, qui ab ipsa fuisti Deo dicatus pueritia. Quare, optime Pater, transfere sine mora Basilium ipsum. . . . Hoc mane adsignavit tibi Ioannes Aretinus Basilii complura opuscula. Vide si quid est, quod rei nostrae, quae modo agitatur conducat. Perge etiam crastino die ad Monasterium Florentinum, ubi hodie dicebas esse eiusdem Basilii epistolas, et vide si est illa, de qua loquebatur Colocensis Archiepiscopus ad Canonicos, quod Spiritus Sanctus est tertius ordine, et dignitate." XXIV: 6. Luiso assigns this undated letter to the period February-June 1439. It is clear, however, from the reference to Eugenicus' argument and from Montenero's subsequent reference to Traversari's translation of Basil's work, that this letter must have been written after the end of the third session and before the beginning of the fourth, i.e., 7-9 March 1439.

33 *Actorum Graecorum,* pp. 354-57.

34 Gill, *Council of Florence,* pp. 204-05.

35 *Ibid.,* 223-24.

36 "Nudius tertius, hoc est die dominico, fui apud reverendum dominum sanctae Sabinae; erat quoque frater Ambrosius, qui praesens est et magno interpretandi dono excellit. Allatus est Graecus codex longe vetustissimus in membranis ab erudito quodam Graecarum litterarum interprete, Leonardo Aretino huius civitatis cancellario. Cum librum in manibus haberet et quandam epistolam quaereremus, occurrit homilia quaedam beati Basilii de Spiritu Sancto. Confestim dixi huic reverendo patri ut totam mihi homiliam perlegeret; sperabam enim fore ut sine dubio Spiritus Sanctus mirum quid efficeret. Nam si a Basilio, qui fuit Spiritu plenus, dici oportebat aliquid firmum ac solidum de Spiritus Sancti fide, in hac certe homilia dicendum erat. Audivi integram atque ad finem magnas egi gratias Spiritui Sancto." *Actorum Graecorum,* p. 327.

37 *Ibid.,* pp. 327-29; Gill, *Council of Florence,* pp. 203-04.

38 Gill, *Council of Florencce,* p. 208.

39 *Ibid.,* 207-66.

40 This manuscript is examined in detail by I. Ortiz de Urbina, S. J., "Un codice fiorentino de raccolte patristiche," *Orientalia Christiana periodica,* IV (1938), pp. 423-40.

41 See above, pp. 206-07, 210, 212-13.

42 "Reperi libellum istum Auctoritatum, quem mitto tibi, ut post Basilium etiam transferas, sicut mihi polliceri dignatus es." XXIV: 6. Note Gill's comments, *Council of Florence,* p.165.

43 Mercati, *Traversariana,* pp. 31-33.

44 Ortiz de Urbina, "Un codice fiorentino," pp. 439-40.

45 Gill, *Council of Florence,* p. 287.

46 X: 21 (21, 14 July 1439).

47 "Magna hic nuntiantur de spe certa conversionis Turcarum. Armeni venerunt parati cedere sanctae Romanae Ecclesiae; et alia plurima plena spei optimae." The Armenians signed a decree of union with the Roman Church in November 1439, as subsequently also did the Coptic Church (1442) and the Syrian Church (1444): Gill, *Council of Florence*, Ch. 8.

48 "Fateor, Laurenti carissime, ita me delectat ista tranquillitas mea, ut in portu fere navigare mihi videar, qui hactenus turbulentissimis fluctibus iactatus eram periculo proximus. Licet enim in caussa illa Graecanica perlibenter laborarim (quippe ad hanc tempestatem, atque ad hanc rem Graecae linguae qualemcumque notitiam divino munere mihi obvenisse putarem) ea tamen oculis, atque auribus in dies haurire cogebar, quae animum longe alienis innutritum studiis excruciarent. At nunc, tametsi non desunt occupationes quotidianae et variae, sedatiores illae longe, mitioresque sunt, quam barathri illius, et labyrinthi inextricabiles curae, gratiusque multo, ac iucundius rusticis nostris, quam cardinibus terrae, Pontificique congredior summo. . . . . me ipsum, et vitam meam, atque omne tempus solitariae quieti dedicavi. . . . Polliceor tibi, Deo auspice, et duce, dulces, et uberes, et periucundos fructus desertum istud pariturum, ubi discussa ignavia, et torpore omni, me piissimis studiis dedam, inque his deliciis perpetua cum voluptate adquiescam." VII: 18 (17, 20 September 1439).

49 Dini-Traversari, pp. 315-21.

Conclusion

1 Camporeale, *Lorenzo Valla,* esp. pp. 277-403.

2 See above Ch. III, n. 270. Note also Sister Agnes Clare Way, "S. Gregorius Nazianzenus," *Catalogus translationum,* II, pp. 136-38.

3 Ficino translated the works attributed to Hermes Trismegistos and the Chaldean Oracles attributed to Zoroaster: see Karl H. Dannenfeldt in *Catalogus translationum,* I, pp. 137-64. For Giles of Viterbo, see John W. O'Malley, S.J., *Giles of Viterbo on Church and Reform: A Study in Renaissance Thought* (Leiden, 1968); *id.,* "Historical Thought and the Reform Crisis of the Early Sixteenth Century," *Theological Studies,* 28 (1967), pp. 531-48; and *id.,* "Giles of Viterbo: A Reformer's Thought on Renaissance Rome," *Renaissance Quarterly,* XX (1967), pp. 1-11.

4 Lucia Cesarini, "La versione del Poliziano di un opuscolo di S. Atanasio." *Rinascimento,* 2nd series, VIII (1968), pp. 311-21. Note Ch. III, pp. 139-40.

5 Sister Agnes Clare Way, "Gregorius Nazianzenus," pp. 65-68, 140-42.

6 E.g. S. Ephraem, *Sermones,* publ. Florence 1481, Brescia 1490, Nuremburg 1492 (Koberger); and Chrysostom, *De providentia Dei,* 1487: see Cosenza, *Biog. and Biblio. Dict. of Italian Humanists,* pp. 3455-63. The diffusion of the patristic translations made by Traversari and other Italian scholars needs to be examined in more detail.

7 Percy S. Allen, "Erasmus' Service to Learning," *Proceedings of the British Academy,* XI (1924-25), pp. 349-68; Denys Gorce, "La patristique dans la reforme d'Erasme," *Festgabe Joseph Lortz* (Baden-Baden, 1958), Vol. I. pp. 233-76; Lewis W. Spitz, *The Religious Renaissance of the German Humanists* (Cambridge, Mass., 1963), Ch, IX, "Erasmus: Philosopher of Christ," pp. 197-236; Robert Peters, "Erasmus and the Fathers: Their Practical Value," *Church History,* XXXVI (1967), pp. 254-61; André Godin, "De Vitrier à Origène: Recherches sur la patristique Érasmienne," *Colloquium Erasmianum: Actes du Colloque International réuni à Mons du 26 au 29 octobre 1967 à l'occasion du cinquième centenaire de la naissance d'Érasme* (Mons, 1968). pp. 47-57; Jean Hadot, "Le Nouveau Testament d'Érasme," *ibid.,* pp. 59-65; C.A.L. Jarrott, "Erasmus' Biblical Humanism," *Studies in the Renaissance,* XVII (1970), pp. 119-52; Desiderius Erasmus, *Prefaces to the Fathers, the New Testament, On Study,* ed. Robert Peters (Menston, England, 1970).

8 Paul Oskar Kristeller, "Erasmus from an Italian Perspective," *Renaissance Quarterly,* XXIII (1970), pp. 1-14.

9 Eugene F. Rice, "The Humanist Idea of Christian Antiquity: Lefèvre d'Étaples and His Circle," *Studies in the Renaissance,* IX (1962), pp. 126 ff. Note also Augustin Renaudet, "Un problème historique: la pensée religeuse de J. Lefèvre d'Étaples," *Medioevo e Rinascimento: Studi in onore di Bruno Nardi* (Firenze, 1955), Vol. II, pp. 621-50.

10 Lewis W. Spitz, "Humanism in the Reformation," in *Renaissance Studies in Honor of Hans Baron,* pp. 641-62; Peter Fraenkel, *Testimonia Patrum: The Function of the Patristic Argument in the Theology of Philip Melanchthon* (Geneva, 1961).

11 Marvin W. Anderson, "Biblical Humanism and Roman Catholic Reform (1501-42): Contarini, Pole, and Giberti," *Concordia Theological Monthly* XXXIX (1968), pp. 686-707; J. B. Ross, "Gasparo Contarini and His Friends," *Studies in the Renaissance,* XVII (1970), pp. 192-232; *id.,* "The Emergence of Gasparo Contarini: A Bibliographical Essay," *Church History,* 41 (1972), pp. 22-45; Felix Gilbert, "Religion and Politics in the Thought of Gasparo Contarini," in *Action and Conviction in Early Modern Europe: Essays in Memory of E. H. Harbison,* eds. Theodore K. Rabb and Jerrold E. Seigel (Princeton, 1969), pp. 90-116; William J. Bouwsma, *Venice and the Defense of Republican Liberty: Renaissance Values in the Age o Counter-Reformation* (Berkeley, 1968), pp. 123-33.

12 Bouwsma, *Venice,* esp. Chs. I and X.

13 Émile Léonard, *Histoire générale du Protestantisme,* (Paris, 1961), II, pp. 10-18, 194-204.

BIBLIOGRAPHY

I. SOURCES

A. Traversari's Writings

Battelli, Guido. "Una dedica inedita di Ambrogio Traversari all'Infante Don Pedro di Portogallo, Duca di Coimbra." *Rinascita,* II (1939), pp. 613-16.

Bertalot, Ludwig. "Zwölf Briefe des Ambrogio Traversari." *Romische Quartalschrift,* XXIX (1915), pp. 91*-106*.

Bulletti, P. Enrico. "Due lettere inedite di Ambrogio Traversari." *Bullettino senese di storia patria,* LI-LIV (1944-47), pp. 97-105.

Martène, E. and Durand, U. *Veterum scriptorum et monumentorum amplissima collectio.* Paris, 1724.

Mehus, Laurentius. *Ambrosii Traversarii Generalis Camaldulensium . . . latinae epistolae.* 2 vols. Florentiae, 1759. Reprinted Bologna, 1968. Vol. I reprinted, ed. Eckhard Kessler, Munich, 1968.

B. Other Works

[Aeneas Gazeus] Enea di Gaza. *Teofrasto.* Ed. Maria Elisabetta Colonna. Napoli, 1958.

Aurispa, Giovanni. *Carteggio di Giovanni Aurispa.* Ed. Remigio Sabbadini. *Fonti per la storia d'Italia pubblicate dall' Istituto Storico Italiano,* Vol. LXX. Roma, 1931.

Barbaro, Francesco. *Centotrente lettere inedite di Francesco Barbaro.* Ed. Remigio Sabbadini. Salerno, 1884.

Basil, Saint. *Letters.* Trans. Sister Agnes Clare Way, C.D.P. 2 vols. *The Fathers of the Church,* Vol. 13. Washington, D.C., 1951.

Bracciolini, Poggio. *Opera omnia.* Ed. Riccardo Fubini. 4 vols. Torino, 1964-69.

Bruni Aretino, Leonardo. *Humanistisch-philosophische Schriften.* Ed. Hans Baron. Leipzig, 1928.

Cassirer, Ernst, *et al. The Renaissance Philosophy of Man.* Phoenix PB ed. Chicago, 1956.

Chrysostome, Jean. *Sur la providence de Dieu.* Ed. and trans. Anne-Marie Malingrey. Nº 79 in *Sources Chretiennes.* Eds. H. de Lubac, S.J., J. Daniélou, S.J. and C. Mondésert, S.J. Paris, 1961.

Cusanus, Nicolaus. Josef Koch, *Cusanus-Texte,* IV: *Briefwechsel des Nikolaus von Cues* in *Sitzungsberichte der Heidelberger Akademie der Wissenschaften* (1942-43).

Diogenes Laertius. *Lives of Eminent Philosophers.* Trans. R.D. Hicks. Cambridge, Mass., 1942.

Dominici, Johannes. *Lucula noctis.* Ed. Edmund Hunt. Notre Dame, 1940.

Erasmus, Desiderius. *Prefaces to the Fathers, the New Testament, On Study.* Ed. Robert Peters. Menston, England, 1970.

Fubini, Riccardo. "Un'orazione di Poggio Bracciolini sui vizi del clero scritta al tempo del Concilio di Costanza." *Giornale storico della letteratura italiana,* CXLII (1965), pp. 24-33.

Ghiberti, Lorenzo. *Lorenzo Ghibertis Denkwürdigkeiten.* Ed. Julius von Schlosser. 2 vols. Berlin, 1912.

Gill, Joseph, S. J. *Quae supersunt Actorum Graecorum Concilii Florentini.* 2 vols. Roma, 1953.

Gordan, Phyllis Walter Goodhart, ed. and trans. *Two Renaissance Book Hunters: The Letters of Poggius Bracciolini to Nicolaus de Niccolis.* New York, 1974.

Guarino da Verona. *Epistolario di Guarino Veronese.* Ed. Remigio Sabbadini. 3 vols. Venezia, 1915-19.

Haller, Johannes. *Concilium Basiliense: Studien und Dokumente.* 8 vols. Basel, 1896-1936. Reprinted Liechtenstein, 1971.

–––. *Piero da Monte: Ein Gelehrter und Päpstlicher Beamter des 15. Jahrhunderts: Seine Briefsammlung.* Bibliothek des Deutschen Historischen in Rom, XIX. Rome, 1941.

Lefèvre d'Étaples, Jacques. *The Prefatory Epistles of Jacques Lefèvre d'Étaples and Related Texts.* Ed. Eugene F. Rice, Jr. New York, 1972.

Mansi, Joannes Dominicus. *Sacrorum conciliorum nova et amplissima collectio.* Vol. 29. Paris, 1904. Reprinted Graz, Austria, 1961.

Petrarca, Francesco. *De otio religioso.* Ed. Giuseppe Rotundi. *Studi e Testi,* 195. Città del Vaticano, 1958.

Ps.-Dionysius the Areopagite. Chevalier, P., O.S.B. *Dionysiaca: Recueil donnat l'ensemble des traductions latines des ouvrages attribués au Denys de l'Aréopage.* 2 vols. Paris, 1937-50.

Ricci, Pier Giorgio. "Una consolatoria inedita del Marsuppini." *Rinascita,* III (1940), pp. 363-433.

Robinson, Rodney P. "The Inventory of Niccolò Niccoli," *Classical Philology,* XVI (1921), pp. 251-55.

Rubinstein, Nicolai. "An Unknown Letter by Jacopo di Poggio Bracciolini on Discoveries of Classical Texts." *Italia medioevale e umanistica,* I (1958), pp. 383-400.

Salutati, Coluccio. *Epistolario di Coluccio Salutati.* Ed. Francesco Novati. 4 vols. *Fonti per la storia d'Italia pubblicate dall'Istituto Storico Italiano,* Vols. XV-XVIII. Roma, 1891-1911.

Thomas, Antoine. "Les lettres à la cour des papes: Extraits des Archives du Vatican pour servir à l'histoire littéraire du moyen-âge, 1290-1423." *Melanges d'archéologie et d'histoire par l'École Française de Rome,* II (1882), pp. 113-35, 435-60; and IV (1884), pp. 9-52.

Valla, Lorenzo. *De vero falsoque bono.* Critical edition by Maristella de Panizza Lorch. Bari, 1970.

———. *Opera omnia.* Ed. Eugenio Garin. 2 vols. Torino, 1962.

———. "In Praise of Saint Thomas Aquinas." Trans. Leonard A. Kennedy in *Renaissance Philosophy.* The Hague, 1973.

Vasoli, Cesari. "La 'Regola per ben confessarsi' di Luigi Marsili." In *Studi sulla cultura del Rinascimento.* Manduria, 1968. Pp. 40-47. (First publ. *Rinascimento,* IV [1953], pp. 39-44.)

Vespasiano da Bisticci. *Vite di uomini illustri del secolo XV.* Eds. Paolo d'Ancona and Erhard Aeschlimann. Milano, 1951.

———. *Le vite.* Edizione critica di Aulo Greco. Vol. I: Firenze, 1970.

II. SCHOLARLY STUDIES AND INTERPRETATIVE WORKS

Allen, Percy S. "Erasmus' Service to Learning." *Proceedings of the British Academy,* XI (1924-25), pp. 349-68.

Altaner, Berthold. "Altlateinische Übersetzungen von Schriften des Athanasios von Alexandreia." *Byzantinische Zeitschrift,* 41 (1941), pp. 45-59.

———. "Die Kenntnis des Griechischen in den Missionsorden während des 13. und 14. Jahrhunderts." *Zeitschrift für Kirchengeschichte,* 53 (1934), pp. 436-93.

———. *Patrology.* Trans., Hilda Graef. New York, 1961.

Anderson, Marvin W. "Biblical Humanism and Roman Catholic Reform (1501-42): Contarini, Pole, and Giberti." *Concordia Theological Monthly,* XXXIX (1968), pp. 686-707.

———. "Laurentius Valla (1407-1457): Renaissance Critic and Biblical Theologian." *Concordia Theological Monthly,* XXXIX (1968), pp. 10-27.

Arbesmann, Rudolph, O.S.A. *Der Augustiner-Eremitenorden und der Beginn der humanistischen Bewegung.* Würzburg, 1965.

Bandini, Angelo Maria. *Catalogus Codicum Latinorum Bibliothecae Mediceae Laurentianae.* 4 vols. Florentiae, 1774-77.

———. *Catalogus Codicum ... Bibliothecae Leopoldinae sive Supplementi ad Catalogum Codicum ... Bibl. Laur.* 3 vols. Florentiae, 1791-93.

Baron, Hans. *The Crisis of the Early Italian Renaissance.* 1st ed., 2 vols., Princeton, 1955. 2nd ed., 1 vol., Princeton, 1966.

———. *From Petrarch to Leonardo Bruni: Studies in Humanistic and Political Literature.* Chicago, 1968.

———. *Humanistic and Political Literature in Florence and Venice at the Beginning of the Quattrocento.* Cambridge, Mass., 1955.

Barozzi, L. and Sabbadini, R. *Studi sul Panormita e sul Valla.* Firenze, 1891.

Baur, Chrysostome, O.S.B. "L'entrée littéraire de Saint Chrysostome dans le monde latin." *Revue d'histoire ecclésiastique,* VIII (1907), pp. 249-65.

Baynes, Norman H. and Moss, H. St. L.B., eds. *Byzantium: An Introduction to East Roman Civilization.* Oxford, 1968.

Becker, Marvin B. "Aspects of Lay Piety in Early Renaissance Florence."

In *The Pursuit of Holiness in Late Medieval and Renaissance Religion: Papers from the University of Michigan Conference.* Eds. Charles Trinkaus and Heiko A. Oberman. *Studies in Medieval and Reformation Thought,* X. Leiden, 1974. Pp. 177-99.

———. "An Essay on the Quest for Identity in the Early Italian Renaissance." *Florilegium Historiale: Essays Presented to Wallace K. Ferguson.* Eds. J.G. Rowe and W.H. Stockdale. Toronto, 1971. Pp. 294-312.

———. "Individualism in the Early Italian Renaissance: Burden and Blessing." *Studies in the Renaissance,* XIX (1972), pp. 273-97.

Blatt, Franz. "Remarques sur l'histoire des traductions latines." *Classica et medioevalia,* I (1938), pp. 217-42.

Blum, Rudolf. *La Biblioteca della Badia Fiorentina e i codici di Antonio Corbinelli. Studi e Testi,* 155. Città del Vaticano, 1951.

Bodnar, Edward W., S.J. *Cyriacus of Ancona and Athens.* Bruxelles, 1960.

Bolgar, R.R. *The Classical Heritage and Its Beneficiaries: From the Carolingian Age to the End of the Renaissance.* New York, 1964. (First publ. Cambridge, 1954.)

Boskovits, Miklòs. "Su Don Silvestro, Don Simone e la 'scuola degli Angeli'." *Paragone,* 265 (March 1972), pp. 35-61.

Bouwsma, William J. *Venice and the Defense of Republican Liberty: Renaissance Values in the Age of the Counter-Reformation.* Berkeley, 1968.

Brown, Alison M. "The Humanist Portrait of Cosimo de' Medici, *Pater Patriae."* *Journal of the Warburg and Courtauld Institutes,* XXIV (1961), pp. 186-221.

Brucker, Gene. *Renaissance Florence.* New York, 1969.

Cacciamani, Fr. Joseph. "La réclusion dans l'Ordre Camaldule." *Revue d'ascétique et mystique,* 38 (1962), pp. 137-54, 273-87.

Callus, D.A., ed. *Robert Grosseteste Scholar and Bishop: Essays in Commemoration of the Seventh Centerary of his Death.* Oxford, 1955.

Cammelli, Giuseppe. *I dotti bizantini e le origini dell'umanesimo.* Vol. I: *Manuele Crisolora.* Firenze, 1941.

Campana, A. "Il codice ravennate di S. Ambrogio." *Italia medioevale e umanistica,* I (1958), pp. 15-68.

Camporeale, Salvatore I. *Lorenzo Valla: Umanesimo e teologia.* Firenze, 1972.

Cappuyns, Maieul, O.S.B. *Jean Scot Erigene: sa vie, son oeuvre, sa pensée.* Bruxelles, 1964.

Cassuto, Umberto. *Gli Ebrei a Firenze nell'età del Rinascimento.* Firenze, 1918.

Cast, David. "Aurispa, Petrarch, and Lucian: An Aspect of Renaissance Translation." *Renaissance Quarterly, XXVII* (1974), pp. 157-73.

Cesarini, Lucia. "La versione del Poliziano di un opuscolo di S. Atanasio." *Rinascimento,* 2nd s., 8 (1968), pp. 311-21.

Châtillon, l'Abbé Jean. "L'influence de S. Bernard sur la pensée scolastique au XIIe et au XIIIe siècles." In *Saint Bernard theologien, Actes du Congrès de Dijon 15-19 Septembre 1953. Analecta Sacri Ordinis Cisterciensis,* IX (1953), Fasc. 3-4 / Iul.-Dec. Pp. 268-88.

Cherubini, Serenella Baldelli. "I manoscritti della Biblioteca fiorentina di S. Maria degli Angeli attraverso i suoi inventari." *La Bibliofilia,* LXXIV (1972), pp. 9-47.

Cirillo, Salvatore. *Codices graeci mss. Regiae Bibliothecae Borbonicae.* 2 vols. Napoli, 1826-32.

Cochrane, Eric. *Florence in the Forgotten Centuries, 1527-1800.* Chicago, 1973.

Constable, Giles. "The Popularity of Twelfth-Century Spiritual Writers in the Late Middle Ages." In *Renaissance Studies in Honor of Hans Baron.* Eds. Anthony Molho and John A. Tedeschi. Dekalb, Ill, 1971. Pp. 5-28.

Corsano, Antonio. *Per la storia del Rinascimento religioso in Italia: Dal Traversari a G.F. Pico.* Napoli, 1935.

Cosenza, Mario Emilio. *Biographical and Bibliographical Dictionary of the Italian Humanists and of the World of Classical Scholarship in Italy 1300-1800.* 6 vols. Boston, 1962-67.

Courcelle, Pierre. *Late Latin Writers and Their Greek Sources.* Trans. Harry E. Wedeck. Cambridge, Mass., 1969.

Creighton, Mandell. *A History of the Papacy from the Great Schism to the Sack of Rome, 1378-1527.* 5 vols. London, 1892.

Daniélou, R.P.J., S.J. "S. Bernard et les Pères grecs." In *Saint Bernard théologien, Actes du Congrès de Dijon 15-19 Septembre 1953. Analecta Sacri Ordinis Cisterciensis,* IX (1953), Fasc. 3-4 / Iul.-Dec. Pp. 46-55.

Davis, Charles T. "The Early Collection of Books of S. Croce in Florence." *Proceedings of the American Philosophical Society,* CVII (1963), pp. 399-414.

Decarreau, Jean. "Un moine helléniste et diplomate: Ambroise Traversari." *Revue des études italiennes* (1957), pp. 101-43.

Delaruelle, E. *et al. L'Église au temps du Grand Schisme et de la crise conciliaire (1378-1449).* 2 vols. Tournai, 1962-64. Vol. 14 of *Histoire de l'Église.* Eds. Augustin Fliche and Victor Martin.

Della Torre, A. *Storia dell'Accademia Platonica di Firenze.* Firenze, 1902.

Diller, Aubrey. "Greek Codices of Palla Strozzi and Guarino Veronese." *Journal of the Warburg and Courtauld Institutes,* XXIV (1961), pp. 313-21.

———. "The Library of Francesco and Ermolao Barbaro." *Italia medioevale e umanistica,* VI (1963), pp. 253-62.

Dini-Traversari, Alessandro. *Ambrogio Traversari e i suoi tempi.* Firenze, 1912.

Douglas, David C. *The Norman Achievement 1050-1100.* Berkeley, 1969.

Dufner, Georg. *Die 'Moralia' Gregors des Grossen in ihren italienischen Volgarizzamenti.* Padova, 1958.

Ettlinger, L.D. *The Sistine Chapel before Michelangelo: Religious Imagery and Papal Primacy.* Oxford, 1965.

Flecchia, Mario. "La traduzione di Burgundio Pisano delle Omelie di S. Giovanni Crisostomo sopra Matteo." *Aevum*, 26 (1962), pp. 113-30.

Fois, Mario, S.J. *Il pensiero di Lorenzo Valla nel quadro storico-culturale del suo ambiente. Analecta Gregoriana*, 174. Roma, 1969.

Fraenkel, Peter. *Testimonia Patrum: The Function of the Patristic Argument in the Theology of Philip Melanchthon*. Geneva, 1961.

Franceschini, Ezio. "Leonardo Bruni e il 'Vetus Interpres' dell' Ethica a Nicomaco." *Medioevo e Rinascimento: Studi in onore di Bruno Nardi*. Firenze, 1955. Vol. I, pp. 297-319.

Fubini, Riccardo. "Intendimenti umanistici e riferimenti patristici dal Petrarca al Valla." *Giornale storico della letteratura italiana*, CLI (1974), pp. 520-78.

———. *Introduzione alla lettura del 'Contra Hypocritas' di Poggio Bracciolini*. Torino, 1971.

———. "Tra umanesimo e concili." *Studi medievali*, ser. 3, VII (1966), pp. 323-70.

Garin, Eugenio. *La cultura filosofica del Rinascimento italiano*. Firenze, 1961.

———. "La *dignitas hominis* e la letteratura patristica." *Rinascita*, I (1938), pp. 102-46.

———. *L'educazione in Europa (1400-1600)*. Bari, 1957.

———. "Ricerche sulle traduzioni di Platone nella prima metà del sec. XV." *Medioevo e Rinascimento: Studi in onore di Bruno Nardi*. Firenze, 1955. Vol. I, pp. 339-74.

———. *Dal Rinascimento all'Illuminismo: Studi e ricerche*. Pisa, 1970.

———. "Le traduzioni umanistiche di Aristotele nel secolo XV." *Atti dell'Accademia Fiorentina di Scienze Morali 'La Colombaria'*, XVI (n.s. II) (1947-50), pp. 55-104.

———. *L'Umanesimo italiano: Filosofia e vita civile del Rinascimento*. Bari, 1964 (First publ. Bern, 1947.)

Geanakoplos, Deno J. *Byzantine East and Latin West: Two Worlds of Christendom in Middle Ages and Renaissance*. New York, 1966.

———. *Greek Scholars in Venice: Studies in the Dissemination of Greek Learning from Byzantium to Western Europe*. Cambridge, Mass., 1962.

Ghellinck, J. de, S.J. *Le mouvement théologique du XIIe siècle*. 2nd ed. Bruges, 1948.

Giabbani, Anselmo. *L'Eremo: Vita e spiritualita eremetica nel monachismo camaldolese primitivo*. Brescia, 1945.

Gilbert, Felix. "Religion and Politics in the Thought of Gasparo Contarini." In *Action and Conviction in Early Modern Europe: Essays in Memory of E.H. Harbison*. Eds. Theodore K. Rabb and Jerrold E. Seigel. Princeton, 1969. Pp. 90-116.

Gill, Joseph, S.J. *The Council of Florence*. Cambridge, 1959.

———. *Eugenius IV: Pope of Christian Union*. Westminister, Md., 1961.

———. *Personalities of the Council of Florence*. Oxford, 1964.

Godin, André. "De Vitrier à Origène: Recherches sur la patristique

Érasmienne." *Colloquium Erasmianum: Actes du Colloque International reúni à Mons du 26 au 29 Octobre 1967 à l'occasion du cinquième centenaire de la naissance d'Érasme.* Mons, 1968. Pp. 47-57.

Gombrich, E.H. "From the Revival of Letters to the Reform of the Arts: Niccolò Niccoli and Filippo Brunelleschi." In *Essays in the History of Art Presented to Rudolf Wittkower.* Eds. Douglas Fraser, *et al.* London, 1967. Pp. 71-82.

Gorce, Denys. "La patristique dans la réforme d'Érasme." In *Festgabe Joseph Lortz.* Baden-Baden, 1958. Pp. 233-76.

Gothein, Percy. *Francesco Barbaro: Früh-Humanismus und Staatskunst in Venedig.* Berlin, 1932.

Gray, Hanna H. "Renaissance Humanism: The Pursuit of Eloquence." *Journal of the History of Ideas,* XXIV (1963), pp. 497-514.

———. "Valla's 'Encomium of St. Thomas Aquinas' and the Humanist Conception of Christian Antiquity." In *Essays in History and Literature Presented by the Fellows of the Newberry Library to Stanley Pargellis.* Ed. Heinz Bluhm. Chicago, 1965. Pp. 37-51.

Gullotta, Giuseppe. *Gli antichi cataloghi e i codici della Abbazia di Nonantola. Studi e Testi,* 182. Città del Vaticano, 1955.

Gutiérrez, D. "La Biblioteca di Santo Spirito in Firenze nella metà del secolo XV." *Analecta Augustiniana,* XXV (1962), pp. 5-88.

Gutkind, Curt S. *Cosimo de' Medici, Pater Patriae (1389-1464).* Oxford, 1938.

Hadot, Jean. "Le Nouveau Testament d'Érasme." In *Colloquium Erasmianum: Actes du Colloque International reúni à Mons du 26 au 29 octobre 1967 à l'occasion du cinquième centenaire de la naissance d'Érasme.* Mons, 1968. Pp. 59-65.

Hartt, Frederick, *et al. The Chapel of the Cardinal of Portugal (1434-1459) at San Miniato in Florence.* Philadelphia, 1964.

Haskins, Charles Homer. *Studies in the History of Mediaeval Science.* Cambridge, Mass., 1924.

Haubst, Rudolf. "Die Thomas- und Proklos-Exzerpte des 'Nicolaus Treverensis' in Codicillus Strassburg 84." *Mitteilungen und Forschungensbeiträge der Cusanus-Gesellschaft,* I (1961), pp. 17-51.

Hefele, Charles-Joseph and Leclercq, Dom H. *Histoire des Conciles.* Vol. VII, Pt. 2. Paris, 1916.

Herlihy, David. *Medieval and Renaissance Pistoia: The Social History of an Italian Town.* New Haven, 1967.

Holmes, George. *The Florentine Enlightenment 1400-50.* New York, 1969.

Honigmann, Ernest. "Anianus, Deacon of Celeda (415 A.D.)." In *Patristic Studies. Studi e Testi,* 173. Città del Vaticano, 1953. Pp. 54-58.

Hope, Richard. *The Book of Diogenes Laertius: Its Spirit and Method.* New York, 1930.

Huizinga, Johan. *Erasmus and the Age of the Reformation.* Trans. Barbara Flowers. New York, Harper Torchbook edition, 1957.

Humphreys, K.W. *The Library of the Carmelites at Florence at the End of the Fourteenth Century.* Amsterdam, 1964.

———. *The Library of the Franciscans of the Convent of St. Antony, Padua, at the Beginning of the Fifteenth Century.* Amsterdam, 1966.

Hutton, James. *The Greek Anthology to the Year 1800.* Ithaca, N.Y., 1935.

Jaeger, Werner. *Early Christianity and Greek Paideia.* Cambridge, Mass., 1961.

Jarrott, C.A.L. "Erasmus' Biblical Humanism." *Studies in the Renaissance,* XVII (1970), pp. 119-52.

Jayne, Sears. *John Colet and Marsilio Ficino.* Oxford, 1963.

Jones, P.J. "A Tuscan Monastic Lordship in the Later Middle Ages: Camaldoli." *Journal of Ecclesiastical History,* V (1954), pp. 168-83.

Klibansky, R. "Plato's *Parmenides* in the Middle Ages and the Renaissance." *Mediaeval and Renaissance Studies,* I (1944), pp. 281-330.

Knowles, David. *Christian Monasticism.* New York, 1969.

———. *From Pachomius to Ignatius: A Study in the Constitutional History of the Religious Orders.* Oxford, 1966.

Krautheimer, Richard. *Lorenzo Ghiberti.* Princeton, 1956.

Kristeller, Paul Oskar. "The Contribution of the Religious Orders to Renaissance Thought and Learning." *American Benedictine Review,* XXI (1970), pp. 1-55.

———. "Erasmus from an Italian Perspective." *Renaissance Quarterly,* XXIII (1970), pp. 1-14.

———. *Iter Italicum.* 2 vols. Leiden, 1963-67.

———. "A Latin Translation of Gemistos Plethon's *De fato* by Johannes Sophianos Dedicated to Nicholas of Cusa." In *Niccolò Cusano agli inizi del mondo moderno.* Firenze, 1970.

———. *Medieval Aspects of Renaissance Learning.* Durham, North Carolina, 1974.

———. *The Philosophy of Marsilio Ficino.* New York, 1943.

———. *Renaissance Concepts of Man and Other Essays.* New York, 1972.

——— *Renaissance Thought: The Classic, Scholastic, and Humanist Strains.* New York, 1961.

———. *Renaissance Thought II: Papers on Humanism and the Arts.* New York, 1965.

———. *Studies in Renaissance Thought and Letters.* Roma, 1956.

———. "Studies on Renaissance Humanism during the Last Twenty Years." *Studies in the Renaissance,* IX (1962), pp. 7-30.

———. *Le Thomisme et la pensée italienne de la Renaissance.* Montreal, 1967.

Kristeller, Paul Oskar and Cranz, F. Edward, eds. *Catalogus Translationum et Commentariorum: Medieval and Renaissance Latin Translations and Commentaries.* 2 vols. Washington, D.C., 1960-71,

Labalme, Patricia H. *Bernardo Giustiniani: A Venetian of the Quattrocento. Uomini e dottrine,* 13. Roma, 1969.

Ladner, Gerhart R. *The Idea of Reform: Its Impact on Christian Thought and Action in the Age of the Fathers.* Cambridge, Mass., 1959.

Larner, John. *The Lords of the Romagna: Romagnol Society and the Origins of the Signoria.* Ithaca, N.Y., 1965.

Lasinio, Ernesto. "Della Biblioteca di Settimo e di alcuni suoi manoscritti passati nella Mediceo-Laurenziana." *Rivista delle Biblioteche e degli Archivi,* XV (1904), pp. 169-77.

Leclercq, Dom Jean. *Recueil d'études sur Saint Bernard et ses écrits.* 3 vols. Roma, 1962-69.

Lecoy de la Marche, A. *Le Roi René: Sa vie, son administration, ses trauvaux artistiques et littéraires.* 2 vols. Paris, 1875.

Leff, Gordon. *Gregory of Rimini: Tradition and Innovation in Fourteenth Century Thought.* Manchester, England, 1961.

Léonard, Émile. *Histoire générale du Protestantisme.* 2 vols. Paris, 1961.

Linacher, Arturo. "Il 'Tempio degli Scolari'." *Atti della Società Colombaria di Firenze,* 1918-19 / 1919-20, pp. 47-65.

Lockwood, D.P. "De Rinuccio Aretino graecarum litterarum interprete." *Harvard Studies in Classical Philology,* XXIV (1913), pp. 51-109.

Lubac, Henri de. *Exégèse médiévale: Les quatre sens de l'Écriture.* 4 vols. Paris, 1959-64.

Luiso, F.P. *Riordinamento dell'epistolario di A. Traversari con lettere inedite e note storico-cronologiche.* Firenze, 1898-1903.

Magnuson, Torgil. *Studies in Roman Quattrocento Architecture. Figura: Studies Edited by the Institute of Art History, University of Uppsala.* Vol. 9. Stockholm, 1958.

Mallett, Michael E. *The Florentine Galleys in the Fifteenth Century.* Oxford, 1967.

Mariani, Ugo, O.E.S.A. *Il Petrarca e gli Agostiniani.* 2nd ed. Roma, 1959.

Martin, John Rupert. *The Illustration of the Heavenly Ladder of John Climacus. Studies in Manuscript Illumination.* Number 5. Princeton, 1954.

Masai, Francois. *Pléthon e le platonisme de Mistra.* Paris, 1956.

Mattesini, P. Francesco, O.F.M. "La Biblioteca di Santa Croce e Fra Tebaldo Della Casa." *Studi Francescani,* LVII (1954), pp. 254-316.

Mazza, Antonia. "L'inventario della 'Parva Libraria' di Santo Spirito e la biblioteca del Boccaccio." *Italia medioevale e umanistica,* IX (1966), pp. 1-74.

Mazzi, C. "L'inventario quattrocentesco della Biblioteca di Santa Croce di Firenze." *Rivista delle Biblioteche e degli Archivi,* VIII (1897), pp. 16-31, 99-113, 129-47.

Meiss, Millard. *Andrea Mantegna as Illuminator: An Episode in Renaissance Art, Humanism and Diplomacy.* New York, 1957.

———. "Towards a More Comprehensive Renaissance Palaeography." *The Art Bulletin,* XLII (1960), pp. 97-112.

Mercati, Giovanni Cardinal. *Codici latini Pico Grimani Pio . . . e i codici greci Pio di Modena . . . Studi e Testi,* 75. Città del Vaticano, 1938.

–––. *Notizie di Procoro e Demetrio Cidone, Manuele Caleca e Tedoro Meliteniota ed altri appunti per la storia della teologia e della letteratura bizantina del secolo XIV. Studi e Testi,* 56. Città del Vaticano, 1931.

–––. *Ultimi contributi alla storia degli umanisti.* Fasc. I: *Traversariana. Studi e Testi,* 90. Città del Vaticano, 1939.

Minio-Paluello, L. "Iacobus Veneticus Grecus: Canonist and Translator of Aristotle." *Traditio,* VIII (1952), pp. 265-304.

Mioni, E. "Le *Vitae Patrum* nella traduzione di Ambrogio Traversari." *Aevum,* XXIV (1950), pp. 319-31.

Mitchell, Charles. "Archaeology and Romance in Renaissance Italy." In *Italian Renaissance Studies,* ed. E.F. Jacob, London, 1960. Pp. 455-83.

Mittarelli, J.B. and Costadoni, A. *Annales Camaldulenses.* 9 vols. Venice, 1755-73.

Muckle, J.T., C.S.B. "Greek Works Translated Directly into Latin before 1350." *Mediaeval Studies,* IV (1942), pp. 33-42; and V (1943), pp. 102-14.

Oberdorfer, Aldo, "Di Leonardo Giustiniano umanista." *Giornale storico della letteratura italiana,* LVI (1910), pp. 107-20.

Oberman, Heiko A. *Archbishop Thomas Bradwardine, A Fourteenth Century Augustinian: A Study of His Theology in Its Historical Context.* Utrecht, 1958.

–––. *Forerunners of the Reformation: The Shape of Late Medieval Thought.* New York, 1966.

–––. *The Harvest of Medieval Theology.* Cambridge, Mass., 1963.

Oliger, P. Livarius, O.F.M. *Expositio Regulae Fratrum Minorum auctore Fr. Angelo Clareno.* Quaracchi, 1912.

O'Malley, John W., S.J. *Giles of Viterbo on Church and Reform: A Study in Renaissance Thought.* Leiden, 1968.

–––. "Giles of Viterbo: A Reformer's Thought on Renaissance Rome." *Renaissance Quarterly,* XX (1967), pp. 1-11.

–––. "Historical Thought and the Reform Crisis of the Early Sixteenth Century." *Theological Studies,* 28 (1967), pp. 531-48.

–––. "A Note on Gregory of Rimini: Church, Scripture, Tradition." *Augustinianum,* V (1965), pp. 365-78.

–––. "Preaching for the Popes." In *The Pursuit of Holiness in Late Medieval and Renaissance Religion: Papers from the University of Michigan Conference.* Eds. Charles Trinkaus and Heiko A. Oberman. *Studies in Medieval and Reformation Thought,* X. Leiden, 1974. Pp. 408-43.

Origo, Iris. *The World of San Bernardino.* New York, 1962.

Orlandi, S. *La Biblioteca di S. Maria Novella in Firenze nel secolo XIV al secolo XVI.* Firenze, 1952.

Ortiz de Urbina, I., S.J. "Un codice fiorentino di raccolte patristiche." *Orientalia Christiana periodica,* IV (1938), pp. 423-40.

Paatz, Walter and Elisabeth. *Die Kirchen von Florenz.* 6 vols. Frankfurt am Main, 1952-55.

Pagnani, D.A. *Storia dei Benedettini Camaldolesi: Cenobiti, eremiti, monache, ed oblati.* Sassoferrato, 1949.

Panofsky, Erwin. *Renaissance and Renascences in Western Art.* New York, Harper Torchbook ed., 1969. (First publ. Stockholm, 1960.)

Paredi, Angelo. *La biblioteca del Pizolpasso.* Milano, 1961.

Partner, Peter. "The 'Budget' of the Roman Church in the Renaissance Period." In *Italian Renaissance Studies,* ed. E.F. Jacob. London, 1960, Pp. 256-78.

Peebles, Bernard M. "The Verse Embellishments of the *Milleloquium Sancti Augustini." Traditio,* X (1954), pp. 555-66.

Penco, Gregorio, O.S.B. *Storia del monachismo in Italia.* Roma, 1961.

Peters, Robert. "Erasmus and the Fathers: Their Practical Value." *Church History,* XXXVI (1967), pp. 254-61.

Pintor, F. "La libreria di Cosimo de' Medici nel 1418." *Italia medioevale e umanistica,* III (1960), pp. 190-99.

Post, R.R. *The Modern Devotion: Confrontation with Reformation and Humanism.* Leiden, 1968.

Quasten, Johannes. *Patrology.* 3 vols. Utrecht, 1949-60.

Renaudet, Augustin. "Un problème historique: la pensée religieuse de J. Lefèvre d'Étaples." *Medioevo e Rinascimento: Studi in onore di Bruno Nardi.* Firenze, 1955. Vol. II, pp. 621-50.

Ricci, Pier Giorgio. "Ambrogio Traversari." *Rinascita,* II (1939), pp. 578-612.

Rice, Eugene F. "The Humanist Idea of Christian Antiquity: Lefèvre d'Étaples and His Circle." *Studies in the Renaissance,* IX (1962), pp. 126-41.

———. *The Renaissance Idea of Wisdom.* Cambridge, Mass., 1958.

Rich, Theodore F. "Giovanni da Sanminiato and Coluccio Salutati." *Speculum,* XI (1936), pp. 386-90.

Robey, D.J.B. "Virgil's Statue at Mantua and the Defense of Poetry: An Unpublished Letter of 1397." *Rinascimento,* 2nd s., IX (1969), pp. 183-203.

Rose, Paul Lawrence. "Humanist Culture and Renaissance Mathematics: The Italian Libraries of the Quattrocento." *Studies in the Renaissance,* XX (1973), pp. 46-105.

Rose, Valentin. "Die Lücke im Diogenes Laertius und der alte Übersetzer," *Hermes,* I (1866), pp. 367-97.

Rosmini, Carlo de'. *Vita di Francesco Filelfo da Tolentino.* Milano, 1808.

Ross, J.B. "The Emergence of Gasparo Contarini: A Bibliographical Essay." *Church History,* 41 (1972), pp. 22-45.

———. "Gasparo Contarini and His Friends." *Studies in the Renaissance,* XVII (1970), pp. 192-232.

Rostagno E. and Festa, N. *Catalogus Codicum mss. Bibl. Med-Laur. . . . supplementa tria.* 3 vols. Lipsiae, 1961.

Rousseau, Dom Olivier. "S. Bernard 'Le dernier des Pères'." In *Saint Bernard théologien, Actes du Congrès de Dijon 15-19 Septembre 1953.*

Analecta sacri Ordinis Cisterciensis, IX (1953), Fasc. 3-4 / Iul.-Dec., pp. 300-08.

Runciman, Steven. *The Last Byzantine Renaissance.* Cambridge, 1970.

Ruysschaert, José. "Le manuscrit *Romae descriptum* de l'édition érasmienne d'Irenée de Lyon." In *Scrimium Erasmianum,* ed. J. Coppens, Leiden, 1969, Vol. I, pp. 263-76.

―――. *Les manuscrits de l'Abbaye de Nonantola. Table de concordance annotée et index des manuscrits. Studi e Testi,* 182 bis. Città del Vaticano, 1955.

Sabbadini, Remigio. "La gita di Francesco Barbaro a Firenze nel 1415." *Miscellanea di studi in onore di Attilio Hortis.* Trieste, 1910. Pp. 615-27.

―――. *Il metodo degli Umanisti.* Firenze, 1920.

―――. *Le scoperte dei codici latini e greci ne' secoli XIV e XV.* 2 vols. Firenze, 1905-14. Reprinted, ed. E. Garin, Firenze, 1967.

―――. *La scuola e gli studi di Guarino Guarini Veronese.* Catania, 1896. Reissued as Pt. II of *Guariniana,* Torino, 1964.

―――. *Storia e critica di testi latini.* Catania, 1914. Reprinted Padova, 1971.

―――. *Vita di Guarino Veronese.* Genova, 1891. Reissued as Pt. I of *Guariniana,* Torino, 1964.

Schucan, L. *Das Nachleben von Basilius Magnus 'Ad adolescentes'.* Geneva, 1973.

Schwarz, W. "The Meaning of *Fidus interpres* in Medieval Translation." *The Journal of Theological Studies,* XLV (1944), pp. 73-78.

―――. *Principles and Problems of Biblical Translation.* Cambridge, 1955.

Seigel, Jerrold E. *Rhetoric and Philosophy in Renaissance Humanism.* Princeton, 1968.

Setton, Kenneth M. "The Byzantine Background to the Italian Renaissance." *Proceedings of the American Philosophical Society,* C (1956), pp. 1-76.

Siegmund, P. Albert, O.S.B. *Die Überlieferung der griechischen christlichen Literatur in der lateinischen Kirche bis zum zwölften Jahrhundert.* München-Pasing, 1949.

Sigmund, Paul E. *Nicholas of Cusa and Medieval Political Thought.* Cambridge, Mass., 1963.

Smalley, Beryl. *The Study of the Bible in the Middle Ages.* 2nd ed. Oxford, 1952.

Somigli, Costanzo, O. Camald. *Un amico dei Greci: Ambrogio Traversari.* Arezzo, 1964.

Sottili, Agostino. "Ambrogio Traversari, Francesco Pizolpasso, Giovanni Aurispa: Traduzioni e letture." *Romanische Forschungen,* LXXVIII (1966), pp. 42-63.

―――. "Autografi e traduzioni di Ambrogio Traversari." *Rinascimento,* 2nd S., V (1965), pp. 3-15.

Soudek, Josef. "The Genesis and Tradition of Leonardo Bruni's Annotated

Latin Version of the (Pseudo-) Aristotelian *Economics." Scriptorium,* XII (1958), pp. 260-68.

Spitz, Lewis W. "Humanism in the Reformation." In *Renaissance Studies in Honor of Hans Baron,* eds. Anthony Molho and John A. Tedeschi. Dekalb, Ill, 1971. Pp. 641-62.

———. *The Religious Renaissance of the German Humanists.* Cambridge, Mass., 1963.

Stornajolo, Cosimo. *Codices Urbinates latini Bibliotecae Vaticanae.* 3 vols. Romae, 1902-21.

Struever, Nancy S. *The Language of History in the Renaissance: Rhetoric and Historical Consciousness in Florentine Humanism.* Princeton, 1970.

Tatakis, Basile. *La philosophie byzantine.* 2nd ed. Paris, 1959. 2ᵉ Fasc. supplémentaire to Émile Brehier, *Histoire de la philosophie.*

Trapp, P. Damasus, O.E.S.A. "Augustinian Theology of the Fourteenth Century: Notes on Editions, Marginalia, Opinions, and Book-lore." *Augustiniana,* VI (1956), pp. 146-274.

Trexler, Richard C. "Death and Testament in the Episcopal Constitutions of Florence (1327)." In *Renaissance Studies in Honor of Hans Baron,* eds. Anthony Molho and John A. Tedeschi. Dekalb, Ill., 1971. Pp. 29-74.

———. "Florentine Religious Experience: The Sacred Image." *Studies in the Renaissance,* XIX (1972), pp. 7-41.

———. "Ritual in Florence: Adolescence and Salvation in the Renaissance." in *The Pursuit of Holiness in Late Medieval and Renaissance Religion: Papers from the University of Michigan Conference,* eds. Charles Trinkaus and Heiko A. Oberman. *Studies in Medieval and Reformation Thought,* X. Leiden, 1974. Pp. 200-64.

———. *The Spiritual Power: Republican Florence under the Interdict. Studies in Medieval and Reformation Thought.* IX, Leiden, 1974.

Trinkaus, Charles. *In Our Image and Likeness: Humanity and Divinity in Italian Humanist Thought.* 2 vols. Chicago, 1970.

Ullman, Berthold L. *The Humanism of Coluccio Salutati.* Padova, 1963.

———. *The Origin and Development of Humanistic Script.* Rome, 1960.

———. *Studies in the Italian Renaissance.* Rome, 1955.

Ullman, Berthold L. and Stadter, Phillp A. *The Public Library of the Renaissance: Niccolò Niccoli, Cosimo de' Medici and the Library of San Marco. Medioevo e Umanesimo,* 10. Padova, 1972.

Uzielli, G. *La vita e i tempi di Paolo dal Pozzo Toscanelli: Ricerche e studi.* Roma, 1894.

Vacalopoulos, A. "The Exodus of Scholars from Byzantium in the Fifteenth Century." *Cahiers d'histoire mondiale,* X (1967), pp. 463-80.

Vansteenberghe, Edmund. *Le Cardinal Nicolas de Cues (1401-64).* Paris, 1920. Reprinted Frankfurt am Main, 1963.

Vasoli, Cesare. "Profilo di un Papa umanista: Tommaso Parentucelli." In *Studi sulla cultura del Rinascimento.* Manduria, 1968. Pp. 69-121.

Verbeke, Gérard. "Guillaume de Moerbeke et sa méthode de traduction."

In *Medioevo e Rinascimento: Studi in onore di Bruno Nardi.* Firenze, 1955. Vol II, pp. 779-800.

Viller, M. "La question de l'union des Églises entre Grecs et Latins depuis le Concile de Lyon jusqu'à celui de Florence, 1274-1438." *Revue d'histoire ecclésiastique,* XVII (1921), pp. 260-305, 515-32; XVIII (1922), pp. 20-60.

Waley, Daniel. *The Papal State in the Thirteenth Century.* London, 1961.

Walser, Ernst. *Poggius Florentinus: Leben und Werke.* Berlin, 1914.

Watanabe, Morimichi. *The Political Ideas of Nicholas of Cusa with Special Reference to His 'De Concordantia Catholica'.* Geneva, 1963.

Way, Sister Agnes Clare. "The Lost Translations Made by Ambrosius Traversarius of the Orations of Gregory Nazianzene." *Renaissance News,* XIV (1961), pp. 91-96.

Weinstein, Donald. "The Myth of Florence." In *Florentine Studies: Politics and Society in Renaissance Florence,* ed. Nicolai Rubinstein. London, 1968. Pp. 15-44.

–––. *Savonarola and Florence: Prophecy and Patriotism in the Renaissance.* Princeton, 1970.

Weisinger, Herbert. "Who Began the Revival of Learning? The Renaissance Point of View." *Papers of the Michigan Academy of Science, Art, and Letters,* XXX (1944), pp. 625-38.

Weiss, Roberto. *Humanism in England during the Fifteenth Century.* 2nd ed. Oxford, 1957.

–––. "Jacopo Angeli da Scarperia (c. 1360-1410 / 11)." In *Medioevo e Rinascimento: Studi in onore di Bruno Nardi.* Firenze, 1955. Vol. II, pp. 801-27.

–––. *The Renaissance Discovery of Classical Antiquity.* Oxford, 1969.

Wilmart, André. "La collection des 38 Homélies latines de Saint Jean Chrysostome." *The Journal of Theological Studies,* 19 (1917), pp. 305-27.

Wind, Edgar. "The Revival of Origen." In *Studies in Art and Literature for Belle da Costa Greene,* ed. Dorothy Miner. Princeton, 1954. Pp. 412-24.

Woodward, William H. *Studies in Education during the Age of the Renaissance.* New York, 1906. Reprinted New York, 1965.

–––. *Vittorino da Feltre and Other Humanist Educators.* Cambridge, 1899.

Zippel, G. *Carlo Marsuppini d'Arezzo.* Trento, 1897.

–––. *Il Filelfo a Firenze.* Roma, 1899.

–––. *Niccolò Niccoli.* Firenze, 1890.

INDEX

Abelard, 94

Acciauoli, Donato, 185

Ademarus Beneventanus, 275

Aeneas Gazeus, *Theophrastus,* 77-79, 82, 120, 143

Aeschylus, 37

Aesop, *Fables,* 30

Agostino (Trionfo) d'Ancona, *Flores Beati Augustini,* 96

Agostino da Portico, 4, 69-70, 181, 251

Albergati, Cardinal Niccolò, 26, 32, 39, 121, 143-44, 160-61, 223, 273, 295, 296

Alberti, Leon Battista, xv, 185

Alberto da Sarteano, 24, 45, 49, 62, 114; Sermon "De sacramento Corporis Christi," 39

Albertus Magnus, 159

Albizzi, Rinaldo degli, 31, 32, 185

Aldobrandus, Jacobus, 46

Alexander the Great, 34, 56, 65, 90

Alexander III, Pope, 191

Alfonsus of Toledo, 95

Alighieri, Dante, 1-2; *Paradiso,* 91

Aliotti, Girolamo, xv, 49

Allegri, Mariotto, 67-68, 79, 250-51, 269, 290

Alonzo de Cartagena, 106, 147-48, 188

Amaseo, Pompilio, 271

Ambrose, St., 59, 114-17, 162, 194, 218, 259; *Epistolae,* xiii, 39, 54, 115, 124; *Hexaemeron,* 8, 84; medieval study of, 88; Trecento humanism and, 8, 9, 100, 103, 117; Guarino's life of, 45

Andrew of St. Victor, 89

Andronicus II, 203

Angeli da Scarperia, Jacopo, 135

Angelico, Fra, 4, 185

Anianus, 85, 93, 104, 154, 156, 260

Anselm, 259

Anselm of Laon, 93

Antonino, Sant', 171, 185

Antonio da Massa, 71, 72, 135, 142, 273

Antonio da Pistoia, 115

Antonio da S. Vito, 186-87

Antonio di Mario, 268, 271, 273

Antony, St., 178; *Letters,* 116, 129-30

Apollinaris of Laodicea, 162

Apollo, 80

Apostolic Fathers, 84, 143-44

Aquinas, St. Thomas, 61, 89, 91, 94-95, 106, 159, 203, 226; *Summa contra Gentiles,* 90; *Summa theologiae,* 90; Byzantine study of, 90, 135; Valla's assessment of, 59-60, 223.

Aratus, 42; *Phaenomena*, 243

Archimedes, 35

Aretino, Giovanni, 262

Argyropoulos, John, 86, 92, 225

Arian heresy, 132, 138-39, 145, 168

Aristides, 28

Aristippus, Henricus, 72, 87, 104-05, 257

Aristophanes, 38

Aristotle, 34, 65, 205, 210, 252; *De anima,* 26; *Eudemian Ethics,* 36, 77; *Metaphysics,* 106, 113, 254; *Nicomachean Ethics,* 7, 50, 105-07, 147; *Physics,* 26, 88, 106; *Poetics* 99, *Politics,* 50, 106-07; *Posterior Analytics,* 17, 88, 107; medieval translations of, 85-89, 106, 108; Bruni's translations of, 50, 105-07; and scholastic theology, 94-97, 106, 108

Arius, 60, 190

Arnobius, 139

Arragazzi da Montepulciano, Bar-

315